Music in American Life

Blacks in the New World

Edited by
August Meier and John H. Bracey

*Lists of books in the series appear
at the end of this volume.*

The Creation of Jazz

The Creation of JAZZ

Music, Race, and Culture in Urban America

BURTON W. PERETTI

University of Illinois Press

Urbana and Chicago

This book is printed on acid-free paper.

Library of Congress Cataloging-in-Publication Data

Peretti, Burton W. (Burton William), 1961–
   The creation of jazz : music, race, and culture in urban America /
Burton W. Peretti.
      p.   cm. — (Music in American life) (Blacks in the New World)
   Includes bibliographical references and index.
   ISBN 0-252-01708-0
   1. Jazz—History and criticism.   2. Afro-Americans—Music—History
and criticism.   I. Title.   II. Series.   III. Series: Blacks in the
New World.
ML3508.P45   1992
306.4'84—dc20   91-34772
                                                                    CIP
                                                                    MN

For my family and friends

Contents

Acknowledgments   xi

Introduction   1

1. *"I Couldn't See Anything but Music"*
   African and Rural Roots   11

2. *"He Should Throw That Club at You"*
   Urban Origins in New Orleans   22

3. *"Therefore, I Got to Go"*
   Jazz and the Great Northern Migration   39

4. *"Changing, Changing"*
   The Forging of Northern Black Communities   58

5. *"The Great Travelers"*
   White Jazz Musicians of the 1920s   76

6. *"Turn the Bitters into Sweets"*
   The Musical Culture of Jazz   100

7. *"Being Crazy Don't Make Music"*
   Searching for a Jazz Subculture   120

8.   *"Money-Finding Music"*
         Jazz as a Commodity   145

9.   *"Wacky State of Affairs"*
         The Depression, Swing Era, and Revolt   164

10.   *"The Wedding of the Races"?*
         Jazz and the Color Line   177

     Epilogue   211

     Notes   219
     Oral Histories Consulted   261
     Index   263

     Illustrations follow page 132.

Acknowledgments

Lawrence W. Levine counseled me on the formulation of this project, critiqued and helped to reshape the many drafts, and provided me with essential support and encouragement in many ways. It was a privilege for me to watch Professor Levine himself at work, to assist him in his research, and to participate in his fabulously helpful (and quite entertaining) research round-tables at his home. (With regard to the latter I must also thank Cornelia Levine for her hospitality.) Olly W. Wilson was most generous with his time and expertise, and was a very helpful critic of early chapter drafts. Leon F. Litwack also assisted in the development of the topic and provided encouragement and helpful criticism. Many other members of the faculty of the Department of History, University of California, Berkeley, provided me with ideas and all varieties of assistance during my graduate career. I am grateful to the department, the university's Graduate Division, and the Hall Center for the Humanities at the University of Kansas for financial assistance during the course of the research and writing.

Other friends and colleagues in California, Kansas, and elsewhere helped in many different ways. Paul Gorman, David Katzman, Shirley Moore, Mary Odem, Michael O'Malley, Steven Petrow, Madelon Powers, Ann Schofield, Charles Zappia, and the members of my American studies graduate research seminar provided perceptive analyses of chapter drafts. Steve Leikin assisted me at the last minute with some research on copyrights. Meg Moss and Margaret Welsh of the Chicago Historical Society provided helpful criticism of chapter 5 in its early form, and I thank the Society for permitting us to produce a final version of the original article in *Chicago History*.

At the University of Illinois Press, I have been supported from the earliest stages by Judith McCulloh, the executive editor, and by the Press's director and editor, Richard L. Wentworth. Nat Hentoff, Theodore Peterson, Charles Joyner, August Meier, and John Bracey provided vital suggestions during the writing process. Rita D. Disroe was the splendid copyeditor.

Curtis D. Jerde, Bruce Boyd Raeburn, and Alma Williams of the William Ransom Hogan Jazz Archive, Tulane University, were of enormous assistance. Even more central to this project was the guidance of Dan Morgenstern, Edward Berger, Don Luck, and Fran Cosgrove of the Institute of Jazz Studies, Rutgers University at Newark. Wayne Shirley and Samuel Brylawski of the Library of Congress and John Edward Hasse, curator of American music, National Museum of American History, were very helpful during my brief visit to Washington. Richard Schwegel, Chicago Public Library, and especially Donald F. Phillips gave me vital assistance during my sole trip to Chicago. I am grateful to Wilbert and Ellen Odem, Wilfred and Julie McClay, Nina Silber and Louis Hutchins, and George and Gloria Torrice for their hospitality during my research trips.

The Kansas American studies and women's studies program staffs, Terrence H. Cross, and my father, William H. Peretti, assisted in the production of chapter drafts and put up with my frustrations and constant need to correct the mistakes I discovered in print. My mother, Giken G. Peretti, and my brother, Bryan A. Peretti, were very patient as I labored and complained, seemingly forever, about this project, continuing to give me plenty of support. Finally, I am grateful to the late Bud Freeman for granting me six hours of his time in 1987, a visit that incalculably enhanced my enthusiasm for this project.

The Creation of Jazz

Introduction

Jazz, for years a popular and respected music in the entertainment world, is finally receiving serious attention from cultural historians. In this book, I place the creation of jazz within the great contexts of American culture—urbanization, race relations, individual development, professionalization, and capitalism—to synthesize the work and testimony of musicians and writers whom the academy has largely disregarded and to initiate new paths of inquiry in jazz historiography.

"Louis Armstrong's trumpet," Wynton Marsalis declared with no apparent irony, "speaks to the possibilities available to the individual in a democracy."[1] Probably the most incisive attempt to define the importance of jazz as a social and cultural phenomenon, this statement, coming as it did from a jazz musician, implies that if we are to understand jazz's significance, we must above all listen to the creators of the music. It was the first generation of jazz musicians, in the decades before the Second World War, who chose to abandon new musical styles and to enter risky stylistic and social terrain. As Marsalis has suggested, their careers were a series of choices, but (as he is well aware, of course) the democracy through which they moved was flawed, and the possibilities were limited. The creation of jazz is therefore a story of expanding creative alternatives, energized by new educational resources, profit-making opportunities, and social connections in urban America; but it is also a story of individual and group aspirations stymied, and sometimes crushed, by a partially undemocratic society that upheld policies of exclusion, unbridled economic competition, and atomizing individualism.

Marsalis's interpretation places jazz within a clear social and

political context and is therefore an attractive hypothesis with
which to initiate this book. Here, social historians and American
studies scholars will be able to appreciate how fully the early jazz
story illuminates the general American culture of the inter–world
war eras. Jazz's shining path through these years has been spied
from a distance by some of the most vital studies of 1920s and
1930s culture, which as usual focus on the white majority. Warren I. Susman, underpinning Marsalis's claim, argued that after
the First World War Americans "sought to build on knowledge,
technique . . . to find methods and ways of expressing and communicating . . . trying to mend what had become apparent to many,
each often in his own way, as a broken world." In the thirties, Susman argued, a "culture of commitment" arose in which Americans
sought communities where they could apply the knowledge they
had gathered in the previous decade. Nathan Irvin Huggins noted
that "the jazzmen were . . . creating a cultural renaissance" in the
twenties, which he implied proved superior to Harlem's flawed literary "renaissance" (alas, the sole focus of Huggins's great study).
Lewis A. Erenberg and Elaine Tyler May, among other recent scholars of twenties culture, stress the search for knowledge and new
life-styles and activities in a post-Victorian world. Kathy J. Ogren,
the first cultural historian to focus specifically on jazz in the twenties, shows that the print controversy over jazz was a means through
which Americans could "argue about the nature of change itself." [2]

The consideration of the nature of change, the search for
knowledge and technique, the creation of a cultural renaissance,
the revolt against Victorianism, a culture of commitment—these
findings suggest that early musicians' explorations of democratic
possibilities coursed through certain channels. Jazz evolved along
all these lines in some ways. Social change was the engine driving the creation of jazz. More specifically, jazz came about because
America was urbanizing on a massive scale. The education of jazz
musicians, their economic subsistence, their audience, and their
specific personal and career aspirations would never have materi-
alized if the United States had not urbanized as it did after, say,
1900, when 70 percent of all Americans lived on farms or towns
with fewer than twenty-five hundred residents. The knowledge
and technique of jazz musicians expanded radically as well; in an
age when most American workers were falling under corporate
regimes and obtaining lightly skilled clerical work or unskilled fac-
tory jobs, the creators of jazz laid the foundation of a highly skilled
and highly learned art form, through the use of African and Euro-

pean creative traditions, which allowed for the development of manifold creative "possibilities" in the future. Huggins's claim that jazz musicians created a "cultural renaissance"—a black cultural renaissance—is more problematic, but their technical and creative achievement broke with the past and energized continuing innovation in the future. The first white jazz musicians especially revolted against "Victorian" codes of behavior, and their music rode the wave of a new, less-inhibited culture of urban amusement— although many musicians admired and retained certain elements of the old code. Finally, it is clear that jazz musicians in the thirties shared an artistic commitment that was generally typical of American communitarianism during the Depression. Here again, though, jazz musicians differed from other Americans in disdaining *political* involvement, for the most part, perpetuating the search for knowledge and technique they had begun as youths in previous decades.

Jazz, thus, does not fit perfectly into prevailing interpretations of twenties and thirties culture, and its deviation from our current "jazz age" paradigm should encourage some modification of those concepts. Any scholar in American studies or history who endorses the truism that jazz is "America's greatest art form" or its "classical music" should develop a more sophisticated notion of what its establishment tells us about its originators and creative methods. Although I work toward that end in this book, I also have a more specific scholarly goal. I seek to unite and redirect three major streams of jazz studies that have proven of limited use to cultural historians: musicology, social science fieldwork, and aficionado history.

Musicologists and others who have studied jazz have produced the richest and most cohesive and methodologically sound body of jazz scholarship. In 1968 Gunther Schuller's *Early Jazz* (followed by *The Swing Era* in 1989) established a remarkable standard for the examination of jazz's general components, the transcription and harmonic and rhythmic analysis of recorded selections, and the description of the evolving styles of players and bands. Subsequently, Olly W. Wilson and John Storm Roberts produced penetrating analyses of the African roots of jazz and other African-American music, and Thomas Owens, Milton Lee Stewart, Scott K. DeVeaux, and James Lincoln Collier developed sophisticated methods of studying jazz music.[3] This work is accessible to trained musicians but unfortunately might scare off those who cannot read music or analyze harmony. The bridge between these readers and the "stuff" of which music is made might best be supplied by the methods of ethnomusicology, the anthropological study of music *in* and *as* culture. Beyond Alan P. Merriam's brief reflections, though, ethnomusicologists have barely investigated jazz. Other studies, however, especially Jeff Todd Titon's and David Evans's analyses of jazz's cousin, the rural blues, show nonmusicians how music might be analyzed as a system of expression and interpretation within larger American subcultures.[4] Here, I neither delve into the specific sounds of jazz nor present transcribed musical examples; rather, I discuss the general musical techniques of jazz players, since they are a major source of information about the musicians' thoughts and deeds. This analysis takes place in part of chapter 2 and in chapter 6. Throughout the study, in addition, the findings of Merriam, Bruno Nettl, and other ethnomusicologists have animated my explorations of jazz's relation to the whole culture and its parts.[5]

A large and disparate body of social scientific work on jazz, in which the thought and activity of jazz musicians have been explored to test a variety of behavioral and cognitive theories, has appeared in the last half-century. Beginning in the 1940s, for example, many scholars (including Carlo Lastrucci, Morroe Berger, Norman Margolis, and Aaron H. Esman) briefly examined jazz as a social rebellion; Howard S. Becker pioneered the study of deviance among some white players in his 1963 study, *Outsiders;* Louis H. Levy analyzed New Orleans jazz culture as an example of formalization and social distance; and Neil Leonard wrote both the pioneering book on jazz as rebellion in the 1920s and a recent study of the ritualistic elements in jazz.[6]

The primary accomplishment of social scientists was to demonstrate that after 1940 certain young jazz musicians in big cities imitated the bebop rebels and created a *subculture* of learned behavior and beliefs, involving drug use, certain styles of speech and dress, and hostile attitudes toward audiences and other kinds of musicians.[7] This vital contribution held great promise as a key to a theory of postwar American culture as a whole, which Greil Marcus and James B. Gilbert have resuscitated in their discussions of music, "delinquency," and the interaction between the mainstream and marginal.[8] At the time, this scholarship was never synthesized into a comprehensive statement: the relation of the music to behavior, the role of racial differences, the evolution of the subculture, and its relation to the life cycle of musicians were among the subjects that were not covered. The upheavals of the 1960s and 1970s brought new music and subcultures into existence and lured scholars away from musicians without causes, and it did not help that jazz itself entered a period of stylistic confusion and "fusion."[9] The 1970s did yield two detailed sociological examinations, by Jack V. Buerkle and Danny Barker and by Charles Nanry and Edward Berger, that offered helpful but tentative interpretations of behavior and attitudes that developed along with the music.[10] All these studies are of value to students of jazz musicians before 1940. However, while the issues of subcultural and deviant identity are stimulating, they cannot be adequately tested from a historical distance. More generally (as I argue in chapter 7), the evidence available suggests that it is much harder to conclude that early jazz musicians formed a subculture fixed upon particular modes of language, thought, and behavior (deviant or otherwise).

The vast historical literature on jazz written by and for devotees of the music is indispensable to historians. Aficionados of jazz have been well served by critics recounting their listening experiences, discographers listing hard-won information about obscure and famous recordings, biographers who chronicle painstakingly the activities of their subjects, and the more documentary-minded players who wrote memoirs. While these writings, like all aficionado literature, tend toward either fact-laden positivism or impressionistic nostalgia, the authors (especially such dedicated historians as Al Rose, Ira Gitler, and James Lincoln Collier) often set high standards of research and writing, and thus ensure that they warrant the attention of any critical student of jazz.

A more recently minted type of source, the oral history, has assisted me greatly. In the past twenty years, jazz researchers have adopted the stricter interviewing methods of the oral history movement to obtain fuller, more careful, and more valuable testimony from reminiscing jazz pioneers. Far richer than the autobiographies or published interview compendia, the copious oral history projects of the William Ransom Hogan Jazz Archive at Tulane University, and the National Endowment of the Arts' Jazz Oral History Project (supervised by the Smithsonian Institution and the Institute of Jazz Studies at Rutgers University, Newark, which now houses the collection) have proved to be my most valued source. These archives contain the voices of hundreds of musicians and their relatives and a wealth of largely working-class reflections on socialization, musicianship, class, race, and many other topics. I have made great effort to ensure that the oral historical evidence here is factual and relevant. The fanciful storytelling and imprecise memories of some older musicians are notorious,[11] so I have concentrated on

verifiable anecdotes, testimony that avoids self-serving, and the in-
advertent and indicative revelations that memoirists make while
concentrating on other subjects. Whenever possible, I have used
newspapers, field studies, and other material from the period, as
well as secondary material on jazz and related subjects, to substantiate and clarify the musicians' stories.[12] I use oral history critically, as
a fundamental component of the analysis, taking as my model John
Bodnar, Roger Simon, and Michael P. Weber's innovative study of
ethnic groups in early twentieth-century Pittsburgh.[13]

I proceed chronologically from about 1900 to 1940. My successive concentration on the rural South, New Orleans, and such
northern cities as Chicago and New York is a familiar progression
in jazz history, from which I deviate sometimes (especially in my
treatment of the West Coast in chapter 3) but have generally found
useful and valid. The first four chapters form a unit that traces
the development of jazz among African Americans. Many writers
have already contributed to the sociocultural analysis of black jazz,
beginning with Imamu Amiri Baraka's study *Blues People* in 1963,
continuing with the work of Lawrence W. Levine, Albert Murray,
and others, and finding recent elaboration in the fine studies of
Katrina Hazzard-Gordon and Daphne Duval Harrison.[14] Still lack-
ing, however, is a synthesis, a sense of the interrelation of the
practice of jazz with the maturation of its creators, the African-
American identities they were led to acquire, and the social settings
in which they made the music. Baraka wrote a brief synthesis of
this kind in 1963, but since then so much work has appeared on
black cultural history, race relations, and the urban migrations in
the South and North that jazz's role must receive a more careful
delineation.

The first chapter is a rural prologue, a gathering together of
the evidence that defines the social and intellectual functions of
instrumental music on the so-called plantations of the lower Mississippi Delta. Since many of these instrumental musicians migrated
to New Orleans around 1900 and played a major role in initiating
jazz, their rural origins deserve discussion. Also, it is necessary to
explain what jazz's relation to that other great black Delta music,
the blues, really was—where their social and expressive roles were
similar and, more crucially, where they diverged. My brief analysis of this divergence might stimulate further investigation of how
rural culture produced differing expressions (by no means limited to jazz and the blues, of course) out of the same African and
slave traditions and under the same regime of Jim Crow. The next

three chapters spell out my basic thesis: jazz was essentially an urban music that grew out of city stimuli and fulfilled uniquely urban social functions. Chapter 2 covers the familiar territory of New Orleans from 1900 to 1917, but with a new emphasis on how rural newcomers and longtime city residents (often light-skinned "Creoles of color") created jazz out of their two traditions while both groups confronted the special social tensions of the Jim Crow era. Despite the Bourbon Street and Storyville nostalgia that New Orleans jazz inspires, the dearth of serious social history on the city in this era is only now being overcome. In chapters 3 and 4, I show how jazz was basically created by the "Great Migration" of southern blacks to the North from 1915 to 1930 and how jazz only acquired its expressive potential and social meaning when it left the South along commercial and migratory routes. Here, too, the socialization of early black musicians shaped their professional activity. Specifically, they and their music were encouraged by the development of northern urban nightlife, were frustrated by the division of black communities by class and skin tone, and were finally encouraged by the coming together of these communities. Also, jazz and its creators were walled into the ghettos that came to imprison most northern blacks. It is possible, in fact, to classify the story of jazz's rise in African-American culture as a triumph within an unexpected tragedy.

These chapters might be controversial, for in a time when scholars are demonstrating the abiding strength and centrality of African-American traditions among blacks from slave times to the present,[15] I give space and attention to the considerable influence of European-American traditions, especially "classical" music, on early jazz musicians. I might be accused of perpetuating what Dizzy Gillespie has called "a whitewashed look to our music" that is going to "ooze off as much as they can to other whites."[16] In response, I would note that the European influence I found came as a surprise and is a factor that unpleasantly complicated my hypothesis about jazz and migration. Black music had always been influenced by white styles and instrumentation, but even the limited exposure jazz's creators gained to northern white urban musical culture ensured that jazz would be particularly enmeshed in this dominant culture. It casts no discredit on the great black folk tradition to note that it was under constant seige. As Gunther Schuller was the first to argue, to the extent that jazz musicians had taken up European instruments and learned Western musical practice, early jazz was a weak or compromised episode in the development of African-

American music. Still, as Gillespie implies, jazz again became "our music," but this largely occurred after 1940 (in part due to Gillespie's own work), a period of jazz that must receive sociocultural study elsewhere.

Whites did begin to play jazz in the black style in the 1920s, and no cultural study of jazz can ignore their role. Chapter 5 begins in New Orleans, where the Dixieland players remained at the margins of jazz by allowing racial ideology to block their further absorption of black influences. Following the traditional jazz chronology, chapter 5 focuses next on the white Chicagoans who embraced black jazz earliest and most fully. These players used jazz to combat their early Victorian and immigrant upbringings and to Americanize themselves in a casual, urban manner. They were similar to other white rebels of the 1920s in their dissatisfaction with placid traditions, but they were also very different, as the music gave them the impetus to explore a newer, more biracial set of values and behaviors.

In the sixth and seventh chapters, I focus respectively on black and white players' musical practices and their extramusical lives. In the chapter on musical culture, I examine how players created jazz works, paying special attention to group composition, the advent of notated jazz, the development of instrument timbres, the technique of improvisation, "signature" playing styles, and band arrangement. In chapter 7, taking my cue from the field studies of the jazz subculture of the 1940s and 1950s, I ask if earlier jazz musicians of either race also developed a clear cultural identity, bound up in such extramusical aspects as language, dress, behavior, narcotics use, and spending habits. Here, I analyze the overwhelming male dominance of early jazz, along with women players' reactions to this condition. Beyond this, the lore of early jazz depicts other trappings of a subculture, but I conclude that the musicians were united only by the music and by any features of African-American culture that sustained their advocacy of the music. I am opposed to the theory that early jazz musicians founded one of the first countercultures, presaging the Beats and the Hippies, and would rather argue that they largely remained dependent on what could be called America's time-honored *black* counterculture.

In the final three chapters, I examine in detail issues that I only allude to briefly in earlier parts. In chapters 8 and 9, I discuss the role of commercial forces in early jazz. In their baldest form, these forces sought to make the music a commodity and its creators producers for the mass market, and of course jazz was also spread and sold in *re*production via the new electrical media: sound film, phonograph records, and radio. After sketching the rapidly changing structure of the music business—and the efforts of the musicians' labor union to fight this structure—I show how jazz players responded with both anger and encouragement to the lure of profits and the impersonality of the studio microphone. In chapter 9, I cover the effect on musicians of the economic convulsions of the 1930s—the crippling Depression, which was particularly severe for entertainers, and the booming Big Band era. Both periods placed the greatest pressure on musicians to decide whether or not they would commercialize, to accept what Frederic Jameson might call "the cultural logic of capitalism" and its implications.[17]

In the final chapter, I return to the central issue of jazz and race relations. Jazz players dealt with the powerful racist traditions in American musical entertainment—the "specter of minstrelsy" that froze blacks and their music into a powerful white construct of demeaning subservience. Although minstrelsy was a dying tradition by 1920, the attitudes that fostered it remained strong. Southern tours by black bands are given special attention, because on these tours the musicians were most clearly told to conform to the minstrel paradigm—and here they most explicitly challenged it. Some white musicians also adhered to racist views, even as they began to work with blacks in the 1930s. The solidifying sense of group professionalism among jazz musicians, however, gave some of them enough mutual respect and resourcefulness to initiate some color blindness in their ranks. This development, despite some support from listeners and promoters, was always fragile and partial, but it enabled some jazz enclaves to become unusual experiments in racial parity and understanding.

The bittersweet nature of jazz's racial identity, on the eve of Pearl Harbor, typified how the creators of jazz, drawing on ancient traditions and fighting against ghettos and profiteers and sometimes among themselves, were able to develop a specialized professional fraternity, somewhat cut off from the folk cultures that had nurtured them. This fraternity was unique, insular, and atypical in important ways, but its characteristics and travails also made it deeply representative of the American experience in that era.

"I Couldn't See Anything but Music"
African and Rural Roots

In the beginning, there were Africans in America, striving to hold onto Africa. The black slaves were not cultureless blank slates upon which the white masters wrote their names, faith, and language. The translation of Africa to the United States, however, was surreptitious and partial, and it was terminated along with the international slave trade in 1807. West African culture survived the Middle Passage, the sea voyage to the New World, but only a few cores of the old experience persisted under the slave regime. All social and political norms, and most language, handcrafts, dress, and cuisines were excised from the slaves' existence; and African cultural survivals grew weaker among the later generations in America.

The basic core of African cultures, religion, did persist, however. The West African groups that yielded the bulk of slaves to the New World believed in a world of spirit gods, aswirl in the landscapes and rivers and embodied in certain animals. The goal of each believer was to be possessed by a spirit, to join with the more elemental being in moments of physical and mental convulsion. In Haiti, where African-American slaves were in the majority and white hegemony was weak, they found easy analogues to the spirits in the Catholic saints, and rites of spirit possession gained a new herbaceous foundation and terminology and evolved into voodoo. Not incidentally, it was in Haiti that slaves by 1804 had overthrown their masters and established the first African-American state.[1] In what became the United States, religious Africanisms gained the strongest foothold on the southernmost fringes. In the bayou and canebrake regions of the lower Mississippi River, in Louisiana and Mississippi, and on the sea islands and delta lands of Georgia and South Carolina, slaves were in a majority, thick swamplands provided private worship space, tropical herbs and materials grew, and the African survivals were easily absorbed and reabsorbed through a constant influx of West Indians. Possession religion took hold in these regions, as did such African-American rites as the John Canoe celebration (at Christmastime), derived perhaps from the West African *yankoro,* or buzzard festival.[2]

To the north, though, the cultural hegemony of whites was stronger, and Christianity's quashing of spirit religion was more complete. The farther north slaves were settled in the American South, the less space, time, and materials were granted to slave spirit religion. Whites were usually the majority in these regions, and Christian hegemony here was greatest. The black revival meeting took the place of possession ceremonies; the preacher replaced the *griot* and the root doctor; the church replaced the village square; and pews often supplanted the circle of standing worshipers. But here, too, Christianity was Africanized, as spirit possession became shouting or evangelical ecstasy, African circle dances became ring shouts, and the preacher called and the congregations responded in the manner of the African communal religious rite.[3]

Music and dance were interwoven with African religion and its American adaptations. West African religions integrated spirit lore, possession rites, communal gathering, singing, dancing, and the playing of instruments—elements impossible to disassociate from one another. Drums housed specific spirits and dances represented them; an individual could become possessed by a spirit only within a group; that group had to dance and sing (to the accompaniment of sacred drums and other instruments) in order to call up the spirit; and the *griot* was often inseparable from his drum. The music, because of its rich spiritual and social role, was complex. Melodically characterized by both long and short strains, it often repeated and featured melismatic sliding between pitches. The timbre of voices and instruments often derived from speech patterns, especially in certain tone languages, in which pitch helped to define words. Most distinctly, the music was highly rhythmic, the contribution of the drums and of its symbiotic relation to dance. As dance brought all kinds of villagers together, this diversity was represented in the polyrhythms of drummers and clappers, the complex interweaving of pulses which Western listeners characterized as extreme "syncopation" (a misleading term, since no single rhythm was irregularly accented).[4]

In the slave states of America, the repression of the musical component of African religion was especially severe. Many states, counties, and owners forbade the playing of drums by slaves, believing that the taps relayed rebellious messages, and they also banned daytime dances and communal singing. The slaves adapted: dances took place at night and during permitted holidays, and communal singing shifted more to the fields of labor. The call and response thus rang out among cotton pickers and stevedores as well as in slave churches.[5]

These efforts at cultural maintenance were swept up, along with everything else, in the sudden destruction of slavery by the Union armies in the 1860s. For Frederick Douglass and other black intellectuals, emancipation and reconstruction heralded the acceleration of trends that had already Americanized the slaves, and they yearned for the day when the freed men and women would be completely integrated into capitalist, secular white society.[6] W. E. B. Du Bois gave a late but definitive expression of this view in 1902, writing that "the end" of the African American's "striving" was "to be a co-worker in the kingdom of culture, to escape both death and isolation, to husband and use [the Negro's] best powers and his latent genius." Du Bois emphasized that blacks had a unique contribution to make, and throughout *The Souls of Black Folk* he stressed the "double consciousness" of blacks, who remained both culturally distinct (due to their African heritage) and part of the United States as a whole. In Du Bois's view, music and dance were the strands of black heritage that would perpetuate the integration of religion, community, time, and space. He saw in the Georgia hills how rural blacks used music to retain their expressive culture: "The music of Negro religion is that plaintive rhythmic melody, with its touching minor cadences, which, despite caricature and defilement, still remains the most original and beautiful expression of human life and longing yet born on American soil."[7]

As every student of American history knows, however, whites hesitated to embrace the former slave's double identity as an African American and as an American and instead worked to suppress it. For a decade after the Civil War, the five million ex-slaves had reason to think that their integration was taking place, as Union forces in the South guarded their ballot boxes and the black officials they elected, and as they and others built schools and other facilities. However, northern whites gradually lost interest in reconstruction, and their elected officials soon decided to discontinue the reforms, which had in any case failed to cause major change. Blacks' economic conditions, handicapped by the widespread dev-

astation of the South, remained wretched, and the rural majority
was faced with the choice of either sharecropping or tenant farming
on the old plantation grounds of their birth or moving to another
rural region, a southern city, or similar locales in the North. Educational, medical, and other facilities were scarce enough to ensure
a deprived, separate culture; but the white South compounded the
misery by cheating blacks out of the vote and instituting Jim Crow
laws promoting the near-total segregation of the races. Dismayed
reformers, both white and black, argued that as a result blacks were
culturally and spiritually impoverished. As late as 1902, Du Bois
argued that the duty of educators was "to scatter [white] civilization among a people whose ignorance was not simply of letters, but
of life itself." To him, the sharecroppers living in shacks "did not
demand better; they do not know what better houses mean."[8]

Du Bois was wrong. Emancipation, while stagnant and disheartening in many ways, led to a profound ferment and evolution
in African-American culture. Freedom gave black families the opportunity to reestablish cohesive, stable units, no longer threatened
by the slave trade, and to perpetuate links with in-laws, cousins,
and other relatives through frequent visits, reunions, and temporary living arrangements. The family unit, legitimized or not by
the justice of the peace or the church, became the primary locus
of socialization.[9] As blacks gained the right to travel, they used
trains, horses, and boats to range across the South and eventually
the country, breaking down the spiritual and material barriers of
the plantation. Such uprooting was both a trial and an exhilarating
new life of motion, which only accelerated as the twentieth century approached. The first free generations, it might be said, also
had a double consciousness of tradition and discontinuity. As Lawrence W. Levine has argued, "the sacred world view so central to
black slaves," which involved "an intimate relationship between the
world of sound and the world of sacred time and space . . . was
to be shattered in the twentieth century." Many of the forces that
secularized black culture were at work before 1900, as freedom of
travel, the sharecropping system, and both the confinement and
concentrated ambition found in segregated neighborhoods robbed
slave religion of its liberationist significance.[10]

The musical culture of the free blacks was rife with these conflicting forces, and as a result its variety was dazzling. The clearest
musical evidence of black absorption into the white culture was the
rise of the spiritual. Spirituals originated as slave songs, but they
were now carefully arranged in the European classical style and

sung by clean-cut choirs of Negro-college students. Appreciative white listeners valued little black music besides these spirituals.[11] Other musics illustrated other impulses, however, as traditional bone bands kept playing on the Georgia Sea Islands, while itinerant songster guitarists wandered in Appalachia, fiddlers thrived in the Carolinas and Virginia, work and prison gangs called and responded with chants, the ring shouts of evangelical congregations rose from fancier settings, and piano "professors" edified the growing urban black classes.

After emancipation, music in black life increasingly expressed secular rites and functions. Music also migrated along with its creators in the new world of upheaval and partial freedom. This is best illustrated by the entry of black musicians into white musical institutions. After 1875, black singers, dancers, and songwriters— such as James Bland, Billy Kersands, J. Rosamond Johnson, and Bert Williams—began to dominate the popular minstrel shows and coon song industry that provided stereotypical fare for both races. In the realm of art music, black musical clubs, vocal quartets and choirs, brass bands, and even a black opera company (founded in Washington, D. C., in 1872) were formed after the Civil War, and a remarkable group of African-American virtuosi managed to establish prominent careers in the South and beyond.[12] Thomas Greene Bethune (1849–1908), a blind pianist and ex-slave from a Georgia plantation, had a unique life, but his experience highlighted the obstacles facing black musicians. As early as 1858 his masters had exhibited "Blind Tom" before paying audiences to supplement the plantation's earnings. Bethune may have been the greatest American pianist of his time. A composer of many works, able to perform hundreds of other compositions from memory, he also regaled his audiences with staggeringly difficult improvisations on requested themes. Until 1904, Bethune was forced to go on national and European tours whenever the white Bethunes needed additional income. "Blind Tom" was a striking example of the intellectual and artistic potential of former slaves and the simultaneous exploitation and degradation by whites of those qualities.[13]

Perhaps inevitably, new black musics were created in this era of change. The origins of ragtime, the blues, and jazz in these decades remain obscure today, but what is much clearer is what these new styles brought together, and how they charted new courses of thought and behavior for African Americans. Pianists in urban saloons created a style with slight hints of African polyrhythms, and through a gradual process of promotion and commercial standard-

ization in the 1890s ragtime emerged. Other innovations were more
closely tied to the countryside, where the vast majority of blacks still
lived in 1900; these changes took longer to publicize. The blues,
in its earliest rural manifestation, was a song style for singing guitarists that featured three-line stanzas and certain standard melismatic and harmonic features that seemed to have been chosen for
their distinctly non-European sound. (When some players called
these blues values "dirty," perhaps the rural, antebellum, and even
African nature of the blues was being highlighted with pride.)
Moans expressing a "blue" state had been heard among slaves and
stevedores in the 1850s, and W. C. Handy claimed that he heard
a one-line blues in 1892. But not until about 1903 was the style
identifiable among the players and listeners in its home regions of
western Mississippi and east Texas.[14]

The country blues were potent evidence that the West African
integration of music, dance, and spirituality lived on in the decades
after emancipation. For country folk, as one sharecropper noted,
freedom "didn't amount to a hill of beans" in their everyday lives,
and thus they had no reason to desert slave culture and every reason to nurture it.[15] The blues was dance music, played in outdoor
gatherings or in the confines of jook joints, whose very name came
from West African antecedents (although the exact derivation remains a mystery). What Katrina Hazzard-Gordon calls "the jook
continuum" maintained the music's connection to dance, which now
flowered into expressive, sensual "hops" and "shimmies," "itches"
and "snake hips." Snakes and other animals were prominent symbols in lyrics and dances, suggesting a connection to the old spirit
gods, and the musicians' vocal emanations almost gave voice to a
kind of spiritual possession. Blues singers cultivated an interest
in voodoo charms and lore and promoted the notion that they
had bargained at the crossroads with Satan to sing the blues—the
"devil's music"—well. Historians of the blues argue convincingly
that the music was part of a folk movement that reacted against the
heavy postemancipation white Christian influence among blacks.
Blues lyrics usually avoided Christian references, but they certainly
did not neglect basic spiritual concerns. Churchgoing folk, in fact,
accepted the blues as a secular version of their shouting, perhaps
taking comfort in noting (with a Louisiana man) that "dancin' ain't
sinful iffen de foots ain't crossed." [16]

The blues and jazz plainly were musical cousins. Both came
to feature specific harmonic and pitch features (blues harmony),
melismatic phrasing, and instrumental improvisation. While they

would differ in other ways, and resonate at first in very different social settings, their origins and characteristics were similar (and much later they would entertain the same audiences in the North). Both, in fact, were in part nurtured in the same general region, in the "Delta" along the Mississippi River between Memphis and New Orleans. Many musicians who later became important early jazz musicians in New Orleans began their lives in the Delta's plantations, the large riverside settlements worked by white farmers and black sharecroppers.[17] The music these instrumentalists made, however, marked them as men who broke with tradition, as well as with the resolutely rural orientation of the Delta blues and the jook joint.

The family band was perhaps at the heart of the Louisiana plantation tenants' musical life. Family relations brought children into the bands, and the band as an institution reinforced both the communal warmth and the strict cohesiveness supplied by families. George "Pops" Foster was born in 1892 on the McCall Plantation, upriver from New Orleans. By the age of eight he and his brother were playing in a plantation band under the apparent coercion of their father. The instruments were owned collectively, and when he joined the band George was given a string bass by the older members. His father, Charley, managed the group (which included nonrelations as well) and promoted beer parties at a local shack on Saturday nights. The boys' uncle was angered by this situation and came "around telling my daddy that he was ruining us kids by keeping us up late playing dances." In George's case, the band may have been his father's preferred substitute for the family structure. The McCall setting was typical for the region: fruit orchards, sugar cane, and vegetable gardens were cultivated by tenants, and the community was cosmopolitan (George's mother spoke seven languages and his band often played for Cajun dances, "mostly country or hillbilly music . . . a lot like Jewish music").[18]

James Humphrey of New Orleans, born a slave in 1859, instructed his family members in musical instruments and made a career of founding family bands in the plantations upriver. His son Willie E. Humphrey recalled that he "taught music in the country, at the Magnolia Plantation, Reserve, Louisiana; St. Charles Parish; St. James Parish; and in Mississippi" and formed bands. James Humphrey regularly brought his own Onward Band to towns between New Orleans and Reserve, thirty miles away. Upon returning from his travels, he would treat his children with "pecans, sweet potatoes, sugar cane, and all from the country." At home, Humphrey's fig garden supplemented his musical income. He was able to persuade his children that music was both a worthwhile occupation and an extension of their cooperative, nurturing family. Willie Humphrey himself became a successful clarinetist and raised his own sons to be musicians.[19]

Children alone tended to band together and teach themselves music. The pioneer jazz trombonist Edward "Kid" Ory grew up on the Woodland Plantation in La Place, five miles downriver from Reserve. The tenant families on this plantation were light-skinned Creoles who spoke only French. Ory made his first mark as a "kid" in the 1890s, organizing a humming band of playmates. "We used to stand on the bridge, you know, at night . . . in the dark, just couldn't see anyone, no one could see us [or] hear us, you know, singing on the bridge. Get us a few ginger cakes, and we was all right." Ory beat a drum rhythm to keep his charges together, and he was already able to harmonize their singing in three or four parts, although "sometimes we couldn't get the correct chord . . . we couldn't get it all the way through." This ceremony mimicked the riverside services of black churches and thus evoked the West African attachment to living, spirit-possessed rivers. Other early syncopators, such as the cornetist Ernest Miller and the guitarist Lonnie Johnson (from Raceland, on Bayou Lafourche), and players in jug bands—small ensembles featuring one or more jug blowers—on the docks of Vicksburg, Mississippi, also practiced their craft near the waters. The jazz bassist and Vicksburg native Milt Hinton noted that "they had to play something that could be quiet, and not disturb, yet audible for people to hear and wake up pleasantly, and say, 'I like that song, and I'll give you guys a nickel.' "[20]

This new generation of young rural musicians had a clear urge to innovate. Like other plantation children, Ory created his own instruments and formed playmate bands. He built a banjo, a guitar, a violin, and a bass, using "thread and fishing cord" and metal wire for strings, cigar and soap boxes for the bodies, and a hot iron to burn sound holes into each chamber. His first band played these instruments, and Ory put the group to profitable use. They caught their own fish, made potato salad, and held fish fries inside an empty house (so that "the music could be heard"). Admission was charged, and Ory later hired girls to prepare the food. He soon brought his band to local baseball games, and earned enough money in the process to buy seven factory-made instruments for his employees. This successful enterprise gained the blessing of Ory's father, who exhorted that "everyone is good for something in this world." Ory's activity, and his father's approval, were clearly driven by the family's constant impoverishment. "We had lost our place, and then my dad and mother had taken ill, and had too much mortgage on [the house], and I couldn't get enough money to pay it off, so I sold it and gave the money to my sisters." When his father died, Ory's relatives encouraged him to take a good field job, but he "didn't like plantation work" and pursued his musical business. Still, he found it necessary to labor on weekends at the plantation's sugar mill.[21]

From the start Kid Ory was a discerning musician. As his wife expressed it, there were a "number of children on that plantation, and . . . he picked them over carefully to find the ones that were even slightly interested in the first place, to start a humming group." Music occupied him intellectually and emotionally: "I couldn't see anything but music. . . . The girls was worrying me. . . . I liked girls all right, but . . . I was sure if I learned music, I can get a girl, you know."[22] Ory clearly was inspired by rich musical traditions and resources, which also inspired future jazz musicians elsewhere in the Deep South. For example, the trumpeter Herman Autrey was raised in central Alabama, where (as in the Delta) music was firmly integrated into religion, work, and community. The landowner's field "was full of people . . . down the road picking cotton. . . . And for some reason, at different intervals . . . somebody would start the song, and they would all chime in, and you never heard such things in your life, such sounds, such harmonies." The music began after workers related stories to one another, "like reading the paper," and "then we'd go into a religious theme" that then led to singing. Here too the folk were discerning: "They didn't stop working, they just stood up and looked at each other, [and said] 'watch out, you get a little flat, you get a little sharp.'" On Sundays, church members cared for sick friends, plowing their land and doing their cooking, and the children picked berries. After the meal "they would start singing . . . and naturally I was playing the trumpet," which Autrey played in church as well. The music, he concluded, "happened to all the people together, singing, shaking hands, praying."[23]

It is plain, however, that the river region in Louisiana was uniquely rife with black instrumental bands by 1900. Ory's was not the only kid band there, as others sprang up on neighboring plantations. Networks of musicians were soon formed, so that Ory met Freddy Keppard, a youth learning the trumpet, and other adoles-

cent players traveling upriver from New Orleans. Ory was nurtured
by the examples of touring professional black bands from the city—
Dave Payton's, Buddy Bolden's, Charlie Galloway's and others—
that made whistle stops at the LaPlace station on the Yazoo and
Mississippi line. The stops were designed to "get people to go" to
their urban dances—a practice showing that plantation blacks, as
well as whites, traveled to cities for infrequent entertainment.[24]

James Humphrey's Onward Band of New Orleans was the
most respected black band. Like most touring bands, the Onward
was well schooled, read notation, and played European-American
light music: waltzes, schottisches, and sentimental favorites. This
band and others made a strong impression on rural children. "We
kids," Ory recalled, "we used to bet. If we'd hear a brass band
playing, say about a block from us, we'd bet to see which key the
band was playing in." Kid bands derived many of their attitudes
about deportment and group identity from these black bands. Ory
gradually acquired band uniforms, first buying matching coats and
then obtaining further components from door-to-door peddlers.
As adolescents, his crew posed smartly in white shirts, bow ties, and
new suits costing $7.95, which Ory kept and protected after each
engagement.[25]

The plantation was a place in which folk traditions of music
making, communality, and childhood play merged with a spirit of
economic enterprise. Markets for musical entertainment were created and cultivated, and the introduction of admission charges at
fish fries and other events showed that this black vernacular music
was entering the commercial market. These ambitious enterprises
culminated in travel and eventual migration to the city. By the age
of ten, Ory claimed, he had already taken his bands on tours of saw-
mill towns between Baton Rouge and Kenner, a sixty-mile stretch
of road. The adolescent Ory walked many times to New Orleans—
"29.3 miles [from] the plantation door"—to hear music, but he had
promised not to move there until he reached twenty-one. "I [be-
came] twenty-one at 4:30 in the morning; at 8 o'clock I was on the
train [for New Orleans]. I've been gone ever since."[26] Migration to
New Orleans would transform Ory's instrumental blues into jazz.
The long list of important early players who migrated to the city
from nearby rural regions includes the cornetists Joe Oliver and
Buddy Petit, the pianist Myknee Jones, the bassist John Lindsey,
the clarinetist Jimmy Noone, the trumpeters Tommy Ladnier, Kid
Thomas, and Mutt Carey, and many others. Many parents of other

jazz pioneers, such as Louis Armstrong's, also migrated down the river to New Orleans.[27]

Jazz, born through this migration to New Orleans, can be defined as instrumental blues, featuring individual and collective improvisation and a unique "swinging" of the beat. It seems certain that all of these elements were integrated only in New Orleans. Various testimony disputes this contention, of course: Herman Autrey said that jazz originated anywhere blacks were "singing, shaking hands, [and] praying," and the bandleader Sam Wooding, who heard swinging in Philadelphia and blues singers from Baltimore in 1909, felt that jazz "spontaneously originated all over the United States."[28]

Certainly, African survivals, as well as the tensions created by Jim Crow laws and hopes for the future, were shared across the nation. The music of the lower Mississippi differed from black music in other regions largely because of its intensity and cultural significance, not due to any special content or role. If we ignore the protojazz developments outside the Delta we obviously will fail to learn about much of what contributed to the classic jazz culture of the 1920s and 1930s. However, the unique rate of musical change in black New Orleans after 1880 was crucial, and musicians there did face special circumstances. The New Orleans experience presented challenges deriving from slavery, plantation life, racial classification, and the Afro-Caribbean heritage, which especially stimulated the growth of the instrumental blues. If we fail to focus on jazz's origins in New Orleans, therefore, we miss what was essential in determining the cultural role of the music and the nature of the jazz musicians' profession.

2

"He Should Throw That Club at You"
Urban Origins in New Orleans

Between 1890 and 1920, African-American musicians in many cities developed instrumental music featuring some syncopation, improvisation, and blues harmony,[1] but it is the musical history of New Orleans that looms large in early jazz chronicles. The city's distinctiveness has been so widely noted, its title as "the cradle of jazz" so secure, that it is very tempting to promote any scrap of evidence that might lessen its reputation. Such evidence certainly exists: early players there called the music ragtime, and the term "jazz" was rarely heard in New Orleans before 1920. Startlingly, the first printed reference to a jazz music appeared in a San Francisco newspaper in 1913, and the word first gained common use in the North.[2]

Ever since 1920, though, the New Orleans music has been called jazz, and historians have at least casually traced jazz's sociocultural significance back to the city's special musical culture. Revisionists find this consensus a tempting target. While it would be valid to explore the limits of New Orleans's role and perhaps to debunk the cradle legend, I only strive here to broaden the inquiry of jazz historiography. The New Orleans scene, so well documented with published and archival material, is the obvious place to begin this broadening. This documentation itself suggests that the exotic lore of the Place Congo and Storyville has been overvalued and that more mundane aspects of daily life and social change will reveal more about the musicians' lives and thoughts. Similarly, the myth of the jazz infant moving up the river to maturity, while based in part on fact, is used here as a heuristic structure for the narrative, which focuses on more pivotal social and commercial processes.

As many writers have observed, New Orleans was in many

ways a well-preserved arena of Afro-Caribbean culture; the integration of music, dance, religion, and community thrived there to 1900. The Sunday slave dances at the Place Congo were held regularly until 1835, and the highly organized practice of voodoo reached its peak with the reign of Queen Marie Laveau in the following decades. The colorful French and Spanish traditions of opera, military bands, parades, and dance have also been richly chronicled.[3] These elements were central ingredients in the formulation of early jazz, but no less important were the plainer, newer, and more wrenching forces that molded New Orleans life (especially among blacks) in the decades before World War One. These forces made jazz an emblem of discontinuity as much as an heir to tradition, a cry of despair as well as a Mardi Gras cheer; and they ensured that its creators would be as likely to flee the city as they would be to revel in it.

Just as on the nearby plantations, emancipation brought to New Orleans a resurgence of racism that seemed more severe in some ways than white attitudes before the war. To an extent, ex-slaves were able to make a smoother transition to freedom than their counterparts in other communities. The city traditionally had flaunted a comparatively relaxed racial code. A large proportion of the antebellum black population had been free, and the celebrated social and sexual interaction among the races in certain milieux had made barriers comparatively porous. The historian John W. Blassingame found that the "successful adjustment of the New Orleans Negro to freedom" was common, because of "the radical difference between the treatment of the slaves on the plantations and their treatment" in the city, and his evidence partially supports this conclusion. Few unions restricted black membership in such skilled trades as shoemaking, carpentry, cooperage, masonry, plastering, and cigarmaking.[4]

New Orleans probably had the best facilities in the South for the education of blacks, possessing twenty-eight primary schools and three "universities" (secondary schools) by 1877. The longer blacks spent living in the city, the more likely they were to gain literacy and arithmetic skills. While more than 57 percent of Louisiana's rural blacks were listed in the 1910 Census as illiterate, only 28.4 percent of urban blacks received that designation. This was still a very high figure—only 2 percent of Louisiana's urban whites were listed as illiterate in 1910—but a sign of progress nonetheless. Indeed, the jazz pioneer Buddy Bolden, a primitive musician to some, was able to read and write, as could every member of his band and family (besides his wife).[5] Blassingame argues that blacks, along with the light-skinned Creoles of color, "created a mosaic in race relations without design. . . . In New Orleans, as perhaps in no other American city, there were many cracks in the color line."[6]

Another historian, David C. Rankin, however, argues that since antebellum free blacks, former slaves, and Creoles of color failed to reach an alliance after the Civil War, they doomed their chances for political and social influence after the Union soldiers left. Instead, Rankin writes, "the war . . . destroyed [the Creoles'] intermediate caste position." Differing from other blacks in their Catholicism and use of French, the *gens de couleur* sought the support of white Creoles while English-speaking blacks cast their lot with the Reconstruction forces.[7] Thus, despite certain economic and social advantages, New Orleans blacks still bore the double onus of Anglo and united Creole discrimination and abuse. Their economic situation was as desperate as that of other ex-slaves, and black mortality and morbidity rates remained high for many decades. In a broader sense, the entire city remained backward even for a Southern city, as it did not adopt Progressive reforms in sanitation, health care, city politics and finance, and housing until well into the twentieth century.[8] This stasis helped to ensure that New Orleans preserved miseries from a previous era that otherwise might have been avoided.

Within white and nonwhite neighborhoods alike, political splits and economic difficulties proved explosive. No American city of the Progressive era suffered greater ethnic conflict than New Orleans. Tensions between Italian and Irish residents climaxed in the 1891 lynch murders of eleven Sicilians—after their exoneration in the death of an Irish policeman. "Cracks in the color line" did exist, but bullets and bricks were often fired through them, such as in 1894 and 1895, when black and white dockworkers engaged in fatal clashes over vanishing jobs. The depths of this conflict were reached in July 1900 during the rioting that followed the capture and murder of Robert Charles (a black suspected in the killing of a policeman), causing at least twenty deaths.[9] The corruption and ethnic tension of what may have been the nation's least progressive city especially stifled the hopes of black residents. "A hardening of white racial prejudices" set in, as the first segregation laws were passed after the Supreme Court's 1896 decision in *Plessy v. Ferguson* (which involved a New Orleans streetcar), and in 1898 blacks were denied the vote.[10]

The Creoles of color (referred to henceforth simply as Creoles), caught between a growing "American Negro" population and increasingly intolerant whites, developed an intense caste consciousness in these years. As the Creole musician Paul Dominguez told Alan Lomax, "Downtown people, we try to be intelligent. Everybody learn a trade . . . [and] try to get an easy job that our education qualifies us for. We try to bar jail. . . . Uptown, cross Canal yonder, they [American blacks] *used* to jail. . . . Uptown folk all ruffians, cut up in the face and live on the river. All cotton— be longshoremen, screwmen. And me, I ain't never been on the river a *day in my life*." [11] Similarly, in the 1920s New Orleans blacks told Langston Hughes that Creoles refused to associate with any "English-speaking Negroes" living "across Canal Street." Although the Creoles themselves had begun to learn English and to shed many traditional folkways in an attempt to brake their fall in status, they nevertheless continued to consider themselves separate from and superior to other African Americans. [12]

Thus, New Orleans presented a novel and oppressive system of racial strictures and tensions. However, it also held some equally novel opportunities and attractions. Like other southern cities, New Orleans became a magnet for thousands of rural migrants. The rural black settlement there from 1870 to 1915 was significant for the era. White migration was heavy as well, so the black proportion of the population was static, remaining at about 27 percent during this period, but from 1860 to 1880 the Negro and mulatto count increased from 25,423 to 57,617, and by 1910 the number had expanded to almost 100,000. [13] Overpopulation only worsened the life of black migrants, who were generally crammed into three segregated districts upriver from the city's center. As early as 1880, almost 40 percent of the families there did not have male heads. Underemployment and unemployment were chronic in the period from 1880 to 1915, mostly due to the city's increasing difficulties in an era of stagnant cotton prices. [14] These uptown blacks traded plantation life for a more complex and dangerous challenge.

Since the early 1800s the English-speaking black community had possessed a thriving musical culture, ranging from the efforts of classically trained impresarios to the ring shouts of the evangelical churches. The religious music was especially potent. When Kid Ory frequented the city after 1900 he attended the "holy rollers'" services to absorb the exuberant music. "Drums and pianos" reinforced the singing and clapping of the parishioners, whom Ory found "would get to swinging." Other Creole musicians, like Edmond Hall, also drew inspiration from the Protestant church music, and evangelical musicians themselves—such as the cornetists Buddy Bolden and Joe Oliver—obtained much of their basic repertoire and expressive style from these church services.[15]

The black brass bands, forerunners of the early jazz groups, flourished as early as the 1870s. New Orleans's rich band heritage derived from the French military-band tradition and the wide availability of Confederate band instruments after the Civil War. By 1880, such black bands as the St. Bernard, Kelly's, and the Excelsior played at parks, picnics, and other public gatherings. It will never be known which of these bands was the first to syncopate their music in the ragtime fashion, or swing it in the jazz manner, or improvise solos; it has been suggested that the guitarist Charlie "Sweet Lovin'" Galloway's 1889 band was the first to swing its beat. Many oral histories, however, have led most historians to attribute the honor to Buddy Bolden's band, active from about 1897 to 1907.[16] Whatever its origins may have been, the style had caught on with many bands by 1907, the year Kid Ory moved from the plantation. Blacks and Creoles alike began to swing the beat, underpinning the already jumpy syncopations of ragtime melodies. The strict military-march beat gave way to the undulating slow drag and up-tempo strut, which became basic forms of the New Orleans jazz style.

The city's crowded and impoverished conditions, however, situated black musicians within a challenging, even hostile, milieu. Black neighborhoods were rarely guarded by the New Orleans police, which like other urban American forces was preoccupied with keeping vagrants and the poor out of "respectable" white neighborhoods.[17] On the contrary, black children (including future musicians) became the victims of strict curfews, which were sometimes violently enforced by white policemen. In Storyville, the city's famous district of legal prostitution, the bassist Montudie Garland noted, "policemen's catch you down there [with] short pants, oh-oh, he should throw that club at you. . . . and you run into it and get your legs crossed on the club, and throw you down." The club featured rawhide straps with which "they used to whip you," and it symbolized the stigmas associated with dark skin and youth in the city.[18]

Urban black instrumental music, like the plantation music before it, developed in an environment of physical violence. As Ory recalled, "the toughest place I ever played in was Funky Butt Hall," as Kenna's Hall was nicknamed, where "if you didn't have a razor or a gun, you couldn't get in there." Racial antagonisms, on the rise by 1900, sparked violence around musicians. Sidney Bechet's father was absent from his band's rehearsal when a white policeman attempted to stop their playing. A band member hit the policeman, and the incident escalated into a neighborhood race fight. The city's most terrible conflagration, the Robert Charles riot of 1900, had made Charles (an Afrophile and opponent of lynching) a folk hero among poor blacks. Charles killed seven white men and wounded twenty after police confronted him; when a white mob set fire to his outpost, Charles himself was killed and his body was pumped with hundreds of bullets and beaten beyond recognition. For a time, "The Robert Charles Song" was popular among black bands and audiences, although the pianist Ferdinand "Jelly Roll" Morton "found out it was best for me to forget it . . . in order to go along with the world on the peaceful side." [19]

As a result of this environment, vicarious violence, in the form of harsh language and simulated battles and killings, characterized the culture of poor black New Orleans. Funerals for pimps, gamblers, and other club regulars became rituals that reaffirmed the toughness and stoicism of the living. At one ceremony Kid Ory noted that "the men was hollering, 'I'm glad you're dead, you rascal you.'" In the case of Ory and other musicians, the atmosphere of violence inspired the barely restrained form of competition between bands called "cutting contests." [20]

Barney Bigard, a Creole who later became a major jazz clarinetist, witnessed many such events, which frequently dramatized black and Creole rivalry. "One [band] might be giving a ball uptown and the other might have one downtown and they would be out on the streets advertising and they would meet up at one corner or another and have a 'battle' to see who was going to 'cut' the other. If one was getting cut real bad the people would chain the wagon wheels together," perhaps out of a latent desire to see the victors actually carve up the losers. "Black Benny," a street hustler, has been mentioned as a spectral figure who often handled the chains. Bigard recalled that "the winner was decided by the people and that's the ball they would go to that night." Violence was further sublimated through the crowd's belief that "whichever band had the nastiest lyrics would win. Like Ory had a tune to which the band sang 'If you don't like the way I play, then kiss my funky ass.' This went over big with all the whores." The leader Frankie Dusen was another "real foul-mouthed man" who cut many opponents. It is striking that Ory, who knew only French before his teens, gained popular success with a volatile mixture of syncopated music and scatological English. Derived in equal measures from the

African-American traditions of oral virtuosity, communal insult, and musical ritual, the cutting contest sublimated violence, putting aggression to creative use.[21]

The earliest black jazz bands, exemplified by Ory's "Woodland Band" (named after their native plantation) and Bolden's outfit, found regular work in riverfront taverns, which housed saloons, gambling dens, and houses of prostitution that served the city's large population of transient sailors and boatmen. The saloon-keeper Pete Lala hired Ory's band in 1907, paying each member the subsistence wage of $1.50 a night. Lala and other tavern owners flourished because their competition was suppressed by the owners' friends in city hall, the police, and in the crime organizations, which profited from the vices the city outlawed. Club owners were the best-connected exploiters of labor in working-class New Orleans.[22]

Rural migrants occasionally could mine some prosperity out of this environment, as Kid Ory's success in the city demonstrated. Ory was among the first black bandleaders to mount his group on a horse-drawn wagon to advertise its engagements. After a few years of working in the city, Ory began renting two dance halls. His band would play in the Economy Hall while he "kept [the Co-operator Hall] dark, until I couldn't accommodate [all] the people at Economy Hall." He would then open the Cooperator and have his second band play there. "I tied them [the halls] up for a whole year," depriving his competition of a site while ensuring the greatest profits for his first band. Other young players displayed similar skills. Willie Hightower, a trumpet player from Nashville who grew up in New Orleans, had built his own instruments as a child, started his own spasm band (as children's bands were known), and used his profits to buy real estate. In 1906, he purchased a small saloon and installed his band. At only seventeen, he was not legally permitted to enter saloons, but his ownership of one was not challenged. Hightower also opened a horseshoe lawn, where he employed the young Freddy Keppard's band as the resident entertainment.[23]

The variety of paid musical jobs available in black New Orleans is revealed by the testimony of Manuel "Fess" Manetta, a downtown non-Creole black who became one of New Orleans's leading teachers of jazz cornet in later years. Manetta began his working life as a janitor in the Odd Fellow's Hall in the early 1900s, where the "ratty" clientele at the hall's nightly dances held "ham kicking contests" (dances) and other rural amusements. Polite black society, in Manetta's opinion, held its functions at Sacred Heart of Mary's Hall, the Catholic name of which suggested that Creoles were polite society in his view. As a cornetist, Manetta worked across a wide social spectrum, playing at "lawn parties for white and for colored." For Manetta the term "lawn party" included less-genteel events in the Irish Channel (a riverfront neighborhood of mixed ethnic population), where the band would "be forced to play beyond the scheduled hours, until all members of the party collapsed from drinking, exhaustion or fighting," and at saloon-sponsored events, such as those held by the prominent pimp Napoleon "Toodlum" Johnson. Brothels, as Manetta and many others noted, generally did not employ bands. A woman friend of his operated a brothel in Storyville, "with white and colored stalls," in which Manetta, Jelly Roll Morton, "Birmingham," and other pianists provided the only musical entertainment.[24]

On the whole, however, blacks and Creoles found themselves unable—even at the height of the dance-hall culture in the mid-1910s—to support themselves and their families as musicians. Music was a side occupation for almost all non-Creole black players, who thus remained folk musicians in a sense, amateurs playing occasionally and for the community. Although renowned for its musical cultures, New Orleans had never hosted a large permanent contingent of musical professionals. In 1870, among the city's 40,000 blacks, only 7 listed their major occupation as musician in the census survey. This compared to 177 black policemen, 397 cigarmakers, and 249 shoemakers. Ten years later the number of black musicians rose to only 53.[25]

While some early jazz players were pushed into folk or amateur status by the lack of a musical profession, many others were pulled toward bands in the first place because of the chance for badly needed side income. In 1879, one-quarter of all laborers in New Orleans, nearly as many carpenters, masons, and steamboatmen, and about one in ten cigarmakers and blacksmiths—an overall rate of 18 percent—were out of work for most of the year. This situation only worsened during the depressed 1890s, when New Orleans jazz began to take shape. Alphonse Picou, a Creole born in 1878, was an accomplished clarinetist by his late teens, but he continued to work as a tinsmith and plumber. "He never considered himself a musician as such until he was asked to join the Bloom Symphony," a Creole classical group. Louis Armstrong hauled coal, the guitarist Johnny St. Cyr was a builder, the drummer Arthur "Zutty" Singleton worked as a drayman, and Pops Foster (who had migrated from the McCall plantation) was a longshoreman. The dockworkers' union leader, Foster recalled, "had all the best musicians working on longshore work," which was facilitated (until 1908) by the union council's "half-half" policy of biracial dock employment. The trumpeter Anatie "Natty" Dominique, like his teacher, Manuel Perez, and many of his Creole friends, worked in the cigarmaking trade in the 1900s and 1910s. "That was compulsory then, working making cigars in the day time. . . . You had to do that. You can't get along just playing two or three nights with th[at] salary." [26]

Perhaps because the poor envied their added income, and the bourgeoisie and the wealthy considered them of meager status, musicians held a very low reputation among New Orleans townspeople. As Pops Foster remembered, "back then everybody," including his new in-laws, "classified musicians as bums." In a bit of bravado, Foster claimed that musicians actually "weren't no good either" and that "all of us made a lot of noise and had a lot of pleasure," but this boastfulness does not conceal his obvious resentment of the low status. "Musicians were nowhere in the South," he noted. "If a girl was with you at a dance nobody would talk to her. . . . It was very hard to find a room to rent if you were a musician." White musicians encountered the same attitude in the city decades later, such as when a woman told the trumpeter Wingy Manone that his band "was a disgrace." "In New Orleans it *is* a disgrace" to play jazz, in Manone's opinion. [27]

Heightened racial tensions in New Orleans after 1890 generally limited musicians' freedom of employment and association. In fact, divisions between blacks, whites, and Creoles underlay most of the social and career difficulties that confronted black and Creole jazz musicians. Activity in the streets and dance halls brought creative, racially diverse people together, but centuries of racial mores and customs strained to keep them apart. The patterns of mixing and dividing in New Orleans were complex, as two teams of black sociologists found in the 1930s, when after extensive fieldwork they arrived at conflicting conclusions. John Dollard and Allison Davis argued that New Orleans possessed a racial *caste* system in which mixing took place with the greatest difficulty and infrequency, while Charles S. Johnson concluded that the caste system was largely a product of illusion and rhetoric, and that too much mixing occurred for such a system to take hold. [28]

The musicians' experience provides evidence for both conclusions, since the city was a bastion of strict racial exclusion that also featured important exceptions to the rule. Interracial bands were

largely forbidden. Around 1900, the white leader Jack Laine had
hired a man for his Reliance Band, but "when I found out he was a
nigger, that's when I stopped hiring him. . . . I never knew he was
colored. . . . [But] one fine day I passed on Ursuline Street, where
he lived, and I saw his daddy and that was enough." Laine had
been fooled in part because the man had married a white woman
(white, at least, to Laine) and lived in the Seventh Ward, known as
the "Can't Tell Ward" because of its extreme racial mixture. Creoles were equally intolerant of darker townsmen. Jelly Roll Morton,
born Ferdinand Lemott into a Creole family, told Alan Lomax that
his grandmother, Mimi Pechet, disowned him when she learned
that he played "common music with the sons of fieldhands."[29]

No significant early mixing in bands occurred. The cornetist
Geary "Bunk" Johnson was one of the few black musicians before
1915 who often played downtown with Creoles, and such light-
skinned, wavy-haired Creoles as Baptist Aucoin, Achille Baquet,
and Dave Perkins could infiltrate white bands on occasion. Before
1920, though, such Creoles as Bechet and Ory rarely formed or
joined non-Creole black bands. Those "black-and-tan" groups that
were permitted faced constraints. As Pops Foster noted, "the uptown clubs and societies were the strictest" places; at the Francs
Amis Hall, only the lightest player was allowed to leave the bandstand to get drinks for the musicians.[30]

Sharp racial divisions generally ensured that bands of specific skin tones could only play before specific audiences. In 1910,
under new management, the Tuxedo Dance Hall, a former brothel,
became an exclusive whites-only ballroom, and only then hired
the Creole leader Oscar "Sonny" (later "Papa") Celestin. Celestin
was told only to hire Creole musicians from downtown who could
read notes. Other halls, including those that featured John Robichaux's popular Creole band, also only admitted white customers.
Storyville was strictly segregated; at Lulu White's brothel, which
employed Fess Manetta and other good pianists, "all of the customers . . . were white, with no exceptions." While white audiences
apparently preferred Creole over black bands, some venues did
offer white patrons the "cornfield" blues style of the migrants. Pops
Foster noted that "it was a rule in New Orleans if you didn't play
any blues you didn't get any colored jobs, and if you didn't play
lancers you didn't get Cajun jobs. White jobs didn't care what you
played."[31]

Whites' ignorance of African-American music thus even led

them to hire and pay disreputable black jazz musicians. For white listeners, therefore, the barriers were low, and the full array of black music was available to them. Black musicians could play in certain downtown regions, but were kept out of many halls and saloons, and black customers were strictly segregated into clubs in all-black neighborhoods. Creoles were caught in a marginal state somewhere (or everywhere) between racial and economic polar opposites.

To further complicate this varied arrangement, New Orleanians institutionalized a number of rituals involving jazz that accentuated racial barriers by seeming to deny them. During the annual Mardi Gras celebration, for example, tradition dictated that blacks and whites wore different kinds of masks. As the white trombonist Georg Brunis explained, whites considered this necessary because masked people went from door to door sampling "doughnuts and chocolate," and hosts wanted to "tell who it was" they were serving. In the parade, however, subtle subversion of this race-conscious masking was possible. As Pops Foster remembered, "they didn't have any colored bands playing in the parade. Some of the colored guys played in the bands but they passed for whites." The Mardi Gras parade also gave blacks a rare chance to see and hear white bands. The trombonist Preston Jackson saw "the white musicians in Mardi Gras parades" wearing masks, "he didn't know who they were"—but at least this way Jackson became exposed to white playing that was usually banned to him.[32]

The Mardi Gras did very little to boost the cause of jazz, but as Samuel Kinser points out, in the same years blacks developed New Orleans jazz they also invented the Zulu clubs and their own separate parade, "aimed at satire, both of themselves—that is, of blacks in their situation—and no less of the whites who lorded it over them." Clearly, both jazz and the Zulu parades were part of the same cultural ferment before 1910.[33]

Other rituals allowed for the musical cross-fertilization of different racial groups. For example, the funeral procession accompanied by brass band began as a white tradition but became a black practice after the Civil War; but the transition was decades in the making, and for years bands of both races met each other on the street. Similarly, in the 1910s Georg Brunis participated in an extraordinary interracial bandwagon battle. His adolescent white band met up with Buddy Petit's Creoles in an intersection, "and we'd challenge each other; and they'd pull one direction, we'd go another direction, and play 'Get over dirty' with the instruments . . .

then maybe an hour or so later, we'd meet on another street."[34] When white and black musicians met, it was usually accidentally, on the streets. In these situations, as in those instances where the Creole was the whites' society musician and perhaps close to looking white himself, racial barriers were temporarily surmounted. Whites and blacks thus briefly enjoyed shared audiences and learned each other's criteria for musical excellence.

Nevertheless, white racism was too persistent and black internal divisions were too deep to be overcome in any lasting way. What Tony Russell noted with regard to the shared blues heritage of blacks and whites applied even more firmly to Jim Crow New Orleans: "the barriers were not to fall; what God, in the eyes of the Southern white man, had put asunder, no musical communion could join together."[35]

In part to soften the harm inflicted by these racial barriers, musicians made their bands insular, nurturing, and fraternal organizations. The bands were an important socializing force for young musicians, especially rural migrants. Some of these bands were established by official agencies. Civic-minded black New Orleanians formed societies and remedial programs for orphans and delinquents that offered music and band instruction. The celebrated Colored Waifs' Home, founded by the black Army veteran Joseph Jones, was even recognized by the city government as a worthwhile remedial institution for black boys who had difficulties with the police. Famed as the man who gave Louis Armstrong his first cornet lessons, the Home's music teacher, Peter Davis, also trained such future jazz musicians as the trombonists Preston Jackson and George Washington. As Jackson remembered, Armstrong's "ability was evident even though he wasn't but twelve years old then."[36]

Whether or not they were sponsored by reformers, bands socialized young followers into the ways of both the musician and urban life. Barney Bigard noted that "my first interest in music" came from "watching the brass bands." On Saturday parades "we would try to follow the band as far as our folks would let us . . . for four blocks or so." The second line of nonplaying marchers was already a black New Orleans tradition, a marching adaptation of the field holler and the ring shout, and it gained new prominence when jazz brass came to lead the children, prostitutes, gamblers, and novice musicians. The bands, like earlier marching groups, bonded these diverse groups in the second line, which shared a traditional powerlessness in urban society and provided the musicians with a community of admirers that literally followed their careers.

Some found the lines disreputable. Bigard's parents "didn't want us to get hung up in those 'second lines' because they were kind of bad." Zutty Singleton followed funeral band processionals, and his mother too "caught me, all engrossed, and jerked me out of the parade. Mothers did not approve of it. The kids who did it were tough [such as] Louis [Armstrong]. And Bechet was a raggedy man." The New Orleans street parade was thus a special lure for young blacks, away from the sheltered world of childhood and toward the intriguing fraternities of adulthood.[37]

The band fraternity was the musical manifestation of urban blacks' strong need for voluntary association. Like white Americans on the frontier or in rapidly industrializing northern towns, blacks in New Orleans responded to their hazardous environment by joining together in recreational, political, business, and even secret societies.[38] As Singleton noted, funeral processions were usually sponsored by such black associations as the Masons, Odd Fellows, Druids, Eagles, Moose, Knights of St. Pythias, and trade unions. "When the member died, he had to have a band [at the funeral]. He was nothing if he didn't have a band." These groups usually sponsored dances, rented halls and other indoor gathering places, or held the outdoor picnics at Milneburg, by Lake Pontchartrain. More informally, as Pops Foster recollected, bands would "go around to your house and serenade you if it was your birthday," and "a lot of times we'd go serenade good customers, or people we just liked. If a guy was building a house, we'd show up and play and help him build it. . . . The pay sometimes just made it a little bit sweeter." Jazz, like most African-American music, was inseparable from group dancing. Ory, for example, noted that his largely Catholic audiences "did not dance during Lent, and it was at that time of year that his band had to find work in Storyville [which generally did not employ bands]."[39]

In New Orleans, early jazz drew upon black traditions of parental musical instruction, which reinforced the familial nature of the bands. Many of the bands reflected what James Lincoln Collier called the intense "clannishness" of New Orleans worklife, involving "a strong tradition of handing down trades from father to son, including music." James Humphrey instructed his son Willie in the clarinet and his daughters Lillan and Jamesetta in the bass, and Willie's three sons, born at the turn of the century, collectively learned the clarinet, trumpet, drums, saxophone, and trombone. Another professor, W. H. Young of the black New Orleans University, dispensed lessons at home as well, where his children Lester, Lee, and Irma, nephews Boots and Sports, and two successive wives were trained for the family's touring band.[40]

As a reflection of this familial quality, enterprising mentors, especially Creoles, sought out and developed broods of young pupils. Natty Dominique remembered that in the 1900s the cornetist Manuel Perez gave free lessons to boys he believed possessed musical talent. "Perez [would] see a kid that he liked on the street, he'd call him, 'hey'—'Come here.' He'd say, 'I'm gonna make a cornet player out of you.' . . . That kid better take that lesson because if he don't, the father gonna find out." Perez, of Afro-Caribbean descent, supported himself as a cigarmaker and as the leader of the popular Imperial Brass Band. Other important Creole teachers included George Baquet, a well-schooled clarinetist who played in classical and early jazz groups and taught the great player Sidney Bechet, and Lorenzo "Papa" Tio, the instructor of Barney Bigard and other Creole clarinetists. After about 1907, jazz bands had a patriarchal air to them, especially when the public began to identify them by their leaders' names and personalities. As Pops Foster noted, Kid Ory was again the pioneer: "People liked his music and it was very hot. . . . He made such a big hit that all the other bands started changing the names of their band to the leader's name to copy Ory." The city's working-class white bands also displayed patriarchal features.[41]

Patriarchy, in turn, reflected the strongly male general orientation of the black musicians' fraternity. James Humphrey, who instructed his daughters, was a rare exception in New Orleans. Linda Dahl notes that women musicians were excluded from many good jobs by a "musical male brotherhood" that was both "a natural support system (though highly competitive) and a response to the economic difficulties of the profession." Bands would often provide music for figures-cutting gatherings, in which men danced as closely as possible around jugs without knocking them over. "There wouldn't be *any* women where these men got together," Sidney Bechet recalled. In New Orleans almost all of the women active in early jazz circles were singers or pianists, and most of them tended to be employed in Storyville saloons and brothels as hostesses or prostitutes. (Important exceptions included Emma Barrett and Jeanette Salvant, who worked in Sonny Celestin's band because, as one historian noted, "Celestin liked to have a woman on piano.") In New Orleans, where more than two thousand prostitutes were registered at city hall, these women and their profession strongly colored the gender perceptions of musicians and other working-class males. "All the musicians back in New Orleans wanted to be pimps," Pops Foster claimed. Foster noted that this ambition resulted in part from the police's strict enforcement of vagrancy laws: "you had to prove you were doing some kind of work or they'd put you in jail."[42]

Two other sets of beliefs helped to segregate women into the brothel and away from participation in instrumental music. First, male musicians of all colors subscribed firmly to the general American belief that musical instruments were gender-specific. Band musicians in New Orleans "thought piano was for women," for example, and taunted male saloon pianists with calls of "'Sissies' and 'look at that faggot up there.'" Second, musically talented women in New Orleans's poorer quarters were associated, often inaccurately, with the socially disreputable voodoo possession religion. Jazz scholarship has shown only a patchy relation between early jazzwomen and voodoo. A strong tradition of matriarchy in New Orleans voodoo had been established during the long reign of queen Marie Laveau, and the earliest report of female blues singing and piano playing involved Mamie Desdoumes, another voodoo priestess whom Jelly Roll Morton had heard singing the "2:19 Blues" in the 1890s. On the basis of such lore, the musicians and future writers repeatedly stressed the relation between jazzwomen and voodoo. Correctly or errantly, musical women were associated by men, almost certainly excessively, with the underworld status of the prostitute and the priestess.[43]

To a large degree, this male-oriented jazz fraternity was a mechanism for socializing young migrants to new urban ways. They adapted rural values to urban life as they entered street parades and the more organized city professions, but they also brought the blues and its social and spiritual connotations into the city, which altered urbanites' perception of their surroundings. Alphonse Picou, an urbane Creole, recalled that around 1900 the bass player Jimmy Brown often "took him down to the railroad tracks," where he taught Picou to sing the blues.[44] This pilgrimage translated the riverside singing tradition of rural times into a ritual alongside the modern pathway of commerce, and symbolized how the spirit of rural life—more specifically, its interrelation of community, music, and environment—infused the culture of the Southern city in which they settled.

Migrant musicians who were drawn into the jazz enterprise were also introduced to European traditions in the city. The French Opera, visits by European companies and soloists, and the very atmosphere of aristocratic filigree and pretense in New Orleans took the players' imagination to worlds beyond the plantation. For these reasons, Jelly Roll Morton—one of the greatest New Orleans innovators—came to argue that "jazz is based on strictly music. You have the finest ideas from the greatest operas, symphonies and overtures in jazz music. There is nothing finer than jazz music because it comes from everything of the finest class music." As a result of urban influences, New Orleans musicians began to conceive of themselves as artists in the European sense, as elite notions became wedded to African-American concepts of the skilled instrumentalist. Montudie Garland, when asked in 1977 whether he felt like a craftsman or an artist in the early days, answered ambiguously, "I feel like an artist. . . . [But] not all the time." Asked about other New Orleans musicians, Garland answered unequivocally that they considered themselves artists.[45]

These views evolved as musicians developed discriminating and exacting standards for jazz. For example, as bands shifted more rapidly indoors, acoustical standards were developed and articulated. The drummer Warren "Baby" Dodds indicated that early bands cared deeply about how their music sounded amid noise, noting that they preferred to play on platforms about four feet high. "Music is more even when it comes down on people's heads, because it hits the ceiling and comes down on them," and "a band will sound better if the best place in the room is picked out to set up the band." As Natty Dominique noted, drummers, like other musicians, cultivated trademark techniques that served as emblems of professionalism. Louis Cottrell mastered the technique of the soft solo roll in rhythm, in which he "barely don't move his fingers, just like that," and Tubby Hall executed a similar eight-bar-long roll "like [he was] tearing a piece of paper." Even the profane master of the new swinging music, Kid Ory, wanted his band to cultivate a soft sound on the ad wagon: "Bring them to me with sweetness, I guess."[46] The general aesthetic remained African-American, but the instruments and the specialized knowledge were indicative of a Euro-American cultural influence that, at the very least, showed how the city changed rural black musicians.[47]

In the space of a generation, a music advocated by all classes of black New Orleanians promoted improvisation and the blues in a winning, forward-looking fashion. At the same time, the burdens of violence and oppression persisted and ensured that musicians in the South would never really liberate themselves through musical innovation. "You know, the Negro doesn't want to cling to music," Sidney Bechet wrote in 1960; "people are always putting him to music. 'That's your place,' they say." But blacks needed music, Bechet concluded: "it means something; and *he* can mean something."[48] Perhaps Bechet intended to say that they only needed to remind themselves that they and their culture, of which music was a vital pillar, had always "meant something." New Orleanians had been able to do this, mainly because urban life gave them some of the tools with which to resurrect those traditional sources of meaning—in the street play of children, in the second line, through the guidance of patriarchs, and in the close quarters of the secret societies, dance halls, and jook joints.

By 1917, New Orleans jazz signified, among other things, a conjunction of rural and urban culture, Africa and Europe, individual skill and communal fraternizing, Protestant and Creole sensibilities, and the violent past and an encouraging future. Jazz's meaning as the art of the urbanizing African American would become even more significant as large numbers of Southern blacks moved North, during the Great Migration of the coming decade.

3

"Therefore, I Got to Go"
Jazz and the Great Northern Migration

New Orleans musicians were not circumscribed professionally by the city limits. Just as many of them had taken to plantation roads to seek opportunities in the city, by 1910 they were already spreading their new instrumental blues through the national channels of the entertainment industry.

As we have seen, the railroad brought bands northward from New Orleans, and for jazz musicians it remained their most crucial link to the world. Mississippi riverboats did not bring the first swinging blues to points north before 1910, but the boats offered a dramatic new opportunity for job travel for blacks just as New Orleans jazz became a discernible music. As the boat-line owner Verne Streckfus has pointed out, until the 1930s the river was the least expensive means of transporting large entertainment operations. The Streckfus line began operating out of New Orleans in 1903, sending floating summer dance halls as far north as Minneapolis. After 1915, the riverboats featured black dance bands, and many talented jazz players received their first exposure to the outside world as Streckfus employees. (The major black bandleaders on the boats, Fate Marable and Charlie Creath, were from Kentucky and Missouri, however.) Streckfus remembered that Louis Armstrong "couldn't read [music] at all" when he was hired, and that "he had never played for whites before he played on the *Capitol*." The dance clientele was largely white, and even at the Monday night "black dances . . . there were as many whites as colored." As a result, the bands were trained to play "straight" dance music (fox trots, waltzes, and one-steps) during much of each session. Streck-

fus even hired "a Russian" to teach the band "how to tune up" and
"to play waltzes and other pieces a bit more gracefully." Even as they
spread the New Orleans style, therefore, these musicians adapted
further to the European-style tastes of the commercial audience.[1]

The lure of jobs on the riverboats made musicians less likely
to put up with the special difficulties of the New Orleans nightclub trade and other push-factors. The cornetist Joe Oliver, as his
widow Stella Oliver recalled, was "content to stay in New Orleans
until the time he got arrested" in a police raid of the Winter Garden in early 1919. Oliver was working in Kid Ory's band at the
time, and Ory later agreed that "it was on this night that Oliver
decided to leave for Chicago." Police raids were a common feature of New Orleans club life, shutting down places under a variety
of legal pretexts at the instigation of well-connected rivals. In the
case of the Winter Garden, the owner of the Roof Garden cafe
was "jealous" (in Ory's view) of the former club's success and had
the police sent in to enforce a largely ignored prohibition law. Ory
had previously suffered from the influence of the powerful saloon
owner Pete Lala. The bandleader had left Lala's club to run his own
dance-hall operation, and Lala demanded a share of the profits.
When Ory refused, Lala "got about fifty cops to go around to his
dances and run all the customers away." These recurring incidents,
as well as ill health, persuaded Ory to depart for Los Angeles in
1919.[2] Oliver and Ory both sought to escape the hazards of the
racket run by club owners and city hall by leaving New Orleans,
probably assuming (incorrectly) that nonsouthern cities were free
of these kinds of exploitation and ill-treatment.

As New Orleans musicians traveled, they found that the rest
of the nation offered them job opportunities and networks of like-
minded African-American instrumentalists. The riverboats exemplified how river transportation bound together cities and musical cultures throughout the nation's middle section. New Orleans
was at the base of a lattice of port cities along the Mississippi and
Ohio River valleys, including Baton Rouge, Memphis, St. Louis,
Minneapolis, Louisville, and Cincinnati.[3] The similarities in the
black music of these cities often outweighed their differences. New
Orleanians felt that their music was somewhat similar to that of
other river towns; one musician found that a Baton Rouge band
played in a pure New Orleans style, and another believed that
"medium[-tempo] and slow blues were pretty much the same everywhere."[4] A small city such as Vicksburg, Mississippi, spawned diverse musical activity. The bassist Milt Hinton's mother taught

piano there, and he remembered that "there was always music" in the town, including vocal quartets and spirituals, and "there was always music in our home."[5]

Farther north, St. Louis musicians impressed New Orleanians with their strong advocacy of the blues. Charlie Creath's St. Louis band played on the Streckfus boats, where their slow blues "could really rock the crowd." Creath, a trumpeter, excelled at challenging others, and when he "blew those first few notes of the blues on his cornet," Zutty Singleton recalled, he "cut the other band to pieces."[6] Cincinnati, similarly, hosted a lively black musical culture that was centered on the riverfront neighborhoods. By the 1910s, blacks were concentrated in an area near 6th and John streets, up against the red-light districts. The young Bill Coleman "did not know anything about jazz or styles," but one wildly syncopating band coming to town "sounded good to me, and it was different from the way the parade bands played." Jug bands, parades, and pianists also contributed to black Cincinnati's musical life, along with bands in minstrel shows who advertised themselves from horse-drawn wagons. As in New Orleans, band members usually could not read music and were hired by word of mouth.[7] In these respects the river port cities belonged in a general musical culture region, although it is fair to conclude that New Orleans's jazz style uniquely exploited brass and wind instruments and Afro-Caribbean dance traditions.

From these port cities, New Orleanians rode the railroads to the major market in the Midwest—Chicago. The pianists Tony Jackson and Jelly Roll Morton worked at the Midway saloon district before 1910, along with such occasional blowing players as the cornetist Willie Hightower. After that year New Orleans band visits to Chicago became frequent: Montudie Garland first arrived in 1911, Natty Dominique in 1912, the Bill Johnson-Freddy Keppard band in 1915, and Jimmy Wade's band in 1916.[8] Another midwestern city, Minneapolis, also benefited from the presence of New Orleans musicians in the 1910s, when professor W. H. Young moved his musical family there.

Damning evidence refutes the up-the-Mississippi thesis of jazz history, however. For New Orleans jazz musicians before 1917, distant California was as important a market as Chicago. As Tom Stoddard first showed in his study of early San Francisco jazz, they knew as early as 1909 that California offered many locales for new types of dance music, as well as mild climate in the summers. In that year, the bassist Bill Johnson moved to Los Angeles, and proceeded to invite other New Orleanians to explore opportunities there. In

1914, Freddy Keppard brought his band to the coast, and in 1919 Kid Ory (whose lungs resisted New Orleans's heat and humidity) began a six-year stay in Los Angeles and Oakland.[9] By 1921, Los Angeles contained some of the most proficient and innovative jazz bands, including Satchel McVea's group and the Black and Tan Orchestra, and in 1922 the Ory band made probably the first purely instrumental black jazz recording at the Sunshine Records studio on Santa Monica Boulevard.[10]

At the same time that New Orleanians began to travel, black musicians in all regions of the nation were also beginning to develop instrumental blues, departing from ragtime but still drawing on European instruments and techniques. This combined effort created black America's first substantial generation of musical professionals. In the Southwest—including Missouri, Arkansas, Oklahoma, and Texas—ragtime resulted from a stimulating convergence of black syncopation and white musical notation. The region also spawned a biracial folk music later called "hillbilly" or "country," although black and native American contributions were largely ignored by the white majority.[11]

Future black jazz players, such as Jay McShann of Oklahoma and Eddie Durham of Texas, have remarked on this unique interaction of ethnic groups. McShann believed that native Americans had considerable influence on jazz, and he had heard jazz-like music played in a club on the Oklahoma plains, frequented by "whites, Indians, blacks, everybody." Durham, whose father was Irish-Mexican and mother was black-Indian, grew up in San Marcos in central Texas. His father, a sharecropper and horse-breaker, instructed him in such folk music practices as tapping his cigar-box fiddle's fingerboard with hatpins and filling its sound-box with snake rattles. The influence of Europe was felt here as well, however, and Durham (as well as McShann and other southwesterners) attended schools at which teachers suppressed blues singing and instructed students in the classics. The onetime musician Ralph Ellison, also, has discussed with great sensitivity how music appreciation classes in Oklahoma City complemented black students' extracurricular interest in the blues.[12]

In other regions of the nation, black musicians also produced striking new combinations of African- and European-American styles. The Gulf and Southeast coast cities, like New Orleans, had been enriched by the nearby Caribbean continuum of music and religion. Players in Charleston, South Carolina, such as the guitarist Freddie Green, benefited from a rich array of marching bands, clubs, and music instruction. The Jenkins Orphanage, a Charleston home for black boys, trained dozens for its bands, which toured the country to raise money for the institution.[13]

Far from the West Indies, though, black musicians were perpetuating polyrhythms and the blues, and even swung a bit, despite the dominance of European traditions. In New York, David Mannes's musical settlement house for black students gave them tutelage in Western instruments and notation, but they also gained inspiration from James Reese Europe's commercially successful ragtime band (with whom they performed in Carnegie Hall in the 1910s). The New York saxophonist Benny Carter has stated boldly that the New Orleans jazz style was recognized by Harlem musicians after 1917 but had little influence: "if there had been no players coming from New Orleans, New York music would have gone on the way it did, more or less the same," presumably developing an indigenous form of jazz.[14] In a small city like Springfield, Ohio, such future jazz musicians as Garvin Bushell and Freddie Jenkins benefited from tolerant white teachers and musicians and the music program at Wilberforce University, a major black college. Wherever they lived, though, African-American musicians labored under great burdens. For example, musicians' unions in Philadelphia, Boston, Hartford, Pittsburgh, and Dayton (but not in New York) forbade blacks, forcing them to form their own locals.[15]

It was this mixture of dynamic black musical activity, occasional assistance from white institutions (which usually Europeanized the black musician), and persistent racial discrimination that New Orleans musicians faced as they began to migrate to the North after 1917.

From 1916 to 1930, nearly one million blacks left the cities, towns, and farms of the South to seek improved economic and political conditions. The North, most of them believed, would provide their families with well-paying jobs and the benefits of America's civil liberties. This migration, more than any other historical event, defined the social and intellectual significance of jazz for African Americans. John Chilton's authoritative *Who's Who of Jazz* traces extensively the lives of 427 Southern black jazz musicians born before 1915. (See table 1, parts A and B.) Of this group, 270 (63.2 percent) left the South (the old Confederacy and Missouri) for permanent or long-term residence in the North, Midwest, or West between 1917 and 1930. Another twenty-eight (6.6 percent) had migrated before the general exodus between about 1900 and

Table 1. Origins and Migration Pattern of Early Black Jazz Musicians

A. Birthplace and/or Childhood Residence (Total sample: 775)

Urban South (cities 10,000+ population, 1910)

LA	80	GA	14
MO	49	SC	11
AL	29	FL	7
TN	23	MS	6
TX	21	AR	5
VA	20	NC	2

Subtotal: 267 (34.5% of total)

Rural South

LA	29	VA	13
TX	23	TN	10
MO	15	AL	9
SC	14	NC	8
GA	13	AR	7
MS	13	FL	6

Subtotal: 160 (20.7%)

Urban Border States

MD	20	DC	8
KY	19	WV	6

Subtotal: 53 (6.8%)

Rural Border States

KY	17	MD	4
WV	6		

Subtotal: 27 (3.5%)

Urban North and West

NY	46	CA	5
PA	28	NB	4
IL	27	CO	2
NJ	19	RI	2
OH	18	IA	1
OK	11	KS	1
MA	8	MN	1
CT	7	NM	1

Subtotal: 192 (24.8%)

Rural North and West

OH	20	NM	2
OK	12	MI	2
KS	11	ND	1
PA	5	AZ	1
IL	5	IA	1
IN	5	NV	1
CA	4		

Subtotal: 70 (9%)

Caribbean and West Indies 6 (0.8%)

B. Northern Migration (total sample: 644)

Southerners to North

1900–1916	28	(7.5%)
1917–1930	270	(72.2%)
1931–1941	76	(20.3%)

Total: 374 (100.0%)
(86.4% of all Southerners)

Initial Destinations 1917–30

New York City	103	(38.2%)
Chicago	94	(34.8%)
Pittsburgh	7	(2.6%)
Detroit	5	(1.9%)
Other Cities	61	(22.2%)

Total: 270 (100.0%)

Source: John Chilton, *Who's Who of Jazz: Storyville to Swing Street*, 3d rev. ed. (New York: Da Capo, 1985). Musicians included were those born before 1915 and documented with the relevant information.

1916, and seventy-six (17.8 percent) followed the major group between 1931 and 1941. All told, about six out of seven major black jazz musicians born in the South before 1915 migrated to the North in the four decades preceding World War Two. Even if some errors of exclusion, inclusion, and fact on Chilton's part are assumed (New Orleans musicians, he notes, are more heavily represented in other biographical dictionaries), this proportion is far greater than the northern migration figure of about 20 percent for southern blacks as a whole in the same forty-year period. Another eighty musicians from the border region of Kentucky, West Virginia, Maryland, and the District of Columbia, as well as 262 individuals native to twenty-two other nonsouthern states, are listed by Chilton as important black contributors to pre-1940 jazz. Black jazz, as it came to be defined then and as it is still defined today, was thus largely the music of northerners and of southern migrants to the North.

Black musicians from the Mississippi and western Ohio River valleys, like their neighbors and relatives, made Chicago their prime destination. More than 60,000 southern blacks migrated to the city in the five years after 1915, more than doubling the black population there, and as many as 120,000 followed them in the 1920s. Before about 1919, Chicago's South Side had not been able to support many full-time black musicians. The crime-ridden Midway district of bars and brothels had been a fitful employer of pianists and singers—Alberta Hunter of Memphis sang at Dago Frank's as early as 1907—and a few New Orleans bands had played residences in nightclubs. According to Sidney Bechet, by 1917 black movie theater bands were already dominated by New Orleans musicians; the clarinetist Darnell Howard "was the only man who wasn't out of New Orleans who played with us." In general, however, the area, unlike New Orleans then, lacked entertainment facilities and markets for most blacks.[16]

As a result, most musician migrants found other work at first. The meatpacking industry, which probably employed about 11,000 black men and women by 1919, was a major employer of unskilled blacks in Chicago.[17] The drummer Paul Barbarin of New Orleans and the trumpeter Andrew Blakeney of Mississippi were among the musicians who worked day jobs in the stockyards and packinghouses; Blakeney was employed full-time there until 1924. Steel mills (expanding with wartime demand), unskilled laborers' work, and such service occupations as porters, janitors, and waiters also employed large numbers of southern black men, and women usually found work as domestics (as they had in the South). As Milt Hinton remembered, Mississippians "always seem[ed] to want to work. . . . they were looking to get to Chicago, where they could get a job rather than be a shoeshine cat in one of them barbershops in Mississippi, and make $2.00 a week, man. Here they could make $25.00 or $30.00 a week." (Hinton's estimate almost exactly matches the actual range of average stockyard and steel mill wages.) [18]

Chicago's native black population also produced syncopating musicians, and they too had to maintain regular jobs early in the migration years. William E. Samuels, a trumpeter and later a union activist, worked at a post office and as an elevator operator and meter reader while playing at society parties at night. This pattern of daily unskilled work by aspiring musicians was repeated across the North, such as in Pittsburgh, where the North Carolina–born trombonist Clyde Bernhardt worked as a scrap collector in a steel mill, and in Harrisburg, where he cleaned streets as part of a work force controlled by the city's leading black politician.[19]

The northern job market was a complex hierarchy that black newcomers were allowed to enter at the bottom, in unskilled wage positions plagued by dangerous and unsanitary working conditions, frequent layoffs, and hostile white coworkers and labor unions. Blacks could circumvent some of these hazards by obtaining jobs from white crime syndicates, whose control of leisure and gambling industries on the South Side, Harlem, and elsewhere intensified during the migration and grew exponentially during Prohibition. Future musicians who spent their childhoods on the South Side, such as Milt Hinton, Red Saunders, Ray Nance, Nat Cole, and Happy Caldwell, were introduced early into what blacks and whites alike considered an illicit but effective and well-paying job market.

Racket organizations headed in turn by Jim Colosimo and Alphonse Capone dominated the service industries, labor organizations, and general economic life of the South Side. Hinton's uncle, for example, owned a clothes-cleaning store that served as a front for one of Capone's whiskey-jugging operations. Young Hinton, as well as other youths from Vicksburg, worked there during summers filling gallon jugs with bootleg whiskey. The operation was protected by Capone's bribery of the police, and Hinton's work there was kept secret from his mother and other female relatives. As he grew older, Hinton sought a career in the underworld, but his elders considered him unsuited for this milieu. Chicago's largest numbers-betting racket, operated by the black Jones brothers even after Capone commandeered it, was known for giving migrants from Mississippi "good, responsible, reliable jobs." Since Capone also controlled nightclubs and speakeasies, the underworld's role in the employment of musicians would be especially significant.[20]

New York City's Harlem was the largest and most celebrated destination for African-American migrants. Although Harlem's job market for musicians was similar to Chicago's, its role as the black cultural capital especially attracted musicians. Bernard "Cootie" Williams, a trumpeter in Mobile, Alabama, long dreamed of making a career in New York. "When I used to say my prayers at night, I used to say, 'Dear Lord, please hurry up and let me grow up so I can get to New York.'" A survey of Chilton's biographical dictionary (see table 1, part B) indicates that New York attracted slightly more migrants (103) than Chicago (94) during the 1917–30 migration period, and that it tended to draw more musicians from the Ohio River valley, Appalachia, the Carolinas, and Alabama.[21]

New York was also the center for commercial popular music and the musical theater, and thus it also attracted those musicians most eager to attain commercial success. The dancer and singer John "Bubbles" Sublett began as a child stage performer in Louisville and Nashville, but realized very early that New York was his ultimate professional goal. His first advancement came when his family moved to Indianapolis in 1911. "See, being born in the country to go to the city, then [to] a city on top of a city" was the means by which Sublett hoped to advance his career. "Indianapolis was more popular [populous] than Nashville," but he soon learned that "in Louisville and in Indianapolis the field is much smaller than what it is in New York or Chicago in the entertainment world. Therefore, I got to go." Arriving in New York in 1920 with his pianist partner Ford "Buck" Washington, Sublett celebrated his arrival by rollerskating down Fifth Avenue while hanging onto car bumpers.[22]

At this time, many important performers began to relocate to Harlem. Some, like Alberta Hunter of Memphis and Chicago, lived on 139th Street, near Striver's Row and amidst the black elite on Sugar Hill. Musicians and dancers were enthralled by the relative wealth and pageantry of Harlem's nightlife. The young Edward "Duke" Ellington, who moved to New York permanently in 1923, found that "New York is a dream of a song, a feeling of aliveness, a rush and flow of vitality that pulses like the giant heartbeat of humanity. The whole world revolves around New York, especially my world." New York's concentration on commercial success fostered a fascination in Harlem with conspicuous consumption, a component of the Renaissance façade presented to the white public in the twenties. Clyde Bernhardt's impressions in 1928 of showgirls "strolling around in big furs with old snooty Chow dogs on their long chains" and men "wearing form-fitting suits—oxford grey with pinstripe pants, jackets very short, . . . vests and spats . . . shiny shoes in black patent leather [and] long, fancy handkerchief[s] hanging out the breast pocket" typified the excited responses that Harlem's special ostentatiousness evoked.[23]

Despite the discrimination, violence, and limited economic opportunity which whites inflicted on the migrants, some of them— especially show people—were significantly more confident during their first years in the North. For the trumpet player Lee Collins, Chicago seemed, as it had for Joe Oliver, to release him from the musician's role as pawn in the struggle between New Orleans club owners and law enforcement. Like other musicians there, Collins had tried to supplement his income by pimping, but he had been forced out of the business by established operators. "My going to Chicago" in 1924 "changed everything. . . . after I left Joe Oliver's band I didn't know my own power."[24]

Power became a major concern for South Side blacks. In the early years of the migration, poor housing conditions, job discrimination, and outbreaks of racial rioting did not at first result in disillusion, but in proud efforts to mobilize and respond aggressively. As Milt Hinton recalled, "Chicago was a hotbed for" Marcus Garvey's black nationalism, "because you could solidify all these black people together, and there were great marches with uniforms, and [the message] 'let's get back to Africa'" was promoted. "The black people began to get this sense of, 'Hey, we do need more than what we're getting. And if we're not going to get it—.' They began to solidify and seal themselves in the ghetto of the South Side." In the early 1920s, Hinton saw Garvey in parades and met black politicians who visited his family's home.[25]

The migrants' initial hopefulness created an urge for cultural activity that was not limited to Afrophilia. Children such as Hinton were urged by their parents (who, like Hinton's, may have been among the more bourgeois-minded migrants) to take violin lessons and to cultivate other genteel practices. Hinton was one young migrant who saw Chicago only in positive terms. "All the kids were playing either violin or taking piano lessons, all these black people that had come up from the South were really utilizing their education—[taking] advantage of getting a better shot for their children, and they're making more money, their men are working in the stockyards, or they're porters." His family "had this nice apartment," and most families had "these nice clean places." A few years later the teenaged Hinton was an accomplished violinist who cherished his ability and the rewards it brought. "And I'm playing violin. I'm a superstar. Got nice clothes, you know, everything. . . . Instead of taking girls to the cafeteria, I took them across the street to the restaurant and buy them a steak. . . . It was just like the happiest thing that could happen. And everybody's kids are doing fine, everybody's working, all these great jazz musicians are playing in all these places."[26]

As Hinton suggested, northern music jobs brought skilled southern musicians unprecedented financial success. Whereas a musician in New Orleans, Florida, or elsewhere in the South rarely earned as much as $5.00 a night (or $30.00 a week) in wages and tips, union scale in northern areas surpassed these averages. Musicians Local 208's scale in the South Side, according to the jazz musician and member Ralph Brown, rose from $25.00 a week in 1920 to $52.50 in 1922, the result of a successful strike and the rise of the bootleg-liquor empire (with which the Chicago union locals colluded). By 1928, Brown recalled, the scale in 1928 was $75.00 for a forty-three-hour week, a salary almost three times what Henry Ford was then paying black auto workers under his heralded "five-dollar-a-day" wage. This total did not include gratuities, which amounted to as much as $100.00 per week at Chicago's Plantation Café and other exclusive clubs. These earnings placed the members of Joe Oliver's band at the Plantation in the top 10 percent of *all* American workers in the late 1920s. While this high living was irregular and confined to perhaps a few hundred of the nation's most-skilled black musicians, it still represented to them a promising break with the past.[27]

Among all northern black locales, Chicago's neighborhoods and nightclubs would be the most fondly remembered by musicians. Alberta Hunter believed that "these clubs in New York haven't got a chance [compared] with what the Dreamland [in Chicago] was. Only the Cotton Club. . . . no, it didn't compare with the Dreamland." Earl Hines of Pittsburgh, who had visited New York before settling in Chicago in 1924, felt that Chicago "wasn't as congested as New York . . . and some of the apartment buildings on Prairie Avenue had little lawns in front. . . . the planning of it was very fine." For Hines "the atmosphere was different altogether [from New York]. There seemed to be more night life, maybe because it was more centralized."[28]

Hines's comments suggest that migrants to Chicago were most able to transplant the "face-to-face" orientation of black culture

in both the rural and urban South. "Nobody bothered anybody,"
William Samuels believed. "You could walk up and down the streets,
and [there were] no holdups or snatching pocketbooks." Alberta
Hunter recalled that in Chicago "if you'd lose . . . $100 or some-
thing, they see you drop it, they'd say, 'Hey, fellow, you dropped this
money.'" New York compared to Chicago, for Hunter, was "nothing. Chicago was the greatest." For the first time, Samuels recalled,
black men could parade like proud flaneurs down a crowded street,
sporting flamboyant clothing and a distinctive walk, or motor down
the same street in a car with a rumbling muffler and squealing
tires. Certainly these memories were nostalgic. Situated historically
between the violent South of the early twentieth century and the
more crime-ridden urban North of succeeding decades, the 1920s
South Side, although awash in danger, seemed in hindsight to be
an urban oasis of relative freedom, civility, safety, and creativity.[29]

   In the North, jazz served the migrant audience in three locales:
the dance hall, the theater, and the nightclub. The dance hall,
the major venue for jazz in New Orleans, retained its role in the
North as the incubator for the most rhythmic jazz. Here, the relations between music and dance and between professionals and the
community, dating back to slavery, were closest and most fully retained. The black bottom, turkey trot, snake hips, and later the
lindy hop and the Charleston testified to the southern dominance
of popular dance in the migrants' halls. As in the South, dance halls
were operated by owners with political and underworld connections, who nurtured thriving businesses by commercializing black
musical culture.[30]
   The theater, playing host to vaudeville, musical comedy, and
the fading minstrel genre, gradually replaced ragtime standards
with jazz in black areas. Migrants in the North probably heard
more jazz music in theaters than in any other locale. Vaudeville
troupes, black musical shows shown on Broadway and interstate
tours (epitomized by Eubie Blake's and Noble Sissle's *Shuffle Along*
of 1922), variety shows held between films at movie theaters, and
amateur nights and revues always featured groups of black instrumentalists, and the number of them who could improvise skillfully
grew during the twenties.[31]
   The nightclub was the newest phenomenon, in some ways a
mixture of the theater and the dance hall, which also featured the
intimacy of the jook joint. The term, though, came into fashion
among New York whites in 1914 to describe members-only saloons

that mimicked the decor and ambience of fashionable restaurants and featured musicians performing on the dining room floor. The proximity of entertainers to patrons created an appealing intimacy that served as the model for public nightclubs.[32]

By 1920, the nightclub had spread from New York to other northern cities. In Chicago, the saloons of the Midway region were overshadowed by the Panama Club and other more elegant operations. The Black Belt on the South Side, a five-block area of theaters, dance halls, and nightclubs stretching down 35th Street, became the major incubator for the classic 1920s "hot" jazz of Louis Armstrong and his colleagues. At the intersection of 35th and Calumet, black and white patrons could dine at the Sunset Cafe while listening to Armstrong and Carroll Dickerson's Orchestra, cross 35th street to dance to King Oliver's Dixie Syncopators at the Plantation, and spend the morning hours with off-duty musicians at the Nest, a nightclub that featured the clarinetist Jimmie Noone and other New Orleans musicians. As the white musician Eddie Condon described the musical excitement at 35th and Calumet, "around midnight you could hold an instrument in the middle of the street and the air would play it. That was music."[33]

The dominant white society, perhaps motivated by the dominant doctrine of separate but equal facilities for the races, increased musicians' opportunities within the South Side. In 1927 and 1928, New York investors, the Balaban and Katz theater chain, and other whites built a large entertainment complex at the southern edge of the South Side, in part to draw blacks far away from downtown. The site contained the three-thousand-seat Regal Theater, the Savoy Ballroom, an outdoor boxing arena, a Chinese restaurant, the South Center shopping mall, and a drugstore. The Regal was far larger than any other theater in the South Side or other black urban centers (the famous Apollo Theater in Harlem seated only sixteen hundred) and the Savoy was outsized as well. As the Local 208 official William Samuels noted, these huge venues helped to ensure that "salaries for the black artists were greater than in New York or Los Angeles until the 1950s."[34]

While they were not permitted to play downtown, Chicago blacks could work in some other fringe areas, such as a small area to the north along North Clark Street known as the valley. New Orleanian Lee Collins played there in the early thirties before "politicians, lawyers, doctors, musicians, pickpockets, pimps, prostitutes, and drug addicts." This area was musically eclectic, featuring "jazz, ballads, and hillbilly music." Collins played at the Paradise Club,

which also featured Joe Stacks's New Orleans "drifters' band," a
lingering folk group that "made their own instruments" and preferred to "hustle on the streets or play from one joint to another,"
despite their growing popularity as a novelty band in "high-class
cabarets" in New York and Chicago. Stacks's band was a vivid relic
of the plantation past at a time when jazz culture was becoming
thoroughly urban.[35]

The black clubs in Chicago perpetuated the communal aspects
of southern musical culture in modern commercial settings. The
core of southern music—vocal and instrumental blues—was shared
by audiences and performers. "The people at that time were blues
crazy," Alberta Hunter recalled; "I always sang the blues." There
had never been floor shows in New Orleans, but now nightclubs
brought celebrities within the touch of the customers, in an innovative blending of folk communality and commercial professionalism.
Hunter noted that blues singing and improvisation could germi-
nate and blossom collectively and reaffirm the communal traditions
of African-American music. "We'd just sit there and make up something among ourselves or start humming a tune and do something
like that, and no music around, and the orchestra would pick it up.
Now, how would they know what we had on our minds[?] . . . many
times I've gotten out on the floor and other people, too, not just
me, gotten out on the floor and start singing something, and the
musicians would pick it up. Now, how would they know to go from
one note to the other?" The migrant clarinetist Albert Nicholas believed that the syncopation infected all who listened. "People at the
Plantation moved in rhythm. Waiters, hat check girls, all bouncing,
moved in rhythm."[36]

In many nightclubs, the intense and prolonged improvisations
of the most skilled musicians caused the greatest excitement among
listeners. The white cornetist Bill Davison, visiting the Sunset Café
in the late twenties, heard Louis Armstrong and Joe Oliver in an
improvising contest in which "they played about 125 choruses of
'Tiger Rag'—exchanging choruses. . . . People went insane—they
threw their clothes on the floor. . . . it was the most exciting thing I
ever heard in my life." Other cities' audiences surrendered to communal bursts of emotion in the presence of improvising masters.
As Mary Lou Williams remembered a performance by her senior
pianist colleague, Thomas "Fats" Waller, "he was just a sensation
in New York, when they'd turn the light on, people would scream,
when he sat down, people would scream. I never saw such a thing.
When he finished, that was the end; they had to let it cool off."[37]

Every large northern city developed a center for black musical entertainment. In Pittsburgh, for example, Wylie Avenue on the Hill (the major black district) contained a string of nightclubs and hotel cabarets, such places as the Crawford Grill, the Leader House, and the Benjamin Harrison Literary Club (a speakeasy). Harlem's two parallel Black Belts, stretching down Seventh Avenue and Lenox Avenue, hosted what became by the late 1920s the largest and most competitive jazz site in the nation. Big bands (with eight or more members) held forth in Small's Paradise, Herman's, and the Lafayette and Apollo Theaters—as well as at such whites-only locales as the Cotton Club, Barron Wilken's, and Connie's Inn—while smaller groups inhabited such places as the Yeah Man, the Lenox Club, the Oriental Café, Herman's Inn, and Jungle Alley (for white tourists).[38]

From the viewpoint of migrant blacks in the audiences, these musical emporia (at least the ones that admitted them) were symbols of their hopes and ambitions in the North. Black community and culture were preserved in elite-looking surroundings that presented visions of the good life embodied in music, dance, and elegant dress. The performers themselves realized what their eminence signified for migrants.

Black comedians often performed along with bands, and, as Earl Hines recalled, they "were very successful. . . . Their funny comments on everyday life, and on what happened in the Southland, were all mixed with references to segregation that were particularly funny to us Negroes who knew what it was all about. It was a relief to the distress and turmoil and the obligations we always had, and that is where a lot of that great soul feeling came from." Eubie Blake and Noble Sissle, the ragtime performers who produced important musical comedies in the 1920s, were very articulate about what they felt their efforts meant. "All understand," they told the *Baltimore Afro-American* in 1924, "we are not trying to be white actors because we know we have something of our own to develop. Jazz originated with the American Negro. It was his way of expressing his religious emotions," and by entertaining whites as well as blacks, they were impressing the world with the musical heritage of African Americans.[39]

By the mid-1920s, John "Bubbles" Sublett, the ambitious dancing star, worked his way into the mainstream musical theater, where he and Buck Washington performed before largely white audiences. Nevertheless, he wrote and sang songs that reflected his ambition and his ambivalence as a black man forced to leave the

South to gain professional success and dignity. One song, "Rhythm For Sale," was "a history of the Negro in the world" that stressed how blacks now had some control over the commercialization of their culture:

> All the world wants rhythm bad
> Colored folks are might' glad
>   'Cause they've got rhythm for sale . . .
>
> Up in Harlem they are doing swell
>   Nature gave them something
>   they can sell . . .
>
> Since the emancipation came
>   Jungle rhythm has made a name
> But the terms ain't quite the same
>   'Cause we've got rhythm for sale.

The lyrics, with their intimations of jungle rhythms, were not free of the primitivism that attracted white listeners, but they nevertheless portrayed the new demand for black music and the sense of autonomy in the black entertainment profession ("the terms ain't quite the same"). They also suggested that such expressions of cultural and racial politics were permitted onstage, despite promoters' desires to control the aggressiveness and rhetoric of black performers (which caused Sublett to suffer on other occasions).[40]

In a broader context, this flowering of jazz in the new black neighborhoods was a rare triumph of culture and spirit over uncertainty and adversity. The great migration was a wrenching passage for most southern blacks. Many found their experiences in New York, Chicago, Detroit, Pittsburgh, and elsewhere to be puzzling at best and often disillusioning and cruel. Initial contact with whites was often hostile. Whites who lived in the neighborhoods in which blacks settled began the panicked "white flight," which unsettled white areas nearby. As the all-black areas expanded block by block, white realtors and landlords overcharged the migrants, and flashpoints at the racial boundaries erupted into "race riots" and other forms of antiblack harassment and violence. Black families suffered from insufficient jobs and housing, and the black churches found it difficult to ameliorate urban vice and crime. In general, the migrants were the ill-informed and ill-prepared victims of deep, nationwide white racism. They struggled as best as they could to establish strong individual, family, and group identities within the corrosive industrial marketplace, but often in vain; and the dream of economic opportunity coupled with racial progress inevitably became "a dream deferred."[41]

With these conditions in mind, it has become commonplace for scholars to discount the optimism of black cultural figures of this time. This is especially true with respect to the Harlem educated elite, which strove to create a renaissance of artistic activity to provide African-American civilization with a distinct and autonomous moral and aesthetic foundation. Their task was difficult, and their efforts were only partially successful at best. Nathan Irvin Huggins and David L. Lewis have argued that such writers as Countee Cullen, Zora Neale Hurston, Langston Hughes, and Claude McKay fell afoul of intrusive patronage, sentimental primitivism, and literary provincialism.[42]

By contrast, though, Huggins noted: "It is very ironic that a generation that was searching for a new Negro and his distinctive cultural experience would have passed up the only really creative thing that was going on. But then, it is not too surprising. The jazzmen were too busy creating a cultural renaissance to think about the implications of what they were doing."[43] This analysis is somewhat inaccurate: jazz musicians *did* think about the implications of their work, as their career strivings and future statements indicate, and they were just as likely as the Harlem poets to enter compromised realms of expression (as we shall see). But Huggins is correct to suggest that jazz's role in the migration was of paramount importance and that jazz had a far greater impact on black and white America than any of the Harlem intellectuals' writings. Jazz may not have been "the *only* really creative thing . . . going on" in Harlem, or the South Side, or on Pittsburgh's Wylie Avenue, but it was perhaps the only new art form that achieved the difficult task of bringing the "new" black aesthetic to the approving attention of the world.

It is no exaggeration to say that jazz caught the world's attention. It did so more rapidly than any black music preceding it. Among the 1 million black migrants of the 1910s and 1920s, the early jazz musicians stand out as the greatest travelers of all. As early as 1917, James Reese Europe's 369th Division Band entertained troops and natives in Paris, and in 1919 Will Marion Cook's orchestra (which included one skilled improviser, Sidney Bechet) was received by royalty in London and gained the admiration of classical musicians. From 1925 to 1927, Sam Wooding's quasi-jazz orchestra toured Europe and the Soviet Union; in 1926 Jack Carter and Teddy Weatherford began leading bands in China, Singapore, India, and other Asian locales; beginning in 1929, Valaida Snow, from Carter's Shanghai band, toured the Middle East and the Soviet Union; and many others also helped to bring jazz to all parts of the world.

Not all musicians particularly enjoyed their protracted stays overseas. For some, Europe was only a safety valve, allowing them to escape family and community difficulties. As the trumpeter Doc Cheatham noted, "I think a lot of guys [in Paris] had family problems. They wanted to get away from them—alimony and so forth." Benny Carter left for Europe with his daughter in 1935 to prevent his former wife from obtaining custody (which had been awarded to her by a court).[44] Those who were in Europe willingly sometimes felt uncomfortable in alien settings. Cheatham recalled that "in Germany we couldn't go out in the street because we'd have a crowd of people following us," and in "a lot of places, . . . people would come into the place just to see a black musician sitting up there because it was such a novelty." The singer and leader Elliot Carpenter even believed that the French "didn't care too much for Americans . . . [and] they figured the black ones were just as bad." As a result, "Negroes had a way of isolating themselves" and "got to fussing and fighting among themselves and making trouble." Duke Ellington undoubtedly had mixed feelings in 1931 when a London hotel provided him with a room only after he had proved that he was not a West Indian.[45]

Nevertheless, most blacks who lived in Europe before 1940 savored various freedoms and the absence of Jim Crow. The trumpeter Arthur Briggs delighted in the "nice little colony of blacks" in Paris, where there were "certain facilities . . . that we didn't have in the States," and the bandleader Claude Hopkins felt that Europeans "were more receptive to the music than the Americans." The adulation jazz received from European admirers had important emotional and intellectual effects on the players. Prominent European art musicians, such as Igor Stravinsky and Ernest Ansermet, publicly praised black ragtime and jazz and incorporated their properties into compositions. In Germany the clarinetist Garvin Bushell, a member of the Wooding band, received instruction in the clarinet and bassoon. "We were youngsters and we were highly impressed with the people and the attitude and the mannerisms of Europeans and we sort of took on some of that and we assumed some of that air." Alberta Hunter, Cootie Williams, Duke Ellington, Benny Carter, and many other black musicians had similar memories of the somewhat ennobling effect that successful European tours engendered; even Canada seemed to Bill Coleman to be a haven of racial tolerance in the twenties.[46]

When they returned to the United States, musicians shared the sense of self-worth (if not the European chauvinism) of Reginald Foresythe, a black English arranger in America, who told Charlie Carpenter in jest that "American Negroes . . . don't compare with me. You can't go here, you can't go there. I go anywhere I damn well please!" As Bushell put it, when the Wooding band returned to America "we didn't fall back into the same groove that we had been in when we left, because we were more matured, [and] some of Europe had rubbed off on us and we felt that we were something special." Jazz musicians, when acting upon these sentiments, were behaving just as the Harlem writers might have expected "the New Negro" to behave in the twenties.[47]

In this sense, as in others, musicians abroad migrated far from their origins while also honing and perfecting a particular expression of the original southern black culture. Those musicians who returned or who had remained members of the migrant neighborhoods also shared in this enterprise, of course, but they also played an extra social role. Along with their neighbors, they became deeply involved in northern blacks' efforts to construct united communities and cultures in the face of internal divisions and external oppression.

4

"Changing, Changing"
The Forging of Northern Black Communities

After 1865, African Americans in New Orleans divided along class, educational, cultural, and color lines, and their divisions directly influenced how jazz musicians worked, thought, and interacted with one another and their communities. Such divisions affected blacks in other southern cities and towns to a lesser extent, and they also persisted among the 1 million southern blacks who migrated to northern cities in the 1910s and 1920s. The growing northern populations faced new difficulties as well. The migrants suffered constant shortages in jobs and housing, insufficient city services, white attacks and exploitation, as well as other complications.

As a result, even though the white majority perceived them as a single, despised group, blacks in the North initially found it difficult to coalesce into unified communities. Longtime black residents in the North were hostile to the newcomers, and the migrants themselves used old and new measurements of social status to create their own hierarchies. Just as in New Orleans, jazz was buffeted, strained, and shaped by tensions between black groups in northern cities. Over time, however, the southern folk and northern bourgeois styles and beliefs of urban blacks gradually blended into an urban African-American culture that could at least absorb the blows inflicted upon it. More than any other art form, jazz was shaped by, and spoke of, these cultural reconciliations and compromises.

As had happened in New Orleans, some of the social and cultural divisions that split black populations north of the Ohio River also drove wedges between musicians. Differences in education, religion, and above all skin tone, continued to divide musicians and their families and neighbors. Creole musicians from New Orleans and other southern locales took North with them their prejudice against dark skin. Jelly Roll Morton, who left New Orleans in 1907, was noted for his antipathy toward blacks. By 1930, "Jelly Roll's whole life," the folklorist Alan Lomax wrote in his biography of Morton, "was constructed around his denial of his Negro status. He was a mulatto, a New Orleans man, a higher-up, a Number One recording artist, but not quite a Negro. Of course this is typical of New Orleans Creoles." Morton's intense musical ambitions apparently exacerbated his Creole sense of elitism, as Lomax pointed out melodramatically: "Outcast and intellectual, he felt none of the finicky reservations and fears of the mulatto, nor suffered from the undisciplined anger and melancholy of the rejected blacks." The pianist Lovie Austin, a colleague and rare friend of Morton's, agreed in simpler terms. "Jelly Roll Morton was a loner. Since he couldn't read" music, "he wouldn't go around with" musicians who could, and he also shunned dark-skinned blacks for their lack of refinement.[1]

Light-skinned southern blacks generally strove to perpetuate their elite status in the North. As Milt Hinton recalled, the "Blue Vein Societies" of rural Mississippi were carried on "straight through to Chicago." In the city, "they had groups, and they got the better jobs. . . . and these people had a better chance at education." Migrants reinforced the membership of such mixed-couple groups as Chicago's Nassau Society and Manasseh Club, which enjoyed special status, and black churches were often distinguished by their black or yellow congregations.[2]

More generally, musicians from specific southern cities practiced exclusion. For Hinton, beginning his career as a jazz bassist in the late twenties, musicians from New Orleans and St. Louis "were the breed that was working" regularly. Hinton's own cohort of young Chicago musicians, at Wendell Phillips High School and elsewhere, challenged the southerners' clannishness. Hinton would never be permitted to join the brotherhood: "I'm from Mississippi, which ain't too far away, but I'm still not from Louisiana." Since Hinton "was surrounded with [New Orleans jazzmen] in Chicago," he found that "the one way to . . . really get into [the profession], since they control the real hotbed of jazz, is [to] accept it." Hinton faced further difficulty when he entered the New York market in the early thirties. Jelly Roll Morton and others were blue veins who shunned him, and darker "West Indian guys didn't say too much to the ordinary black guy" either. As a result, "the Mississippi in me" made Hinton feel inferior. "You always had to fight with yourself, whether you could do it, because we'd been told so long, 'You ain't nothing.' You almost believe you aren't anything."[3]

Similarly, dissension among older South Side musicians often resulted from discrimination on the basis of skin tone. In the twenties, the trombonist Preston Jackson noted, "the New Orleans musicians had Chicago locked up, but they began fighting among themselves." Freddy Keppard's New Orleans band included such light-skinned jazzmen as Manuel Perez, Jimmie Noone, Paul Barbarin, and Bill Johnson, who differentiated themselves from the "generally darker" musicians in Joe Oliver's band (such as Johnny and Baby Dodds, Honoré Dutrey, Louis Armstrong, Lil Hardin, and Oliver himself). This division, Jackson noted, perpetuated the downtown-uptown antagonism between blacks in New Orleans. Oliver later hired the Creoles Barney Bigard and Albert Nicholas but probably regretted this integration since Bigard made the very dark bandleader the butt of a string of practical jokes. Oliver was further nettled by the taunting of other Creoles, such as Morton, who once made a point of shouting "Hi, Blondie" at the cornetist while the latter was playing a solo.[4]

Significantly, as a result of this abuse, Oliver—the orphaned son of a Louisiana sharecropper, blind in one eye, who had risen in Lincolnesque fashion to the top of Chicago's entertainment world—developed a crippling fixation on the stigma Creoles attached to his dark skin. Clyde Bernhardt, who played with Oliver's band in 1930, recalled that Oliver "always seemed conscious of" his darkness, and forced jokes about it. "When he see somebody real dark he strike a match and whisper: 'Who dat out dare? Who dat movin'?' . . . He laughed at his joke and then added, 'I'm black and I only seen two other damn people in the world blacker'n me,' and then he laughed some more." Oliver and others were deeply hurt by prejudice in jazz against dark skin, and the self-deprecating joking with which Oliver struck back did not possess the beneficial, healing effects of traditional black humor.[5]

New Orleans, with its special heritage of racial mixing, was the source of much of the color consciousness in black jazz. As Clyde Bernhardt expressed it, "some New Orleanians have peculiar ways. You just have to understand them—they critical of others and very critical of themselves." Cootie Williams, Duke Ellington's new trumpet from Mobile in 1930, found a similar peculiarity in

Barney Bigard and the bassist Wellman Braud. "I don't know how to describe it. . . . They had that New Orleans thing going. . . . They would be over there talking that half-Creole stuff, and we didn't like that so much." By that time, perhaps, Bigard, Braud, and other Creoles were feeling inferior as well, outnumbered in the vast reaches of Harlem and New York's booming jazz scene. In any case, their Creole identity persisted, perhaps in unhealthy ways.[6]

Class divisions also caused significant conflict in northern black communities. Black ministers, lawyers, doctors, and educators—what W. E. B. Du Bois called the "talented tenth"—strove to exercise civic leadership for all blacks in the realms of culture, morals, religion, and politics. Their values and culture were often close to those of genteel, Victorian whites, which called for a strict code of education, self-control, male authority, female domesticity, and industriousness. In Chicago, many black professionals were Old Settlers who had lived in Chicago for many years before the migration, and they tended to look down at newcomers. As one of them argued, their class "were just about civilized and didn't make apes out of themselves like the ones who came here during 1917–18." These southerners, she felt, "brought discrimination with them" when they arrived. Perceiving themselves as an elite, the native northerners made efforts to welcome migrant southerners into their schools, churches, and other institutions, but often expected the new arrivals to adopt middle-class culture in return.[7]

As part of this assistance, the black elite encouraged the migrants to admire, play, and listen to genteel white art music and to pursue formal musical instruction. In his column "The Musical Bunch," the theater bandleader Dave Peyton often articulated this group's beliefs and exhorted his musician readers to aspire to Victorian models of behavior and training. He criticized "many of us" who "learn to blow or fiddle a tune on our instruments . . . make a wild squeal . . . do some eccentric jazz figures, and . . . think we are 'the berries.' . . . We cannot go wrong by hard study, we cannot go wrong by trying to live right and be ladies and gentlemen, we cannot go wrong applying ourselves to hard instrument practice. If we do these things[,] when that door of opportunity opens to us, we can walk in with chests poked out and with the determination to win." Another prominent columnist, Lucien White of the *New York Age,* attacked jazz in 1921 as a symbol of "unthinking" musicality. In his opinion, the jazz musician did not appreciate "serious application and hard work. He failed to realize the connection between mentality and musicianship." Groups such as the National

Association of Negro Musicians, based in Chicago, and the Hampton Institute's publication *The Southern Workman* condemned some bands for improvising on spirituals (which it claimed was a typical jazz heresy).[8]

The South Side's migrants were often receptive to these calls for refinement. Theodore "Red" Saunders, a future drummer, was inspired to pursue a musical career when John Philip Sousa visited to conduct the Tilden High School band, and he often attended Chicago Symphony Orchestra concerts. The women who headed the household in which Milt Hinton grew up considered it their duty to involve the boy in music, and his school music teacher, Dr. Mildred Bryan Jones, combined music classes with a pronounced emphasis on social uplift. "She was so concerned with us black kids having dignity, because she knew we came out of homes where our people didn't know about protocol." Dr. Jones instructed her students in etiquette because "she wanted us to know about these things before we went so we wouldn't embarrass ourselves and our community." Hinton began to pursue the violin seriously and plan a classical career. At the time he "had no desire to play jazz," but rather "wanted to be like Eddie South," a society orchestra violin soloist who incorporated gentle syncopation into his improvisations.[9]

Even the black underworld professed some genteel musical values. When Hinton asked the Jones brothers for a job in their numbers racket, they "turned me down cold" because Hinton was already "doing well . . . playing with all these bands" as a violinist. "They were as proud of me as if I'd won a world's championship, because I'm something from Mississippi, from Vicksburg, that's into legitimacy, into artistry."[10] Some black musicians soon after the migration, then, turned away from the folk past and looked toward dominant cultural values.

With this encouragement, Hinton looked upon a young man like Quinn Wilson (also a future jazz bassist) as a role model. Wilson "played piano, played violin, he was a captain in the ROTC. The kind of guy that you looked up to and said, 'Hey, man, I really want to be like this cat.'" Wilson's parents had come to Chicago from Mississippi in the 1870s, and he had begun his violin studies in 1920 under a German immigrant teacher.[11]

Another son of Old Settlers, William Samuels, recalled that "my father believed strongly in the value of music from a cultural standpoint. . . . He thought that everybody should know something about music, so you would have . . . music appreciation." While at

Wendell Phillips High School, Samuels learned the trumpet and played in the school orchestra, pursuing a highly traditional curriculum of Latin, geometry, and other subjects as well. ("I had the wrong courses," he noted in 1980. "I should have taken a business course.") In the 1920s Samuels, like other longtime Chicagoans, held an elitist disdain for migrant musicians. As he recalled, "Most of the musicians in my era could read music. . . . If you didn't you just got you a job as a porter or something and got by the best way you could." Nonreaders did get some playing jobs, "but they would work in second-class places. We've always had cheaper places like taverns—we called 'em toilets." Samuels's sweeter brand of syncopated music often found its way to white society parties, where southern blues bands were rarely heard.[12]

The bourgeois-minded in other northern cities reacted in similar ways to southern culture and music. Earl Hines felt disdain for some of the migrants who inundated Duquesne, Pennsylvania after 1917. "A lot of them were good people. . . . but along with them were a lot of roustabouts who had no good intentions at all, and when they came north and found a freedom they hadn't had, they began to get excited." The migration "changed the whole picture of life in Duquesne. We didn't know what it was to lock doors before they came. . . . for most of the people it was a complete change, getting out from under the hammer." Hines's father and others tried to educate and provide "wholesome" recreation for the migrants, but activity still "went on after hours that [migrants] tried to keep the police from knowing about." Hines also remembered with some bitterness that he never saw antiblack discrimination until after migration greatly increased the black population in the Pittsburgh area. Hines's family, for similar reasons, also strenuously opposed his growing interest in jazz piano.[13]

Nonsouthern blacks elsewhere were also told that jazz was beneath their station. Andrew Blakeney noted that among blacks in twenties Los Angeles, jazz musicians were "considered loud and unprofessional" by some, and Lawrence Brown of Pasadena was warned by his father that after only two weeks on the road with a jazz band, "you're going to be in jail." In Harlem, as Benny Carter recalled, "jazz was looked down upon . . . by the people . . . that were involved in the Renaissance." His mother held Victorian aspirations, and "I think it was a bit appalling to her that I was making a living like this." The ambitious John "Bubbles" Sublett, fixing his sights on a Broadway career, heartily disliked the time he spent in Harlem clubs, learning to dance with "underclass people."[14]

Alberta Hunter, who moved to New York in 1920, had little interest in preserving a black folk or southern identity: "I was one of the dicties' [elite's] entertainers." She attended parties given by the wives of Pullman porters and whites' cooks and butlers, who "belonged with the better people" by virtue of their employment. Bessie Smith, the great blues singer who frequented Harlem at that time, did not cut the proper figure among respectable Harlemites. "Lord, Bessie Smith, they wouldn't think of looking at Bessie. Bessie was too raucous like, you know." Harlem society "cared about your background. . . . my background was poor, but it was humble, you know. But Bessie, hers was a little too fantastic," Hunter noted, presumably referring to Smith's vaudeville background and turbulent private life. "We never associated with Bessie, although she was human. . . . I can't stand a rough woman." The songwriter Porter Grainger, elegant in spats and walking stick, would "take and tell Bessie, 'Bessie, don't be rough, don't be loud.' " Smith was thus both guided through and restrained from elite society, a predicament that caused her much social and psychological discomfort. This social mechanism, Hunter recalled regally, ensured that Bessie Smith "didn't have a chance to like me or dislike me." [15]

In spite of these divisions based on class, attitudes, and skin color, some groups of the new black urban North, including musicians, worked to blend the rural and urban traditions of the South with the self-conscious striving of the bourgeois-minded. The migrants maintained many cultural and leisure traditions in northern cities. Regarding Chicago in 1919, James Grossman has written that "despite the pleas of Old Settlers to 'give us more grand opera and less plantation melodies,' the migrants did not leave their cultural baggage at the train station" when they arrived. Often, the entire southern social terrain was transplanted. In Cincinnati the downtown region provided most of the migrants with homes, as well as eating places, nightclubs, and gambling houses that preserved the spirit of black riverside communities in southern cities. The southern penchant for parade and costumes, exemplified by Mardi Gras, was transferred to Cincinnati. "My mother used to masquerade in a suit of my father's on Halloween," Bill Coleman recalled, "and go into Gaither's gambling houses because women were not allowed in there. Everybody mostly put on some kind of mask on Halloween day and it was just as much fun for grown people as it was for young ones." [16]

Young musicians who moved North maintained traditional

folk beliefs. As a boy in North Carolina, Clyde Bernhardt believed in a supernatural world that usually appeared in his dreams, "nightmares" and "hants," particularly a ghostly Indian who "took me out the window and . . . flew [me] all around the countryside." While childhood "was the most fearful time in my life," in part because the dreams came to him after his father's death, Bernhardt kept believing in the spirit world when he matured and moved North. As they had been in the South, ghosts for Bernhardt continued to be symbols both of fear and of protection from distress.[17]

In the case of the pianist Mary Lou Williams, who grew up in Atlanta, "stories about spooks and ghosts" led her to have visions of "weird things" as a child and an adult, such as dogs that grew into cows and headless men who glided down staircases. Williams later felt that this kind of cognition helped her as a pianist and composer. "At one time I could hear a musician playing and could hear the note he was going to make next. . . . It was just like seeing spirit[s] or telling someone's fortune." Williams believed that her musical and psychic inclinations "may have something to do with the fastness of the mind and hearing." She retained her folk beliefs and realized her musical talents after her family migrated to Pittsburgh in 1916.[18]

Superstitions were among the other folk beliefs that persisted in the northern jazz culture. Duke Ellington, while raised in a bourgeois environment in Washington, was one generation removed from small-town North Carolina. While some of Ellington's famous phobias were basic show business traditions, such as his contention (according to Juan Tizol) that it was bad luck to take down opening night telegrams, or from general lore, like his refusal to hire a thirteenth band member until a fourteenth was available. Others, though, were more typical of black folk beliefs. Examples of these included his fear of losing a button or finding one on a piano keyboard, or of receiving gifts of shoes or socks, which signified that the giver was soon going to desert him. These and similar fears amused such northern band members as the trombonist Lawrence Brown, the thirteenth band member Ellington hesitated to hire. (Revealing his middle-class roots, Brown claimed that "my only superstition was I never got enough money.") The stereotype of the southern musician as a superstitious primitive was common in the North, and some jazzmen exploited it: Pops Foster and a New Orleans friend made extra income by masquerading before gullible northerners as expert practitioners of voodoo.[19]

Musicians in the North preserved some elements of the role

their southern counterparts had fulfilled in rural folk culture. Once migrant musicians settled into bands, they toured restlessly during the summers, and thus perpetuated the spirit of the itinerant southern musicianer. In 1927, Clyde Bernhardt worked with Charles C. Grear's Original Midnite Ramblers, known across the Midwest for its raucous down-home music and humor. The band "looked like a band of gypsies. . . . When we drove up to the colored dancehall . . . we all treated as heroes."[20] Similarly, early jazz often featured comic routines, which perpetuated the laughter-inducing traditions of the minstrel and medicine shows. As Barney Bigard recalled, New Orleans migrants used a host of techniques that encouraged listeners to laugh. Slap-tonguing on a saxophone mouthpiece, which caused Bigard to break many reeds, sounded "like knocking on wood," and drummers were specialists in noisemaking, hitting and shaking gourds, firing pistols, beating rugs and washtubs, and even screaming through their snare drums. Such musicians as Jelly Roll Morton would dress in bell-bottom pants and cowboy hat, presenting a clownish image to listeners.[21]

More significantly, this onstage humor showed that their work was serious, and that they were aware of new conditions and pressures. Their humor sometimes reflected newfound dignity and pride, as southern customs became both symbols of and means toward professional advancement. When the young Milt Hinton saw Sonny Greer, Ellington's drummer, perched behind his panoply of rhinestone-studded drums, cymbals, blocks, and bells, the sight was not primarily humorous but dignified and reassuring. "He sat high up there, like way up in the clouds, high above the band, and he was a very regal man, still is to this very day." Like saxophonists, New Orleans bassists developed a slapping technique, using both hands to turn the bass's fingerboard, strings, and body into a percussive instrument. Hinton, seeing Pops Foster and others slap their basses, felt that "I've got to outdo these cats. So not only would I slap it, I would put the bass between the legs and ride it like a horse across the stage and slap it." While Hinton was pleased that crowds found his showmanship "sensational," he also used the stunt to develop complex new slapping techniques that had some artistic value. "I found out how to make triple slaps and quadruple slaps[,] and mixed it up."[22]

Groups also worked to keep their comic skills in control. Bill Samuels' Society Syncopators, while not strictly a jazz band, also indulged in humorous stunts, but Samuels insisted that "there wasn't no Uncle Tom stuff at all with me"; "we were not alienated at the places we played." Entertaining at Chicago society functions,

Samuels featured a man who played the saxophone and clarinet simultaneously, and a trombonist who played on his back, using his foot on the slide. He did have "to be a bit careful about taking" the double-woodwind player "because they expected him to do it," but he was certain that audiences did not usually "expect us to put on any antics."[23] Whatever the reactions of white audiences to these stunts may have been, it is clear that black musicians were aware of the professionalism and skill that produced successful comic effects, and certain that their audiences were aware of this as well.

Though southern traditions were preserved within northern jazz, the music and its creators were also strongly influenced by middle-class and professional values and urban ways of life. The northern city modernized, often subtly, the function and content of southern jazz. As Pops Foster noticed when he moved to New York in 1929, the New Orleans fish fry found its northern equivalent in the "rent party." At each affair, admission money was collected to assist the host in paying the rent, and food, drink, and music were provided for all in return. For pianists, Foster noted, the rent party was as central to employment in New York as the brothel had been in New Orleans.[24]

Similarly, the stronger attachment among northern blacks to the traditional, Victorian domestic role for women significantly altered the connotations attached to female blues singing. Prostitution's sponsorship of jazz music and locales—an important force in New Orleans, especially for pianists and singers—was much less evident in more bourgeois northern cities. As Linda Dahl has pointed out, New Orleans's most prominent early female jazz singers tended to be prostitutes congregating in Storyville. As early as about 1910, however, Alberta Hunter found herself groomed for a different role at Hugh Hoskin's saloon on the South Side. Big Harry and Little Harry, the resident confidence men, "saw that I was a young person, naive, [who] didn't know whether it was raining, so they taught me how not to let anybody make a bad girl out of me." Hunter's mother, who had also moved to Chicago from Memphis, seemed to have been satisfied with this arrangement, "as long as I was a good girl. . . . she always told me, be a lady."[25]

In 1918, Hunter worked at one of Chicago's first nightclubs, the Panama Club. Significantly, the Panama's identity was divided, as its two floors played to different classes and moral environments. As Hunter remembered, "Bricktop [Ada Smith], Cora Green, Matty Hite, Nettie Compton and Florence Mills were downstairs. Now, they were like the nice, quiet girls, you know, that sang the nice, sophisticated stuff and like that. But upstairs, they called us barrelhousers. . . . That means you were kind of rough and ready. . . . that was Nelly Carr, Mamie Carter, Twinkle Davis, Goldie Crosby and me."[26]

The Panama, despite its "rough and ready" floor and stable of blueswomen, did not attempt to replicate the ambience of the New Orleans (or Chicago) brothel. Hunter wore "street clothes" when she sang there, "smart blouses" with high collars. "We didn't bother about being sexy, although we wanted to be smartly dressed." All the management wanted "was for the women to make money, you know, and that's all." Nightclubs, transformed into speakeasies during Prohibition, thus exploited female sexuality without selling sex, as women were paid to keep company with male patrons and encourage them to buy drinks. In these respects as in others, the nightclub reflected the introduction of new codes of restrained and commercial-oriented employee behavior to working-class leisure locales.[27]

While Hunter had her barrelhouse tendencies as a singer, she consistently kept away from music and stage demeanor that suggested sexuality or prostitution. Some of her songs "were a little naughty, and my mother didn't approve of that . . . I was singing them because I could make the money from singing them." Hunter like W. C. Handy and other migrant blues exponents, preferred a more dignified brand of purely sorrowful blues. Hunter came to see her role as that of a *lady* who sang the blues. She deplored singers who "get out on the street and sell [their] wares right out on the corner . . . where's the refinement?" She belonged onstage, where "you had to enter properly and exit properly."[28]

Younger female vocalists also retained this kind of Victorian reserve as they became blues singers. Helen Humes, the daughter of a Louisville attorney, made her recording debut at the age of fourteen in 1923, singing "Papa has Outside Lovin' and Mama Has Outside Lovin'" and "Do What You Did Last Night." At the time "I said, 'now what does all this mean?' " but generally her reaction was to "pay no mind" to blues lyrics. In the North, therefore, the rough-living blues queen was also highly conscious of style and wealth, and their often dignified and sorrowful reactions to adversity suggested that northern-style restraint was influencing their presentations. This transformation was completed in the 1930s when Billie Holiday rose to fame.[29]

The southern newcomers were not the only ones who changed their thought and behavior in the ghettos; northerners also accommodated to the manners and musical culture of the migrants.

Genteel-minded women, in the obverse of the blues phenomenon, figured prominently in admitting "rougher" southern folkways into the artistic spheres they controlled. In 1917, Lil Hardin, formerly of Memphis, moved to Chicago, where she attended music school. In 1919, she was hired as a pianist at the DeLuxe Café on the South Side. Hardin told her family that she was playing in a dance studio, but they soon discovered the truth. Hardin's stepfather visited the nightclub and found it to be "a regular sporting house," but her mother was more easily persuaded that the club was "respectable." She "was flattered and charmed by Mr. Shaw, the owner, who had been forewarned" by Hardin. She "was allowed to continue working, but her mother came to escort her home every night" until a "suitable" chaperone in the band was found.[30]

In the next decade Milt Hinton faced similar difficulties in gaining his mother's and grandmother's approval of his jazz bass playing, for which he had left Northwestern University. "Their dream for me was a classical thing, being the director of a choir, and this was a constant thing in the house." When Hinton dropped out of Northwestern, though, his mother and grandmother were partially relieved because "they [had not been] able to finance anything" for him, while he could easily support himself by working in nightclubs.[31]

At personal and musical levels of experience, therefore, native and migrant musicians in the North broke down regional differences and barriers. As Lil Hardin became one of black Chicago's leading pianists, she joined Oliver's band, and later married the second cornetist, Louis Armstrong. Alberta Hunter recalled that "Lil's mother thought she was too good for Louis," who had been raised in New Orleans's poorest uptown region. Nevertheless the marriage took place, and it highlighted the induction of Hardin, a well-educated "bourgeois" female pianist from Memphis, into the quintessential working-class New Orleans band.[32]

In the clarinetist Ralph Brown's words, black middle-class attitudes toward jazz, although generally hostile at first, were "changing, changing, changing. . . . Just changing, I guess, maybe about '25, maybe the thirties." Even such bourgeois society bands as William Samuels's began to call their music jazz, which had previously been a taboo designation. While "we played the melody a lot . . . soft and sweet," the band also played "anything you wanted. . . . Syncopation was new back then," and Samuels felt then that "I was at the forefront of the jazz movement." Erskine Tate's popular theater orchestra usually began the evening with a concert overture, but the audience would then "want one of these wild things—he'd satisfy the older people, see, and the younger people," as Ralph Brown described it.[33]

Most surprisingly, Dave Peyton, who attacked jazz in his *Chicago Defender* column, began to supply written arrangements to such jazz nightclubs as the Plantation Café. According to Barney Bigard, who played the arrangements while in Oliver's band at the Plantation, Peyton wrote very difficult music in an attempt "to get us out of there." Oliver, however, "was smart and he hired different guys who could play all that hard stuff to play lead." Even Peyton changed his attitude toward jazz in time. In the 1930s, when he led a successful band at the Regal Theater, Peyton "always had the highest type of jazz musician he could find in his orchestra. . . . every one of them had an ability to improvise and also play the classical thing too," as Scoville Browne recalled.[34]

Blacks had wide musical tastes, as Browne discovered on the South Side: "There were a few who liked classics, some who liked jazz." The North satisfied these diverse tastes more readily. In Pittsburgh, Mary Lou Williams had three relatives, all Georgia migrants, who "would give me a weekly allowance to play their favorite songs. My uncle liked Irish songs. My grandfather liked the classics and my stepfather liked boogie-woogie." Further investigation would probably reveal additional examples of a wide array of musical preferences among blacks.[35]

In general, southern traditions evolved the most drastically during this formation of large northern black communities, as migrants became part of a more formalized and eclectic black society. Kid Ory, the prototypical rural folk-jazzman, took the first music lessons of his life from "some German guy" in Cicero, near Chicago. Ory learned more about what he called "toning," although his teacher "couldn't play jazz for nothing at all." The role of parades became diminished for jazz musicians in the North. Milt Hinton noted that there was a "transition" in which the southern bands "are beginning to get this softer sound, not that parade sound. . . . the tuba's a little harsh, so they're beginning to use the bass players [instead]." In numerous other ways—such as when the young Mary Lou Williams learned classical piano works by following the moving keys of her parents' player piano—southern jazz musicians became acculturated to the more European-oriented musical ways of the North.[36]

During the twenties, in Kansas City, Pittsburgh, and above all in Chicago, New York, and the other largest northern cities, some black musicians began to conceive of jazz as the African-American art or classical music. The white publicists and critics who first defined jazz for the mass public rarely praised the music as an art form, and in fact they usually ignored the central role of blacks in its creation. White Americans felt that the odd-sounding word applied only to the frenetic, ragtime-like music of white bands which received the greatest publicity in the mainstream white market. This "jazz" was generally considered to be an interesting (and mildly licentious) diversion, created not by blacks but by what one writer called "the Semitic purveyors of Broadway 'hits.'"[37] Black jazz, and the black origins of swinging syncopation and blues harmony, were rarely acknowledged in the white press. The white listeners who came to the South Side and Harlem often shared the notion that the "jungle music" they heard was a debased black form of white popular music.

Blacks themselves had to draw attention to the new style, but this was not something they were inclined to do. Although black bands had begun to use the word "jazz" in their names in the 1910s, they did not promote the notion that jazz was a discrete, novel music, distinguishable from other musical forms. The early New Orleans player Natty Dominique, interviewed in the 1950s, provided a hint of this attitude when he said that "there's no musicians that have any love for music, [who] will . . . take any interest in bop music." Music, not jazz, served as Dominique's referent for the most satisfying sounds he had ever experienced (what we now call early New Orleans jazz). His colleague Alphonse Picou, no less active in the 1910s Creole music scene, told the Tulane project that he had not even heard the word "jazz" until Mamie Smith's popular blues recordings were issued in 1920.[38]

Yet another Creole, Sidney Bechet, argued that jazz was merely "a name the white people have given to the music. . . . That doesn't explain the music." Bechet found musicians with similar views, such as Duke Ellington, in New York in 1924. When they played together, "there was none of this trying to give a name to Jazz, Orchestral Jazz, Concert Jazz, Fancy-Arrangement Jazz— there wasn't any of that kind of pushing from Duke."[39] It seems likely that these sentiments were a response to white use of the word to exoticize and make light of black music, and also an indication that jazz players, by preferring to call their music "music," felt a kinship with all proud and dedicated musicians.

Once southern and northern black dance musicians had

blended together by 1930, some musicians came to hold a new, elitist view that jazz had freed itself of the "low" qualities of rural southern music. Some urban musicians denigrated the southern roots of jazz. Milt Hinton, a member of Cab Calloway's New York band in the 1930s, developed such a view after the band's first southern tour. "To my thinking, and Cab's way of thinking—I guess I got the idea from him—that [rural blues music] kept the black mind in the South down. He [the black southerner] had nothing really musically uplifting to listen to. It was all this old crud."[40] The postmigration music of the North, by contrast, was usually called "artistic," and its creators "artists." Edwin "Squirrel" Ashcraft, a white observer of South Side music in the 1920s, felt that the New Orleans players were "quite artful" and made "many conscious efforts to draw progress and high virtuosity out of the men, and draw the most out of the music."[41]

This resulted from attitudes in northern black communities that valorized artistry, such as those expressed by the bootleggers who refused to hire Milt Hinton for a job since he was "something from Vicksburg, that's into legitimacy, into artistry." The Chicagoan Scoville Browne stressed that music "*was* a good profession in those days. It was a white collar thing and it was an artistic thing, and you were in a high income bracket. . . . There weren't too many of those people around then . . . in the same category, unless they were professional doctors and lawyers."[42] Soon after the migration subsided, musicians and many other blacks began to consider their finest music the product of unusual taste and talent.

Early jazz, it has been argued, marked the emergence of players who asserted their individuality and their distinctiveness from others in their culture. When this happened, jazz musicians adopted one of the central principles of the European art-music tradition. Individuality, and even alienation from the mainstream of musical culture, had characterized the personalities of European composers since Beethoven provided the example soon after 1800.[43] To a remarkable extent, some jazzmen drew away from a sense of oneness with their folk culture and toward a self-centered view of their creativity. As Montudie Garland put it, "I wouldn't try to imitate nobody else. I wanted my own style." In a highly revealing comment, Benny Carter indicated that in 1920s Harlem, "I think everybody was just trying to do their thing without a great deal of thought about what was black or Afro-American or jazz. . . . I think everybody was just trying to play what they heard, what they felt, without even thinking in terms of roots."[44] Carter suggested that after the musicians had absorbed the education and diverse stimuli provided by the experience of migration, they entered a stage of independent self-definition, in which the materials of the common musical culture became elements of distinctive and acknowledged personal styles (the content of which will be my focus in chapter 6). As musicians adopted these new views, jazz shed some of its early identity as a folk music and acquired a few of the formal characteristics of an elite or art musical culture.[45]

Whatever attitudes they held or steps they took to associate their work with dominant traditions, however, musicians always ran up against white America's refusal to acknowledge their achievement. In addition, the limitations imposed on all blacks by the white majority ensured that black jazz musicians could not escape the burdens of second-class citizenship. By 1930, black jazz played an important but disturbing function in American music and culture: it was the art music of a civilization confined to northern ghettos. The spirit of progress and racial pride that animated both the black migration and black music up to the mid-twenties became tempered by a growing awareness of the severe limits placed on black advancement across the nation. Milt Hinton knew as a boy that his family was accustomed to and was still encountering barriers, even as they welcomed Chicago's relative freedom: "they didn't know about all the gratuities of the Constitution that everybody's entitled to, so even though Chicago was so much better than Mississippi, they . . . never dreamed about going places where white people go, because nobody had ever done that."[46]

Musicians, though, had special skills that they directed toward the task of hurdling those barriers. Early in the migration era, some of them cast African-American harmonies and rhythms in traditional European classical forms. The Harlem pianist James P. Johnson went beyond composing rags, and like Scott Joplin before him wrote an opera, as well as symphonies and other concert pieces for full orchestra. Don Redman, Fletcher Henderson's saxophonist and arranger, also began to compose extended works in the 1920s; and William Grant Still, an oboist who worked with W. C. Handy and Sissle and Blake and later arranged for many jazz bands, also wrote "classical" compositions.[47]

Still and other black composers found, however, that their realm of activity was severely restricted. In a 1931 letter to a white friend, the critic Irving Schwerké, Still lamented that "it is unfortunate for a man of color who is ambitious to live in America."

While Still had known "many splendid [white] people here; broad minded; unselfish," he found that "friends who would lend me a helping hand, who would make it possible for me to make a living for my family[,] are unable to do anything because of those who are opposed to placing a colored man in any position of prominence." Still was aware he faced two disheartening courses of action. "Unless there is a change soon I will be forced to abandon my aspirations and look to other means of gaining a livlihood [*sic*] or to go where such conditions do not exist."[48] The "other means" available in America, for Still and other ambitious blacks, was the jazz world, broadly defined as the composition, performance, and recording of the blues and sweet and hot jazz. Described in large measure by the commercial and social dictates of the music and entertainment industries, this realm was the cultural equivalent of the residential ghettos to which all urban blacks were being confined.[49]

Milt Hinton experienced the constraints of the musical ghetto as a young violinist, when he learned that he could never pursue a career on this instrument. "I saw the guys were getting work, . . . and all the violin players were out of work. . . . There's no place for a black violin player in this world." Benny Carter, growing up in Manhattan in a time when black musicians' jobs were largely confined to Harlem, and when whites owned many of Harlem's bars and clubs, learned that jazz became a symbol of his culture's ghetto-ization. He and others knew that the downtown realm of café and club jobs "was definitely closed to them." The jazz scholar Morroe Berger asked Carter if he had "goals specifically directed towards jazz music." Carter's career decisions were ultimately dictated by the confines of prejudice: "Well, I guess I did, because I suppose that, as a black or a Negro, as I termed myself at the time, I felt that there was no future in being a symphonic musician. I didn't know of any black musicians playing with symphony orchestras, and I knew even very few string players; just a couple of violinists, and those that I knew played jazz . . . or what they called jazz."[50]

Black musical aspirations, like black aspirations in general in the twenties, had expanded greatly, creating an enthusiasm and creative impulse that transformed the attitudes and behavior of the younger generation of black migrant musicians. These aspirations, however, ultimately were confined by the restrictive wall of segregation and prejudice, to the extent that black jazz became defined as much by the limits imposed on it as by the growth and optimism it represented.

The self-consciousness and mature activity of the jazz profession, however, were only initiated in the late twenties, and were in effect the seeds of important new thoughts and strategies that would blossom and bear fruit in the near future. By that time, however, black jazz musicians would not be the only Americans winning prominence as practitioners of improvisation and the blues—white players soon filled the scene. Blacks' careers and efforts would be both enhanced and retarded by the words and deeds of these white Americans who also claimed jazz as their own.

5

"The Great Travelers"
White Jazz Musicians of the 1920s

The story of early jazz is unusual in American cultural history. Our historiographical tradition has invariably treated white history as the mainstream of the American past, but white jazz history is an appendix to an African-American mainstream. In creating jazz, black players exercised a kind of cultural leadership in America that has rarely been permitted or acknowledged. Neither jazz histories nor white musicians' memoirs explore the teacher-student relationship between blacks and whites. The four memoirs published in the late 1940s (by Mezz Mezzrow, Wingy Manone, Eddie Condon, and Hoagy Carmichael) are not very reflective, except for Mezzrow's, which is so full of hyperbole about blacks that it is suspect.[1] Before the civil rights revolution, writers played down the dynamics of race in jazz, and afterward, they took racial progress for granted. If we are to understand the first white jazz players' attraction to the music and the true nature of their relation to black musicians, then it is necessary to reinvestigate and reinterpret their story.

Steeped in the heritage of French military ensembles and musical entertainment, New Orleans's whites possessed a vibrant band culture in the late nineteenth and early twentieth centuries. Because they belonged to the privileged race, until 1920 white bands had far greater access than black outfits to formal education, profitable touring, comfortable locales in the city, and well-paying legitimate customers. Dixieland—the syncopated style of white band music that grew up alongside New Orleans black jazz—was nurtured by particular elements of the city's white band culture.[2] Like black jazz, Dixieland grew out of the folk practices of a working-class, upward-aspiring group of young men.

Dixieland players and their black jazz neighbors were culturally similar in many ways. George "Jack" Laine was the first prominent figure in Dixieland music. Like Kid Ory, Laine first organized a band as a child. At the Cotton and Sugar Exposition in 1884, Laine played the drums in his first spasm band, and while still in grade school he organized five separate groups. His musicians, like their black counterparts, received only basic instruction. "We all played by ear," Laine recalled, "all of us until we got this man Meade or Perkins. . . . he begin to learn us notes." Perkins may have been a forebear of Dave Perkins, a Creole music teacher, which suggests that Dixieland might have tapped authentic black roots from the start. In any case, Laine's groups were firmly imbedded in working-class culture. They played at carnivals, where "they danced the two-step, the schottische, etc. to the ragtime music," but not to the genteel waltz. Laine, in fact, mistakenly believed that waltz time was "⅝ or something like that," but he knew well enough that the waltz was the "wrong time" for these crowds.[3]

Laine grew up among the more comfortable elements of the white working class in New Orleans. His father was a contractor, and his band members "were also from fairly well-off working people": Nick LaRocca's father was a shoe merchant, and Georg Brunis's worked as the maitre d' for a chain of Gulf hotel restaurants.[4] Like the black protojazz bands, Laine's early groups emerged from a culture of childhood communality and experimentation. "We used to go around the street with a bunch of kids, flags and torchlights and stuff like that playing. Every night we'd go out in the street playing music, and marching. This was for pleasure, not for profit." His first professional band, recruited in the 1890s, was also made up of a "lot of children." Laine had "brought them all in, and ever since then, why they began a picking up playing music, and they made remarkable musicians. . . . I used to have around 30 maybe 30, 35 children there. . . . My old folks used to get angry [at] me, for having 'em there," in a woodshed where they were taught to play; "they played the mischief, . . . course I include myself, I wasn't no angel. . . . A good deal of the boys they picked note[s] wonderfully, and some of 'em couldn't, they couldn't knock it in their heads."

Laine developed such future musicians as the leader Tom Brown, the clarinetists Leon Rappollo and Harry Shields, and the trombonist Georg Brunis: "I picked them boys up playing with me when they were just small children . . . in knee pants." Laine bought them uniforms, and soon spread his operation to Biloxi, Mississippi. In New Orleans, as Brunis recalled, "I'd play with his

Reliance Band. . . . we played a dance, we get fifty cents an hour, Crescent Park, Owls' Hall, Suburban Park, Alvero Park in Algiers," and parades.[5]

Laine, like black leaders, acquired a paternal role and a fitting nickname. Laine called his band "a bunch of Papa's kids out, all little fellows, young kids." As the Reliance veteran Nick LaRocca noted, the boys "used to come down to Laine's house during the day . . . Mrs. Laine mothered them all, every one of them. Papa had a place upstairs, over the main floor, had beds in there. The boys used to come there sometimes at night and sleep. The boys' mother would call or come by the house to find out where the boys were. The boys would break the feather pillows open, throw feathers all around."[6]

The white Dixieland experience thus bore a resemblance to the close relationship between professors and novices in black music in the same region. The two cultures also shared folk beliefs; for example, George Brunies shortened his name to Georg Brunis when a numerologist told him that entertainers with thirteen letters in their names risked bad luck in their work. Jack Laine's band and others developed their renditions in a communal folk manner, without written music. As the Tulane interviewers wrote, "a member might come in with a new idea, so a rehearsal would be called, and everyone in the band would work at the idea until it became a full-fledged tune. . . . the 'boys' named all the tunes." The pianist Elmer Schoebel was the only member of Brunis's future band in Chicago who could read music.[7]

Nick LaRocca, however, Laine's most ambitious pupil, infused Dixieland with more elite musical values. As a boy, he had been eager to learn musical notation, and had gained inspiration at the opera, where "I seen how they played background contramelody and different melodies against one another. . . . In later years," when he led the Original Dixieland Jazz Band (ODJB), he "incorporated that and what we had was nothing but a conversation of instruments. You take the *Livery Stable Blues*, for instance. . . . they're three distinct melodies working together." LaRocca characterized himself as "just an ignorant scholar of music but I went to too many . . . opera place[s] where I could hear good music."[8] He would be the first Dixieland musician to make a conscious effort to record tunes on paper and to obtain copyrights.

Like their black counterparts, Laine's and other bands played in many social settings, as entertainment during leisure functions. Bands often played at lawn parties in the Irish Channel, a white ethnic neighborhood where they informally contracted, and were not even paid if these affairs degenerated into drunken battles. When fighting broke out, musicians became signal men for the brawling factions, which formed along ethnic, residential, or age divisions. Laine's band continued the practice (then dying out among whites) of playing in funeral marches, and it participated in Mardi Gras and other parades as well.[9] Street activity introduced young players to the varieties of urban life. Brunis's own kid band took to the streets and played "for the butchers [at the French Market, and] they'd hand us money." Brunis and others played on advertising wagons, promoting boxing matches, balls, football games, and other events. The term "tailgate," denoting the New Orleans style of trombone playing, originated on advertising wagons (but the term only gained wide usage in later years, in Chicago). These bands occasionally met and battled mobile black musicians.[10]

Laine's operation had its folk qualities, but from the early years (like Kid Ory's Creole band) it was also commercial in intent. Laine "left school after he started playing for money," and as an adult, with his wife as paymaster, he operated many street bands, as well as outfits that toured with Wild West and minstrel shows. Laine was even known to take over independent children's bands, such as Eddie Edwards's. As the Tulane oral historians wrote, "it seems to him that no other band had a chance when his was around, and that his band played for anything that required music." When the Streckfus family began to hire white (as well as black) syncopating bands for their riverboat tours, Laine supplied much of the personnel.[11] Nevertheless, all Laine players needed other jobs as well. The drummer Ray Bauduc worked as a clerk at Werlein's music store, the trombonist Eddie Edwards worked as a salesman, and Laine himself as a blacksmith, bartender, fireman, and an occasional prizefighter. He retired from music in 1918, when it was no longer profitable.[12]

In its syncopation, timbre, and measured pace, Dixieland resembled early black jazz. As 1910s recordings indicate, Dixieland was a syncopated modification of traditional two-step dance music. The ODJB's 1917 Victor disks (which began the nationwide jazz trend) also exhibit a variety of glissandi and rough timbral effects clearly related to African-American techniques. In the 1950s, Laine could differentiate this music clearly from the northern jazz of later years: "We didn't have as much swing in the music in them days. . . . we played almost straight stuff. Now and then, we might have a little racket in the music," but generally the syncopation, as the recordings attest, was comparatively slight. The tempi were moderate, unlike the jazz of twenties musicians, who, in Georg Brunis's opinion, had "a tendency to play a lot of fast music." By accentuating only two beats to a measure, unlike the four-beat accentuation of the 1920s (and the eight-beat foundation of 1930s boogie-woogie), Dixieland seemed then as now to be more of a marching than a dancing music.[13]

Despite their cultural similarities to black jazz players, these musicians insisted that blacks had no role in creating jazz. Tom Brown, for example, argued that "the colored are not responsible" for jazz; "the colored only played 'plantation' [music]." Nick LaRocca believed that "St. Louis Blues" was a white tune, since "that chord construction is not from Africa," and claimed that if black jazz "existed in New Orleans I'm certain these [white] people here would have known about it." Jack Laine believed that Manuel Perez's was the only "colored band" in 1900 New Orleans (in fact, many were active), and he actually argued that blacks learned to syncopate from his own band: black children trailed and emulated the band when it marched on the streets, and he thus accused Buddy Bolden, Jelly Roll Morton, and W. C. Handy of copying him.[14]

Racism had not restrained other whites in New Orleans from encountering black and Creole syncopating bands, but the Dixieland players offer a study in contrast. The social distance between uptown blacks and the skilled white working class, which spawned Dixieland, was unusually large. Laine insisted that "I didn't go around them places like" Johnny Lala's and other gambling centers, which for Laine signified the presence of black bands. These men blanched at the thought of racial mixing; thus LaRocca asserted falsely that "in my day no negroes sang or played on [any river]boat." As LaRocca himself noted when he later attacked blacks' claims to jazz, "the only thing I had in my mind was against mixing." One black musician, Zutty Singleton, disputed these memories, arguing that "all the white boys were influenced from the downtown gang. From Tio and them boys." In any case, whites' perception of their social distance from blacks might have overrode their perception or memory of any real encounters.[15]

This distancing allowed whites to claim, at least when questioned, that their group had invented syncopated New Orleans music. As Tulane's oral historians noted, Jack Laine "believe[d] he is [the] first one to ever have a ragtime band on the street." Ragtime originated, according to Laine, in the everyday expression of his people in the 1880s. "There used to be plenty of people whistling it. There used to be an organ grinder who would stop at the corner. . . . there was one tune that he used to rag the mischief out of." Tom Brown, who brought the first Dixieland band to Chicago in 1915, claimed to have invented jazz (a term he does not define), which northern bands then imitated. In his last years, LaRocca aggressively claimed that he composed the Dixieland standard "Tiger Rag," and told Tulane researchers that a bout of youthful flatulence had suggested the tune's basic rhythm to him one evening.[16]

The cornetist's homely anecdote illustrates the players' general attempt to stress their modest beginnings and talents, a kind of aggressive humility that might have reflected the cultural populism of poorer southern whites.[17] Poorer whites, as well as European immigrants, who swelled New Orleans's population after 1890, were especially vulnerable and guarded, and it was they who manned the white-supremacist Democratic political machine run by John Kirkpatrick and Martin Behrman, which ran the city for nearly all of the coming half-century.[18] In part, Dixieland was an expression of this wary group's identity and pride. Laine's band was multiethnic, including such persons as Achille Baquet (a passing Creole of color, unbeknownst to Laine), Manuel Mello, Lawrence Vega, and "Zimmermann," and Laine's wife, Blanche, was Cuban. In addition, the bandleader lived his entire life in one small neighborhood of the city, in the area of Mandeville and Clouet Streets.[19]

For these white residents, Latinos and southern European immigrants were allies, and wealthy Anglo-Saxons and nonwhites were enemies. Nick LaRocca expressed his resentment against the Protestant ruling class in New Orleans, who treated him like "a poor dago boy on the other side of the tracks" when he returned there in 1925. The trumpeter Joe "Wingy" Manone, who like LaRocca migrated North, later vented his ethnic resentments against the Chinese, whose presence in New Orleans both amused and terrified him as a youth.[20] Italians were in a precarious position in this era, as they were both the target of riots and contributors to the white coalition; in Dixieland, at least, they seemed to find a safe haven. This context might help to explain LaRocca's rich outburst: "Not having associated with 'em, not knowing 'em, how was I to give these colored men a break? I couldn't even give myself a break, I had to make that break."[21]

The break LaRocca and a few Dixieland players made for themselves was identical to the solution sought by southern blacks: migration to Chicago and to other northern cities. LaRocca took the ODJB to Chicago in 1916, to New York the following year, on tours of military installations during the Great War, and to London in 1919. He acknowledged that Broadway at that time "was black with Negro musicians, ragtimers," but took pride because "they never was noticed and their music couldn't have been any different than they were playing anywhere else in the world, but they [the public] noticed the DJB. We stood out, made history."[22] The pride in LaRocca's words is evident, but so is his neglect of the racial advantages his band had held as they eclipsed the fame of black bands. He also denied the black contribution to jazz—a typical attitude of early Dixieland players and probably central to their perception of their music and culture.

Although Dixieland was the first genre of syncopated improvisation to gain wide attention, it was largely neglected by the 1920s musicians who created the definitive styles of early jazz. Black jazzmen from that period rarely emulated LaRocca, Brunis, or their partners; and the first white hot players, while they studied the pioneering ODJB recordings, quickly graduated to other styles. Whites who first consciously imitated the black jazz sound were spread across the nation, often grouped in small cliques. Among these cliques was the group of singers in eastern Washington state, living in Spokane amid a strong native American cultural presence: Al Rinker and his sister (later Mildred Bailey, the finest white jazz singer of the Big Band era) and the Crosby brothers, Harry ("Bing") and Bob. Instrumental bands of north central Texas, featuring such players as Jack Teagarden and Peck Kelley, were exposed to black jazz and spirituals. In Boston, Leo Reisman's band was the hub for jazz enthusiasts.[23] These groups shared an interest in race records and attempted to recreate black instrumental or vocal styles.

All of these groups, as well as Hoagy Carmichael's fraternity band in Bloomington, Indiana, and Gil Evans and Jimmy Maxwell's young band in Stockton, California, deserve analysis. I will focus, however, on the most revealing and influential of these white groups, the celebrated Chicagoans. The young players active in 1920s Chicago are generally regarded to have been the first white musicians to fully incorporate the swinging style of the great black players into their jazz.[24] The Austin High Gang, originating in a middle-class neighborhood on Chicago's West Side, was the most aggressive and influential exponent of white hot jazz and included a few of the best early white players: the saxophonist Bud Freeman, the trumpeter Jimmy McPartland, the clarinetist Frank Tesche-macher, and the drummer Dave Tough. Concentric circles of white players formed around this group: from the Chicago vicinity, the saxophonist Milton Mesirow ("Mezz Mezzrow"), the pianist Art Hodes, and the clarinetist Benny Goodman; and from the larger, multistate midwestern region for which Chicago was the urban magnet, the guitarist Eddie Condon, the cornetist Leon Bix Beider-becke, and the clarinetists Rod Cless and Charles "Pee Wee" Russell. These players, in addition, were a focus of Neil Leonard's pioneer-ing 1962 study, *Jazz and the White Americans.* Leonard argued that the Chicagoans were in "revolution" against the dominant values of the era and turned to jazz as a means of combating these values.[25] A more detailed investigation of these issues here, benefiting from the wealth of evidence uncovered in the past three decades, will test and refine Leonard's conclusion.

One of Chicago's first suburbs, Austin was a neighborhood of assimilated Irish- and German-Americans, bordered on the east by the slums of more recently arrived Poles and Italians.[26] Begin-ning in 1921, Freeman, Teschemacher, McPartland and his brother Dick, Jim Lanigan, Dave North, and Floyd O'Brien (later joined by Tough, who visited from Oak Park) spent long hours listen-ing to and discussing jazz records. The first recordings they heard were of Dixieland music, the sweet products of the Paul Whiteman and Art Hickman bands, and Ted Lewis's comic inventions, which "didn't do anything to us somehow," as McPartland recalled. The records of the New Orleans Rhythm Kings, a younger group that consciously tried to play in a black style, excited them more.[27]

The listeners in Austin acquired instruments and taught them-selves to play. Some had already learned the violin and had "played classical things and operas," McPartland noted, but they had not been "that interested in playing an instrument." However, "when we heard this jazz we flipped. That was it." Freeman now played the C-melody saxophone, Jimmy McPartland the cornet, Dick McPart-land the guitar, Teschemacher the clarinet, North the piano, Lani-gan the string bass, and Tough the drums. After months of prac-tice, their sounds were reasonable imitations of the recordings, and the band began contracting to play at dances, fraternity parties, weddings, Chinese restaurants, and other low-paying sites.[28]

The Chicago hot style featured a trio of solo instruments (usually the trumpet, clarinet, and saxophone) that incited each other rhythmically, creating a driving, accumulating effect that released itself in unison "explosions," aided by the work of the drummer. The jazz historian Richard Hadlock has argued that "no group of jazzmen had ever *attacked* music with more vigor and bravado than did this eager fraternity."[29] Until 1929, when economic troubles encouraged them to leave Chicago, they remained a cohesive and rapidly improving group of jazz innovators.

The Chicago musicians' acceptance of black jazz grew out of their early reaction to the social pressures, opportunities, and conditions around them. The Austin natives were restless products of the suburban life-style that expanded quickly (especially around Chicago) after the Great War. The Chicagoans' recollections indicate that suburbs almost instantly inspired adolescent restlessness. Bud Freeman recalled that when he and his brother "were in our teens, we were not very ambitious in the way that most people think they're supposed to be." In Austin, his "neighbors were forever butting into one another's business" and asking Freeman's widowed father why the boys did not work. "After being brain-washed by the community, my father came into our room at seven one morning and announced, 'You boys are getting up and going out to look for jobs and amount to something like other people,'" to which Arny Freeman replied, "'How dare you wake us up before the weekend!'" Other rebellions against conformity were more pointed and angry. Social workers in Austin classified the McPartland boys as delinquents: as children of a broken home, they lived in a spartan Baptist orphanage for years, and later became gang members who landed in jail before their teen years. Jimmy McPartland believed "that this [experience] has affected me throughout my life somehow or other."[30]

Delinquency took other forms. Mezz Mezzrow, a young adult veteran of reform school and youth gangs, lived with his family in the north suburb of Sunnyside when, in a fit of contempt, he apparently provoked an incident that severed his relations with them. Angry that his sister's transcription of blues lyrics from race records "kept 'correcting' Bessie's grammar, straightening out her words and putting them in 'good' English," he decided "to turn my back once and for all on that hincty [snobbish], killjoy world of my sister's and move over to Bessie Smith's world of body and soul." Showing a flair for symbolic ritual, Mezzrow "sneaked into the house and stole my sister's Hudson-seal fur coat out of the closet, then I beat it down to the whorehouse and sold it to the madam for $150. With the dough[,] I made for the Conn Music Company and bought an alto sax for cash." True or not, the story leaves no question about Mezzrow's desire to escape his family, "as respectable as Sunday morning." With similar desires to leave the world of the Victorian family behind them, men across the country who shared a love of black jazz—Bill Davison in Defiance, Ohio; Eddie Sauter of Nyack, New York; Jimmy Maxwell of Tracy, California—stole away from home and parents at night to play in bands, often in downtowns many miles away.[31]

White players especially rebelled against the regimentation of formalized learning. Like other players, Freeman "had a difficult time in school because I was always thinking about music and couldn't wait to get home to play the music [on the victrola]." Mezzrow claimed that he "took my public-school training in three jails and a plenty of poolrooms [*sic*], went to college in a gang of teapads [marijuana dens], earned my Ph.D. in more creep joints and speakeasies and dancehalls than the law allows." To a man, the Austin High Gang dropped out of that school before their senior year, and, symbolically (according to McPartland), they earned the status of gang by using their fists against college fraternity members who heckled their playing.[32]

Mezzrow evaluated the white jazz movement in Chicago with typical grandiloquence: "there was a revolution simmering in Chicago . . . a collectively improvised nose-thumbing at all pillars of all communities, one big syncopated Bronx cheer for the righteous squares everywhere. . . . they wanted to blast every highminded citizen clear out of his easy chair with their yarddog growls and gully-low howls . . . jazz was the only language they could find to preach their fire-eating message." More than one musician from Austin agreed with Jimmy McPartland that "if it hadn't been for the music, I'm sure we all would have become hoodlums." The young Bud Freeman "was around Chicago during the bootleg era and I could have easily gone the wrong way, because I knew many of the people that were to later get involved in that and get killed and go to jail." The Chicagoans were, in short, comparatively privileged young whites who made a quasi-existential flight from the quiet suburb and formal education.[33]

In the 1920s—and in the 1940s, when Mezzrow and others wrote their memoirs—the sociological concept of juvenile delinquency as adolescent rebellion was widely discussed in America. Possibly the public discourse inspired the young musicians to define themselves as rebels, although their interaction with their families and communities may have been different or more complex. Today, sociologists argue that the *society* at large, rather than self-conscious rebels, defines those who are deviant.[34] The criticisms of the Freeman boys by their Austin neighbors and the attitude of Mezzrow's sister illustrate this kind of dynamic, but generally it is difficult to detect a pattern of ascription before the musicians entered jazz. Almost all of them, for example, seemed to have shared the apoliticism of other white adolescents of the twenties (a situation greatly decried by adults then). The jazz world, though, clearly was assigned a deviant status by whites in the twenties, and all of them would feel the onus of their association with it.[35]

The Chicagoans were not alone. In Indiana, Hoagy Carmichael also sensed that "there was rebellion, then, against the accepted, the proper and the old . . . the First World War had been fought, and in the backwash conventions had tumbled." As a high school student in Indianapolis, he "was filled with rebellion rather than learning" and concentrated on the piano. At Bloomington, though, he followed convention by attending the university and the law school. In contrast to the more forthright Chicago experience of rebellion, Carmichael was an ambivalent deviant who cultivated his jazz heresies in a fraternity hangout on evenings after class. His "rebellion" was never pronounced, and his sense of family duty and of tradition seemed to haunt him: "we like to hear the rumble of the ice wagon and the querulous barking of a familiar dog. These sounds are right. We *know* they are right and perhaps they make us afraid."[36]

Despite its nostalgic veneer, though, Carmichael's memoirs suggest that his rebellion, while mostly latent, was filled with anger. In a bitter and cryptic reference to Buddy Bolden's early institutionalization, he boasted that "they got Buddy, but they never got us." This bitterness seems to have been the result of the social and cultural isolation of expressive white adolescents in rural Indiana. Fear stalked them on their road dates, huddled in dingy hotel rooms—"six little children of jazz, brave in our long pants, and then the candle sputters out and we are afraid."[37] Carmichael was apparently haunted by a sense of the futility of tradition and his generation's possible inability to guarantee a future.

As these men struggled against the demands of their families and communities, they found urban life to be an irresistible lure and an arena for experimentation. The musicians who came to 1920s Chicago, whether from the suburbs or from distant towns, found extramusical inspiration in the city's ethnic and occupational diversity. In 1920, three-tenths of Chicago's population of 2.7 million was foreign-born, and German, Polish, Russian, Italian, Swedish, Irish, Austrian, and black ethnic groups in the city each possessed more than 100,000 members.[38] The trumpeter Max Kaminsky, a native of Boston, arrived in 1928 to discover "the bursting feeling of life in the city, engendered by the hordes of young people who swarmed into Chicago by the thousands . . . the gamblers, the promoters, the bootleggers, and the gangsters, [who made] Chicago a wide-open, rip-roaring town, where cattlemen and hillbillies rubbed shoulders with poets and G men, tycoons and politicians, baseball players and B girls, racketeers and reformers."[39]

Native Chicagoans were similarly entranced by the streets. Mezz Mezzrow recalled that "the streets of Chicago's Northwest Side were like a magnet to me . . . the sidewalks were always jammed, big gamblers and racketeers, dressed sharp as a tack, strutted by with their diamond stickpins, chicks you heard stories about would tip up and down the avenue real cool, the cops toured the neighborhood in big Cadillacs filled with shotguns. . . . the sights and sounds of the Northwest Side . . . were all jumbled up in my head." Jimmy McPartland, son of a Scottish mother and an Irish-American father, was born on the equally diverse West Side, where "we had everyone, . . . all kinds—Polish, Italian, Irish, Negro. . . . We were tough little monkeys in those days [when the epithet] "shanty Irishman" [were] fighting words."[40]

For good or for ill, these young men also viewed the jazz scene on the black South Side primarily as an exotic, ethnic, antisuburban attraction. In the 1920s, the South Side, Harlem, and other ghettos attracted large numbers of thrill-seeking whites who patronized black clubs (usually owned by the white underworld) for a new kind of entertainment. The Chicagoans, like these whites, were ensconced in safe, segregated suburbs, but felt bold enough to make excursions to black enclaves to view the migrants' culture. George Wettling, a drummer originally from Kansas, rode his bicycle from a suburb to the South Side and found easy entry into the cabarets. Bud Freeman, disregarding his father's concerns about safety, attended black church services as well as nightclubs, where one doorman would say, "I see you've come to get your music lessons!" The younger players were assisted by students from Northwestern and the University of Chicago, who served as chaperones while satisfying their own curiosity about South Side night life.[41]

Unlike the majority of "slumming" whites, however, some jazz players in Chicago—like other whites scattered across the country—developed a deep and abiding respect for African-American music. The live performances of black musicians thrilled and en-

riched them and sealed their commitment to the jazz vocation. At
a state youth reformatory in the 1910s, Mezz Mezzrow had had
exposure of this kind. The blues the black inmates chanted from
cell to cell at night, "always blending together like the colors in
an artist's picture, the way the syllables were always placed right,
the changes in the words to fit the music—this all hit me like a
millennium would hit a philosopher." Mezzrow learned to play the
saxophone in the reformatory, and "by the time I reached home, I
knew that I was going to spend all my time from then on sticking
to Negroes. . . . I was going to be a musician, a Negro musician,
hipping the world about the blues the way only Negroes can."[42]

In 1923, after hearing King Oliver's band for the first time on
the South Side, Bud Freeman felt that "I had never heard any music
so creative and exciting as this band played, and I really believe that
hearing all this was the greatest education in music I've ever had. I
was not only hearing a new form of music but was experiencing a
whole new way of life."[43] Many tales of first hearings are strikingly
reverent. Eddie Condon's first visit with Freeman and McPartland
to the Café de Paris, where the Oliver band played, "was hypnosis
at first hearing. . . . there was a tone from the trumpets like warm
rain on a cold day. Freeman and McPartland and I were immobi-
lized; the music poured into us like daylight running down a dark
hole." For Hoagy Carmichael, listening to Oliver confirmed for him
that "the muggles and the gin were, in a way, stage props. It was the
music. The music took me and had me and it made me right."[44]

The fact that the white players were moved to take up jazz
as a profession sets them apart from the other white visitors to
the ghetto. Without minimizing the typicality of their socialization in the suburbs, it is fair to conclude that no other identifiable
group of white Americans of this era approached black culture with
such openness and repaid it with comparable gratitude, praise, and
emulation.

There is evidence that some of them who had lived in the city
for all or part of their childhood were able to form positive images
of the other race. Most children raised in urban settings during
the period of rapid industrialization developed powerful territo-
rial allegiances along ethnic and racial divisions, as the experience
of whites in New Orleans showed.[45] By contrast, those jazz musicians who spent their childhood in northern cities before the Great
Migration seem to have benefited from years of relative calm in
black-white relations, in which whites were tolerant of small and
assimilationist black populations. Hoagy Carmichael "grew into a

normal boy" in Indianapolis as "a member of the East Side gang which in the days of screaming youth knew no distinction between blacks and whites." Max Kaminsky of Boston began life in the Roxbury district, "in the heart of the colored section," where he heard gospel singing in churches and "the street cries of the Negro push-cart men on summer nights." Kaminsky was friendly with Harry Carney (later in the Duke Ellington band) and other black youths while he battled gangs of Irish boys after school.[46]

Mezz Mezzrow, George Wettling and Jimmy McPartland, among others, developed early and warm relations with blacks while growing up in Chicago.[47] Like Mezzrow, a few other whites felt that they became Negro musicians after spending time with blacks. For example, the drummer Johnny Otis grew up in the thirties in the racially divided East Bay area around Oakland. "As a kid I decided that if our society dictated that one had to either be black or white, I would be black," because he "reacted to the way of life, the special vitality, the atmosphere of the black community." Otis noted that "my attitude was formed long before I moved into the music field," but music plainly served as the facilitator for sustaining and defining his involvement in black culture.[48]

These musicians' strong attraction to black culture helps us to understand more clearly what they were rebelling against and looking *for*. For some whites, this interracial exploration was part of a general disavowal of ethnic differences. Bud Freeman's comment, "I am concerned with a man as being a man, I am concerned with individual talent," captures and typifies the attitudes of many others. Mezzrow, for one, ignored white ethnicity and emphasized his allegiance to blacks: "being a Jew didn't mean a thing to me." Jewish musicians who worked in vaudeville and Tin Pan Alley were "beat-up old hamfats who sang and played a commercial excuse for the real thing. . . . Around the poolroom I defended the guys I felt were my real brothers, the colored musicians who made music that sent me. . . . I never could dig the phony idea of a race."[49]

Mezzrow, Freeman, and others who echoed them resembled the ideal types of second-generation Americans sociologists once described—young people who fled their parents' old-world roots and became fervent Americans. They differed from this type in a crucial way, however. The jazz musicians used their association with African-American culture to incorporate themselves more fully into a new kind of American urban life. This life embodied the culture of the streets and speakeasies, exciting new mass amusements, and interracial and interethnic exchange, and it was the kind of life disdained by elites who asked immigrants' sons to Americanize in a more suburban, bourgeois-minded way.[50]

No one used jazz music to flee the established paths of ethnic assimilation with more ferocity than Arthur Arshawsky, who became the clarinetist and bandleader Artie Shaw. Born in 1910 on the Lower East Side to Russian immigrant parents, Shaw was moved to New Haven when he was seven. Taunts from gentile schoolmates led him to discover that "I was this strange kind of creature called 'Jew' (and now 'kike' and 'sheeny' and 'Christ-killer' as well)," a stigma (he wrote in 1953) that "had more to do with shaping the course and direction of my entire life than any other single thing that has happened to me, before or since." This experience created "an enormous need to belong, to have some feeling of roots, to become part of a community."[51]

Shaw's future looked dim. "I might very well have become a fair specimen of a juvenile delinquent—and perhaps not only juvenile at that. Given my philosophical outlook, my cynical attitudes toward life as I had known it, plus the goals I had already set up for myself, I was in no mood for any long-range plan involving such activities as schooling or training. . . . I was looking for a short-cut, a quick way out." Shaw therefore, learned the saxophone and later pursued fame and wealth relentlessly, a pursuit that seems also to have been calculated to put his father's immigrant worldview far behind him. Once, while listening to his son practice, Mr. Arshawsky "shook his head in wonder, and finally said: '*America gonniff,*'" which Shaw took to mean, "if people are stupid enough to pay good money to listen to crazy noises coming out of a blower, let them do it, but don't expect me to take it seriously, because I know better." When his father deserted the family for California soon afterward, Shaw felt, "it is even conceivable that my saxophone was the last straw, the one little push he needed to make the break."[52]

In one sense, Artie Shaw's experience had less to do with musical inspiration (although he would become a fine, important musician) than with the general ethnic passion to overcome marginality and to assimilate to what each immigrant's child perceived as being "America." In this respect he seems more intensely alienated than the more optimistically adventurous white players of Chicago. Shaw resembled them, though, in that the "America" he sought was not suburbia, but the urban jazz world, and his candid revelations depict painful emotions that might have been shared (but concealed in the future) by the Chicagoans as well, as they negotiated suburban conformity, youth gangs, territoriality, and ethnic and racial divisions, seeking to feel at home in their city.[53]

White jazz, therefore, was energized by specific ethnic, social, and adolescent impulses, many of them rebellious in nature. During the musicians' early professional careers, their interest in jazz was mixed with a desire to think and act differently. How informed and articulate a revolt was this? Some whites were aggressively anti-intellectual, in a state of primitive rebellion indistinguishable from that of unskilled urban youth.[54] The Dionysian group of musicians who congregated in Wingy Manone and Art Hodes's apartment on Chicago's North Side, in particular, did not actively analyze their world, investigate other arts, or do anything to give jazz a critical thrust. Hodes wrote that "in the two years I lived with Wingy I don't believe I read one book. Our day was so packed with listening to music and playing music and going to see people from our world—mainly Louis Armstrong—that we had no time for reading; we didn't miss it—we didn't know books existed."[55]

Many of the early white jazz musicians, however, were also strongly motivated by a fierce intellectualism. Not only rebelling against the more stultifying aspects of childhood, they also sought knowledge and experience of such breadth that their creation of a new white music seems to have been a by-product. In fact, none of the Austin High players had actually planned on a musical career. Jimmy McPartland noted that "I wasn't that interested in playing an instrument," and Bud Freeman was certain that "if I hadn't become . . . a jazz musician, I would surely have become an actor, or maybe a writer or story teller or something."[56]

Max Kaminsky, who arrived from Boston in 1928, sensed that "all the fellows in the Chicago crowd were on a genius kick." They would "stay up all day [after playing at night] talking about writers and literature and painting and music and all the great new ideas that were in the air." Kaminsky himself, "who up to now had seldom cracked open a book . . . could see myself in them—they expressed all my feelings for me. America was still so young and new then and we all had the feeling of wanting to do something great." Freeman agreed, recalling that he and his friends "were always going to the theatre, going to see films, always there was this constant music. . . . I was involved in the arts." The passions of Chicago musicians were sometimes exotic, such as those of the brothers Boyce and Harvey Brown, who "were both interested in Yogi and Hindu philosophy," as Hodes remembered; "in fact, quite a few of the leading hot musicians in Chicago had gotten interested in it, and there was lots of discussion going on."[57]

As adults, free from the bonds of public schools, some musicians eagerly sought education from books at their leisure. Bix Beiderbecke, often depicted after his early death as anti-intellectual, strove to be "an educated man," Freeman noted, and had "a great regard for the theater, books, for anything artistic," especially avant-garde music and the works of Proust. Although Freeman had quit Austin High to become a musician, he would spend much of his spare time as an adult devouring paperbacks on many subjects, from Latin American poetry to Zen philosophy. One of his happiest intellectual discoveries was the letters of Paul Gaugin, who expressed the resonant opinion that a life of artistic creation was above all a retreat from petty obligations.[58]

Jimmy McPartland, who did not finish his sophomore year at Austin, arranged his own education later in life. Traveling with Ben Pollack's band for extended times in the thirties, McPartland would contact the deans of local colleges, tell them about his interests, and obtain reading lists. Pocket editions of Plato, Shakespeare, and others consumed his free time. "I did it religiously. . . . I quit smoking, quit drinking for two years." Bill Davison, belying his hard-drinking life-style, became a voracious student of history, and Jimmy Maxwell learned many languages during his years as a staff musician with CBS Radio.[59] On their own—and with the aid of jazz—the white players developed a thirst for unencumbered self-education.

On and off the nightclub stages, the white Chicago jazz musicians sported attitudes and manners combining intellect, extravagance, and an experimental sensibility. No jazz musician flaunted these attributes more fully than the drummer Dave Tough. According to those who knew him (Tough did not write memoirs), he was a complex, energetic man who "did everything with immense, deliberate dignity," "was the brightest and most humorous man I've ever known," and "popped with spirit till he couldn't sit still."[60]

Tough was born in 1908 and raised by his widowed father in the wealthy suburb of Oak Park, and by the age of fourteen he could read music and make his way to the South Side clubs. He came to treat the drum set, then a novelty item in most bands, as a serious instrument that delivered many shades of rhythm, timbre, and volume. While many players were content merely to "get a noise out of a drum," Freeman argued, Tough "gets a sound.

It's like another . . . part of the harmony, another note. Dave . . . knew more about this music than any drummer I had ever heard." Max Kaminsky, noting the "biting attack" that the white players shared, added that "I guess we all got some of that bite from Dave Tough. . . . you had to play that hard, biting style to keep less-experienced musicians playing in time."[61]

Freeman believed that "Tough's great mentality made him a great drummer, because he was . . . a sensitive artist, he knew about improvising, he knew about composition, he knew the music he was playing." Tough interested himself in every product of the artistic avant-garde he could locate. He went with his friends to symphony concerts that featured the avant-garde work of Stravinsky, Ravel, and Holst, and he read modernist fiction, including that of his former Oak Park neighbor, Ernest Hemingway. Freeman recalled that "Dave Tough was one of the first people I ever heard speak about Hemingway. He idolized Hemingway," before critics and audiences began praising the writer in 1926. Similarily, Mezzrow noted that "it was little Dave who gave me a knockdown to George Jean Nathan and H. L. Mencken" and "used to read *The American Mercury* from cover to cover," because it was there that "all the bluenoses, bigots, and two-faced killjoys in this land-of-the-free got a going-over they never forgot. That *Mercury* really got to be the Austin High Gang's Bible. . . . [Mencken's] words were practically lyrics to our hot jazz."[62]

The drummer, in his iconoclastic, autodidactic way, seemed to enjoy studying both the special strengths and limitations of forms of artistic expression—a highly modernistic project. He lectured Mezz Mezzrow on "how important it was to keep your speech pure, pointing out that the French and people like that formed their vowels lovingly." The shortcomings of oral communication drew Tough to nonliterary arts besides music. Freeman and Tough often visited the Chicago Art Institute, the city's largest museum, while they were still in high school. "Upon seeing Cezanne's paintings for the first time," Freeman recalled, "I said that I wished I could say something about this magnificent work. Dave replied that that was the best thing I could ever say about it." Tough's interest in the arts, which complemented music, was shared by other players. Abstract painting became an avocation later in life for such musicians as Pee Wee Russell (whose late work gained some attention) and drummer George Wettling, Tough's protegé, who studied painting in New York with Stuart Davis and formed acquaintances with Jackson Pollock and Willem de Kooning.[63]

These intellectual and aesthetic activities indicate that jazz reflected the musicians' general desire to order their experiences in the most pleasing and exciting manner. This desire sprang from the intense new experience of urban life, specifically in Chicago, which offered challenges and solutions that had never been pressed upon young Americans before. As Max Kaminsky put it in his memoirs:

> Each time I return to Chicago nowadays I see the city more clearly—as it is and not through the nostalgia of the past—and when I look at those endless stretches of appallingly ugly, barren streets I think of the Chicago musicians as schoolboys struggling to play the music and holding on to it as something to believe in, something beautiful they were starved for. The Midwesterners, isolated on that vast, empty prairie-land, have always been starved for culture, for art and music and architecture and learning. They're the great travelers, the prototype of the American tourist, in search of the beauty of the ages, the things and places and thoughts of mankind.[64]

Chicago residents had long been notably enamored with aesthetic charms and prestige, and promoted the symphony, opera, a mammoth world's fair, the theater and the acquisition of art works. At the turn of the century, Chicago's architects and writers were the first to capture the emotional and social yearnings of the city and to place them in the appropriate geographical, economic, and ethnic contexts.[65] In a similar way, the white youths who created hot jazz responded to Chicago's hard new realities. As Bud Freeman summarized it, "Jazz music was a way out, [of] finding freedom of expression. I may not have thought of it [in this way] at the time but now, in retrospect, I know."[66]

Were the white jazz musicians representative of twenties white America, or were they not? The role of jazz in the white culture of the twenties has often been depicted misleadingly. Beginning in 1931, with Frederick Lewis Allen's "informal history" of the twenties and F. Scott Fitzgerald's elegy, "Echoes of the Jazz Age," jazz has been characterized as the most outrageous and controversial, and the most representative, product of a decade of controversy. The deception occurred because Allen, Fitzgerald, and most other white commentators of the twenties used the word "jazz" to designate the highly visible and popular dance music—a derivative of ragtime and popularized by Paul Whiteman, Ted Lewis, and Tin Pan Alley—that displaced more sedate popular music after 1919. This music syncopated mildly, rarely used the blues or swung, and it almost never stressed improvisation, and so it is rarely considered part of the great jazz tradition.[67]

Nevertheless, it might be said that the sweet jazz about which commentators wrote did symbolize new patterns in leisure and behavior among the large group of listeners in the white middle classes. For these individuals—as such contemporary observers as Whiteman, Gilbert Seldes, and Sinclair Lewis noted—sweet jazz dancing signified a *temporary* abandonment of Victorian decorum and manners by younger whites who enjoyed increased leisure time and budgets (and perhaps were tempted further by the wide presence of illicit alcohol).[68] Recent scholarship has stressed that this alleged white revolt was largely superficial and confined to leisure hours. College students who participated in gin parties and turkey-trot contests rarely abandoned their support of capitalism and traditional gender and social roles, acceptance of the authority of formal education, and avoidance of mixing with blacks. Contrary to the lamentations of the writer John R. McMahon (who attacked "the jazz path of degradation" in 1922), the intellectual Walter Lippmann (whose erudite 1929 study, *A Preface to Morals*, condemned the behavioral effects of "the acids of modernity"), and many others, it seems apparent that the bourgeois jazz age phenomenon did not signify a radical change in personal morality and behavior in the United States.[69]

Nevertheless, although they were rarely mentioned in the mainstream press, the black, working class, and underworld breeding grounds of authentic jazz *indirectly* fueled the commercial sweet jazz craze. The centrifugal forces of urban nightlife, black culture, and illegal speakeasies did act upon the appetites of middle-class whites. The whites who traveled to Harlem to visit nightclubs may have been "slumming" and avoiding significant contact with blacks, but they were also the first large white group to patronize places of amusement in black communities. The mainstream press's anxiety and bewilderment at the sweet jazz vogue, while overstated, also heralded a new antibourgeois element in urban leisure, in which wealthy boulevardiers and working-class sports joined together in cabarets and nightclubs in an affront to respectable traditions. The bourgeoisie responded with very real concern. Opinions about whether or not sweet jazz was the "true American music," for example, often hinged on the writer's exposure to the new nightlife. For this reason, the controversy over flappers and "dancing the Charleston," while a footnote to true jazz history, was a revealing and pivotal debate.[70]

In some ways, the white musicians who embraced jazz (without quotation marks) and black culture were representative middle-class whites of the 1920s. Some of them, such as Hoagy Carmichael, did not break with their bourgeois origins, were supported by their parents until they could earn money as players, and subscribed to social and political convention. As we will see in chapter 10, some white jazz musicians could not shed early racist attitudes. Carmichael's subsequent pursuit of songwriting success in Hollywood, as well as the search for big band fame of other early jazz musicians in the thirties, indicates that bourgeois origins often helped to determine bourgeois career decisions in later years.

Nevertheless, there were important differences between the white jazz musicians and the less-committed admirers of black and black-inspired music. First, these musicians chose jazz as a vocation. What might have been a passing rebellion against the demands of Victorian society became for these men a career of exploration of the nation's cultural and social demimonde, the only locales in which their craft was taken seriously and developed. The most dedicated players extracted themselves almost permanently from the middle class; memoir after memoir shows that musicians in the twenties worked in working-class gangster-run clubs, low-paying touring bands and shows, and other disreputable locales. Exceptions to these experiences generally involved positions in society bands, which performed among the wealthy, foreign, and dissolute—a segment of society that also gained the moralistic disapproval of *Collier's* and the *Saturday Evening Post*. Their precarious and disreputable careers did not place them clearly within a socioeconomic class, but plainly drew them *out* of the Protestant mainstream's cultural class. Eddie Condon was reminded of this when a six-dollar check he wrote to the father of a friend failed to clear; the father, a corporate official in Chicago, summoned Condon and assailed his alleged desire "to compress as much uninhibited pleasure into as many ungodly hours as it is possible for human ingenuity, physical stamina, and moral disintegration to accommodate."[71]

In addition, the white players who endorsed African-American culture, however narrowly, were entirely atypical. As we shall see, these musicians did not usually investigate or appreciate the whole of black culture, rarely worked to fight racial injustice, and in some cases felt no qualms about exploiting their racial advantage to further their careers in jazz. What distinguished them from others, however, was their persistent exploration of black music, and the maturation of their interest beyond a narrow craving for primitivist release. The musicians shunned the common premise that black culture existed only to serve whites, as an atavistic urban safety valve or diversion. As they came to define themselves as jazz musicians, black music came to be defined as the *norm*, the source of jazz. They, in turn, were the marginal figures, the pupils, and more fully than any other white Americans they became an *appendix* to black culture and history. In a sense, they innovated and rebelled by willingly becoming musically subordinate to a socially and culturally subordinated group. The white Dixieland musicians, adhering to southern white-supremacist ideology, had refused to acknowledge their debt (much less their subordination) to black musicians, and stagnated artistically as a result; the biracial growth of Dixieland-style music after 1940 (in northern cities as much as in New Orleans), nevertheless, shows that later generations of whites in that genre were more flexible.[72]

Finally, the white jazz musicians were among the more radical *adolescent* and *artistic* rebels of the 1920s. Adolescence had intrigued social scientists since the 1890s, and both academic and popular culture began to define a distinct social and educational sphere for Americans making the transition from childhood to maturity. Psychological and sociological thought and literary works of the twenties celebrated the individual, free of group constraints and able to develop independently. Adolescents were thus granted by experts the license to show greater individuality, although the effect of college life in particular often encouraged conformity and submission. In general, it seems that in the twenties certain ideas and social forces encouraged adolescent adventures while others stressed and imposed regimentation. Perceptive adolescents seeking guidance for their own orientation could choose between general patterns of conformity or rebellion.[73]

The white jazz musicians, in their firm rejection of suburban life and secondary education, made a radical break with the conformist ideology, substituting the *Gemeinschaft* of the biracial jazz culture for the dictated and conformist *Gesellschaft* of universities and employers. Thus, they both fulfilled and rejected society's plainly contradictory prescriptions for adolescents: on the one hand, they exerted their youthful wills and blazed new trails of expression and behavior, yet, on the other hand, they refused to conform to dominant white middle-class beliefs.

As Neil Leonard first argued, the white jazz musicians were among the few younger Americans in the twenties who sensed that the First World War had permanently altered the foundation of their lives and values. Hoagy Carmichael, recalling his days in Bloomington, noted that "it was hard for the veterans of my generation to come back from the Argonne and slow down to the prewar

tempo. You get into a higher gear and you never quite drop back."
In his perception, nonveterans like himself were changed as well.
"The shooting war was over but the rebellion was just getting
started. And for us jazz articulated." Few other jazz musicians
alluded to the war in their memoirs—the major effect it had on jazz
in America was to bring like-minded musicians together at various
training camps, such as Camp Beauregard near New Orleans—
but the quickening tempo of their lives compared to that of their
elders, and their radical revision of racial and cultural priorities,
illustrated the effects of the dynamic Carmichael perceived.[74]

The white jazz musicians's sense of urgency and need, in
addition to what they did, showed their similarity to the other
major group of white postadolescent dissenters of the twenties—
the expatriate writers. Both groups fled mainstream neighborhoods, schools, and economic values, what Ernest Hemingway allegedly called the "broad lawns and narrow minds" of his native
Oak Park. As Ben Hecht put it, "you did not [in the 1920s] auto-
matically plunge into the worlds of painting, music, and literature.
You plunged *out* of worlds," and "as long as you 'believed in art'
you remained orphaned from the smothering arms of society. You
shaved only when you wanted to and you felt a contempt in your
head like a third glass of wine for all that was popular and successful." Significantly, Hemingway, Hecht, Sherwood Anderson, and
other expatriates had lived in Chicago in the 1910s, and a vital
avant-garde literary movement in that city had thrived for a few
years, centering on the theatrical presentations of the Dill Pickle
Club, Margaret Anderson's *Little Review*, and Hecht's own short-
lived *Chicago Literary Times*. Freeman, Tough, and other young
musicians knew of this activity, and mimicked it to an extent, developing their own forms of avant-gardist art and nonconformist
attitudes.[75]

The expatriate writers, as the critic Malcolm Cowley especially made clear in his memoirs, were characterized by a sense
of rootlessness in the wake of the war and a desire to roam, and
eventually to leave the United States. Cowley believed "that our
whole training was involuntarily directed toward destroying whatever roots we had in the soil, toward eradicating our local and
regional peculiarities, toward making us homeless citizens of the
world." His Harvard education instilled in him a sense of the European tradition that (along with favorable exchange rates) drew him
to France.[76] Once in Paris, as expatriate memoirs and studies make

painfully clear, these Americans remained rootless, troubled, and fiercely individualistic. Their humanistic, cosmopolitan educations and their shedding of ethnic, regional, or national identity perhaps mandated that these writers would remain a fragmented, if not a lost, generation in Europe.

The white jazz musicians, particularly in Chicago, avoided this fate by orienting themselves musically to the ghettos, to the community of black jazz innovators. In partnership with blacks and by themselves, the white jazz musicians predicated their activity on the fraternal nature of their education, social lives, and employment, a communitarianism that would keep reemerging in later decades. With their sense of urban adventure and anti-Victorian rebellion, the white jazz musicians avoided the stultifying insularity of the Dixieland musicians, and, with their respect for African-American communal musical traditions, they avoided the fragmentation of the Lost Generation. With jazz, they were not lost in urban America.

"Turn the Bitters into Sweets"
The Musical Culture of Jazz

Every distinct group of musicians has a musical culture—a body of ideas and practices relating to their production of music. Jazz players drew on the musical cultures of Europe and Africa, as they had been transformed in the first few centuries of democracy and slavery in North America. The black vocal tradition had retained West African polyrhythms, the singer's role as a relater of folklore, call-and-response with the audience, and the music's intimate ties with dance and the supernatural. The American experience, though, had turned blues singers toward new subjects and forced them to convey encoded messages, use western instruments such as the guitar, and make the best of an oppressive social situation.[1]

European traditions, prevalent among whites and strongest in the cities, valorized the geniuses of the German symphonic tradition. America's economic elites, attempting to direct cultural life, promoted the enshrinement of symphony and opera in stately halls, but art music was also democratized through the mass media and music appreciation education.[2] Africa and Europe thus were the two general traditions upon which jazz drew for its musical identity; both shaped how musicians were educated, how musical standards and the profession of the jazz musician were defined, and how the music was created, discussed, and preserved.

Jazz musical culture was created in a series of laborious steps, and it did not reach a definitive state (in which musicians were conscious of standards and worked to preserve and advance them) until the late 1930s. Players in New Orleans before 1920 took some of the first steps toward crafting a distinct musical culture, which in part involved the growing adoption of European formal musical training and professional practices.

In the early 1900s, many players possessed almost no knowledge of European-style techniques. Buddy Bolden's biographer has suggested that after 1905 the cornetist could not keep up with the innovations applied to his style by trained players and thus was driven to frustration, drink, and perhaps insanity. (Bolden was committed permanently to an asylum in 1907.)[3] Kid Ory recalled that Bolden "was very rough. You have to give him credit for starting the ball rolling [i.e., playing blues in a city band], you know. But he wasn't really a musician. . . . He didn't study, . . . he was gifted, playing with effect, but no tone, you know. He played loud." Many others claimed that Bolden strove mostly to play as loud as possible, which some considered to be an inartistic goal.[4] Bolden personified the down-home tradition in which musicians neither played from written notes nor exhibited the tone, phrasing, and other elements of style that players in the European tradition cultivated.

Instructors such as Dave Perkins and Peter Davis at the Waifs' Home could teach the mechanical and sound-producing properties of the trumpet, the clarinet, and other instruments to students who had no previous exposure to the European tradition. Davis, for example, started the adolescent Louis Armstrong on the tambourine and the peck horn, and eventually shifted him to cornet, teaching him the fundamentals of tonguing, fingering, and tone production in roughly the same way a classical teacher might have. Davis may have given Armstrong flawed instruction in breathing and embouchure—intricacies of horn playing that later gave him painful problems—but the education did enable the boy to begin a career that blossomed quickly. A coarse, unschooled tone quality was considered suitable for some numbers. The clarinetist Edmond Hall recalled that "I got a tendency to get that kind of . . . harsh tone with certain tones [tunes?] you play. . . . playing the blues that fits in good. . . . but if you played a nice ballad that wouldn't go." Overrefinement was a liability for musicians who still knew how rural blues were to be played or sung.[5]

The early rural bands migrating to New Orleans, like many folk ensembles, usually did not possess musical literacy—the ability to read five-stave musical notation. Through 1917, Kid Ory's group always played by ear, and the uptown black musicians were also predominantly nonliterate as long as they lived in New Orleans. The trombonist Preston Jackson could only remember a few non-

Creoles who were able to read music: the students of James Humphrey (including his sons), the pianist James Carrere, the trombonist Roy Palmer, Jackson himself, and the clarinetist Johnny Dodds, whose reading ability was limited. Jackson recalled that he tried to teach the trumpeter Lee Collins to learn to read, without success.[6]

Most of the major jazz musicians from poorer backgrounds, including Creoles like Ory and Bechet, found that they did not require notation literacy to succeed as players. The standard repertory of popular tunes used by New Orleans bands was very small— perhaps as few as fifty marches, rags, and waltzes—and memorizing the entire canon was not difficult for a regular player. Edmond Hall, who did learn to read music, noted that most reading bands had recourse to what was called "the red book," a compilation of popular rags and ballad melodies, but that even those bands used it rarely. "Practically all these tunes[,] everybody knew 'em, you know, and so many band play 'em, you know, they seldom use music." New Orleanians were not unusual; most cultures, even if they have music notation, do not center their musical activity upon this system.[7]

The nonliterates held some surprising advantages over reading colleagues. Fess Manetta met Jelly Roll Morton in the 1900s when Morton "played only blues" on the piano. "He couldn't read music; he played only in the key of D flat, like the other 'ear' players." Morton preferred D flat because it makes heavy use of black keys, which are easier to play, as they are "further apart than the white keys." By contrast, formal piano students usually begin on the white keys alone (in the key of C) and find playing in D flat to be very challenging. Similarly, Preston Jackson recalled "that bands that didn't read, like that of [Henry "Kid"] Rena, played in hard keys [i.e., difficult for reading players] because they didn't know any better." The nonreading musician, while perhaps often prone to "reinventing the wheel," thus was also free to develop some powerful and innovative skills.[8]

The ear bands began to develop their own incipient grammars of instruction and coordination, which became particularly apparent after the northward migration. Finger positions on valves or keys were a crucial source of information. As the white Chicago trumpeter Muggsy Spanier recalled, King Oliver "would cover his fingering hand with a handkerchief so Armstrong [the second cornetist] wouldn't know what break [solo passage] he was going to play, as they had all their breaks numbered. . . . Oliver never dreamed that Armstrong could copy his breaks just by hearing them!"[9]

Cornetists of lesser talent than Armstrong, however, relied on visual clues to learn a master's improvisations. Many stories have been told of how Freddy Keppard, another uptown cornetist, kept his valves covered with a handkerchief so that visiting musicians would not be able to steal his solos. With reading abilities resembling those of Armstrong and Keppard's auditors, some jazz players were able to masquerade as readers in literate bands. Sidney Bechet, a colleague claimed, was able to play in Noble Sissle's Broadway orchestra for thirteen years without his inability to read ever threatening his employment, and the northern saxophonist Eddie Barefield was accused of "putting on" a bandmate when he said he could not read.[10]

By contrast, many more Creoles in New Orleans obtained formal instruction before 1917 and became highly literate musicians. The violinist and jazz bandleader Charles Elgar, born around 1880, was a typical product of the Creole musical system. As a child he studied the violin at the Medard Academy (a private music school), attended the French Opera and classical concerts, and took conducting courses from the major Creole dance musician Luis Tio. Early Creole players, Elgar insisted, "had enough training on the instrument" to play the classics, but "from the very beginning they went into the dance field." Classical training was essential "because until you know your instrument, such as these boys do, you can't be successful in that Dixieland music. . . . Because it calls for a lot of technique."[11]

Thus, Creole musicians believed that notation literacy was necessary. The clarinetist Alphonse Picou insisted "that a student should learn to read music first." Picou claimed that he himself could play anything, "as long as they put the music in front of [me]." Albert Nicholas's pursuit of literacy was unusually narrow: at the age of nine, he studied music-reading with Papa Tio, two years before he began to play the clarinet. Trained musicians came to agree with Preston Jackson that "a musician should be able to read; if he can't he is limited."[12]

Some uptown blacks also sought out formal training. In about 1903, Bunk Johnson began his education at New Orleans University studying the trumpet with Professor Wallace Cutchey. Tom Bethell has noted that henceforth Johnson's "knowledge of music— 'majors, minors, and diminisheds [chords]'—was a source of admiration from those less well-schooled." Willie J. Humphrey directed a symphonic orchestra at the university when he attended classes in the late 1910s. Humphrey also received instruction from his grandfather James, the itinerant bandmaster. Humphrey admitted that "lots of stuff Grandfather taught him went in one ear and out the other," but he did learn much about "major and minor scales almost every night." He was taught to write musical notation: "if Junior didn't get something, he'd make him draw it, write out the music, over and over. He was severe, a strict teacher." [13]

Professor W. H. Young had similar methods, which he used to instruct his children after they had moved north in the 1910s. Young's main instruction tool, his son Lee recalled, was the blackboard. Lester, the older son, generally ignored what his father wrote on the board and played his own melodic inventions on the saxophone. His exasperated father "would pick up the horn and say, 'How can you play it like that? This is the way it goes.' . . . he would give Lester the horn back and Lester would play ba-ba-dee-doo-dee. . . . that was a pretty funny happening." Such great musicians as Lester Young are famous for their independent natures, but even Young learned to read, and he was one of the very few successful players after the 1910s who could safely avoid much formal training. [14]

The frequency of notation and music reading grew gradually. A few musicians have noted that Johnny Dodds and Jimmie Noone, uptown blacks who later dominated jazz clarinet playing in Chicago, were both able to read written parts during their New Orleans years. Similarly, the bassist Montudie Garland testified that he learned only as much reading as he needed to satisfy himself and his colleagues. Disturbed late in life by the probing questions of a white bassist, Garland responded by insisting that "I know . . . a little about reading. I'm not much on it. I ain't an expert on it, but I know my notes. . . . I likes my own basis for playing jazz music." [15] Many musicians probably shared Garland's proudly utilitarian attitude toward notation literacy and its place in their craft.

Early jazzmen, therefore, used both African and European musical culture to develop their own techniques, standards, and literacy. Even the formally trained Creole elite enjoyed a mixed musical experience in New Orleans. They played the swinging-blues style of music as if it were a hobby, although many of them rarely came into contact with the uptown neighborhoods that spawned it. The Creole trumpeter De De Pierce recalled that musicians who used written music when in marching or society bands would play "the jazz . . . mostly by head." Natty Dominique noted that in Papa Tio's society orchestra, "the same musicians who played the concerts . . . which utilized classical music . . . could also play jazz, but they played the melody," which indicates that many different kinds of musicians were moving toward a synthesis of rural and urban black music. Reading musicians may have found that jazz was an expressive *way* of playing standard music, and perhaps of displaying their own instrumental technique.[16]

Folk traditions of education and dissemination gave jazz much of its character and identity as a music with deep roots in African-American culture. Nevertheless, European-oriented musical education greatly aided the growth of many jazz musicians in New Orleans. It ensured that black musicians would become more competitive with their lighter-skinned colleagues, find new ideas and stimuli for their music, and increase their ambitions and prospects for professional advancement.[17]

In the North, black musicians made formal musical education a fundamental basis of their careers. There were some important exceptions to the general trend. Mary Lou Williams's mother, an organist in Atlanta, forbade her daughter to take lessons because she felt instruction would inhibit improvisation. Williams was gifted with perfect pitch (the ability to identify every note or key by ear) and would later believe that there was "a danger in losing it through studying music. . . . everything's on paper and you don't get any more sounds or anything." Williams, like Earl Hines and Lester Young, was a rare and authentic prodigy, a child who picked out tunes on the piano and "didn't know what I was doing . . . . that's the strange thing."[18]

Similarly, Lester Young "couldn't read very well," his brother recalled, "because he didn't like to read." He resisted his father's instruction in notation and instead "liked to get with the records" and play along. Interestingly, few other black musicians recalled learning extensively from records, although recordings had a major effect on the black listening public after 1920. Ralph Brown of Chicago recalled that in "those days, you'd buy the record [and] play it, play it, play it, and write it note for note. . . . I learned on the clarinet first from the record." Brown's recollection of learning from the phonograph is rare; he had been formally trained, so for him the Victrola was a secondary learning tool.[19]

More commonly, musicians relied on teachers and formal study to aid them in understanding and mastering their instruments. A small number of skilled black instructors in various cities trained many future jazz musicians. Besides Lorenzo Tio, Manuel Perez, and Fess Manetta in New Orleans, these teachers included Major N. Clark-Smith of Tuskegee, Kansas City, and Chicago;

P. G. Lankford of St. Louis; John "Fess" Whatley of Birmingham; Mrs. Portia Pittman of Dallas (the daughter of Booker T. Washington and mother of the saxophonist Booker T. Pittman); and Captain F. Eugene Mikell of New York.[20]

Mikell, who directed the 369th Regiment Band after James Reese Europe's death in 1919, became Benny Carter's saxophone teacher. Carter had already had some training in piano and trumpet and was leaving his first saxophone teacher and neighbor Hal Proctor, who could not read music. Superior teachers of both races instructed black musicians nationwide. The trombonist Lawrence Brown grew up in Pasadena, California, where there were "very, very good instructors in the school system," most of them white classical players. In Columbus, Ohio, in 1922, Clyde Bernhardt found a trombone teacher who suggested that he listen to bands, a rare exception in Bernhardt's experience. "Many teachers," he recalled, "warn their students to stay away from jazz bands." In Harrisburg, Bernhardt also studied with a German teacher, who taught him such advanced techniques as lip vibrato and told him that he was "progressing better than his other students." Even on the rural Texas carnival circuit, the guitarist Eddie Durham was able to take lessons and to learn "a lot of Latin [musical] terms."[21]

Usually around the age of eighteen, musicians took control of their own musical developments. Milt Hinton and his friends at Chicago's Crane Junior College often gathered at his grandmother's house in the twenties, where she made "a big old stew, or something" and they would "just sit around there and play . . . and discuss music. . . . I'd write a part to see if you could read it, try to make it as hard as I could write it. And you'd write one and challenge me to see if I could read it. We'd sit on the elevated trains coming home from school and write our parts and pass them across the aisle." Hinton and his friends became autodidacts *after* they had gained a foundation in formal training. Conversely, at least one black musician—the singer/dancer John "Bubbles" Sublett—deeply regretted his lack of early training. Sublett damaged his vocal chords after years of aggressive singing and was confined to dancing after the 1920s. Many years later he admitted that "I just can't get over how—[it is] so sad in my mind for me not to take vocal lessons to . . . preserve my voice."[22]

Adolescent white jazz players, in a telling contrast, characteristically rebelled against formal training. They disliked schooling of any kind, and they also avoided musical instruction early in their careers. Educators considered themselves the guardians of

America's musical future and in the twenties frequently fought the rise of jazz.[23] Wingy Manone's cornet teacher, for example, told the nine-year-old that he would "never be anything but a second-rate musician unless you forget about that jazz." Bud Freeman was given saxophone lessons by Mr. McPartland, but disliked them because "they reminded me of grammar school," but Jimmy Maxwell and others found their parents' informal home instruction on various instruments very beneficial.[24]

Future white jazzmen preferred autodidactic musical learning to the formal music education widely available to them. As with black bands, some white groups educated themselves in childhood. In Defiance, Ohio, the seven-year-old Bill Davison led some friends in choral sessions of popular songs, improvising "barber shop chords and barber shop harmony to songs that we used to play or sing . . . without any instruction at all." Davison taught himself the banjo, made bugles out of discarded pieces of garden hose, and formed his own six-piece band in grade school; "it was amazing when we got together the things we'd put together." Bix Beiderbecke was largely self-taught on the cornet, and his lifelong use of "incorrect" fingerings contributed to the uniqueness of his style. Gil Evans, who grew up in central California, became a highly regarded band arranger, but he had never taken lessons in arranging and never even developed a fluency in playing from a written score.[25]

In the late 1920s, when they were firmly decided on musical careers, Bud Freeman and other whites from this group did gain some formal training in performance and theory, but, significantly, their initial involvement in music was strongly autodidactic.[26] This antischolastic tendency differed markedly from the conscientious search for training of the black jazz musicians they emulated and of the white sweet musicians they disliked. The opposite attitudes of whites and blacks illustrate the differing social and emotional paths the two groups took toward the creation of jazz.

Like all musicians, jazz players were obsessed with music and sound, and their ability to comprehend and make music was a basic determinant of their adult identity. The plainest expressions of this fact are the most eloquent. Wingy Manone wrote at the age of forty-four that "without my horn, I'm lost. I got to have music or I'm nowhere."[27] For Sidney Bechet, music was private therapy. As a child Bechet was chronically lonely, "but he had a song. He kept making that song over and over out of himself, changing it around,

making it fit. . . . as soon as he had the song, he wasn't lonely any
more. . . . he had this thing he could trust, and so he could trust
himself."

For Bechet, the essence of music or jazz was even simpler than
a melody. "My family beat time with their hands on drums. . . .
that's Jazz too. . . . you can just beat on the table and it can be
Jazz."[28] Rhythm was the most obvious and entrancing characteris-
tic of jazz. While riding underneath freight cars to destinations far
from Chicago, Mezz Mezzrow would "dig . . . the riffs the wheels
were knocking out." Musicians were obsessed with rhythm; Art
Hodes felt that Wingy Manone and other white jazzmen "lived to
the beat," and Jimmy McPartland felt that "it's a religion within
itself, the beat." Bud Freeman, echoing many others, argued that
Louis Armstrong was special because he "had the greatest beat
of any trumpet [player] I have ever heard." Manone, Freeman recalled, "was solely influenced by Louis. Louis was his god." Even
saxophonists like the young white Bennie Moylen, who "tried to
play tenor sax like Louis was playing trumpet . . . hearing Louis
all the time" while he played, and Benny Carter and Coleman
Hawkins, among others, sought especially to capture Armstrong's
swinging, invigorating rhythmic sense.[29]

Jazz is often called a very rhythmic music, but this can be a
misleading description. Other African or European musics are performed to much heavier drumbeats than are usually found in early
jazz.[30] What set it apart was its progressively intricate swinging, by
which notes were alternately played ahead or behind a plodding,
steady beat. As Max Kaminsky noted about jazz's main rhythm-
keepers, "the really great drummers can play the top part of the
beat and not rush. Most amateurs play at the bottom part of the
beat, where it's most heavy. The beat is just a stroke of time but
it has so many vibrations to it that the stroke can be hit at the top
or middle or bottom. Most all the early jazz bands played at the
bottom of the beat, and that's why Louis [Armstrong] used to call
out, even on records, 'Swing, man, SWING!' He meant to hit it on the
top." There are other ways of defining swinging. Viewed in a broad
context, swinging was the merging of West African polyrhythm—
in which no beat was privileged—with the strict monorhythm of
European march and dance music. Musicians and others adopted
the Eurocentric notion of the beat and perceived the polyrhythms
as a swinging of that beat.[31]

It took some time before the swinging rhythm of the Chicago
bands enlightened groups on the East Coast, where Kaminsky grew

up and played in the twenties. "They were still playing oompah and ricky-tick, breaking up the rhythm into choppy syncopation" in the ragtime style. "That nervous, ragged, ricky-tick beat of the white dance bands of the twenties—that was one of the factors that had been at the bottom of my confusion when I listened to my records" as a youth in Boston, "trying so desperately to unravel the puzzle of jazz." All serious players worked toward understanding the nature of rhythm and what they considered the components of the beat. Bix Beiderbecke, the best swinger among early white players, gave Kaminsky advice. His secret was "anticipation—playing notes of the melody a hair-breadth before the strict time." This "use of anticipation, without rushing, which is all a part of making the music swing, was just getting to be understood then." Kaminsky boasted that by 1928, when he was twenty, he too "had the innate feeling of the beat and of playing the melody simply and purely without all the little flutings and corny licks that were regarded as 'hot' in those days."[32]

Audiences were especially attracted to the special swing in the jazz rhythm. Lois Deppe, who led a band in Pittsburgh in the twenties, worried that his young pianist, Earl Hines, "was inclined to loaf" and play "just chords. . . . Not being a pianist, I didn't realize that a man got tired just swing-swing-swinging away all the time at the piano. But that's what the people were getting a kick from, his swinging syncopation." So Deppe ordered Hines to swing, convinced that this "way of playing is what drew attention to him." Journalistic proponents and opponents of jazz all recognized the peculiar swinging rhythm of the music, most typically because it inspired the swaying, jerking, and stomping of the newly popular and controversial jazz dances.[33]

As Hines came to realize, musicians lived within rhythm. Wingy Manone, Art Hodes recalled, "had a beat you couldn't get away from. If we had two blocks to walk, we'd walk it in time. Wingy would sing some song as we walked along and we'd both swing along in time. Never real obviously—yet at times Wingy would make himself very obvious. . . . We lived with a beat. . . . I'd wake up with 'Muskrat Rumble' on the vic, and immediately I was back in time, walking to the music, dressing to it, and being walked out of the house." When Hodes moved to New York City in 1938, he found few musicians who shared his rhythmic sense. "I tried to organize a few of us from Chi. . . . But it didn't work so good for me. The drummer and I couldn't get together. With me it's either you're in time or you're not in time." The drummer Zutty Singleton also noted that "so many guys can play when the beat ain't there, but man, I can't do a thing 'til everyone is right in it. Then I can play." [34]

An often overlooked fundamental of jazz playing is tone or timbre—the nature of the sound a musician produces with an instrument. Jazz musicians studied and shaped their tone as assiduously as they cultivated their ability to swing. Like many instrumental musics, jazz gained much of its character from the spoken and sung dialect and inflections of the culture that nurtured it. The moaning, howling, and sometimes ethereal speaking and song of the Delta blues culture directly influenced the uptown jazz pioneers in New Orleans. As Earl Hines described it, "it's a funny thing about these New Orleans guys. That's one thing they dwell upon: the tone. Open, you know, not piercing." Mezz Mezzrow argued that the black New Orleans founders of jazz "never had much training in the classical European school of music, so they weren't taught to get a 'pure' and untainted tone out of each instrument. Their wind instruments played the way that was most natural to them; [they] grunted and growled, sobbed and laughed too, like human voices." [35]

White admirers in the North, such as the Austin High Gang, followed suit, producing the musical equivalent of what Mezzrow called "yarddog growls and gully-low howls." Max Kaminsky noted that Bix Beiderbecke "purposely kept his horn funky, never cleaning out the dried spittle that accumulates in the valves and mouthpiece" to keep a soft, mellow tone, and that other white players emulated him. The black twenties trumpeters, led by Louis Armstrong, also sought to produce a warm, mouthy sound. Earl Hines noted that these players found this kind of "tonation" to be closest to the human voice. By the late twenties black instructors in the North were teaching the Armstrong timbre to young trumpeters. Hines sent the horn players in his band to an instructor in Chicago who would "hang a trumpet" by a string "up in the air" and have his students "walk up and play it" to develop the posture, embouchure, and breathing needed to produce the open Armstrong sound. [36]

As soon as musicians mastered the swing rhythm and their instruments, their jazz styles evolved rapidly, through a kind of natural selection. Certain instruments, including the violin, cornet, tuba, and banjo fell out of favor among jazz players. The violinist Eddie South, classically trained yet able to swing a melody, was one of the South Side's most popular musicians in the twenties. By 1930, however, the violin had gone out of fashion and South often could not find more than one job a month. Furthermore, "Eddie was the only black violin player, after the twenties, that survived that whole scene in Chicago," as Milt Hinton noted. In the mid-1920s, most cornetists, including Joe Oliver and Louis Armstrong, switched to the trumpet, with its more commanding, ringing sound. Oliver was also the major innovator in the use of trumpet mutes, as he covered the bell with a Conn mute, a derby, or a water glass to produce growling or rasping sounds. Clarinetists also broke with southern tradition by adopting instruments with the Boehm system of fingering and keys, which was generally believed to be easier to play at fast tempi than the Albert system, then used in New Orleans and other southern cities.[37]

On their preferred instruments, musicians crafted their own trademark styles. Lawrence Brown played trombone at the Club Alabam in Los Angeles in the 1920s, where players had to mingle among guests' tables to play solos. Brown's "little gimmick" was to "play so soft, open horn, that I would hold the horn in the middle of your table and play an open melody, and you couldn't hear it past the table." This sound "wasn't a sub-tone—the tone wasn't blocked," but a "soft, very soft" sound: "I could control it so evenly that [I] could put it right in your ear."[38] Earl Hines, as a piano prodigy in Pittsburgh before 1920, exhausted the wisdom of two teachers, mastered classical techniques, and then turned to jazz. Hines's smooth improvisational style, a clean break from the syncopated ragtime tradition, originated in part in his imitation of the trumpet's sound. His friend Joe Smith could "play an open horn with just a coconut shell [underneath it] and get a velvet tone, almost like a human voice. . . . I sat and listened to him and marveled at his style, and wanted to play [on piano] what he played on trumpet. It gave me a lot of new ideas."[39]

The mature jazz musician's playing style was individual, balanced, expressive, and relatively easy for an experienced listener to identify. In 1929, Artie Shaw spent a few weeks in Chicago, where he acquainted himself with some of the Austin High Gang, now adult veterans of the nightclub circuit. The trombonist Floyd O'Brien, Shaw later wrote, "would almost, but not quite, crack a note into little pieces, and each time you thought he was about to fall apart he'd recover and make something out of what started out to sound like a fluff—till after a while you began to get the idea that this guy not only wasn't making any mistakes at all, but had complete control over his horn. . . . The things he played went off in altogether unexpected and sometimes quite humorous directions . . . . it's impossible to give the flavor of it in language." The clarinetist Frank Teschemacher had a far different style, spare and angular. "In its own grotesque way it made a kind of musical sense," Shaw wrote, "but [it was] something extremely personal and intimate to himself, something so subtle it could never possibly have had great communicative meaning to anyone but another musician and even then only to a jazz musician who happened to be pretty damn hep to what was going on."[40]

Some of the most talented musicians were extremely individualistic, and became detached and aloof in their pursuit of musical innovation, in the manner of the European Romantic artist. Earl Hines became this kind of musician. As William Samuels remembered, Hines "had a peculiar style. . . . he would just sit there and George Dixon used to rehearse the band for him. . . . they would say to Earl . . . 'Will you take twenty bars of that?' He'd say OK. . . . He has a peculiar way about him—he's not sociable. . . . the fellows would want to come around and talk to him and stuff, and he's very cool, and he wouldn't have nothing to do with you." Samuels felt that "Earl is crazy," but nevertheless "one of the originators of jazz." Jelly Roll Morton, in the portrait compiled by Alan Lomax, appears as a similarly isolated man, as well as a fiercely driven, proud creator who boasted of his ability to "turn the bitters"—life's experiences—"into sweets." As Barney Bigard put it, "if [Morton] needed money he would sit at the piano and compose a tune right there and then take it to his publisher Mr. Melrose and get maybe a thousand dollars as advance royalties." Bigard exaggerated the revenue Morton's tunes brought in, but conveyed accurately the intensity and ease of Morton's creative gift.[41]

Each of the most talented musicians sensed that jazz challenged them to *innovate* constantly. Sidney Bechet spent most of the twenties traveling restlessly to Europe and on touring shows, and he sensed then that "the music, it's got this itch to be going in it—when it loses that, there's not much left. Those days I was getting that itch pretty strong. I really wanted to be moving."[42] For the great originators of early jazz—Hines, Morton, Bechet, and others—jazz's true meaning lay in its rapid innovation and movement. All successful jazz musicians, in fact, developed new styles with varying rates. Louis Armstrong's rhythmic freedoms, reaching the point of joyous near anarchy, and Clyde Bernhardt's use of trombone lip vibrato as a member of a south Pennsylvania road band each signified a different kind of migration across the musical and intellectual territory of the twenties.

Of all the formal and aesthetic properties of jazz, its improvisational nature most effectively set it apart from other urban music. Jazz revitalized improvisation in the music of the Western world. Spontaneous improvisation had been a highly valued talent among European keyboard and string artists well into the mid-nineteenth century, when music critics and pedagogues discouraged the practice and championed the virtues of written scores (which had originated centuries before as heuristic guides for improvising ensembles).[43]

Recordings and dances dictated that musicians come up with discrete jazz numbers, which (like jam sessions of undetermined length) almost always featured a blues or show tune, a rag, or even a folk or classical melody, followed by a string of improvisations on that tune. As Eddie Condon noted, "jazz had never been confined in its material; it was always a way of playing music, and its manner—freedom of improvisation on a basic chordal structure—could be applied to any standard song." (Some musicians, such as Art Hodes, were more selective. His twenties band "didn't bother to learn the pop tunes of the day and we didn't play any tunes we thought weren't any good.")[44]

The improvising jazz musician used the notes from the melody's chord progression, varying rhythmic details and passing tones, to produce harmonizing variations on the original theme. When he heard a New Orleans band on a steamboat in 1922, Condon first noticed that in jazz "you know what the melody is but you don't hear it. The cornet and the clarinet, and sometimes the trombone, treat it like a girl. They hang around it, doing handsprings and all sorts of other tricks, always keeping an eye on it and trying to make an impression. The rhythm section provides transportation, everything floats on its beat." Improvisations usually lasted the same amount of time as the original tune, although star soloists often had twice or four times the space in which to present their ideas.[45]

A jazz musician was evaluated on the basis of his or her improvisational skills. Max Kaminsky felt that good improvisation relied on "an inborn sense of swing, so that you feel the melodic phrases in terms of the jazz beat . . . harmonic sense, good intonation, good taste . . . a sense of order, of structure, of form," and "understanding and teamwork among the musicians." The hot soloist, in Earl Hines's opinion, was one "who had a fast mind, could think far ahead in regard to the chords coming up, and was good on his instrument."[46]

While discipline was required for good jazz improvisation, it was also essential to recognize and transcend the systematic, the structured, and the mundane. As Hoagy Carmichael put it, the twenties "was the great time of experimentation in jazz, with only enough precedents to stimulate individual and original exploration but not enough nailed down examples to set any definite patterns as rigid rules." Jimmy McPartland also valued the spontaneous, chance-oriented nature of improvisation, perhaps more than a Hines or a Kaminsky had. "In my mind when I play I have no idea in which direction I'm going. I know what the melody is and harmony and I can hear all that. These things pop up now and then, which is a compliment to . . . the good taste that your mind . . . retains. Puts it way back there in the recesses some place and then eventually it will pop out and you'll say, where did that come from?" This approach had obvious dangers. Wingy Manone, a rugged improviser in his youth, "wouldn't stay on any set harmony, but went off any way it felt good to go . . . anytime I got off harmony I sounded awful. So I had to learn the proper chords and stay with the right progressions."[47]

Good players, armed with instrumental technique and improvisational skills, improved further by challenging each other. The cutting contests of New Orleans, which sublimated the urban violence surrounding musicians in the 1910s, were refined further in the North into instrument suppers and band battles. In the 1920s, cutting contests were perhaps most intense in Chicago, where the best players from the nation's entire midsection gathered for the first time. Louis Armstrong gained much of his fame from his conquest of other horn players. As a Tulane interview synopsis described one confrontation, Freddy "Keppard challenged Armstrong, borrowing his horn; Keppard played and played; Lil Armstrong said to Armstrong, when Keppard finished, 'Get him!' Armstrong, who really played when he was angry, played so great that people were standing on chairs when he finished." Lester Young, his brother Lee remembered, was a ferocious competitor in 1921, when he was twelve. "Lester wanted some of it, as the saying goes. . . . he really wanted to see who was the better man; it would be just like a prize fighter or a wrestler."[48]

Collective cutting contests—featuring many players of the same instrument—became possible in Chicago and New York, where musicians could always easily be found. By 1930 these sessions were called suppers. As Bill Coleman recalled, saxophone suppers or trumpet suppers would be announced at musicians' gathering spots, such as Harlem's Rhythm Club. "As many as 10 or 15 instrumentalists could be counted on to be at the club when-

ever their particular instrument was announced for a supper."
Pianists or guitarists accompanied the competitors. Removed from
the commercial world, which primarily rewarded entertainers for
their popularity, the suppers provided a workshop environment for
exchanging ideas and honing skills on a particular instrument.[49]

In small instrument combinations or combos, the musician
sought both regular employment and the best setting for his or her
individual playing strengths. Combos quickly learned to work out
in advance when each player would solo, how to link the solos, and
how to introduce and conclude each number. These head arrangements, committed to memory rather than paper, bound players
together. Max Kaminsky has argued that in the twenties, white
players such as the Chicagoans bonded differently than did black
bands, and as a result produced a different, more complex kind
of group improvisation. "The Chicago-style jazz had always been
strong on ensemble improvisation. . . . It was mainly the white musicians who carried on this tradition. With the Negro's strong rhythmic instinct, it was more natural for the colored bands to swing, but
their swing was always based primarily on rhythmic riffs—from the
run-of-the-mill jump bands to the great bands of Count Basie and
Duke Ellington—rather than on ensemble improvisation."[50]

Talk about natural instinct aside, Kaminsky's comment suggests that whites (at least the Chicagoans) were aggressively communal and improvisational, while black bands were more assured
and relaxed in their presentation of solos and ensembles. The
recordings of, say, the McKenzie-Condon Chicagoans, contrasted
with those of Louis Armstrong and His Hot Five the same year,
suggest this also, as does the whites' incessant talk of twenties rebellion (compared to the more sedate recollections of blacks). Cultural
and economic forces certainly dictated the differing evolutions of
white and black band styles, although these styles would not be
segregated for long.

From the earliest years, jazz musicians were not content with
making music on a small scale. Black jazz orchestras, featuring nine
or more musicians, quickly achieved dominance in the North, as
leaders drew on both southern jazz examples and the whole nation's
rich orchestra and band traditions.

The rise of orchestras hastened the advent of notated jazz and
literate musicians. Musicians in the North soon found that reading ability was demanded by almost all theaters and many dance
halls and nightclubs. As Clyde Bernhardt noted, "If you didn't read
[music] by 1927, you got left out. No place for you in a good-quality

band. Even the stock arrangements of 1928 was different . . . , and the pressure was starting to hit nonreaders hard." Jelly Roll Morton apparently learned to read and write music during his years in California and Chicago, and Morton probably was the first New Orleans jazz musician who actually passed out written parts to a band. George Mitchell, the cornetist in Morton's Red Hot Peppers (formed in 1926), said that "Morton wrote parts for the Peppers [recording] session" but "permitted players to discard the parts once they got the idea of the tunes." Mitchell said that he "had to have music to read, so that he could get the idea of the pieces." Mitchell himself, a migrant from Louisville, took no lessons but practiced on his own from instruction books. Louis Armstrong, Joe Oliver, and most major New Orleans musicians learned to read music during the late twenties.[51]

In the twenties, bands began to use written arrangements to achieve cohesion and to permit complex ensemble pieces. The origins of orchestrated black jazz are difficult to trace. While Morton's Red Hot Peppers used sheet music quite early, the first jazz orchestrator may have been a woman. In 1923, Lil Hardin Armstrong was hired by Columbia Records to write six arrangements for a pickup band. Three of the compositions were to bear Louis Armstrong's name to boost sales. (Armstrong, under contract to another company, was not involved in the project, and was infuriated when he learned that his name was used.) For the July 1923 sessions, as the Tulane synopsis of Lil Armstrong's interview states, " 'Perdido Street Blues' was written out entirely, even to the solos. . . . the session was the first recording session made using written arrangements." Whatever the truth of the last claim, it is significant that written music was used by a jazz band as early as 1923.[52]

Jazz band music rapidly increased in complexity. By about 1926, the producer Percy Venable at Chicago's Sunset Cafe had the Earl Hines band play difficult arrangements that required advanced reading abilities. "You had to know your instrument and you had to know what you were doing, because it was never all written out. We might start on page one, jump over to page seven, play eight bars, come back to page three and play all of it, and then turn back to page two. This could be very confusing."[53]

Creative leaders saw that the rise in literacy and musicianship opened new expressive possibilities. Jazz, therefore, became *harmonically* complex in a matter of years. Western art music's recent interest in complex tonalities, chromaticism, and frequent modulation were quickly replicated in early jazz. Older players, like the bassist Montudie Garland, found it difficult to keep up with the changes Hines initiated in Chicago. "Poor old Hines mess you up. . . . Fatha Hines would change on you as quick as daylight. Liable to be playing in A flat and he jump way down to D flat, jump back to C. Oh, he's tricky, you got to watch him, know what you're doing. . . . Don't mess with Fatha Hines."[54]

Fletcher Henderson, a college-trained pharmacist from Georgia, became Hines's New York equivalent as a developer of the virtuoso reading jazz orchestra. Cootie Williams, who toured with Henderson in 1928, felt that he had "terrific" arrangements. "He played in all hard keys, everything. . . . Five flats, five sharps, six sharps, everything." Henderson kept his numbers entertaining, though, by stressing the melodies in his complex arrangements. As Natty Dominique of New Orleans recalled, while Henderson's orchestrations would be "getting harder and harder, . . . his last chorus goes back to the melody," which "people knew. That's what made Fletcher Henderson so great."[55]

The attempts by Morton, Hardin, Hines, Henderson, and others to create the jazz orchestra culminated in the achievement of Edward "Duke" Ellington and his band. More than any other individual, Ellington epitomized the jazz movement's obsession with rapid innovation. As his lead trumpet Cootie Williams remembered, Ellington "was always going forward. He was writing music every day and night. He never did think about going back." The bandleader himself regretted that his musical "past was always getting in the way of my future."[56]

In 1926, Ellington had taken command of a cooperative band made up of old friends from Washington, D.C., and transformed it by 1930 into the most prominent and innovative black orchestra in Harlem. He developed a new method of group composition, in which he would bring snatches of melody into a band rehearsal, expand them into full phrases on the keyboard, have the band learn the phrases and offer ideas, and gradually stitch together a full number. As the pianist Jimmy Jones later said, "What he does is like a chain reaction. Here's a section, here's a section and here's another and, in between, he begins putting the connecting links— the amazing thing about Ellington is that he can think so fast on the spot and create so quickly."[57]

In this way Ellington retained the African-American communal tradition of music making, but also situated this activity within his own compositional framework, in the manner of the European art-music composer. As his recordings from the Cotton Club years (1927–31) attest, the throaty, southern-style sounds of Barney Bigard and Cootie Williams and the rough timbre of Bubber Miley's and Sam Nanton's plunger-mute work blended almost miraculously with Ellington's innovative and urbane voicings and melodic lines.[58]

As a man and musician, Ellington was a magnificent bridge between two continental traditions. In some ways he seemed to have elite aspirations. He had received limited training in composition from Will Marion Cook and Will Vodery, New York's most highly trained black musicians, whose classical ambitions had been thwarted by racism. Ellington used some rules of traditional orchestration and voice-leading, and he knew them well enough to break them when he desired. Interestingly, this placed his musical activity in a rough parallel with that of avant-garde composers of the 1920s who centered their learning and activity in Paris. In a few years, some white listeners (especially in Britain) began to argue that Ellington's music was an African-American manifestation of modernist musical dissonance and rhythmic experimentation.

Ellington welcomed his growing reputation as an avant-garde composer, which he reinforced with a carefully polished self-presentation. The son of a Washington butler, he had gained his nickname because of his aristocratic bearing as a boy, and his later success, as well as his anger at whites who accorded him second-class status, led him to develop a very lofty demeanor. Ellington cared deeply for fellow blacks, but many of them recall that his demeanor was often aloof and inscrutable, inviting others to defer to him. He spent much of his income on fine clothing, food, and apartments, and he always toured in regal style with a large entourage. In the 1930s, his growing ambition to compose what he would call symphonies, concertos, and suites also showed his affinity for aristocratic Euro-American traditions.[59]

At the same time, Duke Ellington cannily preserved the unschooled folk heritage he and his band had only known before 1920. He preserved the rural, rough, musically nonliterate past of black jazz by hiring hard-drinking and combative bad boys for his band, who produced the funky timbre, blues, and wails of the rural tradition. To the irritation of bourgeois-minded band members, Ellington rarely disciplined the rascals, and only fired one musician (Bubber Miley) in his half-century of band leadership. His music was never diluted with genteel gestures: in an interesting subversion of notational practice, he wrote the direction "sloppy" on some band parts. Ellington retained a strong pride in his heritage, and incorporated "black," "Harlem," "Afro," and similar terms into many composition titles.[60]

The move toward complexity in jazz found its next great center in Kansas City, where southwestern dance traditions inspired William "Count" Basie, Andy Kirk, Jay McShann, and other leaders to produce the most aggressively rhythmic jazz band music, often called boogie-woogie or eight-to-a-bar. The arranger Eddie Durham joined Benny Moten's Kansas City band in 1929, and produced complicated, innovative arrangements for the rough-hewn group. "They were using three-part harmony. . . . I added in the sixth [chord degree]." Durham's innovation went against tradition: "the band didn't want to hear that. They'd say, 'that's out of tune,' . . . 'it's too rich.' . . . Every time they'd play in rehearsal and break for intermission, they all wanted to see Benny, without me. They'd get in a corner, talking—'Benny, this guy's out of his mind, that don't sound right, that chording and all that stuff.'" Durham wrote rudimentary arrangements, but found that the Moten band lacked the ability to head arrange his more sophisticated basic ideas.[61] Later in the 1930s, Durham joined the more skilled Basie band, which was much more able to improvise their own ensemble passages (and featured that master of ear playing, Lester Young).

We need much more investigation of the practice of jazz to understand how the musicians worked and thought. Still, it is clear that when Durham, Basie, and others came East from Kansas City in the mid-1930s, the musical culture of jazz was already well established. African-American communities continued to nurture confident and able practitioners of swinging, improvisation, and the blues, even as European traditions seeped into the musical education and practice of those communities. These classical influences, though, were never allowed to absorb or dilute jazz, as such figures as Ellington used white forms and ideas (and pretensions) to strengthen the black statement and to facilitate its introduction to the global audience. And for whites as well as blacks, "living to the beat," individually and collectively, led to a mastery of time and instrument, as well as to the creation of a great, generative, musical tradition. Now it is worth considering whether or not their musical achievement inspired a similar measure of creativity and experimentation in their extramusical lives as well.

"Being Crazy Don't Make Music"
Searching for a Jazz Subculture

The best musicians live to shape their music; it is their avocation and their vocation. If this is true, it follows that the extra-musical details of their lives are of little import in themselves, since they consist perhaps of the necessary activity needed to sustain their lives so that they may continue to make music. Jazz musicians, specifically, were preoccupied with perfecting improvisation and group performance and blending sounds on paper and on the bandstand. Thus, it might be suggested that they were united *fundamentally* by their interest in music; any other cultural or social ties were accidental. Jazz certainly originated in a shared African-American heritage, but after the 1920s players from other cultures championed the music in places and spirits free of Creole, funeral-society, and medicine-show influences. The only culture an Artie Shaw, a Louis Armstrong, and a Bix Beiderbecke might have shared (besides the tenuous social and language ties that bound them together as Americans) were the common musical techniques that we categorize as jazz.

But it is universally believed that jazz was (and is) far more than a professional lingua franca, binding an international elite together in the same way that set theory gives convening mathematicians a common ground. Jazz—popular thought has it—created both a music and a *culture*, a way of life differing from the root culture and the dominant society that now surrounded it. This culture is thought to be the social equivalent of the music, a jiving, swinging, improvisatory mode of existence, as funky in expression as a good horn is in timbre, as collegial as a combo in full cry. After 1940, social scientists and others considered jazz a self-consciously *deviant* subculture, cradling angry young men who wanted to be despised by the squares around them. Their dress, language, behavior, and use of narcotics allegedly set them apart from a larger culture from which they yearned to escape. This analysis applied almost exclusively to white players. Did the first white jazz musicians originate that sense of cultural alienation (as Neil Leonard suggests they did)? Were they as ambitious about creating a new style of life as they were about inventing a new music? And if so, did black musicians share such a life style with them, or stand apart as role models?[1]

Hoagy Carmichael suggested that his coterie of players in central Indiana in the 1920s had based their music on a social reality. "Jazz is after all an abstract art, and so the results the player got were abstract, but based on the world as he knew it, suffered and dreamed it could be." Their subculture, he argued, filtered the superfluous material which burdened those around them: "jazz carried no long words, culture, or phony intellectuals' patter in the playing." Jazz to Carmichael was their way of communicating their specific emotional condition: "The totality of feeling that came out of a brass horn was amazing . . . like all primitive sound, it was an emotion in most ways beyond taking apart and examining." Carmichael, in his memoirs, delineated how the "Bent Eagles"' cacophonous noodlings grew out of a total cultural experience: they were youth who rejected the stock of "patter" their fathers intoned, were conscious of putting their world into an abstraction, and were particularly eager to capture their emotional world in sounds.[2] They invite comparison with other white jazz groups, such as the Chicagoans and their talk of rebellion.

If musicians abstracted their shared behavior, or culture, to create jazz, then perhaps they also on occasion returned their attention to their *extra*musical life as well, applying what the music taught them to their everyday lives. Like twin vines, Carmichael's comment suggests, jazz music and culture sprouted together and clung to one another. The historian Warren Susman has argued that Americans after the Great War were especially eager to tinker with their culture: "the 1920s was a period dedicated to knowledge and experience and the effective use of both. It spent considerable time, energy, and talent in trying to mend what had become apparent to many, each often in his own way, as a broken world." More specifically, twenties America "sought to build on knowledge, technique; it sought to find methods and ways of expressing and communicating."[3]

Susman, like most historians of the twenties, is speaking mostly about white America. While jazz musical culture was largely black in orientation, it was quickly infiltrated by white players and eventually became a subject of interest to whites nationwide. Therefore, it is worthwhile to explore the extent of jazz's relation to the white-majority culture so shaken by the Great War. Did jazz give rise to a "method . . . of expressing and communicating"? Or is the notion of a jazz culture both an exaggeration of music's role in cultural change and an oversimplification of that change in the twenties and thirties? In its baldest form, the question could be phrased like this: was there really a jazz age that accompanied the jazz music?

If early jazz begat a new way of life, then it is most obvious that this way of life would have been dominated by males, and that women held an inferior status. The male dominance of instrumental music was clear in New Orleans, and it persisted and even increased in the North.

Only a few jazzwomen, in a few clearly defined spheres of activity, achieved prominence. The most significant female presence in early jazz was provided by female blues vocalists, who combined the image of the stylish new woman with flourishes of Storyville suggestiveness. To a lesser degree, woman pianists also gained wide attention. The first prominent woman jazz pianist was Cora "Lovie" Austin, a native of Chattanooga who became the music director at Chicago's Monogram Theater. The ten-year-old Mary Lou Williams had seen Austin in a Pittsburgh theater pit, "her legs crossed, with a cigarette in her mouth, playing and writing music for the next act. . . . It was amazing that someone could concentrate like that." For Williams, Austin was a clear role model: "I always wanted to do that, it's so creative." Austin, Williams, and Lil Hardin Armstrong were able to build substantial careers as band pianists, arrangers, and recording artists. Scores of pianists who were active for long periods but never recorded, however, are forgotten, ranging from Julia Lee of Kansas City to Willie Woods and Florida Beck of Pensacola to Zella Hunter of Chicago.[4]

It is clear, in addition, that singing and piano playing were virtual ghettos for jazzwomen. Their restrictions to these roles resulted from general Western traditions that encouraged women to pursue voice or piano, because these musical activities most reinforced women's association with the parlor, the Victorian home, and the domestic sphere as a whole. Female wind and brass players and leaders received scant attention from commercial interests, and little is known about their relation with black audiences vis-à-vis male musicians.

Despite these obstacles, women participated in early jazz across the country in many capacities. As early as 1916, Estella Harris's Ladies Jass Band played in Chicago, and bands led by Garvinia Dickerson, Dolly Hutchinson, Lottie Hightower, Marie Lucas, and Annie Harris were featured there during the next two decades. Valaida Snow, who danced and played cornet in Jack Carter's band in Shanghai for much of the twenties, is the best-remembered female brass player from this era, but there were proficient players in America, often in all-female bands.[5]

Jazzwomen made the most of the opportunities open to them. Mary Lou Williams was never allowed to become a permanent member of the male bands in Kansas City for which she played piano. "It may have been that they didn't want a woman in the band because women during that era was not playing with men. That was another thing that made people scream and carry on, because they saw a woman [onstage] and one that weighed ninety pounds." A musician *in* these bands but not *of* them, Williams developed a deceptively active method of learning the trade, carefully observing the leader Andy Kirk's work habits. "I can learn a lot through watching. That was my bag, see, watching people and doing what they do." Williams became one of the most original performers and composers in jazz, but she felt compelled in 1973 to characterize her early role in Kansas City as a helpmate. "I thought I was helping. There's a peculiar thing about me in life. You know, if you want to really hear me play or write something, give me somebody to help." Williams's subordinate status as a female pianist certainly encouraged her at least to profess this humble attitude.[6]

Successful blueswomen, by contrast, seemed to use their star status and public exposure to construct the strongest and most aggressive personae the male world would allow. Alberta Hunter flourished as a haughty blues queen. "I've always been liberated," Hunter insisted in 1976, noting with pride that she reformed her first husband. At first "I had let him hang around . . . and accept the nickels and dimes from the people where I'm singing," but "he would have never made a man of himself" this way, so Hunter took work in Paris and left her husband in Chicago to fend for himself. Bessie Smith, similarly, always tested the limits of the queenly role she was permitted, behaving and speaking "out of turn" to the distress of the men around her.[7]

Generally, men considered jazz to be their fraternity, thus women were only given minor roles. The infancy of jazz on the plantation and in New Orleans bands, involving patriarchial instructors and boy students in kneepants, had been male-dominated. To some extent, African- and European-American taboos against females playing guitars and wind instruments lay at the root of jazz's marked sexism, and testimony suggests that gender roles were firmly in place during the early development of the music.[8] The trumpeter Andrew Blakeney recalled that men in Los Angeles felt that "the woman pianist wasn't quite as strong as the men would like them to be, especially as the background, the left hand chords; it wasn't as good as the average man." He does not recall that women played any instrument besides the piano. Bill Coleman, as a youth in Cincinnati, was surprised to discover that the pianist Amanda Randolph "played like a man," and that one Dolly Jones played the trumpet in a band; "a girl playing in an orchestra had never been seen in Cincinnati." For young Coleman "a violin was more of an instrument for girls," and he "never told [his violinist friend] Willis what I thought of the violin because we were good friends and did not wish to hurt his feelings." In the 1920s, Coleman played in Cecil Scott's band at the Savoy Ballroom in New York, which hosted an annual Female Impersonator's Ball. "For the Sissies' ball we were in our regular costumes to show at least there were a few men there."[9]

In their relations with women, many jazzmen were conditioned by their high exposure to prostitutes, dancing girls, and other women who functioned in northern entertainment centers as commodified sex objects. In nightclubs, where bargirls served mainly as enticements for lonely men to buy more drinks and waitresses fetched paper-money tips with their thighs or vaginas, jazzmen saw women in roles explicitly associated with sexual liaison. While blueswomen managed to shed the immoral image that singers had borne in Storyville, prostitutes remained a common feature of nightclubs and dance halls in the North, and they often introduced adolescent jazzmen to sex.[10] Milt Hinton—who claimed later he had less interest in girls than in music—joined his musical friends in 1920s Chicago in renting an apartment for rendezvous. Their sex lives were launched along with their professional jazz careers, since they could rent the place only after they had obtained reliable incomes. They kept the place for a year, Hinton recalled, "until finally we got to working and really getting money, so we could go to hotels." Despite the risks ("we came up with a lot of gonorrhea") the young musicians enjoyed the experience, but Hinton was less sanguine when the others spent the group's tips on a private sex show; revolted, he "wanted to take my money out of the kitty."[11]

Marital relations in the realm of jazz, as in other professions that involved traveling, could be strained and volatile. Some players compounded difficult situations by placing little trust in their wives, who waited at home for them. The attitude of the trumpeter Willie Hightower, as remembered by his bandleader Earl Hines, may not have been rare. Hightower's wife Lottie was herself a talented pianist, bandleader, and union activist, but Hightower felt that she needed firm guidance. He told Hines that on his wedding night, after his wife had fixed an elegant meal, he "pulled the tablecloth, the dishes, the whole thing on the floor," in order "to let her know who was master of the house." Hightower was particularly eager to have Lottie "tell him about every penny she spent, and have it all itemized."[12] Such disavowals of wives' autonomy (particularly striking in the case of the talented Lottie Hightower) might reflect a number of root causes: the patriarchal nature of the musicians' guild, the special tensions of working-class couples, and the burdens of black men seeking a form of control in a prejudiced society. In fact, it is surprising that evidence of gender conflict in early jazz is not more widespread.

The intensely male orientation of early jazz invites speculation regarding how pervasive and deep male-only contact was among jazzmen. Long nights away from female partners on tour buses and in alien towns and hotels, hours spent daily in union halls and nightly in clubs, and the scorn heaped on women intruders suggest a highly homosocial environment. Also, the tendency toward falling into hard-living fraternities, and the boyish camaraderie these fraternities seemed to foster, also hint at such an environment. Some homosexual activity and its tacit acceptance would be an expected result of the intense fraternity of early jazzmen, as it was then for other kinds of touring artists, criminals, and other groups of men led by professional or other circumstances into homosocial living patterns.[13] Homosexuality, though, is almost never mentioned in early or recent jazz narratives.

Though acknowledgment of homosexuality is rare, a few of the most candid sources note such activity—Dick Voynow, pianist with the Wolverines, Ellington's future arranger Billy Strayhorn, and such hangers-on as Gene Berton, brother of the Wolverines' drummer, were among the few acknowledged homosexuals. In general, though, its absence is notable. The strong taboos against homosexuality, especially in the black community, cannot be discounted, and the invective against sissies and the decidedly swaggering, dominating nature of cutting competitions suggests hostility to any deviant or submissive behavior. This, however, might have been an evasion of an ever-present tension. In any case, early jazz players certainly did *not* foster a notable oasis of experimentation and tolerance in modern urban America, as the ranks of art-music composers and other occupations did at this time.[14]

The jazz musicians' frequent cohesiveness in small groups could produce satisfaction of a more general sort, however. For young whites, jazz playing served as a form of spiritual therapy— particularly as a communal experience (as it had been for blacks in the South and North) and an escape from boredom and apathy. Hoagy Carmichael's circle of jazz-playing friends in Bloomington, among others, came together to escape mutual anxieties. They voiced their solidarity in unison by means of jazz as well as eccentric group behavior. If Carmichael and his friends walked down campus streets "hissing silly sounds at each other," "throwing their tongues out at each other like a snake," and "screaming such things as 'hydrant!' 'faucet!' or 'buskirk!' " they did so because they "found that it was soothing to the soul. Life had been boring a moment before, but now it was much better."

Carmichael, in fact, tended to stress that this nonsense "was a means of escape from boredom. Maybe it was the expression of jazz in a spiritual sense." The spiritual leader of this group was Bill Moenkhaus, who "made straight 'A's' in a bored sort of way," wrote "surrealistic nonsensical writings" as "the founder and chief spokesman of a campus cult which he named the Bent Eagles," and learned to play "a bass horn when the roots of jazz took hold in Bloomington." "Monk's" motto was a couplet he composed: "Long live the drunken alphabet / The time for us has not come—yet." In a rudimentary way, the group sought moments of transcendent experience.[15]

Carmichael oriented them toward jazz, with the help of no less a figure than Bix Beiderbecke, who befriended Carmichael and Moenkhaus and joined them in nonsensical conversation and poetasting. "Bix, the inarticulate kid, who played the wonderful horn" and "Monk, the surrealistic intellectual" both wore traditions more lightly and felt freer to express their intuitions and jumbled perceptions. "You couldn't be mean and petty and blow stuff like Bix blew. You couldn't be stupid and mundane and write stuff like Monk wrote. . . . And the things I did and the people I knew and loved are reflected in the tunes I was to write."[16]

This whimsical revolt, which even Carmichael admitted was somewhat precious and ineffective, nevertheless mined joy from a rural American way of life that seemed to offer little else besides boredom. Students at Bloomington, "in the exact center of population at that time," felt particularly restless, learning of the urbanizing world in a disconcertingly rural setting. Like the sons of immigrants who embraced jazz in the big cities, these rural white Indianans felt like marginal members of society, as emblematic of "Middletown" (as the sociologists Robert and Helen Lynd found then in nearby Muncie) as the tradition-bound elders from whom they sought escape. Unlike the lonely outsiders of Muncie, however, "each hungry for companionship, but knowing no one else in the city who speaks his language," Carmichael and his friends innovated and developed ways to communicate, paralleling the more sophisticated surrealist attack on traditional expression then raging in Europe.[17] What is significant is that their assault began as an expression of male fraternity and ended in the production of jazz.

For Chicago whites as well, jazz was a therapy made up of meaningful nonsense. Louis Armstrong's purported invention of scat singing—the use of nonsense syllables in the place of words—in 1925 greatly aided whites as they became attracted to black jazz. As Bud Freeman saw it, when Armstrong dropped his lyrics while recording "The Heebie Jeebies" he began "singing improvised notes that developed into a completely original Jazz form of improvised singing. . . . Although man is a thinking reed," Freeman stressed, "he does his best work when he isn't thinking." Mezz Mezzrow recalled that "for months" after the recording was released, "you would hear cats greeting each other with Louis' riffs when they met around town—*I got the heebies,* one would yell out, and the other would answer *I got the jeebies,* and the next minute they were scatting in each other's face. Louis' recording almost drove the English language out of the Windy City for good." Mezzrow and others exposed Bix Beiderbecke to the recording, which inspired the latter to attempt his own recorded scat singing the next year.[18] For whites, this particular inheritance from Louis Armstrong brought verbal communication closer to the music and to the emotional and psychological messages it transmitted. Since scat entered their conversation, it also brought jazz closer into their speaking voices as well.

The experience of playing jazz thus helped to uncover or provide a kind of mental health. Like other 1920s Americans who embraced psychoanalysis and other secular regimens for the soul, jazz musicians found their music to be an effective and holistic therapy. The music Mezz Mezzrow learned to play from Oliver and Armstrong "is dignified, balanced, deeply harmonious, high-spirited but pervaded all through with a mysterious calm and placidity—the music of a personality that hasn't exploded like a fragmentation bomb. . . . *Get yourself together* is the personal slogan for all the guys who want to make this great music." If musical communion was achieved, the results were deeply fulfilling. As Max Kaminsky noted, "everyone [in Chicago] went out of his way to be encouraging. . . . After I'd take a chorus Teschmaker [*sic*] would shake his head unbelievingly and say, 'What a tone!'" and Bud Freeman "was so outgoing and enthusiastic that he was apt to rear back and laugh aloud from pure joy after taking a chorus." The therapy had long-term benefits as well. Freeman felt that "all the good white players . . . were very lucky that they had this music to use because without it, [they] might have gone into the studios where they would have become old and not wanted." The former gang member Jimmy McPartland provided the most succinct evaluation: "since I started to play, why, I've never been a bad boy."[19]

Good music, therefore, could yield both a sense of community and intense personal satisfaction for jazz musicians—perhaps *communitas*, which anthropologists argue is produced by the most-valued social dramas and rituals in any group.[20] Did the white search for therapy and the black continuum of music and culture in the ghetto create one or more jazz subcultures? It has been popular to believe that jazz either before or after 1940 yielded a culture in which jive talk, unusual dress, eccentric behavior, and the use and abuse of alcohol and drugs flourished. Perhaps, as it has been suggested, jazz culture was the predecessor of the great rock counterculture of the 1960s.[21]

Sociologists studying bebop-oriented and other white dance musicians in the forties and fifties argued that these players had formed an important deviant subculture. Howard S. Becker showed that they spoke constantly of their opposition to the mainstream culture of squares. "Squareness," they felt, "penetrates every aspect of the square's behavior just as its opposite, 'hipness,' is evident in everything the musician does. . . . Every item of dress, speech, and behavior which differs from that of the musician is taken as new evidence of the inherent insensitivity and ignorance of the square."[22] As Becker has noted, this insularity resulted directly from special postwar pressures to conform, which forced jazz musicians into a deviant self-image.

By contrast, members of the earlier jazz fraternity altered the rhythm of their lives and actions in more subtle and less-conscious ways. The concept of a jazz culture did not take root among the musicians themselves. Many of them, black and white, even insist that they never labeled their music jazz, a clear indication that they did not seek to differentiate themselves.

Their work did force some deviant behavior onto them, most clearly by causing them to become *nocturnal* creatures. While ragtime and even New Orleans jazz had frequently been associated with daytime parades, minstrel shows and social events, jazz in the North became more of a music to be played at night. Jazz musicians played weddings, tea dances, and other daytime jobs when necessary, and often made Sunday afternoons a regular session time. Jazz, though, became nocturnal as well as diurnal. Small combos in nightclubs, road bands in rural barns, and big bands playing in dance halls all usually began their performances after sunset and rarely finished before early morning. Duke Ellington recalled that in mid-twenties Harlem "the ginmills were wide open at that time, and there weren't restrictive regulations about closing hours. Nobody went to bed at nights, and round three or four in the mornings you'd find everyone making the rounds bringing their horns with them." Chicago club owners evaded ill-enforced local ordinances and kept bands playing until dawn. Earl Hines played in such a band at the Elite Club No. 2, where musicians came to jam after their regular jobs had ended.[23]

The nocturnal urban way of life depended upon electric lights, alarm clocks, and most of all, a booming market for nighttime amusement. Eddie Condon, Max Kaminsky recalled, "was like an owl—he never came to life till the sun went down. If he was up and about at two or three in the afternoon, which was seldom, he'd be silent and morose and take refuge behind a newspaper or a book. As the sun set his star would rise." Kaminsky himself was "young and rugged in those days, and the extra work spurred us to extra play." After getting home in the morning from their nights' work in a Dallas club, his band would play a round of golf, "top [it] off . . . with some refreshing slices of ice-cold watermelon soaked in gin before we tumbled groggily into bed." Later, based in New York in the early thirties, Condon "opened a charge account at a delicatessen for canned tomatoes, to be kept on ice until we called for them in the morning—or the afternoon."

Black musicians were no less nocturnal. Earl Hines noted that players in the South Side in the twenties all "worked seven days a week. There was so much going on that nobody paid any attention to the time of day. You'd go to work, get on the stand, play, come off the stand, go outside, get into all sorts of arguments, go back, play again, and so on like that through the night." In the mornings Hines and his colleagues headed for roadhouses on the outskirts of Chicago for breakfast and informal jam sessions.[24]

Beyond nocturnality, it is difficult to generalize about an alternative beat underlying the jazz life; this rhythmic metaphor, in fact, has generally been exaggerated. It is striking, for example, how few musicians displayed an interest in jazz dance, the most rhythmic means of self-expression available.[25] Manone and Hodes may have woken and walked to the jazz beat, McPartland may have considered the beat as a bridge across the color line, but as a stimulant (or even a metaphor) for an evolving cultural pattern, swinging jazz rhythm was not sufficient. In fact, as they observed swinging, colorful musicians, what white Americans thought was a novel jazz subculture was often actually a group of professionals strongly influenced by the *African-American* mainstream. Like their music, the musicians' behavior and attitudes represented the merging of two great continental cultures, not the creation of a new one. The case of jazz slang, or jive, provides the best illustration of this.

Jazz musicians did not confine themselves to nonsense scatting; they also developed one of the most colorful bodies of slang in American English. Like most originators of new musical forms, jazz musicians created a needed vocabulary relating to aspects of the form—such words as "riffs," "breaks," and "stop time," among many others. The slang, more accurately, was a professional, practical *jargon:* it labeled new rhythmic, improvisatory, and ensemble features and techniques that had never been named before. In the 1910s, for example, Ralph Brown found that New Orleans players in Chicago used their own terms, such as "getting off," which meant that "the band will lay down the drums and the piano, let's say, or the guitar, and this man starts taking a solo." Get-off men, Brown noted, were "strictly" from New Orleans. White players developed vernacular musical terms, too: "when I'm playing ensemble," Georg Brunis recalled, I'll holler 'walk it,' and he knows what I want. That's what I call home cooking." [26]

In addition to musical terminology, however, jazz jargon also described the particulars of their employment ("gigs," "jam sessions"), and their audiences ("cats," "chicks," "squares"). While jargon was needed for practical reasons, therefore, it also constructed terminology defining the nonmusical world as well. To some, this illustrated the insularity and uniqueness—as well as the isolation— of this small group of musicians. Wingy Manone argued that "jive talk got started, *of course,* the same place jazz was born, down in New Orleans," and his comments on jive (the common term for jazz jargon by the late thirties) stressed that it was the special language of New Orleans musicians, used "to 'jam up' the music and make things hot." It was location specific, "to suit the places they were playing in."[27]

Most important, the players guarded their jargon. "Naturally, people began to ask musicians what this lingo was all about, and the expressions caught on just like other types of slang. As other people took up our kind of talk, we musicians had to invent new words, so we would still have our own private language." Mezz Mezzrow also noted that "the reason we hot musicians are always making up new lingo for ourselves" was that "outsiders pick up the jazzman's colloquialisms" and "kick them around until the words lose all their fresh meaning." The word "swing" "was cooked up after the unhip public took over the expression 'hot' and made it corny by getting up in front of a band snapping their fingers in a childish way, yelling 'Get hot! Yeah man, get hot!' "[28] Mezzrow was a white rebel against society, and Manone was one of the most commercial-oriented of all players, but both understood that jive (unlike the music itself) was their verbal "improvisation," reserved for the private use and understanding of the musicians. Many other musical cultures share this trait.[29]

Such testimony suggests that at least some early jazz musicians (most likely white) were alienated and deviant, in this sense paving the way for the highly insular post–World War Two players.[30] In some ways both generations were typically American. The United States, where citizens group together out of necessity to forestall cutthroat competition and real or imagined conspiracies, has seen private languages spring up among many of these groups. The greatest American alternative language, though, had grown up among the slaves and free blacks, dialogues of deception, opposite meanings, protective exaggeration, and veiling slang. Jive gained its form and content—and its insular function—from this black linguistic tradition.[31]

Like the music itself, jive grew as blacks moved to northern cities and carefully experimented with their new opportunities. Mezzrow, who first heard New Orleans musicians speak it on the South Side around 1920, argued that the language grew along with black society in the north. To him the New Orleans language "wasn't very elaborate or full of bubbling energy and unshackled invention; it was the tongue of a *beaten* people." The Chicago jazz slang of the twenties "was the first furious babbling of a people [black migrants], who suddenly woke up to find that their death-sentence had been revoked." In 1930s New York jive "really came of age. These Harlem kids had decided they wouldn't be led back to jail nohow. They spieled a mile a minute, making that clear." [32]

Note that Mezzrow said nothing about jazz having a special role in the fostering of jive; on the contrary, it was the less-musical, less-successful, less-integrated urban blacks who brought jive to its fruition in the late thirties. Drug dealing was often carried out beneath a cloak of thick jive, as Mezzrow (a frequent participant) illustrated:

> SECOND CAT: Hey Mezzie, lay some of that hard-cuttin' mess on me. I'm short a deuce of blips but I'll straighten you later.
> ME: Righteous, gizz, you're a poor boy but a good boy—now don't come up crummy.
> SECOND CAT: Never no crummy, chummy. I'm gonna lay a drape under the trey of knockers for Tenth Street and I'll be on the scene wearin' the green. [33]

It is doubtful that jazz musicians used jive to build a private subculture. H. L. Mencken argued in *The American Language* that jive, while it almost certainly "arose" among jazz musicians, was more specifically "an amalgam of Negro slang from Harlem and the argots of drug addicts and the pettier sort of criminals, with occasional additions from the Broadway gossip columns and the high-school campus." Mencken correctly suggested that a private musicians' language only slightly influenced the shaping of "the queer jargon called *jive,* which had its heyday in the early 1940s." Terms like "groan-box," "box of teeth" (an accordion), "slush-pump" (trombone), "thermometer" (oboe), "licorice-stick" (clarinet), and "pretzel" (French horn) may have originated in night-clubs, but they rarely found their way into regular conversational use among musicians, if the bulk of interviews and memoirs are any guide. [34] Sidney Bechet felt that musicians of the forties indulged in a linguistic cakewalk with "all that crazy jive talk, all that stuff about 'gate' and 'tea' and being real 'cool.' " His main complaint was that "If you really mean to play your instrument, this jive business has got nothing to do with it. . . . Being crazy . . . don't make any music at all." [35]

Before 1940, publicists for jazz overstressed the linkage between jazz musicians and jive. Dan Burley, a Harlem newspaper columnist, Ned Williams (Cab Calloway's press agent, who ghostwrote

A handsome, ambitious group in a rural setting. One of Kid Ory's early bands at his boyhood home, La Place, Louisiana, circa 1908. Ory is second from left. (Al Rose and the William Ransom Hogan Jazz Archive)

Sidney Bechet in 1938. Bechet's background and training epitomized the musical culture of black New Orleans from 1905 to 1917. His music and career, along with those of Jelly Roll Morton and Louis Armstrong, represented the pinnacle of New Orleans jazz. (Institute of Jazz Studies)

Charles "Doc" Cooke's orchestra at Harmon's Dreamland, Chicago, 1924, a quintessentially urbane band in the era of the Great Migration. (Institute of Jazz Studies)

Papa Jack Laine's band in a dynamic yet informal pose, Alexandria, Louisiana, 1919. Laine watches his "boys" from the drums; Alfred Laine plays the bass, Georg Brunis, the trombone. (Institute of Jazz Studies)

Chicagoans in the Red Nichols band felt the full force of the city's urban industrial environment, its cultural yearnings, and its black musical scene on the South Side. This 1929 photo suggests the impact of such accelerated experience. From left, seated: Max Kaminsky, Joe Sullivan, Pee Wee Russell, and non-Chicagoans Red Nichols and Herb Taylor; standing: Mezz Mezzrow, Bud Freeman, Dave Tough, Eddie Condon. (Duncan P. Schiedt)

Eddie Durham, one of the masters of written jazz arrangements in the 1930s, seen here rehearsing his own band in 1940. (Institute of Jazz Studies)

A rarity in the male-dominated world of jazz, the pianist Lottie Hightower enriched the South Side with her band, the Night-Hawks, posing here in the 1927 or 1928. Lottie's husband Willie is the trumpet player on the right. (Institute of Jazz Studies.)

Twenties veterans, entering middle age, enjoying the "hot revival" at Jimmy Ryan's, New York City, circa 1939. From left: Pee Wee Russell, Brad Gowans, Bobby Hackett, Joe Sullivan, Marty Marsala. (Institute of Jazz Studies)

White jazz fans carefully examining the Count Basie Orchestra at the stand of the Famous Door, New York City, 1938. Basie is at the piano, Jo Jones on the drums. (Institute of Jazz Studies)

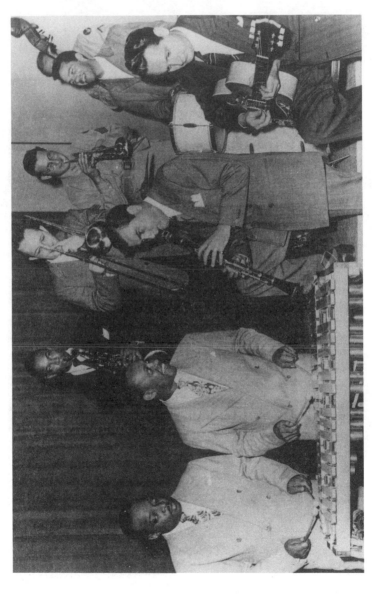

An interracial jam session, early 1940s, depicting wariness, bliss, and casual friendliness among the famous participants. Front, from left: Count Basie, Lionel Hampton, Artie Shaw, Les Paul; rear: Illinois Jacquet, Tommy Dorsey, Ziggy Elman, Buddy Rich, unidentified bassist. (Institute of Jazz Studies)

a *Hepster's Dictionary* for his client in 1938), and Mencken himself (along with their novelty seeking readers) did far more than the musicians to promulgate the use of jive. Aside from the somewhat polemical Mezzrow, the only jazz players who popularized jive were Calloway, Wingy Manone, and other fervent showmen. Manone, who worked in Hollywood in the 1940s, spoke with a reporter to "set him straight on the meaning of 'git-box,' 'riff,' 'killer-diller,' 'lick,'" and other words, and performed such stunts as hosting a Quiz Cats show at the Los Angeles Palladium, spinning a hep wheel and questioning contestants ("When I say a cat is solid like the Rock of Gibraltar, what do I mean?").[36] Manone by then had plainly lost the need to keep his private language private.

Most musicians were selectively colloquial. They used jive musical terms almost universally, and most blacks and a few whites used slang terms for emphasis (especially when expressing affection) in places and quantities revealing both their fine taste in verbal expression and their desire to be understood by a wide audience. In fact, black creators of jazz, due to reticence with white interviewers or other reasons, use surprisingly few African Americanisms in their recorded speech. It seems that their creation of a private jargon in the twenties and thirties grew out of their cultural isolation as blacks, and that their comparative neglect of that jargon in later years (in contrast to its flowering among the young and drug users) reflected their growing involvement with the white mainstream. The relation between musical and verbal creativity, therefore, was not always a direct one.

This is indicated best by the fact that players did not hasten to call their own music jazz. The term "jazz" received wide exposure in the white press after 1917, and columnists and editors speculated at length about the term's true origin. Jazz, it was theorized, derived from an Afro-Creole word meaning "to speed up"; the name of a performer, Jazbo or Charles ("Chas.") Brown; jasmine, added to New Orleans perfumes to give them a sharper fragrance; and the French *chasser*, to hunt or chase.[37] The term "jazz" was rarely used in the twenties and thirties by talented players of either color. "Jazz," Sidney Bechet wrote, "that's a name the white people have given to the music." In Creole society the word "jazz," Bechet reported, "could mean any damn thing: high times, screwing, ballroom. It used to be spelled *Jass*, which *was* screwing." Earl Hines in his memoirs, taped and edited by Stanley Dance in 1977, never calls his music "jazz." Bud Freeman recalled that "musicians never called the music jazz, but they knew what they were hearing and what they were feeling," and his friend Eddie Condon summarized this point in the title of his memoirs: *We Called It Music.*[38]

The choice was not casual. Their language, more than any other aspect of their behavior, showed both their dedication to an insular professional identity and their desire to avoid appearing to the general public as a freakish, jiving subculture. The role of race in the establishment of jazz jargon was clear: black culture supplied all musicians with the means and desire for generating a private jargon. The jargon, in turn, flowed back into the largely black urban culture that had spawned it, even after many musicians no longer craved a secret language.

Other elements of what might be called the jazz subculture came from more diffuse sources. Clothing, for example, has helped many Americans to define their private and public selves, occupation, and status in a fluid, loosely structured society; and it has been suggested that jazz musicians were especially eager to make sartorial statements. Bud Freeman has said that "the most immaculate, clothes-conscious people I know are musicians." There is evidence suggesting that some jazz players did have greater concern for fashion than the average urbanite, but again the concerns of whites and blacks differed somewhat.[39]

Their definition through clothing began in childhood. Jazz was a paying profession, which for both races was a passage into adulthood; and for jazzmen, this meant long pants. American boys at the turn of the century were graduated from infant curls and dresses to short hair and kneepants, a somewhat more masculine identity, but long trousers brought them out of adolescence and into the world of the money-earning adult. Sidney Bechet noted that "wearing long pants" in New Orleans theaters "made me a man," but that boys in short pants were chased out by the police. Lee Collins, a Creole, recalled a stricter regime, in which boys "had to be twenty-one years old before you could put on long pants." In Chicago, a club duel between Louis Armstrong and Jabbo Smith was most memorable to Scoville Browne because "I think I was there in my first pair of long blue pants."[40]

Among white musicians, the most famous pair of exposed knees belonged to the young Benny Goodman. The clarinetist first played professionally at the age of eleven (in 1920) and wore short pants to most jobs. Goodman wrote that even when he traveled to California at eighteen to join Ben Pollack's band, "I probably was a pretty picture when I got out there, a skinny kid in short pants, with a clarinet under my arm." Pollack, though, asked the young man to wear trousers from then on.[41]

New Orleans's elaborate public etiquette encouraged adult musicians of both races to pay special attention to dress. In their free time, Wingy Manone pointed out, New Orleans musicians "go for . . . the funny kicks that they see on the streets," and are careful about dress because "that sharp look is important down there." Once Manone "came into town wearing a sweat shirt, slacks, and sandals. . . . when I went into the saloons I was ignored." But when he bought "a sharp new suit, and came back in style, . . . 'now you're talkin,' they said, and, Cousin, what a welcome I got then." Louis Armstrong similarly flaunted his attire. In the 1932 short film *Rhapsody in Black and Blue*, Armstrong played the "King of Jazzmania" in a leopard skin. Manone reported that Armstrong "stuck his thumb under the lapel of that tiger skin [*sic*] and started to strut," in the manner of a New Orleanian strolling down "the main drag so everybody will see it, up and down with his thumb hooked under the lapel of his coat." The sartorial gesture "really broke me up." [42]

In the North, blacks' initial optimism after migrating—as well as their caution in the face of white hostility—was expressed in their stylish clothing and appearance. In Chicago, young Milt Hinton "got nice clothes, you know, everything. It was paradise, man." In Harlem, newcomer Clyde Bernhardt saw that "everybody seemed so neat and dressed up," men with "vests and spats, . . . camel hair topcoats, . . . derbys and homburgs everywhere. . . . that was *real class*." Furthermore, as Earl Hines found in 1925 Chicago, migrants wore gold chains, watches on chains, gold teeth, diamond tooth implants—"anything to attract attention." Impressed with the local style, Hines "practically lived at the barbershop, getting manicures and massages, as well as getting my hair fixed." This look, while generally an expression of optimism and freedom, also signified the toughness needed to survive in the ghetto. "In those days everybody tried to be half bad, and everybody had a gun," since "somebody was always getting hurt, and you had to have a certain amount of courage to work in those clubs." For black bands, clothing contributed to their professional success. As Hines put it, "All the bands tried to outdress one another, but, with Jimmie Lunceford's and Duke Ellington's, we were considered the best-dressed band on the road. It meant an awful lot, because appearance was almost half the battle." [43]

Musicians' attention to style matched the assertive and impro-

visatory nature of their profession. Whites' often ample earnings in
the twenties bankrolled them to stylish wardrobes. After paydays
Eddie Condon bought "twenty-dollar English hats, thirty-dollar
shoes, and bench-made suits," and by about 1928, as he made $145
for twenty-four hour work weeks, his "bathing suits were being
made of silk." Josh Billings, a nonplaying friend of the Chicagoans,
designed an unusual suit in 1927. According to Bud Freeman, "the
trousers were high peg-top, full in the legs and tapered down to
very narrow, cuffless bottoms. The jacket was long, with wide lapels
and one button, which was not worn buttoned, and there was a
tight vest." Freeman, his brother, and their musician friends "had
suits of this design made immediately." Their neighbors did not pay
"much attention to our dress. We were musicians, and I suppose
they expected anything of us." The freedom that led them to wear
such clothing also allowed them to abandon it at will. "After about
a year, what with our ideas changing many times, we changed to
wearing something more conservative." [44]

Musicians' fashion sense helped them to combat the jazz promoters' habit of dressing them in ridiculous costumes. Managers,
listeners, and even a few musicians, steeped in vaudeville and minstrelsy, cared less for jazz's artistic potential and more for traditional
entertainment values. For a work called *Monotony*, performed in
Chicago in 1925, Paul Whiteman (who often exhorted Americans
to take jazz seriously) made each band member wear "blue smocks
and helmets of papier-maché decorated with cogwheels" and blue
face paint. They played in front of "an enormous time-beating
metronome" which hid Whiteman from the audience. Musicians
at social functions, as Bud Freeman has noted, were "pretty much
treated like waiters," and often had to dress like them; such twenties bands as the Mound City Blue Blowers performed in bellhops'
smocks and caps. Working in New York in 1930, the band was
hired by a profitable speakeasy to perform in prison-style striped
jerseys with lute-shaped guitars and banjos. Imposing uniforms on
jazz musicians was one way in which audiences and commercial-
izers tried to stress jazz's alleged and popular barbaric or nutty
qualities. [45]

This kind of exploitation and trivialization especially confronted black musicians, since costumes always reinforced the caricatures that had dogged all black entertainers. The bandleader Lois
Deppe began his career as a singer in Pittsburgh. At the Duquesne
Gardens nightclub, the owner, Ollie Reed, "passed me as a Hawaiian in a white shirt, white flannel trousers and the lei around my

neck," Deppe recalled a half-century later. The details of his costume were still vivid because they defined his public persona as a performer and member of the Hawaiian race.[46] Like Armstrong's leopard skin, Deppe's outfit showed that clothing was a tool used by promoters to misappropriate jazz and its creators.

Similarly, jazz musicians found their rightful earnings misappropriated as well (a subject fully discussed in the next chapter). But as with clothing, money was used by musicians (especially whites) in an improvisatory, even flamboyant style. Twenties underworld culture, prospering during Prohibition, produced a flow of money and goods that challenged and delighted these young creative people; they had occasion to spend money they had not earned, buy items they never used, and earn more in trivial jobs for the wealthy than in dance halls or clubs. Eddie Condon was twice given hundreds of dollars by bookmakers seeking to divert trailing law officers. Wild Bill Davison, arriving in Chicago in the late 1920s, was hired by Benny Meroff's band and given an annual salary of $11,500. "I didn't know what to do with it. I bought big cars and lots of booze and chased chorus girls." Art Hodes found immediate success as a speakeasy pianist. When a wealthy patron made requests, Hodes played "song after song for him; the gals would come up and stuff the money in my pocket." With these tips Hodes "bought a car, nice clothes, and was in the chips." The windfall of the twenties was unexpected: "the last thing we talked of was getting paid for playing." Hodes and Wingy Manone welcomed scores of musicians to their Chicago apartment, men who "spent all their money for records, gin, food, and stuff."[47]

Jazz arose during the initial era of mass abundance in America, when many found themselves with ample spending money that largely had not been earned through labor but acquired through investments, credit, and working for heavy tippers.[48] Within this culture of easy money Americans were not savers but consumers; the money went toward middle- and working-class forms of conspicuous consumption. Even the rebellious white musicians were susceptible to the consumerist enticement of advertising and motion pictures and fantasized in a conventional twenties manner about success and wealth. Mezzrow and Freeman wanted to travel to Hollywood, and "we all began to dream about that special swimming pool a hundred yards long, filled with imported champagne," the "squad of butlers . . . assigned to do nothing but roll muggles [marijuana] all day long, each one five foot long," and "the whole Ziegfeld chorus . . . hired to fan us with palm leaves as we lounged around in the sun, reading H. L. Mencken and playing Louis Armstrong records over the P.A. system."[49] As with clothing, wealth was something musicians sought and "slipped into" when they could. But it is easy to exaggerate the actual *spending* and wealth of the musicians, many of whom (especially blacks) remained close to the culture (and, often, poverty) that had spawned them. Their wealth rode on the whims of chance.

For this reason, gambling was exceptionally common among jazz musicians. Gambling was a backstage ritual that symbolized their ambivalences about wealth and possessions and decided their socioeconomic fate in compact, brief, and democratically founded rites. Black musicians, perhaps because they were less able to realize consumption fantasies, were most often addicted to gambling. Policy rackets (illegal lotteries) and card clubs flourished in the northern ghettos. Milt Hinton recalled that he was inured to gambling on high-school basketball courts: "They'd stand in the gym all year round, 'I betch'a a nickel I can hit from 10 feet, 15 feet.' There was a heavy accent on gambling," which Hinton witnessed again as a musician.[50] Scoville Browne found that backstage gambling among black players in Chicago "was a ritual. This was part of the night's activities, to have a few games going on." Earl Hines and others working at the Elite Club were often "sucked in" to the club's gaming room, where "you were caught in one of those traps where he didn't have to pay you your salary because you had blown all your money playing the games back there." Louis Armstrong's manager in the thirties was more helpful. Pops Foster, who would "gamble on anything," recalled that "if Joe Glaser didn't have any work, we'd loaf. We didn't get any pay but Joe would loan us money," which they used to raise antes.[51]

White musicians from Chicago were also heavily involved in gambling. Manone claimed that while Californians "go for sports, especially golf," New Yorkers, "shows, wearing good clothes, and jam sessions," and New Orleanians, "food . . . and the funny kicks they see on the streets," Chicagoans "travel faster. They get their kicks mostly from gambling, race horses, pool, dice, fast women, and good whiskey." This characterization was expanded upon by Max Kaminsky, who noted that "I was a card player [in Boston] from way back and I was full of confidence and in about three minutes" of playing with the Austin High Gang, "I lost all my money." Frank Teschemacher was the most skilled; "all he did between sets was play cards, and when we played at the Chinese restaurant at Sixty-second and Cottage Grove he used to take on the waiters—

and the Chinese are the original card sharks of all time." Art Hodes took to gambling on his summer jobs, playing at Wisconsin lake resorts. "Luck stood alongside me all summer—I just couldn't lose. . . . I bought new clothes, records, and came home with a pocket full of dough."[52] For the white musicians as well, success at gambling represented a magical means for obtaining money and prestige— similar to jazz itself—which freed them from mundane social and economic restrictions. Both they, and Americans ever since, have been willing to pair jazz with free earning and spending.

Early jazz has also been paired in lore and legend with the overconsumption of alcohol and other drugs. It was difficult for the musicians to avoid these substances, since illicit traffic in liquor and narcotics took place in many of the same settings in which they worked. Marijuana, long popular among Mexican-Americans in the Southwest, by the turn of the century had gained a following in New Orleans and other Gulf cities. The drug apparently arrived in 1910s Chicago by means of the growing Mexican and southern black population.[53] Those few musicians who became regular marijuana smokers—even New Orleans natives like Manone and Armstrong—were introduced to "muggles," "tea," or "muta" in South Side nightclubs.

Whites apparently did most of the smoking. Pops Foster recalled that "colored musicians mostly drank booze and the white guys started taking dope. Some young colored musicians [active in the twenties] started taking dope after that." Foster singled out Louis Armstrong as one black player who regularly enjoyed marijuana, but the songwriter Charlie Carpenter recalled that a white introduced him to it, in Chicago's Savoy ballroom. "Everybody was standing outside in the back, and I was right there, because I was always with Louis. 'I got a new cigarette, man,' a white arranger said to him. . . . So this guy lit it up, to take a drag or two, and passed it around, and nobody would take it. 'Let me try it,' Louis finally said." "Later on," Carpenter added, "Mezz Mezzrow became Louis's supplier," and the great musician smoked marijuana regularly until his death in 1970, despite a 1930 jail term for possession.[54]

Mezzrow (who became Harlem's major marijuana retailer in the late thirties), more than any other musician, sought to associate creativity in jazz with the weed. A rare early figure in the long and notable roster of jazz addicts, Mezzrow in his memoirs stressed the emotional clarity and resurgence that marijuana produced: "You still see what you saw before but in a different, more tolerant way, through rose-colored glasses, and things that would have irritated you before just tickle you." [55]

Mezzrow argued that marijuana intensified both creativity and the camaraderie of musicians in bands. "Tea puts a musician in a real masterly sphere, and that's why so many jazzmen have used it. You look down on the other members of the band like an old mother hen surveying her brood of chicks. . . . your own accompaniment keeps flashing through your head, just like you were a one-man band. . . . You hear everything at once and you hear it right. When you get that feeling of power and sureness, you're in a solid groove." The entire Austin High Gang, as well as such visitors to Chicago as Hoagy Carmichael, smoked marijuana during social gatherings. Despite Mezzrow's claims, however, they rarely smoked during performances. Jimmy McPartland remembered that "we would smoke it but . . . we wouldn't overdo it." He avoided smoking "when I was playing because it made my mouth too dry," but he felt that "it's better than drinking." [56]

Writers usually exaggerate the role of drugs in jazz before World War Two. Sam Wooding recalled the use of cocaine and opium in Atlantic City clubs in the 1910s, but this use apparently had little relation to musicians' activities. In fact, the black songwriter and promoter Clarence Williams said that "I never knew hardly any musicians that took dope, it was mostly the girls." While heroin was used heavily by musicians after 1940, who claimed that it helped their playing, drugs played no role in the early development of jazz music. No other musicians seemed to have shared Mezzrow's view that marijuana stimulated creativity. Based on his autobiography, it seems that Mezzrow's use of drugs—which progressed in the thirties to a near-fatal opium addiction—was primarily a symbol of his withdrawal from mainstream white society, and (as he eventually admits) drug use slowed rather than hastened his musical development. [57]

Neil Leonard has recently argued that drugs played an important role in loosing the creative energies of jazz musicians: "For some [musicians] drugs seemed to help. There is no evidence that they actually stimulated creativity, but in the short run they relieved stress and allowed the player to focus fully on the ecstatic task." Many musicians expressed the opposite of this opinion. Johnny Otis in the late thirties "knew better than falling for the 'immoral' and 'dangerous to health' propaganda that one still hears," but still did not smoke marijuana, in part because it did not inspire him musically: "Why take a chance on going to jail for something that was quite expensive and did nothing more, really, than put me to sleep[?]" Milt Hinton smoked marijuana once before a job, and while it "felt like I was . . . playing in the most heavenly place in the world, . . . the time was just so slow"; the next morning it took hours for him to drive home, and he never "got high" before a performance again. Sidney Bechet felt that "drinking and reefers and all that stuff, most times they just mess up all the feeling you got inside yourself. . . . When a man goes at the music that way, it's just a sign that there's a lot inside himself he don't know how to answer." The arranger Gil Evans made no artistic claims for marijuana, allowing only that it did not hurt some psychologically, but that "lots of people don't smoke grass" because "it makes them very paranoic." Most memoirs of early jazzmen do not mention any drug use, and those that endorse marijuana as a stimulant to creativity are even rarer.[58]

The role of alcohol—by far the most prevalent drug of the era—in the construction of an alleged jazz subculture remains controversial. Jazzmen writing memoirs in the 1940s depicted a free flow of alcohol during a stereotypical jazz age of the twenties. Eddie Condon recalled how he and other friends, relaxing at a club where Bix Beiderbecke was playing, "stayed to feed him between sets from the stock of ale and Scotch we had brought with us," supposedly to keep him in playing condition. The pianist Joe Sullivan, Condon wrote, would keep a filled glass on his piano at Guyon's Paradise, and often "play a tenth [chord with one hand] and reach for a drink at the same time." Art Hodes believed that the trumpeter Dick Donahoe "had his jug handy so that his nerves would hold up Boy, he sure needed it on that job; waltzes, tangoes, rhumbas, what not," which his band played in ninety-minute sets. Black musicians were also dedicated drinkers. Lee Collins's Illinois roadhouse band during the Depression "did a lot of drinking on this job. There was a big water pitcher filled with gin on the bandstand, and we stayed drunk all the time." Wingy Manone's band sold gin under nightclub pianos and sipped with straws out of hidden bottles during recording sessions; the trombonist Jack Teagarden was never without a whiskey flask on his belt; and Duke Ellington fired the drummer Sonny Greer for drunkenness, but still kept him on the payroll.[59]

The torrent of drinking by twenties jazzmen has been well documented, but was it unusual for the era? And did it mean that alcohol had a central, defining role in a jazz subculture? Bud Freeman has categorically rejected the notion that jazz musicians needed alcohol to play, and in fact argued that "any great player will agree with me when I say that it is *impossible* to play when you're drunk," especially for eight-hour stretches. "The first thing that goes wrong is your breathing and, of course, your brain doesn't function." Indeed, the physiological effects of alcohol—slowed reflexes, depressed production of brain enzymes, impeded breathing and circulation—are exactly those that destroy a musician's ability to improvise creatively and intensely. Freeman noted that "we were all drinkers," but claims that he did not drink "a great deal because, having been an athlete as a child, I loved the idea of health and my father instilled this in me." [60]

Despite Freeman's statement, it appears that many skilled players, particularly nonblowing pianists and drummers, could and did play while drinking. Alcohol may have helped them to forget troubles, block out the crowd noise, and put them in a mood to entertain—if perchance their beloved jazz music alone did not produce these results. It can be safely concluded that alcohol was central neither to the creation of jazz nor to a jazz subculture; rather, it was a ubiquitous component of the twenties urban culture that spawned jazz, and musicians could not avoid it. Wild Bill Davison set the Chicago context well: "it was a fun time in life for musicians. There were so many jobs and there was so many people that liked it and there was so much boot-leg whiskey around . . . at that point, I think, if you tell somebody, you're not allowed to drink—that's when they're going to drink the most and I think, in those days, even the women were getting drunk." [61] Alcohol was unavoidable in the culture of the speakeasy.

At the individual level, musicians found that drinking was more of a curse than a blessing. Addiction to alcohol is largely dependent upon the individual's psychological, physical, and hereditary makeup; cultural trends may encourage alcoholics, but they do not create them. Freeman was almost certainly incorrect to argue that Bix Beiderbecke, Dave Tough, and other reputed alcoholic jazzmen were merely "dipsomaniacs . . . who can smell a cork and go completely beserk" but who drank comparatively little. Regarding Beiderbecke, he protests the fact that "people like to think of him as a knocked out character who was never sober. On the contrary, all of his great recordings were made when he was completely sober." This assertion of Freeman's is more accurate (although Beiderbecke undoubtedly did drink while playing in nightclubs), but it is incomplete. Beiderbecke was an alcoholic whose addiction reveals much about the tensions of the jazz life—and about the *lack* of a supportive subculture. [62]

According to his biographers, Beiderbecke's alcoholism was irritated by his utter inability to handle fame. Louis Armstrong summed up the consensus of opinion in his memoirs: "He had a lot of admirers. In fact that's what mostly killed him. He wasn't the type of lad who had his own strong mind. When he felt bad and wanted to say good night to the gang he ran with, they would always say, 'Aw, man, stay a little longer . . . and have another drink.' Poor Bix would force himself, against his will." Bill Challis, an arranger and friend of Beiderbecke's, implicated Eddie Condon: "Condon has started a lot of [alcoholics?]—well, he was one of the guys who used to always drink with Bix. . . . He was always hanging around Bix—a real Bix fan, a fanatic."[63] While Condon was "an operator," Beiderbecke "was still a kid—naive, not childish, but a trusting sort. . . . But the thing is, they made fun of his drinking. They made fun of his remarks. Good old Bix—everything was funny to them." The clarinetist Pee Wee Russell, his former housemate, recalled that other musicians "never let him alone. . . . They came around at all hours of the day and night. He couldn't even play the goddamn piano without somebody hanging around." Beiderbecke's final three years were plagued by the symptoms of advanced alcoholism—onslaughts of delirium tremens and a dangerously low resistance to disease. Despite months of treatment at a leading sanitarium, he died of pneumonia.[64]

Few other musicians had possessed as much talent and as little self-possession as Beiderbecke, but the early jazz profession did produce many other alcoholics. The trumpeter and bandleader Bernard "Bunny" Berigan, a popular and critically acclaimed performer, died from alcohol at thirty-five; and other white players, such as Pee Wee Russell, George Wettling, and Fud Livingston also failed to control their drinking. The special prevalence of heavy drinking among whites, in addition, suggests that the rebellious nature of white jazz may have produced special insecurities and weaknesses (although it is not likely that blacks in the 1930s had less reason to drink). At the very least, it is clear that whites were most eager to publicize their weaknesses for narcotics and alcohol in a confessional manner.

It would be anachronistic to criticize the jazz fraternity for not weaning musicians away from the bottle, in an era when no one knew that alcohol was an addictive drug, but it is striking that the opposite dynamic developed. Adopting the ultimate misperception of Beiderbecke's talent and problems, younger jazzmen emulated his drinking. "As young people," Bud Freeman recalled, "we were

naive and instead of just idolizing the musicality of our idols, we
wanted to live like them and I think that was a great mistake. . . . In
following Bix's life," Freeman added in an overstatement, "I think
that most cornet players, trumpet players were ruined by him because they all became drunkards." Still, it would be wrong to say
that such emulation produced an alcoholic subculture. As Herman
Autrey has noted, by the late thirties there were too many players
fighting for places in the job market to allow for a tolerance of
alcoholism among them.[65]

Taking these celebrated extramusical aspects of the early jazz
musicians' lives into consideration, it is not possible to argue that
they created a distinct and influential subculture. Their tendencies toward masculine fraternity, therapeutic uses for the music,
nocturnality, slang, unusual dress, gambling, and drug and alcohol
use and abuse most often derived from the tensions and creations
found in the dominant white and African-American cultures. By
no means can their union be called a counterculture of the sort
prominently described among forties jazzmen and youth of the
1960s, for their music, and only their music, held them together as
a group.

"Money-Finding Music"
Jazz as a Commodity

From the start, jazz was not only the music of a folk or of a fraternity of musicians, but it was also a business, a small craft industry in the great market square of modern American capitalism. Until 1900, jazz's forerunners were spread and sold by the means of transportation and technology of the preindustrial era. Ragtime was spread in much the same way as music circulated in 1850—by riverboat, locomotive, horse, and foot from one local dance to the next. Similarly, bands were inseparable from small communities, expressing the moods of local voluntary associations, neighborhood rivalries, annual parades and celebrations, and other institutions of rural and urban communal life.[1] At the turn of the century, however, industrialization and other new social forces helped to sever many connections between music and folk-communal traditions. Mass transportation and the automobile allowed strangers to infiltrate neighborhoods and natives to flee them; education and formal musical training were more widely available to players; and opportunities for national and international travel on entertainment circuits were enlarged.

The southern migrant musicians and their northern colleagues who created jazz were citizens of a more complex, diverse, and wealthy society than their parents' generation had known. Rebellious whites and ambitious blacks alike took advantage of opportunities provided by ample education, transportation, and communications media. These media alternately constrained and liberated jazz players, audiences, and the music itself. To a great extent the musicians were Janus-faced, drawing inspiration from preindustrial folk and art musical practices while they were confronting a dynamic industrial society that rationalized their lives and music. The musicians were not as nostalgic for a folklike past as some jazz historians might be today. (Tom Bethell, for example, argues that New Orleans musical culture "placed one in the center of a colorful way of life," while "the musician who left to go north inevitably became a small cog in the wheel of the entertainment industry.")[2] On the contrary, musicians found the power of the new broadcast technology stimulating, and they realized that their labor union and managers helped to provide more secure structures for employment. While the exigencies of commercial promotion, mass dissemination, and collective unionism bewildered and stymied musicians on many occasions, these resources just as often increased their influence and status as the creators of a vital new music.

The most striking commercial conditions under which jazz musicians worked were provided by the much-heralded gangsters of the Prohibition era, who proved to be generous but difficult employers during the music's early, fragile years. A few musicians did not find the underworld to be unusually exploitative—Scoville Browne argued that with gangland employers, "you do your work and you get paid and that's all there is to it. Same way it is now"— but most held a different perception.[3] By bankrolling speakeasies, nightclubs, and brothels, the underworld became an unusually persistent supporter of jazz musicians, but gangsters exacted a high price for their patronage.[4]

Employers involved in organized crime set the terms of musicians' contracts without negotiation and thus refused to allow players to leave when the contracts expired. This was the norm in Chicago as early as 1916, when future members of the Original Dixieland Jazz Band left Schiller's Café as a group. "We were lucky we were all together when we left," Eddie Edwards recalled, "because, when you leave a cafe like that, they don't like it. And they are liable to give you the Joe [E.] Lewis treatment," a reference to the comedian's well-known punishment at the hands of gangsters (as Mezz Mezzrow recalled, "they beat him unmercifully; he was in the hospital for about three years"). Wingy Manone's band feared the spontaneous violence they confronted while working in Chicago's Manley Club in 1930. They were "ready to give notice and get lost. But we couldn't—the boss wouldn't let us quit. We stayed on, fearing something would happen to us if we left our job." Walter Fuller had planned on joining the Earl Hines Orchestra in 1931, but the "gangster owner" of Fuller's club made veiled threats, forcing Hines's patron to trade another musician for the trumpeter.[5]

Gangsters sometimes harassed, maimed, and even kidnapped musicians who disobeyed them, or who were simply symbolic targets in the employ of rivals. Barney Bigard recalled that Duke Ellington was warned on a visit to Chicago that he had "upset" some gunmen, who now "wanted to burn him, make him limp for a while. . . . the gang weren't making much money out of bootlegging any more and they hadn't yet taken over the numbers racket, so they tried to make their money by bearing down on important people." Ellington used his own connections to obtain suitable protection. Less fortunate was the clarinetist Joe Darensbourg, a New Orleanian playing in Harrisburg, Illinois in the mid-twenties. Angry at their employer, the local gang attacked Darensbourg and his bandmates: "they pistol-whipped me and creased my skull with a bullet, shot me in the arm and leg and left me for dead."[6]

Such casualties, along with the violence inflicted on others around them, alienated musicians from the underworld. After some months of playing in a Chicago club, Garvin Bushell "would come home a nervous wreck. . . . You could sit in your house any night in Chicago and hear a huge explosion down the block—some tailor shop that didn't pay off for protection or a grocery store. . . . I couldn't stay in Chicago. Couldn't take it." Mezz Mezzrow found that Capone's Valentine's Day Massacre of 1929 made the formerly congenial city unbearable. "It looked to me like the whole continent was being drowned in a bath of blood, from coast to coast. . . . It was all one great big underworld, and they'd put their dirty grabbers on the one good thing left on earth, our music, and sucked it down into the mud with them."[7]

Aside from the hazards of the mob environment, the exploitation faced by jazz players was rather typical for performers of this era. Jazz, like minstrelsy and ragtime before it, came under the control of professional promoters who sought to make the music profitable. Adapting the techniques of advertising, song plugging, and vaudeville, jazz promoters turned band battles into events, band members into employees, and leaders into popular personalities. Some promoters, such as Joe Glaser (who managed Louis Armstrong in the thirties) were associates of organized crime who left the underworld when Prohibition was repealed. Glaser apparently had overseen Al Capone's profits from the Sunset Café and a prostitution ring before he became Armstrong's manager in 1935. Many more promoters, however, were veterans of Tin Pan Alley, Manhattan's song-publishing industry, including Irving Mills, a former singer and songwriter who managed Duke Ellington's and other black bands in the thirties. Others began their careers as dance hall managers in various cities, such as "Paddy" Harmon, owner of Chicago's Dreamland Café, who plastered notices in every elevated train station in the city to advertise the Charlie Elgar band and others. The last two promoters sought and gained spurious renown, as Mills took partial credit for many Ellington compositions and Harmon patented and gave his name to a trumpet mute that had long been popular among Joe Oliver and other black players.[8]

The motives and sensibilities of jazz promoters varied widely. Some were virtual privateers, such as certain operators in the new Music Corporation of America (MCA) who bought out, merged, and renamed financially troubled bands beginning in the late twenties. Others were genuine advocates of the music, such as the wealthy Virginian who backed the female band the International Sweethearts of Rhythm in the late 1930s, or the able young impresarios John Hammond and Leonard Feather. While most promoters provided musicians with publicity and opportunities to perform and record, they did not usually pay ample salaries. Irving Mills may have paid the Ellington band for sitting idle during delays in the recording studio, but the International Sweethearts of Rhythm each made only $8 a week on their earliest tours in the thirties. Even promoters who paid well took the lion's share of box-office revenues. Ed Fox, like Joe Glaser a former Capone club operator, managed Earl Hines's touring band in the thirties. Fox paid Hines $150 and each of the eleven musicians $75 to $90 weekly, a total less than one-third of the net receipts of $3,500 Fox gathered in each week from the tours.[9]

Musicians knew that most promoters exploited them. Black players found, as Earl Hines put it, that "whites [in the 1920s] began to realize the talent Negroes had, and they began scheming how to commercialize it." The Theater Owners' Booking Agency pioneered the use of black jazz musicians in its touring shows of the twenties, but gained little respect for its poor wages and discriminatory policies. Loath as they were to "Take Oldman Bailey's Advice," black players depended on TOBA, although it was "Tough On Black Artists" and "Asses." Record company agents did not always pay musicians as they promised, and written record contracts were rarely drawn up. In Alberta Hunter's experience, while Paramount's white agent M. A. Supper "never cheated me out of a dime," J. Mayo Williams "was a thief."[10]

Promoters usually ignored the artistic potential of the music, and thus earned the scorn of black and white musicians alike. For example, while the record producer Jack Kapp became a powerful benefactor to jazz when he wholly dedicated his successful American Decca company to popular dance music, he nevertheless hurt the music by diluting it in the recording studio, simplifying melodic lines and eliminating much improvisation. Musicians accused Kapp of seeking the lowest common musical denominator for Decca releases by requesting that melodies be simple and very prominent; "Where's the melody?" was Kapp's famous, puzzled response to the improvisation of the Eddie Condon band. ("Anybody can play the melody," Condon responded. "These boys are doing better than that.") Bill Challis simplified his arrangements for various bands at the request of Decca engineers. "They would suppress it. Tighten it up. . . . I would ask of the guys, 'Can't you give me more body?' 'No, all you want to hear is the vocal anyway, the lead is all we want.'" To Challis, Kapp's engineer was "a cigar store Indian" who "can't hear" and "doesn't understand the jazz."[11]

Economic exploitation, though, and not matters of taste, most disturbed the musicians. Managers deprived many of them of their freedom of movement, legal rights to intellectual property, and pay guaranteed by contract. Ed Fox's embezzlements during his tenure as manager of the Earl Hines tours were only the most substantial offenses of this kind. Bill Coleman's "first experience in show business as a musician" came when he toured with a band in central Ohio. Hoskin, the manager, consistently kept most of the theater income for himself and only gave the musicians enough money to survive. The band decided to monitor one box office as the money flowed in, and they finally received their share: "we divided the money in equal parts and told Hoskin that we had done our last show for him." The Buck and Bubbles team sued their manager, Nat Nazzaro, when they learned that he had neglected to publicize them and had deprived them of earnings; Nazarro, however, had the pair banned from a chain of theaters in retaliation.[12]

Musicians were most victimized, perhaps, when promoters and leaders systematically deprived them of royalties from their own compositions. Since 1909, published music had been fully covered by copyright, and the American Society of Composers, Authors, and Publishers (ASCAP), founded in 1914, had begun to ensure that at least the best-selling song composers would get their royalties. Jazz musicians only gradually gained an awareness of their royalty rights. Migrant players from the more traditional

South, where the folk concept of anonymous song composition dominated, had to assimilate to the more commercial North before they accepted the concept of individual authorship and royalty rights. Only then did they begin to quarrel over who composed "Tiger Rag" and "High Society."[13]

The folklike disregard of composers' rights also persisted among musicians in the North, however. In the Lloyd and Cecil Scott band in 1920s Ohio, Bill Coleman noted, "nothing was written down on paper. The only problem was that, although [our] musical numbers were worked out together, Cecil used to take the credit when they were recorded, because at that time, we knew nothing about ASCAP or royalties." Duke Ellington knew about royalties, and exploited the lingering precapitalist attitude of his band members when he "borrowed" their musical ideas. He justified his actions by claiming that "everybody else steals from me." Musicians in New York who wrote down their ideas were victimized as well, by the army of white aspirants working in Tin Pan Alley. One white copyist's "room was piled to the ceiling with Benny Carter arrangements, and other people's arrangements," the white leader Charlie Barnet recalled. "And he would go around and sell the arrangements." Carter did not assert his rights: "He's such a nice man that he figured, 'well, if he's making a couple of bucks, what the heck, you know.'"[14]

Many musicians only slowly grew aware of their rights. Ellington did pay his musicians small amounts for ideas that he developed into full band pieces. Juan Tizol sold the rights to "Caravan" to Ellington for $25, but did not receive a percentage of the ample royalties until he reached an agreement with the leader in the 1960s. Barney Bigard, too, sold such tunes as "Mood Indigo"— or portions thereof (the matter is still disputed)—to Ellington or Irving Mills for "twenty-five or fifty dollars," and only gained royalties after legal proceedings. The trombonist Lawrence Brown, therefore, probably spoke for many others when he told Ellington during a heated argument, "I don't consider you a composer. You are a compiler."[15]

Stories regarding Ellington's practices, as well as those of Irving Mills, Clarence Williams, and other promoters, led jazz musicians to become careful and increasingly litigious. In 1938, when Alan Lomax brought Jelly Roll Morton to the Library of Congress to record his oral history, the pianist "began by outlining his plans to sue" MCA and ASCAP for copyright infringement. According to Lomax, Morton's publisher, Lester Melrose, had systematically deprived him of all royalties, and the musician Albert Nicholas has noted that "Morton was heartbroken at the end [of his life, in 1940], because the royalties were tied up." (Morton's sister was able to recover some of the money after his death.) Alberta Hunter received some copyrights and royalties at a late date, which she believed had been impounded by Mills Music, but still felt that she did not receive all of the money she deserved.[16]

The musicians who flourished during and after the Great Depression were often those who seized control of their business affairs away from the promoters. By 1939, Ellington was knowledgeable and self-assured enough to escape his contract with Mills, form a less-exploitative association with the William Morris agency, and begin his own music publishing company. Earl Hines faced many more difficulties in his 1940 attempt to break his ill-designed lifetime contract with Ed Fox. A year of lawsuits and musical dormancy (followed in 1942 by the musicians' union's ban on recording) was suffered by Hines and his musicians before they escaped Fox's control. A few enterprising blacks started their own booking agencies before 1940. One of the most successful was William E. Samuels's Associated Colored Orchestras of Chicago. Samuels enticed clients with whiskey, flattery, and the illusion that his agency was busy enough to take only the best offers, and he came to realize without apparent dismay that "music is a business like everything else."[17] The growth of this business sense, however, was not universal, as it was difficult for musicians of most temperaments and backgrounds to package and market their talents and their products. As Bud Freeman noted, "musicians were never people who could go . . . call up a man who ran a recording company and sell themselves." ("Condon could do it, [Red] McKenzie could do it," Freeman noted, but they were exceptions.)[18]

While the milieux of music publishing, nightclubs, and touring circuits exploited and benefited jazz musicians in ways that performers of earlier generations would have recognized, new and unusual music industries played increasingly important roles in the development of jazz. Phonograph records, radio, and sound motion pictures greatly expanded the national impact of burgeoning jazz styles in New Orleans, Chicago, New York, and other cities, and also captured the music on mechanically reproducible devices that changed the basic nature of music listening in America. Jazz and the new sound media were exact contemporaries, and the first generations of musicians were rarely able to define or advance their craft without being influenced by the powerful properties of these media.

After thirty-five years of methodical development following Edison's creation of the first tin-foil cylinders, the phonograph industry grew at an explosive rate in the years following 1912. Gross receipts from sales of phonographs rose from $27.1 million in 1914 to $158.7 million in 1919, and the Victor Company, the major American producer of "talking machines" and disks, saw its assets rise from $2.7 million in 1902 to $51 million in 1921. In that year Americans purchased more than 100 million records, four times more than in 1914. The rapid rise of the phonograph was also reflected in the accelerating succession of technical gimmicks and improvements offered on new phonographs and the advent of lavish wood-panelled units that appealed to buyers in the growing middle class.[19] Records became an important cultural resource for almost every segment of the population. In a cross section of southern rural black homes in 1939, it was found that 2 percent contained telephones, 13 percent electricity and 17 percent radios, but 28 percent contained phonographs. Records were perhaps black sharecroppers' main contact with the larger world.[20]

Dixieland records, introduced with Victor's Original Dixieland Jazz Band disks of 1917, and race records featuring black jazz performances (beginning in 1920) appeared at the height of the phonograph boom. Records quickly became the chief educational tool for young jazz musicians across the country, as youths in California, Montana, Texas, and Massachusetts alike mimicked and transcribed the new music. They excitingly realized the democratic educational potential of the medium, resembling the ham radio operators and barnstorming pilots of the same period, who used new technology with adolescent glee and experimentation and a disdain for official guidance.[21] Jazz spread and evolved more quickly than any previous new music, as the phonograph stimulated the search for artistic examples and models and fostered autodidacticism among a global village of listeners.[22]

The phonograph helped young musicians to concentrate on the music, for listening to recordings was generally devoid of the extramusical connotations that had become associated with nightclub settings. Bud Freeman had sensed this when he "found that I was learning more about jazz just through listening to records than I was occasioned to learn by going to the clubs, because in the nightclub atmosphere, your attention was not always on the music" but on "a lot of interesting things we had never seen before." When they recorded, the musicians were astounded to hear themselves on disk, disembodied and unadorned. In 1925, Hoagy Carmichael and his Indiana friends made their first recording, and "tears came to our eyes as we listened to it. Tears of affection for each other, tears at the imagined beauty of our playing. Every note an individual thing; a part of the man who played it and that man a friend"—but now every note was apart from the man, and that disembodiment helped to inspire the strong emotion. When Eddie Condon and others heard their first disks in 1928, they knew that their experiences had been translated into oddly satisfying new artifacts. "The nights and years of playing in cellars and saloons and ballrooms, of practicing separately and together, of listening to Louis and Joe Oliver and Jimmy Noone and Leon Rappolo, of losing sleep and breathing bad air and drinking licorice gin, paid off. . . . We had never been an audience for ourselves. . . . At the finish we were all laughing and pounding each other on the back." [23]

This joy was the only substantial payoff recordings gave early jazz players. Record companies kept artist payments as low as possible to maintain their profit margins. Instrumentalists were usually paid flat fees (ranging from $30 to $75) for making both sides of a 78-rpm disk, and they never obtained royalties. Some female vocalists were not paid at all for recording. Promoters like Perry Bradford and such bandleaders as Paul Whiteman, however, made thousands from their exclusive rights to disk royalties. Throughout the interwar era bands needed to tour, appear on radio, and play club engagements to earn money, because (as Charlie Barnet later noted) "records alone wouldn't do it in those days." [24]

The larger reason for this was that the record companies themselves were financially unstable. Smaller companies were often founded by struggling firms in other industries. Gennett Records and Paramount, both important jazz distributors, were owned by the Star Piano Company and the Wisconsin Chair Company, respectively. The early Black Swan recordings were prized by blacks because the company was founded and owned for a time by W. C. Handy, but Paramount purchased Black Swan in 1922 after the company suffered large losses. Columbia Records went into bankruptcy in 1923 when it failed to recover from the sharp recession of 1921, and even the giant Victor Talking Machine Company was sold to financiers in 1926 when its sales began to drop.[25]

This strange decline occurred in large part because *radio* weakened—and perhaps co-opted outright—the phonograph's disseminatory role for music in America. Wireless technology had been strictly controlled by the government during the world war, and regular civilian broadcasting did not begin until station KDKA began transmitting in Pittsburgh in November 1920. The duet of Lois Deppe and Earl Hines, heard on KDKA in 1921, was perhaps the first black musical group ever to perform on a radio station. "The broadcast created a lot of excitement," Deppe recalled, "especially in the colored neighborhood. . . . there was a radio buff on Wylie Avenue who had loudspeakers sticking out his window" for the crowd on the street. Before 1925 most radios did not have speakers, and headphones were used. Young Milt Hinton and his Chicago playmates placed his Atwater Kent headset in his grandmother's cut glass bowl to amplify broadcasts.[26]

In 1922, commercially sponsored broadcasts began in New York, and thereafter, radio's rise was even more meteoric than the phonograph's a decade earlier. In 1925 Americans spent $430 million on radios, and twice that amount three years later. While many early local stations lost money and closed, the formation of networks and radio advertising agencies by 1928 enabled the surviving stations to thrive. When the vaudeville-minstrel program "Amos 'n' Andy" gained an unprecedented national listening audience between 1929 and 1931, it became apparent that radio, unlike records, was a stable and well-funded medium for popular entertainment, especially for music.[27]

At first, however, jazz musicians benefited little from radio. The sweet dance bands dominated programming, and even worse, as Bill Challis noted, with the rise of radio "people were beginning to lose interest in . . . going out to places to dance." As he recognized during a 1927 tour with the Goldkette band, "the business was beginning to get disastrous for dance bands." The gains in radio for musicians, as in recordings, were limited. Hot jazz music was played regularly on some commercial stations (as well as such special frequencies as WEVD, New York's Socialist party mouthpiece), but the more sentimental bands dominated radio into the 1930s. Radio did provide some benefits. It made an important aesthetic contribution: most amplifiers reproduced music far more realistically than 1920s phonograph records (which forced record companies to incorporate radio technology, such as electric microphones, into recording). In addition, musicians were excited by their newfound ability to communicate instantaneously to thousands of listeners. Earl Hines, broadcasting from Chicago's Grand Terrace in 1929, recalled that during the show "people would come up to the mike and say things like, 'Be home very shortly, Mom.' Or, 'We're having a grand time!' Or, 'Hello, honey, how are you?' "[28]

Blacks were rarely employed as actors or writers in radio comedy and drama (although caricatures of blacks by white performers were very common), but they flourished in various kinds of musical programs; radio, like recording, demonstrated that racism could be diminished when the visual stimulus of skin color was concealed. It may have been quite significant, as Milt Hinton has argued, that jazz on radio and records was a purely "auditory art. A guy hears you, he don't see you. It's one of the greatest arts in the world for a black man. . . . because if you can do the work, and qualify, they will hire you." Sam Wooding's band broadcast as early as 1923, and by 1932 such major figures as Ellington, Fats Waller, and Art Tatum had regular series. Nowhere else in jazz was the segregationist ideal of "separate but equal" promoted in a more positive sense than in radio, although the pervasiveness of black stereotypes in nonmusical programs probably undercut the gains of black broadcasting. The ambivalence of blacks toward 1930s radio was expressed very well by Clyde Bernhardt, who said that "I can't help but [re]call how many black people really liked those [racist] programs. And how many black performers got knocked out of work. Didn't seem right because they were damn funny shows."[29]

In the 1930s popular music dominated radio programming. From 1933 to 1939, popular music programs (which, in one researcher's definition, included everything except "classical, semiclassical, religious, hill-billy, and old-time music") accounted for more than 40 percent of the total programming on NBC's Red and Blue networks. The weekday hours after eleven o'clock, as well as Saturday evenings, were dominated by music broadcasting and attracted the most listeners to jazz and other popular music.[30]

It was in radio rather than recording that jazz musicians found their first lucrative jobs in a new communications medium. The Tommy Dorsey band held a fifty-week annual contract with CBS. As the band member Bud Freeman recalled, "it was quite a sum of money, and a few drinking musicians disappeared for a while." A government study showed that during the week beginning October 15, 1939, the three radio networks employed 387 full-time staff musicians, who were compensated an average of $125.90 that week, more than twice the average amount paid to writers, announcers, or "other artists." (705 independent stations employed 1,871 musicians, who were paid far less—a weekly average of $47.53.) Besides playing for musical and dramatic programs, radio musicians also made disk transcriptions for commercials, work which reflected the advertising agencies' domination of radio programming.[31] The radio experience taught musicians that the more commercialized jazz became, the better it paid.

The motion picture industry, even more than recordings and radio, were slow to create work for jazz musicians. Music and sound had become wedded to film only after a long and awkward courtship. Film sound technologies had existed since the 1880s, but the studios had feared that dialogue would drive away immigrant and foreign audiences. Only the advent of electrical recording and improved chemical processes in the mid-1920s made sound films too practical to ignore further. Curiously, the very first sound film, released by in 1927 by Warner Brothers, exploited cultural tensions that were closely related to the jazz experience, telling the story of an immigrant's son who is drawn to American urban life and syncopated music. With such content and with the title *The Jazz Singer,* the film might have caused the Austin High Gang or Artie Shaw to think that it told their own stories, but the Tin Pan Alley songs and the melodramatics removed it far from the reality of twenties white jazz. (Milt Hinton, then a young violinist, was far more enthused by the short sound film appended to *The Jazz Singer,* featuring the eight-year-old violin prodigy Ruggiero Ricci.)[32]

Much experimentation with the recording, and later dubbing, of music onto film took place, which gave some California musicians a variety of roles. Their first roles, in the single-soundtrack era, were clumsy, as technicians found it unusually difficult to mesh sound with familiar shooting procedures. In 1927, when Lawrence Brown played for sound films, "the music was recorded along with the sound and the picture—the camera work—so we had to sit there very quietly. . . . if it was a dance scene on the floor you'd quiet down [the music] so that [it] didn't cover up the voices of the actors." In any event, the studios, awash in profits like no other American industry, paid players (at least the whites) a lucrative ten dollars an hour for such work.[33]

Sound films had a far more deleterious effect, however, on the careers of thousands of moviehouse instrumentalists across the nation. In 1925 the vitaphone, a device that synchronized recorded music with action on a film reel, was first used in theaters. Various booking companies had provided musicians to many theaters for silent film accompaniment and intermission programs, but after 1927 they began to release musicians and to seek profits in the dis-

tribution of newsreels and cartoons.[34] More than any other incident
of technological obsolescence of the 1920s, the sudden unemployment of theater players foreshadowed the great difficulties that
musicians would face in the coming decade of economic depression.

The new technologies and industries affecting music were met
by a powerful countervailing force—the national musicians' union,
the American Federation of Musicians. The AFM responded to
the widespread exploitation of musicians by turning the traditionally disorganized profession into one of America's most solid and
militant labor forces. The union had been chartered in 1896 by
the American Federation of Labor, and it succeeded where earlier
organizations had failed by explicitly defining musicians as neither
artists nor professionals, but as *workers*. The AFM viewed urban
musical employers as capitalists who were prone to exploit their
skilled workforces, and it introduced collective bargaining, strikes,
closed shops, and unfair employers' lists to the economic life of
opera companies, vaudeville houses, cinemas, and hotel pavilions.[35]

Music had long been the most labor-intensive of fields, and
the AFM devoted much of its energy to managing its vast membership, which rose from 83,992 in 1917 to an interwar high of
146,421 (including 15,500 in New York City alone) in 1928. Membership dues were set at $50 a year for most locals by 1920, and in
return the union ensured that local members would receive little
competition from musicians from other towns. Musicians visiting
a city on tour had to apply for "transfers" from that city's local,
and those who moved permanently to a new locale were barred
from musical employment for six months, until their membership
in the new local was finalized. (Chicago's local also required that
musicians were to wait ninety days *after* joining before they began
full-time work.) The locals also published lists of nonunion musicians' names for employers and requested that these individuals
not be hired; in 1928, Chicagoans Eddie Condon and Joe Sullivan
were stigmatized in this way.[36]

In the 1920s, the union focused on confronting the rapid
growth of mechanically reproduced music. Local 10, the whites-
only Chicago Federation of Musicians, pioneered active opposition
to the new technology. The CFM gained its rebellious character
after a bitter and failed strike against theater owners in 1920–21,
which led to new leadership in an election marked by violence and
fraud. Throughout the 1920s, Local 10 was in effect a racket, working in tandem with the Capone nightclubs and enforcers. As the
historian Donald Spivey wrote, "if a [Chicago] club employer re-

fused to hire only union musicians, he might find his establishment ablaze or his kneecaps broken."[37]

The CFM was also able to secure the highest wage scales of any AFM local in the nation. James C. Petrillo, the president of Local 10 from 1922 to 1940 and of the AFM from 1940 to 1958, believed that the diminishing market for theater and dance musicians threatened the musicians' profession with extinction, and he challenged promoters and industries through legal and extralegal channels. In the twenties, Clarence Darrow was Local 10's effective senior counsel. Petrillo and the national union assaulted film sound with print campaigns in union and mainstream newspapers, but the battles were lost. In 1928, for example, a Chicago court rejected the CFM's demand that a minimum of four musicians be employed in every theater wired for sound. The CFM was more effective when it ordered members to shun phonograph recording and radio appearances—part of a strategy to win compensation for musicians placed out of work by vitaphones, radio dance programs, and disk jockeys. Petrillo was also successful in his attack on remote control performances, in which a ballroom band's music was transmitted by radio to a second location in the late 1920s; MCA and other promoters agreed to hire a new group of radio musicians every time they relayed a band's music to secondary audiences. Also, the AFM strongly advocated royalty systems, payable to musicians, for records and radio transcriptions.[38]

Jazz musicians had an unusual relationship with the union. Considering the character of many promoters, few instrumentalists were more in need of the AFM's coercive power. Nevertheless, the regimentation and restrictions that the union demanded of its members—and the racial segregation it enforced in most cities—alienated jazz musicians somewhat from the AFM's cause.

Union musicians had to contend with the mob, which provided racket enforcement on behalf of some AFM locals. Pops Foster found in 1920s New York that gangsters "pretty much told you where you were gonna work. The union didn't say nothin'." After the Chicago café in which Joe Oliver's band worked was bombed in 1924, Local 10, "tied into that gangster bunch," kept the band from seeking jobs in similar clubs. Band member Barney Bigard recalled that "if we tried to take a job in a white place then Petrillo would send the goons in. These characters would tell the owner, 'We're going to bomb you all out.' And they did it too." Oliver, Bigard noted, "was getting disgusted," and took the band on tour;

the man who had left New Orleans when club work became too violent now confronted similar conditions in the North. Scoville Browne also believed that Petrillo had contracted with Capone, and claimed pointedly that the relationship between Local 10 and the black Local 208 "was like father and son—or, I should say, master and slave."[39]

Browne's analysis was not uncommon. Like blacks in other occupations at the time, black musicians associated organized labor with exclusion, segregation, and inferior employment opportunities. Ralph Brown believed that the union aggravated race relations among musicians: whites and blacks were "not too close then. . . . I think the unions stirred up some of it." Job segregation in Chicago kept black players from working in "any kind of choice club, . . . hotels and no radio stations or nothing like that. And no regular bigtime jobs," as Red Saunders noted. Saunders disliked the accommodationist policies of Local 208's longtime president, Harry Gray. "Petrillo and Gray were holding hands. . . . They had an agreement, definitely so." In 1928, Petrillo apparently made an effort to merge Local 208 with Local 10, which was rejected by the black leaders. Black musicians disagree about whether or not the rejection came because 208 did not want to relinquish their property holdings or the ample fees they collected from visiting black bands. Blacks were second-class citizens in the national union as well. Attending AFM conventions from 1938 to 1940 as a Local 208 official, William E. Samuels found it "disgusting" that blacks were not allowed to pick up their credentials at the host local and were not invited to convention dances and functions. Petrillo's cousin did allow a black group to alternate with his band in a Chicago club, but union leaders generally did little to alleviate the discriminatory climate.[40]

Jazz musicians were not usually dedicated unionists. Some avoided the unionized job market, especially in the less-reputable sections of cities, and thus escaped affiliation and the AFM's control. The clarinetist Darnell Howard was expelled from 208 when the school board discovered that he was still in his early teens, but that did not stop him from working. Red Saunders joined 208 in 1933, but "I didn't belong when we were hustling and things like that. Wasn't no cause [to join 208 then], you know." Scoville Browne also recalled "quite a bit of" nonunion music jobbing among South Side musicians. In the downtown area, where whites predominantly worked, Art Hodes found "quite a few" nonunion jobs, although "the best jobs were unionized." In 1929 New York, sixteen-year-old Charlie Barnet had no difficulty finding nonunion work for his first band. "The union was terribly weak at that time," Barnet recalled, and "there wasn't anybody in town that was getting paid union scale, except maybe some studio musicians."[41]

Jazz musicians later tended to characterize the AFM as a force that impeded their working freedom. Wingy Manone was banned from playing in an Oklahoma City restaurant when the union local discovered that he had not deposited his AFM card and applied for a transfer. Earl Hines, the greatest black musician (after Oliver and Armstrong) to migrate to Chicago, was given "the biggest trouble" by Local 208 "because they didn't want any strangers or outsiders there." Cootie Williams and Milt Hinton faced similar difficulties when they came to New York in the late twenties and early thirties. In March 1932 the clarinetist Frank Teschemacher was killed near Chicago when a car driven by Bill Davison collided with a tree. Petrillo, anxious to avoid publicity, banned Davison (who had not been charged by the police) from Local 10 on a contract technicality. He was eventually reinstated, but Petrillo's action (which might have reflected his low opinion of jazz musicians) gave Davison a lasting and bitter memory.[42]

In one respect the temperament of the union coincided with those of most jazz players. The union, like the jam session, served as a locus for almost exclusively male friendship and fraternity, a protection against the impersonal dangers of the city. The Arkansas blues singer Howlin' Wolf (Chester Burnett) came to Chicago in the late 1930s, and the 208 official Bill Samuels offered him guidance. "I said, 'Well, Mr. Wolf, you got to have confidence in somebody. . . . You joined this union for protection and that's what we want to do.'" The black local, thus, served as an aid organization for southern migrants in the 1930s. Union halls were popular meeting places for musicians and were often used for hiring and rehearsing. For young players like Milt Hinton, the union rehearsal room "is where we'd get known."[43]

In the final analysis, however, the union's constant emphasis on the labor-management struggle disenchanted many jazz players. The AFM's historian Robert Leiter, for example, noted in 1953 that "the union has been somewhat fearful that the stimulation of musical interest among public school students unduly increases the number of potential musicians. Even today the policy of the organization on this matter is uncertain." It was unlikely that black and white musicians, whose thirst for music education in and out of the classroom stimulated their creation of jazz, would ever have had a basic philosophical affinity for such an organization.[44]

Jazz musicians confronted technological change with more equanimity than the union. Just as the phonograph for them had been a central learning tool and source of information, rather than a component of the machine age's assault on tradition, the recording and radio studios were the incubators of their most widely distributed musical achievements.

At first, technical limitations were a major frustration to musicians, and the main hindrance to effective recording. Before electrical recording—which translated musical sound waves into electrical energy, which was then molded onto grooved disk surfaces—became standard by the end of the twenties, the far less flattering acoustic process was used. As Bill Davison described recording for Gennett with this process, "there was no electric[ity] and you played through tinhorns into long pieces of hose going directly into this huge thing with a needle," which engraved the sonic impulses onto a wax disk "two feet across" and "an inch-and-a-half to two inches thick." If the band made a mistake, the technicians brought a funnel-shaped object fitted with gas jets down onto the disk "and they would burn a new soft surface on that." As many recordings made in this manner by black and white bands indicate, few such corrections were possible in one session, and disks featuring obviously botched performances were often released.[45] Even faultless performances were distorted by the crude sound horns, which turned very high and low tones into noise. Loud bass sounds (from drums, pianos, or trombones) jolted the needle off of the wax, so the clarinetist Dink Johnson's tapping feet had to be muzzled by a mattress on the floor, and bass drums were swathed in overcoats or replaced by suitcases. In general, as David Baker has argued, the use of drums was so restricted in 1920s recordings that "the drum set as we know it really came into full flowering much later than it might have."[46]

Later innovations, though, allowed jazz listeners to appreciate the capabilities of the best players more fully and to spread their pioneering work more quickly. The new electrical process, which used microphones in the place of horns and acetate instead of wax masters, made the band's sound "fuller" and enabled the listener to "hear the guts of the band," as Bill Challis noted. Whereas it was thought that the mechanical process could not capture more than two saxophones or trombones, Challis, Ellington, and others expanded their arrangements to include three or more of these instruments. Microphone amplification (which, like electrical recording, was a product of radio technology) greatly enhanced bands' presence in noise-filled halls, and came into widespread use in the mid-1930s. Eddie Durham began electrifying his guitar in 1938, and predicted accurately then (he claimed later) that the dominating rhythmic pulse of electric guitars and basses would radically alter black popular music.[47]

The major difficulty jazz musicians incurred stemmed from the radio and recording industries' sole interest in producing commercially marketable commodities. Although their differences with the AFM were great, musicians sensed with the union that the mechanization of music removed it from the creators' control and placed it into the hands of electric-age promoters. In the late thirties radio stations introduced the disk-jockey format, in which announcers supplied with records (now sounding as realistic as live radio) took the place of studio bands. The arranger Eddie Sauter learned that "disk jockeys wouldn't play [a record] unless it was two [minutes] fifty [seconds]" in length; "they wanted it less than three minutes or else it interfered with commercials." Manufacturers of another innovation, the jukebox, made a similar request of recording bands. These machines flooded the nation with reproduced music; as Red Saunders observed, "the disk jockey and the record industry has almost ruined the musician. They took their own product and then just beat them across the head with it."[48]

Similarly, the players' talents were seen by industries as a raw material, an abstract production resource that they alienated from the musicians. The radio network jobs were the best paying in the jazz world, but they were few in number and fell often to those who were the most willing to let producers dictate their musical expression. In the late thirties Artie Shaw perceived a "new type of political musician," with few talents and many business connections, who most often gained studio employment. Jimmy Maxwell, a CBS musician, had a clear view of the studio players' mentality, noting that they always had to "act like you enjoy [playing for radio] because if you make waves, they're not going to hire you; . . . you have to learn to be patient," and "you have to put up with what you think is an injustice."[49]

By contrast, since the 1920s many jazz musicians had mocked and resisted mechanization. Eddie Condon, Bud Freeman, and Dave Tough, playing in a Chicago film theater in 1927, "were supposed to watch the newsreel and play appropriate accompaniment

[but] we seldom did. One night in the middle of *Clarinet Marma-lade* I looked up and saw a French general placing a wreath on the tomb of the Unknown Soldier." Max Kaminsky, playing with a Massachusetts band, also subverted the regimentation of film playing, as "it became a regular gag with the band to tear into 'Hold That Tiger' whenever a heart-rending scene was in progress." In the late thirties, Art Hodes was both amused and angered by the procedures of the recording studio, run by "five 'experts,'" in which "the rhythm section is never seated in a way to help the band, but in the best possible manner to help the engineer." [50]

Radio received a similar rebuke from Hodes. During World War Two, the pianist was hired to play for a patriotic radio drama. "But to me [the drama] wasn't the play. The play was going on all around us—we were the play, every one assembled here on a cold day, drawn by one thing—money."

> The script unfolded, and we got down to a part where it said, "When a fellow has a terrific idea he'll find money," and there a little trouble developed. The orchestra leader had to dig up music that was appropriate "money-finding music," and the first five items he displayed didn't hit right. The producer got short of temper, the band leader got hot under the collar, the cast started looking at the leader. . . . The producer started losing patience. . . . The leader would holler "Will you wait just a minute while we go over this," or else "just listen to this," and the pressure on him grew.

After the session was over, the producer "went up to the orchestra leader and hugged him," even though "a half hour before they were hating each other."

For Hodes, the radio session was public theater, a search for profit masquerading as a communal artistic enterprise. The pianist fled the studio for a bar, "just to get drunk, and not to think about the play. . . . this play we live, these hours we waste, this silliness we engage in." [51] Commodification and technology had thrust life-affirming music into "silly" and inauthentic social and economic relations. The blood and life of jazz, he and so many other musicians implied, could not be captured in commercial situations, or on records or on radio. The commercial and technological revolutions of the 1920s and 1930s, therefore, while they often ensured the survival of some players and helped to spread the music, were not necessarily conducive to the satisfying production of good jazz by musicians.

— 9

"Wacky State of Affairs"
The Depression, Swing Era, and Revolt

The force with which records and radio struck jazz in the 1920s was mild compared to the wild shifts of fortune that musicians faced in the following decade. Having cast their lot with urban life and commercial musical careers, jazz players in the thirties confronted both the worst and the best situations the decade could have offered them—an unprecedented economic depression, followed by the greatest period of acclaim and success jazz would ever receive.

Any musical culture is fragile and deeply dependent upon a structure of support and social contexts in which musicians can work. In Europe, the Napoleonic wars virtually eliminated the continental network of aristocratic patronage of music,[1] and the First World War killed composers' thriving relations with opera houses and orchestras. In the United States, the Great Depression threatened to eradicate the economic and social supports that jazz enjoyed in the twenties. Some jazz musicians, of course, especially blacks, had known nothing but economic depression for years, and had spent the 1920s in impoverished rural and urban environments. Bill Coleman's band had nearly starved during a hiatus in New York in 1929, as had Earl Hines's in San Francisco, and Eddie Durham had earned only twenty dollars a week as a carnival musician in Texas before the Depression.[2] Still, the twenties had generally been a time of prosperity and florid expectations for jazz, fueled by the rapid rise in the public's discretionary spending money.

After 1929 this portion of the nation's wealth nearly vanished; the shrinkage, combined with the growth of mass communications technology, led to unprecedented economic hardship for all American musicians. The membership of the AFM declined from 146,326 in 1928 to 101,111 in 1934, and more than 12,500 of the remaining members received relief employment from the Works Progress Administration. Local 208 in the South Side "was just getting by," William Samuels recalled. The local's savings were lost in 1930 with the collapse of Jesse Binga's bank (founded by the black entrepreneur in 1908 and given a state charter in 1920). Local 208 members "couldn't pay their dues," Samuels noted, so the union held Thursday night dances. "The fellows who would work up there they would make three or four dollars and that would help them pay their dues because we would put 'em up there and deduct the dues and give 'em the balance." In addition, the membership fee was reduced from fifty to twenty-five dollars. Samuels himself made only eight dollars as a bandleader during the month of June 1931 and was forced to move his family into less-expensive housing.[3]

As a subclass of the occupation, jazz musicians suffered further when Prohibition was repealed in 1933 and their music was no longer needed to attract customers into speakeasies and bootleggers' nightclubs. When the liquor racket lost its reason for being, it took such gangland figures as Joe Glaser a few years to adapt to the "legitimate" world of music management. During these difficult times musicians could not look to recording for any kind of income opportunities. After 1930, as wary Americans virtually abandoned their demand for durable items, the recording and phonograph industries were crippled with unique severity. Record sales fell from 104 million in 1927 to a mere six million in 1932, every small company closed, and as Roland Gelatt has written, "by January 1933 the record business in America was practically extinct."[4] In addition, jobs in radio at that time paid poorly; for example, the Ellington band was not paid at all for its broadcasting from Los Angeles' Cotton Club in 1932. From 1926 to 1930 union scale had been set at weekly minimums ranging from thirty to seventy-five dollars, and the best players often earned comfortable salaries exceeding one hundred dollars a week. After 1931 New York and Los Angeles musicians only infrequently worked more than three nights per week, and perhaps earned ten dollars a night in wages and tips. As late as 1935 the AFM's level-C pay scale, in effect in Harlem, was set at only thirty-five dollars a week for band members and twice that for leaders.[5]

In general, as the jazz historian William Russell has noted regarding New Orleans, union membership "wasn't very important in the middle of the Depression." The clarinetist Johnny Dodds "might have belonged to the union because he made some records in 1938, but all the time Russell knew him in [Chicago] he wasn't playing union jobs. During the depression, they would play for anything they could get, even a bag of food." While Milt Hinton's family endured the Depression in Chicago without having to obtain relief, Hinton himself fell into a desperate economic situation when he first traveled to New York in 1933. For months he could not find substantial work, but he did not contact his mother for help. "She would have sent the money, but then she would discourage me about traveling again, going out on the road with bands and experimenting like that. . . . So I didn't call. I just toughed it out, man."[6]

For white musicians from middle-class backgrounds, the Depression was the greatest test of their dedication to jazz careers. In the twenties their embrace of jazz had been facilitated, if not stimulated, by their families' comfortable economic status. It had allowed them to experiment and freed them from the need to enlist in the commercial ranks. When they did join those ranks, as we have seen, musicians spent and gambled away money carelessly and amply. Wild Bill Davison held a typical attitude. He quit the Benny Meroff band in 1931, a "crazy" move at that time, but "with all the money I made, I didn't save any—I always figured—tomorrow is another day." The succeeding months, though, were very difficult. "I even jobbed around in places where the boss would come at the end of the night and say, 'I'm sorry fellows, we didn't make enough to pay you. . . . it was just that tough."[7]

For many musicians, the winter of 1934 was the lowest point in their economic existences. "Prices went down," Eddie Condon noted, "musicians were out of work, and the weather turned cold." Condon and Max Kaminsky, then in New York, were locked out of their hotel room for failing to pay the bill and had to walk through subzero weather to a friend's apartment. In the early thirties, Condon later asserted, "we bled to death; . . . we gnawed at each other's wrists." Kaminsky got a good job the next year and conducted his "own private bread line outside of Delmonico's every night that spring of 1934. I'd be at the side door with a pocketful of fifty-cent pieces for the out-of-work musicians waiting in the cold," including Condon, Bud Freeman, and Pee Wee Russell. Illness and misfortune disoriented their lives: Condon nearly died of a ruptured pancreas, Davison was stigmatized for his alleged role in Frank Teschemacher's death, and Artie Shaw was indicted for vehicular manslaughter after hitting and killing a pedestrian. In their future recollections, the early thirties would be portrayed as a time of troubles of mythic proportions.[8]

Some musicians had to find new and unusual ways to support themselves. In the mid-1930s, Sidney Bechet and the trumpeter Tommy Ladnier ran a dry-cleaning shop in Harlem, one of the few nonmusical ventures entered into by leading players at that time. The trumpeters George Mitchell and William Samuels, the arranger Zilner Randolph, and others joined the WPA's musical organizations. In Chicago Samuels earned ninety-four dollars a month in a forty-piece, all-black WPA orchestra at a time when he paid thirty-five dollars monthly in rent and supported a wife and three children. Samuels also "really got deeply involved with the union in the '30s to survive the Depression," and eventually spent "half of the time with the union, and the other half playing music." The Federal Music Project of the WPA established four music schools in Manhattan and three in Harlem, and hired more than one hundred musicians as part-time instructors. In some instances musicians were able to obtain good jobs; for example, the expiring Capone nightclub chain in Chicago lingered into the 1930s, and in 1931 Milt Hinton held onto a sixty-dollar weekly job in a speakeasy.[9]

The most lucrative alternative facing the impoverished musician in the thirties—entering the commercial dance-band market— was also for some the most artistically problematic. To commercialize, jazz musicians had to travel to New York City, where most of the depression-ravaged, streamlined popular music industry was located. Very few accomplished jazz players remained in Chicago, New Orleans, and other cities during the Depression, and those in New York attempted to sign on with dance bands, radio studios, Broadway pit orchestras, and even the Muzak Corporation and other producers of "musical environments." In 1934 nearly one-fifth of all AFM members belonged to New York's Local 802.[10]

In 1938, Art Hodes, the last major white Chicago player to come to Manhattan in search for work, found it a locus of merciless competition. "I wanted to play—and there was no place to play at. . . . In New York it was all business. If you went somewhere and waited around awhile, you might get asked to play. Then again you might not, and I just had to play." When Clyde Bernhardt arrived from Harrisburg, his uncle warned him that "they only hire the top professionals in this town" and that he was "nothin' but a little old chickenshit, country horn blower with a big head." New York musicians held the same opinion of Bernhardt, insulting him and his technique for days before he earned their respect. This initiation ritual seems to have been especially intense in New York, as the drummer Lee Young and other musicians also found.[11]

From the earliest years jazz musicians characterized New York City as a hostile inferno through which they had to pass, the place where their music was commodified or repudiated. In 1915, when Tom Brown's band made an unprofitable visit, the clarinetist Larry Shields developed a powerful dislike for the city. In the 1950s, his bandmate Eddie Edwards interpreted Shields' solo on their "St. Louis Blues" disk as

> a ribald gross denial. Larry hated New York City, or rather . . . his love for Chicago was so great there appeared a dislike by comparison. This annoyance is carried on to the fourth measure, is followed by a wavering of indecision and inertia, helpless in its efforts to rise above it. On into the blue notes, characteristic of the . . . moods, lights, colors, and shadows of his urban dislikes and indecisions. Noises at times, exuberant and pathetic, and lonely. Chaos is all about. It is dismal and gruesome. This is the first strain of twelve measures. The second chorus of [the] strain follows with screaming hate.

Either Shields or Edwards (or most likely both) were deeply disturbed by the scale, the commercial attitude, and the "indecisions" that in their opinion characterized New York.[12]

Later musicians echoed Edwards. Earl Hines found Manhattan to be "a rat race," where "anybody who didn't live there was considered a damn fool. I used to hate it when I first went there, and I still do." William Samuels "can't stand" the city, Milt Hinton thought it "cold," and Lawrence Brown found that the "homey" Los Angeles area "had a complete[ly] different atmosphere than the eastern part" of the nation. Jack Teagarden expressed his sentiments in a 1928 recording, "Makin' Friends," when he sang, "I'd rather drink muddy water, Lord, sleep in a hollow log / Than to be up here in New York treated like a dirty dog."[13]

Art Hodes wrote that "it was New York that taught me that the customer is always right and you have to please the people, but darn it, that's one lesson I haven't learned well." Some black musicians, who may have found a greater variety of benefits in the commercial activity and sheer density of Manhattan, did not demonize New York so intensely in the 1930s. Scoville Browne of Chicago, foreshadowing Ralph Ellison's antihero, "saw New York as being better. . . . I guess it's because you could hide more in New

York. . . . a person can lose his identity in New York," especially a black person, in a society where whites "don't like to be seen talking to too many black people." [14]

Perhaps as a result of such a willingness to find strength in numbers (at the risk of invisibility), black musicians were not inclined to criticize the market-oriented nature of commercial music. Duke Ellington let his manager, Irving Mills, add lyrics to his pieces, and he had his band play popular radio ballads. The numbers prostituted the group's talents, but were essential to its commercial success. By 1938, band members were making over one hundred dollars a week, and Barney Bigard recalled that "we worked clean through the Depression without even knowing there was one. I guess we were one of the best-paid, best-known bands in the U.S.A." In 1937 Cab Calloway's band members made the same weekly salary.[15] The fraternal and communal nature of large bands had appealed to black musicians since the first years of the jazz era, and in the early thirties these groups were not reluctant to offer a commercial product that might help to sustain them.

The same cannot be said for some of the white hot musicians who emulated the music of Ellington, Bigard, and Calloway. A majority of the first generation of white jazz musicians began to participate in mass market-oriented, commercialized bands, radio programs, and recordings in the 1930s as job options became limited. As Art Hodes (a strong nonconformist) pointed out, "after the crash of '29 it was just too much to try living on the remains. So most of us started looking for better pickings." Starvation, while rarely encountered in reality by white musicians, was often mentioned as a threat that justified their choice of the commercial path. Referring to Hoagy Carmichael, who left Indiana (and jazz) for Hollywood in the thirties, Bill Challis argued that "our business, the way it is, you can't blame a guy for getting commercial. He's going to starve if he doesn't get commercial somehow or other." Wingy Manone, who came to Los Angeles to work in "the big stuff, meaning studios and radio," believed that "the guys who have been havin' it, have got it, and the others have to go out of town and starve. A lot of 'em prefer to starve." Like other musicians, Manone had escaped poverty and felt free to denigrate those who did not embrace commercialism as their professional savior. As early as the twenties, in fact, Manone had felt that "if you weren't in New York, you were nowhere." Music, cut off from its cultural and regional moorings, thus degenerated into a tool for accumulating wealth.[16]

The process of "becoming commercial," like the search for a

steady income during the Depression, was not always this atavistic. Such a devotee of pure jazz music as John Hammond, who promoted Count Basie's band in the late 1930s because it was a fresh, rhythmically exciting group, still thought it necessary to counsel Basie on "refining" the least urbane musical qualities of his band, "the places where people could jump on it" (as Hammond's contemporary Helen Oakley Dance recalled). Like Manone, Hammond realized that commercial success would come to those musicians who presented a particular kind of showmanship that would appeal to the largest audience. Earl Hines learned to become a master of ceremonies in the thirties, studying "stage deportment, and I paid a lot of attention to vocalizing" and to maintaining a big grin onstage. "But one day, up at the Apollo Theatre, I smiled so much that when I got offstage I couldn't get a smile off my face. . . . It was as though my muscles froze. . . . I was really giving them the ivory!" [17]

The trend toward marketing in 1930s jazz held subtle dangers for musicians, as Artie Shaw realized during his commercial success in the late 1930s. The public, he came to believe, desired "engine-turned, slick, flawless, shiny surface perfection" in its music. "We are on the whole a nation of craftsmen, artisans, engineers, rather than artists," who value "the high degree of technical skill and craftsmanship involved in the making of even the worst piece of junk." Since "the mass American public is by and large musically illiterate," "there is always this engrossment with surface detail rather than intrinsic merit." [18] These astute but cynical observations—common among intellectuals in the 1950s, when Shaw wrote—reflect not only musicians' adaptation to commercial techniques of presenting their music, but also how they might now have perceived their audience as a faceless public with which they shared no folk identity. This perception, as Louis H. Levy has shown, was the result of a process by which jazz became "formalized," as musicians were placed on stages apart from the social milieu of audiences. [19]

Musicians found it progressively more difficult to avoid the trend toward mass marketing, as only large and nationally oriented companies survived the turmoil of the Depression. By 1938 the two largest record companies, Victor and Columbia, were subsumed by the owners of the two largest radio networks, RCA and CBS, which had a broad, unprecedented role in deciding what music was heard by or withheld from the public. In 1940, due to a contract dispute, they banned songs licensed by ASCAP and thus severely limited the radio opportunities of most jazz bands. In addition, during the thirties the musicians' intrusive guardian, the American Federation of Musicians, also waged national battles that undermined jazz's exposure and profitability. In 1942, James C. Petrillo brought his antimechanization campaign to a climax when he ordered all AFM members to refrain permanently from recording, a ban the union enforced for two years. Under such conditions, the fortunes of individual jazz players and bands might shift almost uncontrollably.[20]

In general, though, the uneasy mating of jazz and the mass market led to the unexpected and explosive "Big Band Era" of 1935–47. In early 1935, to the surprise of musicians and promoters, young audiences began to attend and cheer concerts by the Benny Goodman, Tommy Dorsey, Bob Crosby, and other large bands, and buy their records and listen to their radio programs, in rapidly growing numbers. Black bands and audiences were not immune to the growth of what was now being marketed as swing music. As the bassist Quinn Wilson recalled, "we changed to swing" in 1935, "started playing Benny Goodman type of music. . . . it was a more subdued type of jazz. . . . Instead of playing oom-pah, oom-pah, I just made it flow from one note to another." In Benny Carter's view, New York had for a decade been the "melting pot" of jazz, and the highly homogenized swing music of the Goodman band may have been the end result. The record and touring industries revived, and the profits were extraordinary. In 1939, after trying a number of different musical approaches, Artie Shaw became a major swing bandleader and earned a personal net income of twenty thousand dollars for every week of touring.[21]

The best jazz musicians—including blacks, whose opportunities increased more modestly—now faced a clear choice between joining the commercial juggernaut or maintaining or creating an alternative. Many of them decided to avoid the big bands and to pursue less-lucrative careers, and their reasons for doing this were revealing. Most of these individuals did not like the heavily arranged and massed sound of the big bands. Throughout the thirties, Jimmy Dorsey implored Bill Davison to join his band, but the trumpeter "couldn't see myself getting buried in a . . . brass section." Art Hodes was "cured" of his desire to play in big bands when one leader added violins to Hodes's group and had it play waltzes. "After I got through expressing my views on leaders in general, and on the violin as an instrument in a dance band, especially a hot band, there was nothing left for me to do but leave." Hodes later did temporary work with a vaudeville band led by Eddie Condon, which mechanically reprised its performances twenty-nine times each week.[22]

In general, the big bands were expected to duplicate their commercial hits with the frequency and precision of a phonograph record; individual soloists, as well as bands, earned livings by playing the same "spontaneous improvisations" countless times. In 1939, after making his famed recording of "Body and Soul," the saxophonist Coleman Hawkins would never be able to escape listeners who asked him to play exact renditions of that solo.[23]

The big bands usually stifled solo and collective improvisation, dissatisfying those musicians who cherished the spontaneity and diversity of jam sessions. Bud Freeman, who had pursued jazz in the 1920s because it presented "an escape" from social restrictions, found that playing in the Goodman and Tommy Dorsey bands— which gave as many as nine performances a day—was a new, musical restriction he had to flee. "You were, in a sense, almost in jail, and the music—if I had not been a player of improvised jazz, I couldn't take it. I loathe the idea of having to do what somebody wants me to do." Milt Hinton, who played with the Cab Calloway band at the new Cotton Club in downtown Manhattan in 1937, perceived harmful psychosocial consequences of a long, repetitious residence. While it was pleasant at first to "be with your family" since "the guys had been on the road, . . . you get sick of that show, man. The same crap every night. . . . After six months it gets kind of dull to you, and maybe you're getting into some altercations with your old lady in town, and you get restless. . . . everybody's anxious to go now."[24]

Despite the mobility, touring also exacted a psychological toll. Speaking of the 1930s, Barney Bigard of the Ellington band said that "of all my years these were the most confusing years. Your head stays in a permanent muddle because of the traveling. . . . The world was now made up of theaters, trains, boats, hotel rooms, movie lots, radio stations, band buses which all come under the all encompassing heading 'The rigors of the never ending road.'" Success in the big band field, as Artie Shaw has argued eloquently, could lead to serious psychological difficulty and confusion. As he earned over $1 million in 1939 and fought off mobs "of milling youngsters who wanted nothing more than to pull out my hair for a souvenir," Shaw came to feel that "any halfway sane person could [not] adjust to any such wacky state of affairs as that." In 1941, Shaw abandoned his band and went to Mexico on a honeymoon—

a pretext for escaping the pressures of commercial success that he would use again many times.[25]

The men who had fewer psychological difficulties leading commercially successful big bands gained a special notoriety among independent jazz players. In the 1920s, such white musicians as Mezz Mezzrow had derided such authoritarian figures as the symphony conductor, "posed up front with his stick, as ungraceful and mechanical as an epileptic metronome," and viewed the large orchestra as "a musical battalion hypnotized by a dictator's baton." The Chicagoans believed that while any good large band needed a guiding spirit—such as a Duke Ellington—the commercial big bandleader was an martinet who suppressed his players' individual gifts to achieve success, and benefited from a cult of personality once that success had been attained.[26]

Some twenties bandleaders, such as Red Nichols, were known more for their business acumen than their musicianship, and in the next decade, many more ambitious players virtually remade themselves into authoritarian commercial entrepreneurs. The trombonist Glenn Miller, his early bandmate Bud Freeman recalled, "was a big drinker in those days . . . for many years," but when "Miller got his own band, he completely stopped drinking and became quite the disciplinarian and . . . a tremendous success." Jimmy McPartland recalled that Miller was "a task master" and "a very competitive guy" who explicitly sought a smooth, simplified jazz sound for his band. He turned down Bill Challis's arrangements because of what he considered their "Bix Beiderbecke" sound, saying that "kids never even heard of him. They don't know anything about Bix." Miller pared down the black arranger Joe Garland's "In the Mood" and made it his band's most successful tune. (Garland's initial version had been an ornate and serious work. Clyde Bernhardt recalled that "that piece was heavy music—had four big manuscript pages just for the trombone parts. We called it his Black Symphony.")[27]

The big-band leaders were required by commercial demands to be disciplinarians. Benny Goodman and Tommy Dorsey, Freeman argued, "were hard men. They had to be." Freeman himself tried to lead a band, but found that "I could not be custodian over other people's lives. . . . I had all I could do to handle myself." Dorsey ruled his men with an explosive temper. Freeman, only briefly in his band, would "often wonder about the guys who had to just sit back and play and take Tommy's insults and all that." Benny Goodman, a greater musician and more complex man, mixed toughness with many other qualities and goals. Freeman noted that he "never saw a man work as hard as he did" to maintain both a band and his own superior clarinet playing. Goodman "knew what he was doing and he knew what he wanted and he was like a machine." Goodman's remoteness, egotism, and sternness were famous among jazz musicians, but they were leavened at times with kindnesses, humor, and a social conscience. Perhaps, as Freeman suggests, no one else strove as mightily as Goodman to maintain his musical and personal integrity while also working to conquer the commercial world. The respect Goodman earned from white and black, commercial and marginal, musicians indicates that he perhaps did manage to reconcile the contradictions of his career.[28]

Goodman characteristically worked to preserve hot jazz by forming small improvisatory groups that performed and recorded along with the big band. Other bandleaders followed Goodman's lead and formed such combos as Artie Shaw's Gramercy Five, Woody Herman's Woodchoppers, Bob Crosby's Bobcats, Tommy Dorsey's Clambake Seven, and Duke Ellington's various small groups. Players who had gained anonymity in big-band sections thus were not always compelled to abandon their mastery of and dedication to improvisation, blues harmonies, working in small groups, and sophisticated syncopation.[29]

This development was particularly significant because it indicated how the success of big bands produced an environment which nurtured and financed their antithesis. In the late 1930s, some white veterans of twenties hot jazz initiated a quasi-commercial movement to preserve small-group improvisation, which strove to remain separate from the big-band milieu. Spontaneous performances by small groups, or jam sessions, were supported financially by small groups of record collectors and musicians.

In New York, these individuals self-consciously sought to recapture the nightclub setting of the early twenties, in which musicians mingled and played together with minimal intrusion from profit-minded promoters, programmed audiences, and technological media. With the help of Columbia University students, the record store owner Milt Gabler, and a group of club owners, the Chicagoans and others virtually recreated their adolescence. Eddie Condon, whom Max Kaminsky described as "a perennial youth of the twenties," used publicists' connections in his wife's family to develop regular concerts and jam sessions at a few clubs on New

York's 52nd and 56th Streets, and eventually opened a club himself in the 1940s. Gabler's Commodore Records label captured these musicians on disk; *Life* magazine ran an approving pictorial article in 1938; hot clubs formed across the country; and the twenties jazz revival began.[30]

The movement was an interesting mixture of new publicity techniques, an authentic folk-musical heritage (black musicians were usually welcomed), and the self-conscious portrayal of jazz as an art form. In the 1930s Milt Gabler (as quoted by Condon) expressed a dual (and contradictory) desire both to popularize hot jazz and to maintain its artistic elitism. "It's recognized now. . . . It's now just a matter of spreading it to a larger number of people. Over here we never think anything is recognized until the entire population takes it up; then we get tired of it and call it common and look for something else. You can't do that with an art; in fact I don't think an art is ever popular; there aren't enough people with taste and understanding to make it popular. It's the cheap imitations of art that are sold by the million."[31]

While Gabler and other aficionados attempted the paradox of popularizing strongly anticommercial music, the musicians participating in the hot revival plainly hoped and expected that they would escape the pressures of the mass white audience. That audience had proven deeply problematic for Artie Shaw (no jam-session rebel) who felt profoundly alienated from the masses, and found greater kinship with noncommercial musicians as the alienation became clearer. "If anything, the larger the crowds and the warmer the waves of admiration and love, . . . the more intense the loneliness and sense of isolation I have felt standing up there between the two separate worlds of my band on the one hand, and the audience on the other." By 1940 the hot musicians realized that articulated anticommercialism expressed much of the rebellion and resentment they had felt for almost two decades. In the late 1930s, the musician Paul Smith articulated the resentment for Eddie Condon, arguing that Americans "misrepresent jazz. . . . They commercialize it, organize it, prostitute it, and convince the public that jazz can be played from arranged music by sixty men whose only qualification is that they read notes. They play on radio programs and tour the country; they pick off the good jazz men one by one and bury them in their tiers of horns and reeds."[32]

The anger had long been simmering in many. Sidney Bechet, out of the dry-cleaning business by 1940, was infuriated when a booking agent told him that he appeared too old to obtain good jobs: "If [a man's] got white hair you don't allow him a soul." Bechet despised "all this commercializing that was happening to ragtime" and became radically opposed to market forces: "if you start taking what's pure in a man and you start putting it on a bill of sale, somehow you can't help destroying it." The one helpful lesson Art Hodes believed that New York taught him, he wrote in the 1940s, was "to hold my head up and keep trying and fighting for my beliefs," and the pianist did this by flagrantly disregarding the opinions of commercial audiences. He allowed New York clubowners to steal his tips and pay him low salaries (and let other musicians deride his "ingenuousness"), and he chose to ignore audiences that praised the worst recordings and neglected the hardest-working musicians. One of Hodes's proudest moments came when Benny Goodman's entourage entered the club in which Hodes played, permitting the latter to ignore pointedly the famous bandleader.[33]

The white revivalist musicians did find an audience in the 52nd Street clubs. This group indulged in pre-Depression, pre–World War Two nostalgia while they welcomed incremental musical innovation, and the audience treated the musicians like artists who could also retain an urban-adolescent brashness. This small community of artists and listeners presented an escape from some (but by no means all) of the dilemmas presented by the growth of mass culture.

The literary critic Dwight Macdonald may have had the hot revival in mind when, in the late 1940s, he began to call for "a number of smaller, more specialized audiences that may still be commercially profitable" as an antidote to the hegemonic effect of mass marketing on folk and elite art. In fact, Macdonald concluded in 1962 that jazz was "the only art form that appeals to both the intelligentsia and the common people."[34] This was a simplistic evaluation, but it reflected quite accurately the dual ambitions of the hot revivalists. The musicians who had spent their 1920s youths striving to incorporate useful aesthetic and musical notions into their new style were able by 1940 to produce an effective and stimulating institutional response—the commercial nightclub—to the dominance of the big bands and mass culture.

10

"*The Wedding of the Races*"?
Jazz and the Color Line

Throughout the economic, social, and technological upheavals that defined the jazz creators' careers and productivity, the American culture of race presented them with their greatest personal and professional challenges. Jazz was a biracial music, but the society that fostered it was violently opposed to biraciality. Jazz almost seems to have been inserted in the American fabric to test the strength of its fundamental, racial strands of thought. Jazz musicians did not seek the assignment of hurdling the barriers of race, but they nevertheless were compelled to face them and to confound them on many occasions. In the 1920s African Americans sought inclusion in urban musical cultures, saw ghetto walls spring up among them, and regrouped inside the sanctioned realm of race music, while white players, in moods of social rebellion and adventure, traveled to the jazz ghettos and welcomed the music and the culture. Did this situation change in the following decade, as the musicians, their jazz, and the institutions surrounding them matured? Did the jazz community become a great American experiment in racial equality, or did it become as hypocritical and segregated as other institutions remained through the Second World War?

In the twenties American society was as intensely segregated and antiblack as it had been at any time since the Civil War. In the South, the descendants of the slaves had been deprived of the vote, many legal remedies, the right to live in many neighborhoods, access to many schools, hospitals, and other social services, as well as most rights and privileges. As C. Vann Woodward has written, "there was no apparent tendency toward abatement or relaxation of the Jim Crow code of discrimination and segregation in the

1920s, and none in the 'thirties until well along in the depression years. . . . in fact the Jim Crow laws were elaborated and further expanded in those years," as new activities pertaining to women, transportation, leisure, and industry inspired new laws restricting black participation.[1] Terrorism, provocation, and lynching complemented the police powers that enforced Jim Crow legislation. The Ku Klux Klan and other white supremacist groups played roles in both the political and social workings of the caste system; and nongovernmental entities, such as churches, businesses, and farm organizations, also systematically excluded blacks from participation.[2]

After jazz acquired its economic and artistic identity in northern cities in the 1920s, many of its practitioners introduced the new music to areas south of the Ohio River and the Mason-Dixon Line. Northern blacks who were the children or grandchildren of southern migrants or migrants themselves almost unanimously found that their tours in the region presented them with surprising challenges. These musicians learned of—or reencountered—a 1930s South that persecuted them systematically. In addition, they, like other black performers, were challenged and upbraided by whites in a public, *theatrical* manner, for racism in the South had always been embodied in public rituals as well as in legislation.

As had happened on Streckfus's Mississippi riverboats, black bands touring the South on land often gave performances for whites or blacks only. "If it was a black dance," Cab Calloway band member Garvin Bushell noted, "there would be white spectators who were not allowed to dance. If it was a white dance, then they didn't have black spectators." In a Florida locale, blacks were allowed to watch from the balcony as Calloway's band played for white dancers. As in the North, though, black bands touring the South sometimes could play before multiracial audiences, but local law usually demanded strict segregation in each dance hall. Dancers were usually segregated by ropes that bisected the floors. Milt Hinton, who was also in Calloway's band then, recalled that ropes were used in dance halls in Texas, Mississippi, Georgia, and Florida. Bushell noted that halls in Greenville and Charleston, South Carolina, were required to trisect their floors with two ropes: "one section in the middle was for the white dancers. This section [on one side] was for blacks. This section [on the other side] was for mulattoes." Bushell observed correctly that "there's a great mulatto caste system in . . . South Carolina."[3]

Segregated dances and clubs, of course, were also common

in the North. Clyde Bernhardt's first downtown New York job was at a speakeasy that used burly doormen to enforce its whites-only policy. Hinton recalled that the Calloway band usually played for all-white audiences in the South and "mostly white" crowds in the North. Southern segregation in jazz locales, as in other public settings, was notable both for its basis in statute and for the symbolic social function it played for whites. The easily surmountable rope that kept the races apart at jazz dances challenged blacks and whites to *enact* and maintain segregationism themselves, even as they enjoyed and danced to the same music. The symbol was not always effective, as in Johnson City, Tennessee, where a huge race fight erupted during a Calloway concert and forced the band to flee through the back door.[4]

Local law officers, when present at such dances, embodied the oppressive force that underlay the Jim Crow system. Their role often was to harass and abuse the least socially powerful dancers—black women—as a lesson to potential transgressors. "If there was a disturbance at any of those dances in the South," Earl Hines recalled, "two policemen could handle the whole hall in those days. They used to beat up on the women, but so long as they [black men] were cutting each other up the police didn't pay much attention." Often no disturbance was needed to provoke police harassment, as the drummer Johnny Otis found while he traveled with a black California band to Texas in the early 1940s. At one hall a second rope separated dancers from the bandstand. When a black woman leaned on this rope to request a song from the band, a white policeman ordered her to "keep offa that goddam rope, and I don't want to have to tell you again," and walked away. The band then began playing, and "the hostile, real world was forgotten momentarily by the crowd as it pulsed in a rhythmic ecstasy." At intermission a different black woman, wearing a similar dress, leaned on the rope. The policeman came forward, swore, and hit the woman. "Hundreds of people stood like frozen zombies. The men—all of us—had been reduced to dogs. To less than dogs." Otis and the other musicians went outside; "as I knelt in the Texas dirt, retching, I realized that one of my bandsmen was standing next to me, crying his heart out."[5]

Otis's story emphasized the explosive nature of racial violence at jazz dances, as well as the white police power's inciting role and the musicians' shocked and pained reaction. As players in a symbolic Jim Crow drama that underlay many of their performances in the South, some black bands were subjected to unambiguous physi-

cal violence. The most straightforward incidents occurred outside
the dance hall, in places where musicians held no special status.
As Bill Coleman, whose Cincinnati band traveled in the summers,
recalled, "It was not always pleasant traveling through West Virginia":

> it was necessary to pass through many small towns and villages where
> mostly white miners and farmers lived and as the bass and drums
> and other baggage was carried on the running board of the car, we
> could be seen coming into a place from a great distance.
>
> The white kids seemed to know that it would be a car with
> negro musicians and they would throw rocks at the car and call us
> niggers. It was a bitter pill to swallow and we could do nothing about
> it. This also happened going through places in Kentucky.

Similarly, Coleman heard a "very well known story in Ohio" regarding a band led by the college-educated trumpeter Freddie Jenkins.
The band was invited to play at a private rural party in Kentucky,
and some whites picked them up and drove them to a house where
"a gang of other white men" awaited. "This was the party but not
like the Whispering Serenaders thought it was going to be. This was
to be a head whipping party for no other reason than that the Serenaders were fine musicians but negroes. Being gentlemen didn't
mean anything to the jealous southern white men." The musicians
were badly beaten and their instruments were destroyed. In this
instance the whites' anger grew out of their envy at the band's financial success. "The only reason for an act of that kind to take place
in the South," Coleman wrote in his memoirs, "is that these musicians were from the North, they played too well for somebody's
taste and they had the nerve to accept an engagement in a white
hotel down South." [6]

At southern dances, black jazz bands were often the racial as
well as the musical focus of the white customers. Threatening the
band with violence perhaps gave some whites a sense of performing at the same level of importance as the musicians, especially
in the context of biracial audiences. Law officers felt particularly
empowered to harass bands. A white policeman once requested
that Earl Hines's band play "Honeysuckle Rose," but went to the
restroom while the band played it. When he returned he asked
Hines when the tune would be played; told that they *had* played
it, he called them liars and "began to use bad language and get
very offensive about race," and the police captain came to the bandstand and ordered the *band* to leave after intermission. The black

musicians, the captain and other whites felt, were the cause of such disruptions. Hines, echoing others, believed that southern whites "couldn't understand our being so well dressed, nor the way we carried ourselves. . . . There were so many illiterate people in the South—on both sides—and they were the people who constantly caused commotion."[7]

The ritual of challenging well-dressed black players had many manifestations, in and out of the dance hall. At one Florida performance by the Calloway band, the musicians had to be cordoned off and guarded everywhere they went; "the security police used to have to have a rope up and make a line for us to go through in intermission at white dances in Florida to go to the men's room." Customers would "stand on each side of the line like a parade and they would be trying to hit us."

There was no end to the provocations Calloway's band suffered before the leader stopped touring the South in the early forties. In Longview, Texas, according to Garvin Bushell, a drunken white offered the sheriff guarding Calloway seven hundred dollars if he would let him hit the bandleader, saying, "I just want to hit him because he's who he is." Milt Hinton told a fuller story about what might have been the same incident. "We're playing up there and one guy says to Cab, [']I'll pay $200.00 to hit that nigger.['] And he's reaching over to try and hit Cab." The white road manager restrained the drunkard.[8]

Further trouble, however, rooted in whites' sexual stereotypes of African-American males, soon developed in this hall. A white woman lured the band's pianist Bennie Payne into a trap by offering Payne a drink. "Of course Bennie knew better than to accept a drink from a white lady from the South with all the white folks sitting right there with her. . . . So she says 'you mean you ain't going to take a drink that's offered to you[?]' Course Bennie gets upset—he says maybe I ought to take it. . . . He takes the drink and he swallows it. And then the white fellow says—'nigger, you taking whiskey from my woman?'—so you couldn't win either way." A fight ensued, from which the band barely managed to flee into a cellar. Pounding on the cellar door, the drunken Texans "started fighting amongst themselves . . . when they didn't see us." The band, "just scared to death," stayed in the cellar until the whites left.[9]

Southern racial incidents involving jazz bands tended to grow out of white patrons' desire to strip black jazz musicians of their prominence as entertainers and prestige as talented artists. This is plainly illustrated by an incident involving the Duke Ellington band in Henderson, Texas. As the musicians boarded the bus after their engagement, an older white man came forward and grabbed "Tricky Sam" Nanton's trombone, saying he was taking it and that "I don't give a damn about the police." Ellington coolly told him that he could take the trombone. "That killed him when he said that," band member Juan Tizol recalled, "and [the man] said, 'No, that's all right; I don't want the trombone—all I wanted to see was how he was gonna act about it.' "[10]

Whites also recruited willing southern blacks to undercut the visitors' status. Milt Hinton recalled that the Calloway band "could get out to some of these small towns and the white people would put the black people against us," saying " 'Now look, them niggers are from New York and they come and they take your women.' " The players "had to be careful about our association with any black community." Hinton remembered "several bad cases" of local blacks attempting to keep band members away from their bars, restaurants, and women: "I almost got killed one night in Louisville." This showed that migrant musicians had a special count against them during southern tours: they had lost a measure of their shared identity with southern blacks, some of whom no longer considered them southerners.[11]

Even north of the Mason-Dixon Line, southern whites could aggravate blacks' submerged guilt over their desertion of the mother region. In York, Pennsylvania, in 1931, one such man approached Marion Hardy and His Alabamians and asked how many members were from Alabama. "We were scared to say no, and scared to say yes," band member Clyde Bernhardt recalled. The man took a wad of money out of his pocket and offered ten dollars to each band member from Alabama. Everyone raised their hands ("somebody raised both hands") and the white man gave them money, saying, "I don't know why . . . so many damn colored boys ashamed to admit they all from the South. Just give 'em some money and they fess up fast." The musicians' reaction is understandable: at that early stage in their careers, it made sense to avoid any association with the South, unless they were to profit from it. Nevertheless, they fell into the white man's theatrical trap, in which the master-sharecropper dynamic of plantation life was recreated, at the humiliating expense of the blacks, in a northern dance hall. Humiliation in the North took other forms, as Bernhardt discovered in the late thirties as a member of Edgar Hayes's band. One Ohio hall manager told the band members that they could neither bring their black girlfriends into the hall nor speak with the white female customers. This manager, it seemed, strove to guard against any display of visible black masculinity.[12] For whites—and not only southern whites by then—black bands were upstarts and targets for public control and humiliation. Perhaps this challenging of black professionals was a bastardized form of the antebellum southern concern for honor, and of the prickly pride and theatricality with which cavaliers always defended it.[13]

White jazz musicians, too, were confronted on occasion by other whites who opposed their advocacy of black music. The pianist Gil Evans, in the army during World War Two, "had a hard time; . . . a lot of people didn't like my [black jazz] albums, my records. . . . I used to have a little metal case full of 78s. Most of the albums were of Duke Ellington, Louis Armstrong. I had some very, very close calls with some soldiers, some draftees. They couldn't stand it."[14] Even in situations far removed from their dance halls, therefore, some whites felt obligated to make a show of their opposition to black musical accomplishments, sometimes by threatening physical conflict.

Musicians reacted to these provocations with a mixture of sorrow and caution. Bill Coleman poignantly remembered the occasion when his band was asked to leave the Greyhound bus waiting room in Gettysburg, Pennsylvania. Coleman "never paid much attention to prejudice at that time [circa 1930] because I was born in to it." Nevertheless, "it was something that I never dreamed could happen in Gettysburg[,] which is in a northern state and especially where Lincoln had made his famous speech about the freedom of mankind." "Of course," Coleman added unconvincingly, "the situation did not upset us." Under these nationwide conditions, bands on tour sought out black families in various towns for housing. An advance agent for the Ellington band found houses in southern towns. Lawrence Brown recalled that "it got so it was real nice because we also usually would eat at the place we stayed."[15]

Less well-established bands, such as Charles C. Grear's Original Midnite Ramblers in 1927, had more difficult experiences on the road. "If we got hungry," Clyde Bernhardt noted, "we roll into the next town and look for colored people—they always had something for us to eat. If the town was all white, we knew not to stop." Frostburg, Maryland, was one such town, as Bill Coleman's band discovered one night. "It was really a frosty place because it was in February and below zero," and the dance hall was unheated and poorly attended. "And we almost had a tragical night because there was no hotel and only one Negro family in the town; . . . what saved us was this one Negro family who offered to let us sit in their living room by a hot fire until it was time to take the bus" the next morning.[16]

As black and white musicians began to work together in the late 1930s, they had to take great care when touring. The white bandleader Charlie Barnet noted that "Cincinnati's pretty close to the jumping-off place as far as [mixed bands were concerned]" in the thirties, and most of them stayed north of the Ohio River. The Ellington band featured one nonblack, Juan Tizol of Puerto Rico, and his presence on the bandstand between fellow trombonists Sam Nanton and Lawrence Brown irritated some white customers. Occasionally the three changed their seating, so that the two black players sat together and Tizol was segregated at the end of the bench. When Teddy Wilson and Lionel Hampton became the Benny Goodman Orchestra's first black members they would always search out separate housing during tours in southern towns. Cootie Williams, who joined Goodman's band in 1940, adopted a different method: he posed as the bandboy and carried baggage into hotels, and would have his meals sent up by room service.[17]

After 1930, jazz was largely a northern music, since most of its creators, promoters, and audiences lived and were active outside the South. Northern racial antagonism in jazz was not as intensely focused on the touring, tuxedoed black band. It was more diffuse in its sources and manifestations and more entangled with other class and ethnic conflicts. This complexity was typical of the less institutionalized nature of discrimination against blacks in the North. In general, blacks outside the South were rarely segregated by law, but they were denied full economic and social equality by most businesses, voluntary associations, labor unions, and other private organizations. These actions, in fact, ensured that blacks in 1920s Chicago or New York were more geographically segregated from whites than they had been in New Orleans or Atlanta.[18]

White northerners' belief in the doctrine of "equality of opportunity"—which held that everyone could advance as far as individual merits allowed—blinded them to the wide discrimination characterizing their own society. Nevertheless, segregation and white supremacy, while evident in the North, had never been enshrined as social ideals by whites there, and thus they had never been the cornerstones of culture they had become in the South. Northern whites tolerated "friends of the Negro" among them and a certain measure of black success in the mainstream. Rituals like lynchings and public humiliation were rare in the North. Black economic advancement in the ghetto was tolerated by whites who did not have an interest in exploiting its residents. The ghettos were largely poor and inferior to white facilities, but they offered educational and health services and job opportunities superior to those found in southern cities.[19]

In the North jazz was dominated by commercial promoters, and thus discrimination was less flamboyant and public than in the South and more related to the cold and calculating search for profits. Blacks were denied (and granted) jobs on the basis of how employers predicted the market would react to their presence. This did lead to simple discrimination in northern clubs, by which blacks were refused employment because they were not white.

In the 1930s, when Scoville Browne courted a woman in Chicago whose apartment overlooked the Grenada Cafe, he was anguished every time he caught a glimpse of that bastion of whites-only hiring. He was reminded that he could never work there. In the 1940s Garvin Bushell, who was employed at the Radio City Music Hall as the only black musician, nearly obtained a position with Paul Whiteman's orchestra, only to be dismissed with a lame apology when the bandleader found out that he was black ("the name Bushell [had] tricked him"). In the 1920s Whiteman had been far more direct with Earl Hines, when (as Hines recalled) he approached the pianist at the Grand Terrace and said simply, "if only you were white." Hines "didn't pay much attention to that then, but later on I realized what he was talking about." Even when blacks were able to gain secure employment, they often had to work in clubs that only admitted whites, such as Chicago's Sunset Café and Harlem's Cotton Club and Connie's Inn.[20]

The radio industry was no less restrictive. As the white player Jimmy Maxwell recalled of CBS, the nation's largest radio network, "the studio worked just like everybody else, they had categories. . . . if you were a black musician you were a jazz player and you didn't get too [many] calls to be a lead player." Similarly, whites who excelled at jazz improvisation lost many assignments to less-talented black players. White studio musicians were especially wont to deride "CPT," "colored people's time," which allegedly made black players undependable for live broadcasting. Commercial sponsors frequently helped to promote discrimination; for example, in 1945 Chesterfield, based in the South like all tobacco companies, at first refused to sponsor a broadcast featuring a mixed band, on the assumption (conveyed to Jimmy Maxwell) that black jazz musicians "can't read" and were "troublemakers."[21] Similarly, in films the white musicians' union local in Los Angeles pressured studios to hire whites to dub music onto soundtracks when black bands were seen playing; whites made an average of eleven dollars an hour, the blacks eleven dollars a day. Only one black musician, the composer Calvin Jackson, was employed full-time by a major film studio in the 1930s, but "he would only show up on the screen credits as the arranger. [MGM] would not give him composer's credits at the time." In the early 1940s, the drummer Lee Young would be MGM's only full-time black studio musician.[22]

Some incidents suggest more complex commercial forces at work, in which race perhaps played a secondary role. In the summer of 1940 Eddie Durham's band played on the seacoast in Bridgeport, Connecticut. His popularity with white listeners challenged that of Harry James's white band (playing nearby), and the racketeers who controlled the local dance halls tried to force Durham away by cutting the power lines to his nightclub. Local politicians encouraged Durham to stay, while union leaders asked him to leave; he compromised and agreed to bar white customers for at least one night a week. In response, Durham's black musicians angrily accused him of segregating. In this case, the black band had powerful white allies and, by compromising somewhat, was not muscled out. It is important for historians to investigate why and how often such situations developed in the generally hostile North.[23]

More than simple hiring discrimination was usually at work in the North. Before the Great Migration, northern whites had allowed the entertainment industries to construct stereotypes of the mass of blacks, deep in the South. The contrasting images of the minstrel stage included the dancing Jim Crow, the presumptuous dandy Zip Coon, the harmless Old Black Joe, the razor-wielding jealous husband and the silly young pickaninny, among others. These images reinforced northerners' sense of difference and distance from the colonized, backwards ex-Confederacy, as well as their own sense of white supremacy, which was less urgent a matter for them than it was for white southerners. During and after the black migration the old stereotypes persisted in films and radio, as northern whites sought assurance in their entertainment that their social order was not changing.[24]

Bemused young black musicians were often expected to comply with this dominant stereotype and were "handed the burnt cork" by employers in the commercialized northern theater of racial hierarchy. In 1927, The singer Lois Deppe was rejected for a part in the original production of *Showboat* in 1927 because "you're mulatto, not negroid enough," but he did find work as an Indian or Hawaiian singer, adapting to employers' racial expectations with the agility of a chameleon. Blacks sometimes had to change their skin tone at the request of audience-conscious promoters. In 1936 the management at Detroit's Fox Theater decided that the pairing of white female stage dancers with Count Basie's band, apparently forced upon them by an unusual Fox contract, was too provocative. As Basie's vocalist Billie Holiday later recalled, the managers fitted the dancers "out with special black masks and mammy dresses" and ordered Holiday herself to apply "special dark grease paint" to her face, since they feared "I was too yellow to sing with all the black men in his band. Somebody might think I was white if the light didn't hit me just right." An angry Basie was unable to break his contract.[25]

Movie studios hired black bands as exotic onscreen per-formers. MGM often asked Lee Young to put together bands of "colored musicians" who could read music, presumably to obtain an effect only black bands were thought able to create. Studios, too, wanted to ensure that the groups actually looked black. When Duke Ellington's band appeared in the "Amos 'n' Andy" film *Check and Doublecheck* (1930), Juan Tizol and the light-skinned Barney Bigard wore blackface makeup. The black players at the second Cotton Club, which opened in midtown Manhattan in 1936, re-ceived a subtler reminder of their neominstrel status: among the only black customers ever allowed in to hear the band were the film actors Clarence Muse and Stepin Fetchit, the greatest (and wealthiest) exponents of the servile stereotypes.[26]

The regional trends in antiblack attitudes and behavior—the-atrical and public in the South, commercial and stereotypical in the North—were unavoidably imprinted on the minds of early white jazz musicians. It was the southern white players, therefore, who adhered to an explicit racist ideology. Three major early figures in Dixieland music, Jack Laine, Tom Brown, and Nick LaRocca, argued that blacks had never played "their kind" of music (a true statement, considered literally) and had never become competent jazz musicians. Laine noted in a late interview that two Creoles of color who managed to infiltrate his band "played so good, . . . we couldn't tell what color they was"—a source of distress to the leader. Musical styles, by Laine's reckoning, were unique to the different races; blacks, in his view, surprised him by playing "good" music.[27]

On this point Brown, Laine's protégé, was uniquely explicit, perhaps even pathological: "niggers ain't no good on clarinet. Them thick, blubbery lips can't make no decent tone. . . . They ain't smart enough to tell where the harmony is, neither. After all, they niggers." For his part, Nick LaRocca initiated a frantic letter-writing campaign in the 1950s to attack musicians and historians who had credited New Orleans blacks with a significant role in the creation of jazz. He wrote to the discographer Brian Rust that jazz "melodies are white mans music and not African in Origin" and that "these men who write on Jazz obtain Grants from Guggenheimer Foundation W. C. Handy NAACP and probably Communist from Russia." Striking out at unfamiliar people and ideas, LaRocca's fears sprang from his desire to protect his white working-class culture: "the colored man must have Culture, so what is the difference if we take it from a Poor Man he cannot say or do us no harm." LaRocca refused to acknowledge the biracial tradition in New Orleans's musical life and the stimulus this provided for jazz, insisting that recent historians "are nothing but Intergraters to Mix white and Colored which can never happen down South."[28]

There is no reason to believe that LaRocca, Brown and others had ever acknowledged or respected black musicians during their playing years. In the 1910s and 1920s, syncopated ragtime was for them a music strictly associated with white clubs and social activities, such as lawn parties in the white working-class Irish Channel. These attitudes were shared by many younger Dixieland musicians in the city, some of whom refused ever to play or record with nonwhites.[29]

In keeping with the more subtle nature of discrimination above the Ohio River, almost no northern musicians were overtly hostile towards blacks. Those who developed racist views often had been embittered by competition from blacks for scarce jobs. In heavily commercial New York City, some whites handicapped black players by giving them a false sense of camaraderie, which weakened their competitiveness. Jimmy Maxwell witnessed incidents in New York at CBS Radio, when the studio band's sole black member fell prey to subtle racism. "The guys would get him out, take him to the bar and drink and [say] 'oh, you're a great guy,' everything like that. . . . I was trying to tell him, 'these guys are not your friends. . . . They're taking you out and making a character out of you, they're not treating you respectfully. . . . you're getting a bad reputation and you're showing up late and you're making it tough for all the [black] guys that are going to want to . . . follow you.' . . . unfortunately, it was too late, I guess, when I told him."[30]

It was common for white musicians to ignore or belittle the black foundations of jazz. The self-proclaimed jazz musicians of the 1920s who played sweet music almost never mentioned blacks when they discussed jazz's origins. *Jazz*, Paul Whiteman's 1926 book, contains no mention of blacks or their music, and "the King of Jazz" felt that jazz mostly consisted of syncopated classical music. Georg Brunis similarly argued that jazz originated in barbershop singing, and that "blues comes from . . . the Jewish hymn, like Eli, Eli. . . . Then they took the African bongos, the tom-tom, and they made rhythm to it. That's my opinion of the blues." His opinion was not favorable: "to me all blues sound alike." Bill Challis, a Whiteman arranger, agreed: "I think the white [players] who got into the playing [of] the blues . . . gave it an up-tempo and dressed it up a little bit so it was a little bit more listenable."[31]

Unlike the Chicagoans, who had been deeply inspired by black jazz on the South Side, musicians from other backgrounds often did not appreciate it. Glenn Miller, born in Iowa and raised in Denver, "thought that Benny Goodman was the first jazz clarinet player who ever lived," his bandmate Bud Freeman recalled. "It was not until Bix took me and Jimmy McPartland up to Harlem to hear [Willie] the Lion [Smith] that the rest of the white guys in the [Ben] Pollack band started to go up to Harlem, Benny Goodman being one of them. Long after us." For some, such ignorance made theft more conscionable. Many white bandleaders stole arrangements from such black arrangers as Don Redman, Fletcher Henderson, Benny Carter, and William Grant Still; Gil Evans singled out Tommy Dorsey as the worst offender.[32]

Even the Chicagoans, the whites who were closest to black musicians and treated their music with the most respect, absorbed racist attitudes of varying degrees of subtlety. These attitudes had been typical of white Chicago in the era of the Great Migration and the 1919 race riot. Bud Freeman was certainly incorrect in stating that in the 1930s "all musicians, all white musicians, were color blind anyway." Freeman noted in 1978 that earlier, on the South Side, "I saw this freedom of spirit that we whites didn't have." As a youth, he was aware that blacks "were having a difficult time getting hold of money and they weren't . . . allowed any of the privileges and life could be difficult for them," but amid the nightlife "they just appeared to be free in spirit and so happy." Freeman's early view thus was that blacks were "naturally" carefree, a notion that certainly derived from his socialization in Chicago to dominant white views. This socialization provided Chicago whites with basic presumptions about the inferiority or marginality of blacks.[33]

Two oddly similar incidents, each involving shared names, illustrate that the Chicagoans could perceive blacks as marginal. The cornetist Ralph Brown noted that the Capone family "used the name Brown" as an alias on occasion, "Al Brown, and his brother was named Ralph, and my name's Ralph Brown. I worked for them at 95th and Westborn, a nightclub, and Ralph would come in and say, 'Oh, yes, my twin brother,' kidding me all the time.'" At that same time, the black musicians "were too little for them to bother with. He told us to see nothing, hear nothing." Patronizing treatment was to be expected from the Capones, but some white Chicago jazz musicians also displayed Ralph's kind of condescension. In 1930s Harlem, Eddie Condon, Dave Tough, and the pianist Joe Sullivan were surprised to discover a black pianist also named Joe Sullivan. "Our Joe Sullivan," Condon recalled, "sitting between us, looked innocently at Tough. Tough patted his arm. 'Every light has its shadow,' he said. 'I like both.'" That the sophisticated Tough viewed the black Sullivan a "shadow" of the white indicates that he and his friends continued to identify themselves primarily as members of a white group and considered blacks and their music as supplements to or opposites of white culture.[34]

More to the point, the minstrel stereotypes shaped the Chicagoans' perception even as they consciously admired and emulated the black musicians they encountered on the South Side. Condon, one of the first important white rhythm players, echoed the standard notion that "the Negro is born with rhythm. . . . We've got to learn it," and he also seemed to have no qualms in the 1920s (or in 1946, when he wrote his memoirs) about performing a blackface minstrel routine with his brother in Chicago. Although they performed "shaking and without a smile" (the director had told them to "smile" like "happy carefree Negroes") the brothers' discomfort was only due to stagefright. The players' lack of innovative thinking on the subject of minstrelsy suggested that their appreciation and advocacy of blacks ran up against deep-rooted perceptual barriers. Hoagy Carmichael, who had played with blacks since his youth, felt compelled in his memoirs to praise Louis Armstrong's appearance in a stereotyped manner: on one occasion, "those big lips of his, at the mike in front of my face, blubbering strange cannibalistic sounds, tickled me to the marrow."[35]

In addition, throughout the North, the racist practices of the commercial world prevented whites from working with blacks, and thus kept them from acquiring more accurate perceptions. When Art Hodes came to New York in 1938, he found that "it was . . . difficult to book any kind of a band. But me wanting a mixed band . . . made it worse." The best white players were "making more money than you can afford to pay them. So you get the best that are black, even though it's going to be hard on you. . . . If you went on a train with blacks, you had problems, and I was doing it. . . . I had all sorts of problems." Jam sessions were not integrated in most settings for many years. Scoville Browne was probably not the only black who could not "remember any mixed jam sessions in Chicago, person-ally . . . for the simple reason that I don't know of anybody who would dare go up with any of the [black] guys who were playing jazz then." Some whites gained a similar opinion. Muggsy Spanier recalled that "white and Negro musicians kept to themselves pretty much; only rarely did they sit in with each other."[36]

Personal and commercial barriers held up the integration of the New York nightclub scene into the 1940s. Billie Holiday ob-served that in the late thirties "white musicians were 'swinging' from one end of 52nd Street to the other, but there wasn't a black face in sight on the street except Teddy Wilson and me." In a reveal-ing rationalization of the situation, Art Hodes argued in 1942 (like other whites certainly would have then) that 52nd Street musicians segregated themselves willingly: "Most of the colored boys hang there [at the White Rose]. But then at Reilly's the opposite is true. So everyone's happy." Despite these oppositions and barriers, progress among musicians was made. The white saxophonist Charlie Barnet often played in Harlem jam sessions, and later recalled that "I've been there when I was the only white guy, and I've been there when it was, you know, three or four white guys there . . . just whoever was there." Barnet noted that the Famous Door on 52nd Street (which in the 1940s became Manhattan's "swing street") dis-couraged racial mixing, while the Onyx Club next door "was very liberally minded." Other New York locations, like the Park Central Hotel, also allowed mixing.[37]

Black musicians worked as effectively as possible within this inconsistent system in New York, and some of them tolerated white players' limited understanding of their predicament. Benny Carter remembered that black musicians welcomed whites to Harlem jam sessions, and did not recall that blacks felt that "white musicians could have tried a little bit harder to open up some opportunities for black musicians. . . . Maybe we just kind of at that moment had . . . sort of resigned ourselves to the situation as it was and [felt] maybe that even the white musicians themselves couldn't do any-thing about it," Carter noted cautiously in 1976. In 1930s Chicago, however, Scoville Browne grew resentful of the fact that Americans "didn't want to accept something from a black musician, but let a white lad learn this same thing and present it and they accepted it. Now, whether this is prejudice or not, I don't know."[38]

Having gained these views, some black musicians made it a policy in the 1930s to exclude whites from their activities. Separatism, of course, lived on among many northern blacks in the thirties. Some musicians hoped to preserve black culture and heritage apart from white influence. Black competition with white ethnic groups had already fueled hostility. As Milt Hinton remembered, "our parents would always speak of the Jews as derogatory. You know, 'Jews own everything.' It was more like a jealous thing."[39]

In jazz these notions had social and economic effects. Of all the black-owned or -managed theaters in Harlem, Garvin Bushell recalled that only the Apollo Theater would occasionally hire white bands, and it was not until 1934 that Charlie Barnet's group began to play there regularly. Black bandleaders did not hire qualified white musicians when the chances arose, even when many white big bands had begun to integrate. Duke Ellington told his saxophonist Ben Webster around 1940 that "I don't want any ofay in the band"—with the white man in question, Jimmy Maxwell, present at the time. Maxwell and many other whites disenchanted by the commercialized big bands would have accepted positions in black groups, but black leaders felt no obligation or inclination to give them steady employment.[40]

In a more abstract form of racial assertiveness, many black players came to feel that white musicians were inferior practitioners of jazz. "Most of the white bands" of the 1920s, Pops Foster believed, "think if you're not blowing loud, you're not playing nothing. None of them want to study intonation." The older Sidney Bechet was passionately separatist. In Bechet's opinion, white jazz "wasn't our music. It wasn't us. . . . it's awful hard for a man who isn't black to play a melody that's come deep out of black people. It's a question of feeling." Dixieland "musicianers" could only "play what they learned from us," but their blues playing was still "a burlesque of the blues. There wasn't nothing serious in it anymore." Mezz Mezzrow, Bechet felt, tried "so hard to be something he isn't, . . . being King of Harlem for a while," with the result that "some of that will show up in his music, the idea of it will be wrong."[41]

These views were a means for black musicians to protect themselves from infiltrations by white players who, consciously or not and in varying degrees, disparaged and stereotyped black culture as a whole. White jazz musicians, of course, felt that black separatists were as guilty as Nick LaRocca of denying that other people could understand and assimilate to jazz. Bud Freeman stressed that such black musicians as the clarinetist Fess Williams showed little talent for syncopation and improvisation, and he has said that "I am concerned with [a] man as being a man, I am concerned with individual talent, because if we are going back to say[ing] [']it's the black man's music['] . . . I say, 'that's fine with me, [but] how many really played it?'" Whites were more likely to celebrate racial mixing, such as when Jimmy McPartland characterized jazz as "the wedding of the races," of the African beat and "European harmonies and melodic lines."[42]

Viewed in historical context, therefore, jazz was not immune to the powerful segregationist and racist sentiments of the interwar era. Besides affronts from hotel clerks and sheriffs and closed paths of employment, black musicians faced the specter of minstrelsy and the lingering prejudice of otherwise sympathetic white colleagues. The climb out of this predicament was not easy, but just as the migration that nurtured jazz had endowed it with an aura of mission, the musicians' move towards professionalism became a challenge to racial barriers. The challenge began, fittingly, in the South. The theatrical confrontations there revealed not only white hostility but also important white ambivalences. Just as New Orleans jazz had evolved in the midst of confusing racial conditions—in which Jack Laine found that light-skinned "blacks" played so well "we couldn't tell what color they was"—so did whites across the South discover that black jazz musicians could obfuscate the color line.

Some black touring musicians gained opportunities to subvert and invert the basic premises of Jim Crow. In Louisville in the 1910s, John Bubbles sensed this power when he and Buck Washington appeared in blackface. "They don't realize we're black—how can they realize it? How are you going to tell?" Perhaps emboldened by this knowledge, Buck and Bubbles sang "Back Home in Indiana," "Shine" (which described the antics of a black folk hero), and the blues, which were not usually sung by minstrels. Light-skinned blacks inspired confusion and queries among southern whites. The bandleader Charles C. Grear used his white complexion and smooth talking to buy food at white grocery stores in the South for his band, as did Count Basie's saxophonist Earle Warren. Railroad conductors often instructed Warren to leave the other members and return to the white car where he "belonged."

Willie Smith, an important saxophonist, played with Jimmy Lunceford and Duke Ellington for long periods, but in the 1940s worked with Harry James's white outfit. For Smith the ambiguity worked both ways: when he played for James, whites easily assumed he was white, and when he played for a black band they viewed this "slumming white" with incredulity. The converse of Smith's liminal identity in the South was experienced by the white man who joined Jay McShann's band in the 1940s. Southerners, McShann recalled, "figured he had to be colored because he was with us," and the bandleader amused himself by "helping" white gas station attendants and hotel clerks to "catch" this man using white facilities.[43]

The infinite gradations of skin tone in jazz played havoc with segregationists. Listeners in a restaurant in Hattiesburg, Mississippi, in 1920 did not know what to make of Lee Collins's touring band, which included a Creole drummer (Jelly Roll Morton's cousin), a Mexican bassist, and "a Japanese fellow" on clarinet. The mixture was too rich: "the white people didn't want the Japanese to play with the band," but they permitted the remaining ethnic mixture.[44] In San Antonio, white efforts to rope off nonwhite dancers at an Earl Hines band performance ran afoul of "dark-complexioned Mexican Indians," who protested that "they were not Negroes." As such social mingling became more frequent in the North and the South, confusion developed among the policers of Jim Crow. At the 1939 World's Fair near San Francisco, Johnny Otis was permitted to attend a blacks-only dance (featuring Count Basie's band) only after a Mississippi-born policeman examined Otis's fingernails and concluded that he was black. Beforehand Otis had thought that "if you look white you are white and the 'man' keeps you white," but this incident changed his mind; sly subversion was possible.[45]

Southern jazz tours also brought listeners and musicians closer together and increased the potential for meaningful exchanges on race. In the 1930s, before a concert in Dallas, whites were curious about Juan Tizol's presence in the Ellington band. One man approached Tizol:

> I thought to myself, "I know he's going to ask me some questions soon." He said, "You don't mind giving me an autograph?" and I said, "You don't want no autograph; I know what you want—you want to ask a question about me." He said, "What are you doing playing with these niggers?" I said, "Let me tell you something; you see that man over there on the piano? You know he is a Negro, but

he got more respect than a lot of white people put together, you know?" So I didn't give him no autograph or nothing.

Many southern whites asked Tizol why he played with Ellington when he was able "to play with a bunch of white men," and Tizol's usual response was, "I don't want to—I learn more with this band. . . . This is a famous band." The white conversers themselves "learned more" when Tizol and Ellington came to their towns: perhaps for the first time, a white man informed them that a black man deserved their respect.[46]

Blacks, too, found that words and personal bearing could weaken the mystique of Jim Crow in individual whites. Garvin Bushell "never had any trouble in the South" because "I approached the southerner with an air that I felt I was his equal, if not better. And when I began to speak, I spoke in the best English that I knew how. . . . I had confidence in myself. I never backed up. I walked into stores in Texas where they didn't even allow black porters, and I said, 'How do you do?' You know, they said, 'Where you from?' 'I'm from New York, does it make any difference?" Loud, see. I used to disarm them that way." When other band members followed the command of a Mississippi lunchroom cook and removed their hats before ordering, Bushell kept his on and went hungry. "You could disarm them down there by just doing another act," in the manner of the theater.[47]

Such gains, of course, came at the expense of southern blacks, who remained the paragon of inferiority for whites. Bushell found that being a northerner helped: "when they found out you weren't from there, it was a different story. Never had any trouble." Similarly, a Texas man told Budd Johnson, "You're not niggers. . . . You're different from what we've got down here." The disruptive nature of this differentiation of blacks by southern whites cannot be underestimated. Nevertheless, this limited racial egalitarianism became more casual in later years, especially when black musicians, growing in confidence, responded to the friendly greetings. By the late 1930s, for example, the trumpeter Oran "Hot Lips" Page had his hand shaken by a white dance hall attendant—who said (according to Max Kaminsky) "Ah want you to know this is the first time Ah ever shook the hand of a colored man"—and he felt comfortable enough to respond, "Well, buddy, that didn't hurt, now, did it?"[48]

The confidence—and courage—of Page, Bushell, and other blacks who tested the strength and limits of racism stemmed in part from growing personal assurance. Even when whites challenged jazz musicians under a bastardized code of honor, they were often tacitly acknowledging the rising prestige or honor of these black men, and in several cases it was clear that their skill and professionalism impressed whites. When the theater of bigotry was met by the theater of black dignity, especially northern black dignity, the opinions of actors on each side may have been changed significantly. Still, it was largely in the North where unambiguous strides toward racial equality in jazz were made.

In the nationwide struggle for equality and integration between the world wars very few bright moments obtained. Despite the efforts of the National Association for the Advancement of Colored People, the National Urban League, and such philanthropists as Julius Rosenwald, there was little effective organized resistance to lynching and Jim Crow, and only a modest "uplifting" of the black poor. During the administration of Woodrow Wilson, the federal government had been counterproductive, and the government in the 1920s did little more than voice encouraging opinions (mostly so that blacks would remain loyal Republicans). During the Great Depression of 1929–40 state and federal relief programs (generally administered by Democratic governments) also discriminated widely against blacks, who received far fewer farm loans, food subsidies, public works jobs, and housing and electrification grants than their numbers warranted. When he left the NAACP in 1934, W. E. B. Du Bois spoke for many blacks, arguing that "segregation may be just as evil today as it was in 1910, but it is more insistent, more prevalent and more unassailable by appeal or argument," and that the NAACP's quarter century of work had produced a net result of "a little less than nothing." [49]

At this time, the nightclubs of Harlem, the South Side, Pittsburgh's "Hill" and other black neighborhoods were virtually the only American venues in which significant numbers of whites increased their contact and involvement with black culture. Showboats and theaters produced special black musical revues for white customers, and such clubs as Chicago's Sunset Cafe accommodated enthusiastic whites who crowded and priced most blacks out of the audience.[50] But even in these venues, most white customers gained little appreciation of black culture, since they came to nightclubs to reinforce their preconceptions about "primitivistic" art and people. White promoters and patrons praised black musicians and dancers, but they also oversimplified and trivialized their motives, perceptions, and actions. In some respects, the 1920s nightclub scene perpetuated the minstrelsy tradition of onstage humiliation and stereotyping. Nevertheless, that whites traveled to the ghettos at all and that they appreciated black music to some degree was an unusual development in America's bleak racial landscape.

In the smaller milieu of black and white jazz musicians, conditions did exist that subtly encouraged them to break down racial barriers. Most important, perhaps, were the opportunities for interracial contact and friendship that musicians-to-be gained as children in certain urban areas. White musicians, as we have seen, gained important friendly exposure to blacks during childhood. Some black musicians also benefited socially and musically from their early relations with white children. Lois Deppe, a future singer and bandleader, found acceptance in the 1910s in Springfield, Ohio. He would sing in the back yard and later gain jobs with his closest friend Albert Caine, a white boy with "a phenomenal voice."[51]

Earl Hines, whose first jazz piano job was with Deppe's band, had similarly happy memories of Duquesne, near Pittsburgh, before the Great War. While children fought, "it wasn't racial fighting, just the Protestant children, white or colored, fighting the Catholic children," and "everybody felt like they were all good friends." There were "only twelve colored families in Duquesne, out of a population of nineteen thousand," and a unified bourgeois mentality lessened racial distinctions. "Anyone's child, white or colored, would be chastised by any adult who saw them getting out of line. . . . there was this understood agreement among all the families." Hines always appreciated how his relaxed upbringing exempted him from the rage and resentment that many African Americans carried into adulthood. "It makes me feel good to think that I had an opportunity to see real people that understood people as people, who helped you to go out in the world and protect yourself and also to know how to help others."[52]

Hines's childhood did not remain arcadian (as white prejudice swelled after the masses of southern blacks migrated to Pittsburgh), but his easy access to musical education and the encouragement given by white townspeople indicates that the urban North could allow talented blacks and whites some creative and expressive equality. The singer Maxine Sullivan agreed with Hines that the Pittsburgh area offered some integration and friendliness among blacks and whites. Sullivan found that segregation in Homestead was based on income not race, although Clyde Bernhardt, who moved there later, did not agree. Integration in the South occurred at times, such as when Bernhardt was taken in by a white family in rural North Carolina. Taunted by his black friends, Bernhardt responded in kind: "Yeah, I'm white. . . . I'm a dark-skinned white boy." In Savannah's Yamacraw district Trummy Young played with whites, once covering an Italian boy with charcoal so that both of them could attend a blacks-only theater. Young and Bernhardt probably shared Alberta Hunter's belief that "the [white] Southerner, if he's your friend, he's your friend. . . . You know how you stand with a Southerner."[53]

For most Americans, such childhood bonds were erased in adulthood, but black and white jazz musicians maintained a link because they shared a music. Sidney Bechet had grown up in New Orleans with an oppressive awareness of black isolation, yet he noticed that when jazz bands played in the 1910s "even the white musicians themselves, began to go with the music. They couldn't stay mad" and joined in. "Pretty soon there was all kinds of dancing and hell raising, everybody having a whole lot of fun, answering to all that rhythm there, feeling all that melody carry them along."[54] (Nevertheless, only those white New Orleanians who migrated North, such as Wingy Manone and Paul Mares, would ever acknowledge their debt to blacks.) In twenties Chicago, musical ideas were both exchanged and appropriated between the white and black jazz camps. As Ralph Brown remembered, "they didn't let us [blacks] play certain places, and [white] guys would steal, some guy would steal what someone was playing, there was some friction, but there wasn't much you could do about it." Nevertheless, despite segregation in downtown nightclubs, Brown and other blacks resolved to " 'steal some of theirs, too.' . . . the white boys had plenty to offer. I listened and got plenty from them. . . . something they'd do on the saxophone, that sounds good to me."[55]

Theft evolved into sharing, as white and black band arrangers circulated their work among themselves. Roy Lodwig of Jean Goldkette's competent white band would trade the group's arrangements (made by Bill Challis and others) for those used by Henderson's group, and Challis actually worked for Henderson in the early 1930s; at the same time, the black arranger Reginald Foresythe was hired by Bill Davison for his white Chicago band. Such communal behavior helped to counteract the continuing thievery of some white leaders, and blacks realized that other whites were charitable and generous with their own musical secrets. No aspect of jazz, however, bonded black and white as closely as interracial jam sessions, which began in twenties Chicago and became far more frequent in New York in the next decade. As Jimmy McPartland correctly noted, the Chicagoans' trips to the South Side's Sunset and Onyx Clubs "started the integration style musically" in Chicago.[56]

The line dividing "good" and "bad" musicians became less of a color line, as the jazz playing of some whites gained the respect and admiration of accomplished black players. In the twenties, Benny Carter and Lester Young had modeled some of their saxophone playing on Frank Trumbauer's recorded solos, and Clyde Bernhardt emulated the trombone sounds of the white players Miff Mole and Abe Lincoln. In later years Albert Nicholas admired Artie Shaw's clarinet, and Cootie Williams felt that the Benny Goodman band was "the only band . . . that really moved me." These players did not indicate that whites were equal or superior to the black pioneers; but rather, they acknowledged that white players brought useful new ideas and elements into jazz.[57] In the 1930s, the pathbreaking black virtuosi—Louis Armstrong, Earl Hines, Coleman Hawkins, Lester Young—set jazz's highest standards, but the lesser ranks contained many innovative and respected white players.

Admiring each other's music, these blacks and whites gradually saw themselves as workers in similar creative enterprises, and developed some personal and professional bonds. Occasionally these bonds were strong enough to overcome deep mistrusts. Sidney Bechet—generally very indignant about white jazz musicians—praised Eddie Condon for his efforts to keep the early style alive in his New York clubs. Louis Armstrong considered his white followers a kind of family, which perhaps gave him the respect and adulation he sought but did not always find among blacks. McPartland recalled that Armstrong's band "loved us and of course we loved them, you know. And Louis and King [Oliver] would come and sit down with us kids. . . . 'My boys,' Louis used to say, 'my boys.'" Bill Davison, however, recalled that he was "about the only white guy [Armstrong] asked to sit in" with his band, which conferred a special status on the Ohio trumpeter. Davison, thus, billed himself in 1932 at an all-black dance at Chicago's Savoy as "Wild Bill Davison—the White Louis Armstrong." Racial identities lessened in importance as skills in jazz were more widely shared.[58]

This musical relationship gave some players the ability to articulate a response to the general racial dilemma. White musicians became aware of how unusual their involvement in black music and culture was in a segregated society. In the 1920s Bud Freeman did not entirely divest himself of the white stereotype of blacks, but he did strive to do so in those years. "I know that I can honestly say that my prejudice never went to anything racial. I think my prejudices were always personal. We are all prejudiced in some way and about something, but it was not possible for me to have it since I admired the black musicians so much and loved the music so much."[59]

White musicians' acquaintances assailed them for admiring blacks. As the jazz historian Charles Edward Smith noted as early as 1930, "such [white] bands as the Wolverines were called 'white niggers'" in the 1920s. Jimmy Maxwell "was kidded in my home-town [Stockton, California] because my neighbors would say, 'Well, you're never going to be happy until you have a green suit and play with a nigger band, or something.'" Maxwell's responded by inverting the small-town white conceit the neighbors challenged him to reassert. "I said, 'that's right, you know.' . . . I always felt kind of flattered" to be considered worthy of a black band, and he said so. "I had the feeling in those days that black people had the edge in jazz. . . . whether it's a matter of race or culture or what-ever . . . that means nothing." For Maxwell, Mezz Mezzrow, and others, their association with black jazz was an assertion of pride and independence.[60]

By 1940, black and white musicians knew that they shared a common musical heritage, the product of a generation of creative integration. When the great controversy within jazz circles regard-ing bop music exploded during World War Two, older players of all colors reacted fiercely against the young innovators. Art Hodes recalled that the writer and composer Leonard Feather, an English-born advocate of the new sound, was the target of fistfights for older black and white players. Muggsy Spanier and Danny Alvin (who were white) as well as Coleman Hawkins, Eddie Heywood, and John Simmons "grabbed" or fought with the zealous young advocate. "There was no color line on who hit Leonard at that time," Hodes noted.[61]

The integration of musicians was helped along by a number of white managers, radio and record producers, and other promoters who also came to discount the color line. The South produced a few willing integrationists well before the thirties. Omar Bechet man-aged to secure what his son Sidney called the first riverboat job for a black band in New Orleans, from a boat manager who "was so fond of him." White passengers protested at first, but the music soon became popular, and the Streckfus family and others soon hired black bands for their boats. In about 1927, when most radio stations prohibited blacks from playing, Alonzo Ross's band made covert broadcasts from a station in Miami Beach. "That wasn't something that you heard of," band member Cootie Williams recalled, "because there wasn't no colored [people] allowed over there on the beach. . . . they used to sneak us over there to the radio station and sneak us back." A New York promoter heard the broadcast and hired the band for an engagement in Brooklyn, where the seventeen-year-old Williams began an illustrious northern career.[62]

In northern cities the AFM and commercial sponsors worked to ensure that no black musicians were permanently employed in network radio before 1940, and a variety of other constraints limited black involvement in recording, theater, and film. Still, the progress made in the thirties was substantial. Blacks had received sporadic exposure on radio since regular broadcasting began in the early twenties, usually on small black-owned stations or as rapid replacements for unavailable white musicians. Pops Foster, for example, played with the white jazzmen Joe Venuti and Eddie Lang on a 1930 program (in a rare trio of jazz violin, guitar, and bass), and other blacks received greater exposure on New York's Socialist station, WEVD. This paved the way for Ellington's, Tatum's, and Waller's local weekly shows, as well as Waller's breakthrough network show on CBS in 1934. After making successful broadcasts from London, Alberta Hunter also was called a pioneer, becoming in 1937 the first black entertainer to have her own radio show on an NBC affiliate; "The Alberta Hunter Show," incongruously featuring sweet white bands, ran on three different stations between 1937 and 1939.[63]

Phonograph recording helped black musicians even more fully, even though the income was meager compared to what radio or touring provided. Blacks benefited from the existence of the race record labels for the enthusiastic black listening public. Recording producers quickly became familiar with the wide array of talent featured on race records and began to hire blacks as replacements or first choices on mainstream-label releases for the white market, usually paired with white musicians. In the summer of 1923 Jelly Roll Morton assisted in a recording by the white New Orleans Rhythm Kings at the Gennett studio in Richmond, Indiana. Alberta Hunter claimed that in 1923 she became "the first Negro girl to record with a white band," the Original Memphis Five (from New York); discographers support her statement.[64]

Most recording executives, though, hesitated to record mixed bands. In 1928, when Eddie Condon and Louis Armstrong asked the OKeh producer Tommy Rockwell if they might record together, Rockwell "looked uneasy," Condon reported. "'I don't know about using a mixed group.' . . . 'If Victor can do it OKeh can do it,' I said." Rockwell was reassured, and the record was made in March 1929. The trumpeter "Ham" Davis also recorded with Condon in that year, and integrated sessions became more frequent.[65]

By the late thirties mixed jazz recordings were an accepted institution. Bud Freeman claimed inaccurately that "record dates" in the thirties "were always black and white"; while Freeman's discography shows that less than one-third of his recordings in that decade featured one or more blacks, his statement indicates that recording was nevertheless a progressive force in jazz race relations. By the late thirties, for example, members of the Ellington band felt free to ask Woody Herman if they could participate in some of Herman's recordings while they "struck" Ellington, protesting his use of their musical ideas.[66]

This commercial integration usually did not spring from conscious attempts to combat racism. The efforts of the young promoter John Henry Hammond, Jr., however, were an important exception to the general trend. Born in 1910 of wealthy parents (his mother was a Vanderbilt), Hammond combined a career as a writer on jazz and social problems with a variety of roles as promoter, record producer, and activist on behalf of white and black musicians, which became formalized in 1939 when Columbia Records made him a producer. A politically active, persistent, and well-connected advocate, Hammond was the most explicitly rebellious white advocate of early jazz. An amateur violinist, Hammond's great gift was his ability to detect new performers with innovative skills. Perhaps because he did not try to master an instrument or jazz techniques, he felt freer than any musician to associate racial progress with the advancement of jazz. His experience as a reporter on the trials of the Scottsboro boys in 1932 sealed his commitment.[67]

Like many white liberals, Hammond dedicated less of his time to radical politics after 1935, when the worst effects of the Depression eased; in that year he joined the executive board of the NAACP, which he felt "was losing some of its middle-class, middle-of-the-road caution." He also concentrated on selectively promoting black bands and soloists. Hammond had already gained enemies by criticizing Duke Ellington for compromising himself by working in whites-only clubs, and by refusing to aid Fletcher Henderson's orchestra. As Hammond claimed later, he felt

"Fletcher had a lassitude born of years of exploitation, so that when opportunities came to help himself he was unprepared to take advantage of them." When Henderson allowed his musicians to show up late for recording dates, Hammond believed that this exemplified "the discouragement Negroes felt as economic victims of the times, and perhaps it was also a small and self-defeating exercise of independence."[68] The promoter felt that leaders and bands with weak social resolve ultimately produced weak music. He used his connections and powers of persuasion to promote certain black bands (particular Count Basie's) over others, and in doing so helped to determine which black jazz musicians and genres would thrive, and which would struggle and wither, into the 1940s.

Controversy regarding Hammond's role still erupts today, but it is clear that Hammond was the individual who worked the hardest to integrate black and white jazz musicians in commercial music. In 1934 Hammond obtained a contract to produce recordings for English Columbia, and he tried to persuade Benny Goodman to lead a mixed big band featuring Benny Carter, Coleman Hawkins, and other black stars. Goodman vacillated and then turned Hammond down, insisting that "if it gets around that I recorded with colored guys I won't get another job in [New York]." Hammond was persistent with Goodman, however, and got him to record with Bessie Smith and Billie Holiday under a pseudonym. In 1936 Goodman hired the pianist Teddy Wilson, a favorite of Hammond's who became the first black to join a major white band. The next year, when the vibraphonist Lionel Hampton joined Goodman, Wilson, and the drummer Gene Krupa to form the Benny Goodman Quartet, jazz received its most dramatic early symbol of integration; "that Quartet," Hammond later wrote, "was a beautiful sight." At the same time Hammond also assisted the Count Basie band, introducing Basie to such future collaborators as Billie Holiday, Helen Humes, and Freddie Green. Hammond then began his work for Columbia in 1939 (after CBS had purchased it and eliminated its discriminatory contract policies) and developed more artists, and during World War Two pressed for the integration of radio bands and the armed forces.[69]

Other white promoters were fitful at best in aiding the cause of black musicians. David Kapp of Decca's notions of progressive behavior were to allow his black maid to audition prospective recording artists, give Woody Herman blues themes taped among southern rural blacks, and offer paltry recording contracts to Basie and others. William Morris, Jr., head of the talent agency of the same name, was an effective advocate of some black performers, aiding Duke Ellington in his fight to gain independence from Irving Mills and paving the way for Charlie Carpenter to become Earl Hines's personal manager (the first black to hold such a position).[70] Besides Morris, Hammond had few compatriots in his fight to orient the record industry toward biracial participation. Despite this and his controversial partiality, however, Hammond's efforts were widely publicized and were emulated more frequently in later decades, as white support for African-American civil rights increased.

White musicians themselves worked to advance black employment through a variety of means. The interracial band battle, a descendent of the band cutting contests in New Orleans, became an irregular fixture of the jazz scene in the late twenties. The OKeh Records Artists' Ball in Chicago on February 27, 1926, featured an exciting clash between the white Wolverines and Cook's Dreamland Orchestra, and in 1928 the Arcadia Ballroom staged a week-long battle between Lloyd and Cecil Scott's Band and the white Buffalodians. Bill Coleman of the Scott band recalled that "jazz battles did not exist in the terms of battles that were to become known a few years later," but the engagement was a success, as "we blew and sang enough to have a big majority of the public applauding for us after each number." By 1930, Chicago's Midway Gardens featured battles between Art Kassell's band and such black bands as Davis Goodman's. Such future band battles as a famous 1937 encounter in Newark between the Basie and Benny Goodman bands helped to establish the event as a jazz institution; the interracial nature of these battles deserves further exploration.[71]

More dramatically, white bandleaders integrated their own groups with greater frequency after 1935. Before this time, white leaders emulated Jack Laine's early efforts in New Orleans to keep his band racially "pure," although Bill Coleman did remember seeing the young Freddie Jenkins in a white Cincinnati band before 1920. In 1920s Chicago, besides working as the offstage arranger, Don Redman rehearsed the white Goldkette band, but he was not allowed to appear onstage with them. Mezz Mezzrow apparently broke the taboo, creating what was likely the first consciously mixed band in 1933 (a year before John Hammond's attempt), primarily for a recording date.[72] It was probably standard (as William E. Samuels recalled) for whites initially to hire blacks to play rhythm instruments, but a few blowing players also eventually found work in white bands. In 1939, while Clyde Bernhardt was freelancing during the Edgar Hayes Band's hiatus, he played with whites for the first time. By the early 1940s interracial hiring took place in the other direction as well. Eddie Durham, who toured with his black All-Star Girls' Band, pointed out that "when I ran out of black girls, I used a lot of white [players]. . . . When we'd go down South, I'd take the white girls out of the band and put them in [another] band."[73] Generally, though, the rate of interracial band hiring remained slow into the 1940s.

Still, a sense of mission grew among some players with respect to race. By the late 1930s many of them sensed that jazz could serve as a weapon against Jim Crow. As a young man in the 1920s Earl Hines had found that mixed audiences in Pittsburgh were rolling back the dominant prejudices: "it was musicians and theatrical people who first began to change the strictly segregated way of life. People in Pittsburgh began to forget about discrimination as we began to play in more places and make friends. . . . soon there was less discrimination and envy there." Similarly, in the 1970s Hines could view his band's tours of the South as exercises that challenged Jim Crow. "My band was among the first Freedom Riders, because we were riding through the South many, many years ago, and creating all kinds of excitement. . . . When Southern whites wanted to board *our* bus, the [white] driver would say, 'This is a private bus.' Of course, he and these people would get into all kinds of arguments."[74]

Important white bandleaders, such as Benny Goodman, Charlie Barnet, and Artie Shaw, made significant and persistent efforts to erase racial divisions in their bands, tours, and concerts. As Billie Holiday recalled of Shaw, "Artie [in 1937] was a guy who never thought in terms of race." On a tour through Kentucky Shaw ensured that Holiday, the only black in his band, roomed in the best (and most segregated) hotels in each town. Clerks would refuse her admittance, "but Artie didn't want to give in." Holiday was frightened at first by Shaw's insistence, but soon became emboldened enough to challenge hecklers herself in St. Louis and other locales. She concluded that Shaw "didn't win. But he didn't lose either." Goodman demanded that his black band members be allowed to enter nightclubs through the front doors (although he once acquiesced to an owner who asked that these players enter the front without their tuxedo jackets), and he viewed Jim Crow as a profound impediment to good music making. Challenging Jim Crow earned these bandleaders no profits and little prestige; their actions added a new dimension to the "leader's" role in the jazz world, but also alienated them from their more conventional white peers. As

Holiday wrote of Shaw in 1956, "people still talk about him as if he were nuts because there were things more important to him than a million damn bucks a year."[75]

As their professional techniques, places of employment, goals, and concepts of jazz converged in the 1930s, the most skilled white and black musicians began to share their private lives and concerns. Their increased contact in nightclubs, recording studios, and jam sessions had allowed them to blend white and black musical styles, attitudes, and speech. This exchange transformed white players in particular, as they gained the clear understanding that African Americans were fully capable of excelling at an important artistic activity and that their work in jazz reflected their seriousness and competence as informed members of a rapidly evolving urban society. "The colored guys," the young Gene Krupa told Mezz Mezzrow in 1927, "really get out in front and set the pace when they're given half a chance."[76] Few white Americans of any region or social class had exposed themselves as fully to blacks, or came to appreciate and advocate their equality as enthusiastically, as had these musicians. Unlike their black counterparts, whites had to divest themselves of racist attitudes toward the other color. For this reason, the illusion persists that the white integrationists were subverting the dominant racial regime more radically, although the rise of the black players was a more dramatic challenge (and the essential precondition for the whites' new attitude).

Whites spoke of jazz as a foundation for a new ethic of biraciality. Many of the incidents that epitomized this attitude were intimate and comparatively modest, such as when Jimmy McPartland spent afternoons in Art Tatum's apartment, drinking beer with the near-blind pianist and reading him adventure stories. Similarly, the Maxwell family's sheltering of a stranded black band in rural California reinforced Jimmy's dedication to jazz, white assistance to Earl Hines and other players in Pennsylvania gave them examples of interracial kindness, and Harlem blacks' general hospitality to whites in and out of jam sessions promoted extramusical friendships and trust. When Bud Freeman strolled the Harlem streets in the early morning, "nobody would bother you . . . word was out that the white musicians were there to hear the music and everything was fine, not that they would have bothered us anyway."[77]

Freeman's view was not unique. Artie Shaw's experience in Harlem, where he played with the great stride pianist Willie "the Lion" Smith, began as a musical odyssey, as he attempted "to latch on to what [Smith] was doing . . . whenever we slid into one of those complicated little modulatory phrases of his." Eventually this music making and interracial openness gave young Shaw "a sense of *belonging*—a feeling of being accepted," which this victim of childhood anti-Semitism sorely needed. "For the most part I was actually living the life of a Negro musician, adopting Negro values and attitudes, and accepting the Negro out-group point of view not only about music but life in general." While Shaw was not a person to believe for long that he had "become" black (in contrast to Mezz Mezzrow, for example), the Harlem experience crystallized Shaw's sense of racial equality and justice, which came into play during his years as a bandleader. Jimmy McPartland also gained this sense in the 1930s, when he came to feel that jazz bands *had* to be mixed racially. "I usually have a six piece band. I usually like to try to get three black and three white. This represents America to me. And it represents music also."[78]

The white attraction to blacks and to jazz was always emotional as well as artistic in nature. When Wingy Manone and Art Hodes visited Louis Armstrong at Chicago's Savoy Ballroom, "Louis would see us at once, and his face would light up—and we'd feel warm inside." For a white admirer of jazz such as William K. Vanderbilt, a visit from black musicians relieved him from his duties—perhaps even his identity—as a New York multimillionaire. As Garvin Bushell recalled, Vanderbilt was a miserable man who told the musicians that he wished "I could have just half the fun that you guys have, but I can't because. . . . I don't know who's genuine, who means what they say in my own family." Trapped by unusually strong Victorian restrictions, Vanderbilt was relieved of his miseries by Fats Waller and the other musicians. "Fats used to say, 'Vanderbilt, you give me some of your money, I'll show you how to have fun.' And that would knock him out." While a John Hammond found ethical and historical reasons for the need to value blacks and their music, other whites such as Vanderbilt—Hammond's great-uncle—saw the African American as a remedy for the heart. This was dangerous, of course; in this incident Waller reprised the minstrel's role to an extent, as the voice of repressed white sensuality. On the other hand, he did so as the emotional and social tutor of one of the nation's wealthiest whites, and in the privacy of the latter's own parlor, at a vast distance from the degrading public ritual of the southern jazz dance. Still, in such cases the danger of misunderstanding and exploitation remained.[79]

It was not surprising, then, that black musicians responded to

this white admiration with a mixture of avuncular pride and cir-
cumspection, proud of their hard-won artistic status but aware of
the continuing precariousness of their economic and social positions. On the positive side, when Louis Armstrong called Bill Davison, Jimmy McPartland and other white disciples "my boys," or
when Willie the Lion Smith tended to "cubs" he nurtured at Pod's
and Jerry's, they expressed as black men a degree of mastery and
authority rarely matched in American race relations.[80]

At the same time, among the more conventionally talented
black players, the cautiously approving attitude of Ralph Brown
was probably common. Brown resented the humiliating restrictions
that the musicians' union placed on black employment and the subservient role blacks were expected to enact in South Side clubs,
but he believed that institutions, not individuals, kept them apart.
"The union hasn't been as close as it could be, but the white and
black musicians have always been close." While Pops Foster played
in few interracial jam sessions in 1920s Chicago, he too recalled
spending leisure hours with Bix Beiderbecke, Rod Cless, Pee Wee
Russell, Frank Trumbauer, and other whites. Attending barbecues
and drinking parties, "we just got together for kicks. The colored
and white musicians were just one," and would even "go out with
the same girls." Bud Freeman corroborated Foster's claim regarding biracial dating, which seemed usually to involve black women.
Dave Tough married one of the two black chorus members whom
he and Freeman courted in the 1930s, and Mezz Mezzrow and Gil
Evans also married black women. (It is certainly not clear, though,
that whites tolerated relations between black musicians and white
women, although none explicitly condemned this.)[81]

When strong interracial friendships were made between musicians, the final individual hurdles created by racist socialization had
been overcome. When he worked at CBS in the 1940s, Milt Hinton became very close to white studio musicians, and he noted that
their friendships were built on a foundation of mutual professional
respect. "This is how this relationship—which is still lasting—had
to come about. We were friends first, we respected each others'
crafts, each others' talents," and eventually "got to be so tight it was
ridiculous." Still, persuading their families (who had not bonded
across the color line through jazz) to follow them remained a challenge. "It was difficult for us to get through to our families about
this." Segregated residentially and socially, some months passed before Hinton's wife and children could interact comfortably with his

white friends and their families: "it took a lot of doing and a lot of loving concern from amongst us to sell to our families this relationship." However, the racial climate in the larger musicians' culture in Manhattan continued to liberalize, in Hinton's view; when he beat out white bassists for freelance jobs, they were disappointed, but they never voiced or indicated any racially based antagonism.[82]

At the deepest personal level, some white musicians found that jazz was a means for dissolving white and black prejudices and geographical barriers. For them it became welcome, and perhaps essential, to ignore real or imagined racial differences. Remarks by such whites as Gil Evans convey the subtle, utilitarian process by which they diminished concepts of racial difference in their lives. "I don't feel black or white. I don't feel like I tried [or] I haven't tried; I just skirted around that one [racial identity]. Because if I didn't skirt around it, I'd be missing out on things in life." Similarly, Jimmy Maxwell noted that "when you're working in a band, you forget who's black and who's white. . . . you've got to start visualizing which is which. You see somebody enough, they don't have a color anymore." In Maxwell's own mind, therefore, the old white-southern confusion about "passing" and racially marginal individuals was transformed into a state of contented ambiguity. During his first years as a player in mixed bands the trumpeter overdid this attitude: "it took me many years to get mad at a black guy. I always sort of backed off. So, in other words, I had a prejudice in reverse, there was a difference in my mind."[83] At least in an individual's mind, then, it was possible for prejudices to be reversed or neutralized.

Maxwell's state of mind could suggest a bittersweet conclusion: that racial equality in jazz before 1940 could not exist anywhere outside certain individuals' perceptions. In fact, integration and equality in jazz were woefully incomplete by that year, and there were fundamental reasons for this. It has been argued incorrectly that the jazz community worked consciously towards cultural integration and biracial understanding.[84] The evidence on this issue, though, is conflicting at best, indicating both the complexity of individual musicians and the difficulties confronting any attempt to build interracial trust in the 1930s. While 1930s jazz resulted from the combined effort of whites and blacks, musicians on the whole did not make integration and racial equality a primary goal. In general, integration before 1940 was a by-product of their searches for professional and artistic stimulation and growth. As it had for other Americans in the thirties, racism presented the advocates of equality in jazz with too many daunting barriers.

In jazz, above all, the specter of blackface minstrelsy stifled personal and commercial exchanges. Viewing black jazz musicians onstage, white audiences—and some white musicians—saw them as heirs to the subservient minstrel and "coon" personae of earlier decades. Blacks fought back by using jazz, with its unique cultural and intellectual properties, to probe, assess, and evade the "dynamic of minstrelsy" on and off bandstands. Sometimes this meant recoiling from involvement with whites, but it also led to confrontations with the persons and the ideology that demeaned them. Although their efforts had little ameliorative effect on white listeners, their attempts on southern tours to maintain and enhance their dignity in the face of hostility give jazz, at least in retrospect, a special cultural significance. Few other black enterprises of this era fostered such a cadre of combative, proud, and innovative professionals.

Before 1940 sensitive white musicians, such as the Chicagoans, became aware of these developments. Despite the persistence of racism everywhere, the 1930s saw a significant increase in the racial integration of jazz, in bands and recording studios and during musicians' leisure hours. The changes certainly were not as extensive or as rapid as they might have been, but the contours of a future victory were evident in the growing activism and assertiveness of jazz advocates of racial equality, in public, in private, and over the airwaves.

Epilogue

Any historian of jazz should keep the words of Hoagy Carmichael and Bill Moenkhaus (Carmichael's boyhood friend in Bloomington, Indiana) in mind as both a goal and a warning. According to Carmichael, Moenkhaus told him in the 1920s that the "real" jazz history would never be written: "Most writers who record the events of the Jazz Age [a term Moenkhaus disliked] really know nothing of the real jazz. They mostly stick to the Ritz." Carmichael, writing in 1965, agreed: "we barnstormed and slept in buses, ate road-house food, met the early jazz giants," "but we didn't write about it, so it went into history all ass-backwards." [1] The jazz aficionados who wrote and read the flood of memoirs, discographies, oral histories, and other writings were dedicated to changing that, but even after these works are published, and after academics and others gather, classify, and re-present the evidence in this literature to fit scholarly molds, Moenkhaus's and Carmichael's challenge remains: can we recover "the real jazz" through scholarship?

Sources in early jazz history are profoundly elusive; written sources are scarce, the large amount of oral testimony is contradictory and often impossible to corroborate, and at this writing most of the richest sources of all—the early jazz musicians and their friends—have run out of their share of years and have taken crucial opinions and recollections with them to the grave. Jazz histories are hobbled by more than their share of the hazards that thinkers have detected in the writing of history—the elusiveness of objectivity, the inevitability of interpretation (*of* and *by* the informants), indecision about context, and the dominance of paradigmatic myths that predetermine our conclusions. [2] Objectivity, judiciousness, factuality, and other traditional standards of historical research are difficult to maintain in jazz histories, but I have tried my best in writing the present work. The book is unavoidably a hermeneutic exercise, however, since it shows how aging musicians interpreted their early lives and also seeks to corroborate and make sense of their interpretations through its own overlay of contexts, sources, and recent social and historiographical concepts. I have not willingly or perversely sought to be so intersubjective; the nature of the documentation often led me in that direction.

Especially because such challenges are endemic to jazz history, further work must be done on all the social and musical phenomena I have discussed in this synthesis. Because of the limits of space, time, and energy, I only sketch the rural and urban communities in which jazz was nurtured, the dozens of musicians' cultures that sprouted up around early jazz, the interrelations of race, individual development and creativity, and the role of economics and commercialism in the development of musicians' and listeners' attitudes. Sources that were not used should be mined to bolster (or refute) the book's statements about the significance of jazz for persons or groups, in fine-grained studies of family relations, education, socialization, and career strategies. Despite the paucity of press coverage of early jazz and the elusiveness of privately held sources, I am convinced that stronger sociocultural analyses can be made on a smaller scale, and that the still-dominant goal of objectivity can be better attained through careful research.

These studies, and others I envision, would in fact take us beyond the accurate recounting of early jazz history that Carmichael and Moenkhaus hoped for. The study of jazz suggests how certain themes in American studies might be reconsidered and rejuvenated. For example, after two decades of growth, community studies has become a moribund genre in United States social history. The imaginative recent work of Roy Rosenzweig, Stuart Blumin, and Mary Ryan notwithstanding, community studies (and the use of new quantitative methods that spawned them) have become less popular, as scholars once again tend to favor impressionistic sources over databases, broad developments over isolated microcosms, and issues of ideology and social change over the everyday life of the "inarticulate."[3]

Some, however, such as Mary Ryan and Samuel Kinser, have reinvigorated the study of communities by focusing upon particular rituals or cultural moments, which may occur at fixed times and places, hold special meaning for community members, and might distinguish their community from others. This work often acknowledges the importance of social dramas (whose primacy was stressed most effectively by the anthropologist Victor Turner), moving away from the search for static structures or an *histoire totale* full of quotidian detail.[4] To an extent, jazz performances were public rituals; they were the focus of social energy among migrating African Americans who held specific notions about education and self-advancement, and among rebellious and quiescent whites who put very different notions of race and self-development into play on the bandstand and in the audience. For local urban communities, jazz performance was a social drama, and the nature of these rituals in hundreds of locales (and the changes in the performances' meaning over time) could be profitably studied in the future.

Among the many subtopics that should be explored, historians perhaps ought to pay the closest attention to the end of the early jazz era. After 1940, the big band or swing style was rejected by the best new black musicians, who pursued a subtler and more complex small-band style which is now usually called bebop. At that time, other young blacks in the northern ghettos foresook jazz for the music of the new rural arrivals—the blues—now amplified and more percussive. Although social historians in the 1960s and 1970s and scholars of African-American letters and culture today have given us a solid set of concepts with which to deal with the migration and settlement periods of 1915 to 1935, we have almost no comparable understanding of black thought and community just before and during the Second World War. The rise of what we now call bebop, I would suggest, rode atop a critical change in black emotions and attitudes during the second (and larger) "great migration."

This is indicated by the testimony in Ira Gitler's oral history of bebop. The younger musicians knew that Charlie Parker's improvisations overshadowed and even effaced the melodies on which they were based (a distinct contrast to early jazz musicians' adherence to clear melodic outlines); at first the new style was "shocking," "unbelievable," and "shatter[ing]." As the guitarist Biddy Fleet noted, the new generation "put art above the commercial side" and used "changes and different keys . . . to separate the sheep from the goats," to establish who were "commune brothers" who "know what's going on." Like their elders, these rebels had like-minded white colleagues, such as the trumpeter Johnny Carisi, who avoided

Eddie Condon's suspicious gaze because he was "that smart kind of person, bullshit-type thing that figured with his bad, bad guitar playing."[5]

The generation gap was indeed wide. To Billy Eckstine, the new dissonances and lines were "just a way of seeking at that particular point," but to most veterans of the 1920s and 1930s, bebop was alien, hostile, and not a little frightening. Mezz Mezzrow called bebop "the music of tics," "the agony of the split, hacked-up personality;" Natty Dominique thought it was "nothing but a mess"; and Louis Armstrong heard only "weird chords that don't mean nothin'."[6] The young players explicitly disavowed the accommodations that Armstrong and other elders had made, to both racism and to commercialism, and in the hands of the young Dizzie Gillespie and others knife-fighting in jazz reemerged, reviving the combat spirit of 1910s New Orleans.[7] A more politically informed, angry, and musically adventurous generation of musicians had arrived.

Future studies need to explore how the growing despair of the ghettos, the fresh worries and opportunities brought by World War Two, and the second great migration of southern blacks to northern cities energized the wrenching change jazz underwent during the war, and how those larger struggles might have been played out in the ritual of jazz performance. Such work might also provide us with badly needed overviews of bebop musical culture and its relation to extramusical life.

With respect to the pre-1940 era, this book hints at many subjects related to jazz musicians that need further attention. In chapter 7, for example, I argue that jazz musicians did not create a subculture. On the one hand, they certainly created a musical culture, but in their extramusical lives they only used and abandoned various elements of white and especially black American shared learned behavior, and they never developed a specific, discrete life style. Scholars with an interest in jazz and in the larger issue of popular music's relation to twentieth-century countercultures should test this argument by doing further research and filling in the details on early jazz. Unfortunately, like community studies, the study of American youth culture, adolescence, and social rebellion is moribund—I was startled to find how fully this subfield dried up in the late 1980s, as I researched this book—and we still do not have a history of how this rebellion was formed (if indeed it had a century-long gestation, as Greil Marcus has argued).[8]

If jazz seemed to detach itself eventually from youth culture, it also seems to have strayed somewhat from black culture as well. Students of the African-American tradition would be well advised to consider how central or marginal jazz (early and recent) has been to that tradition, and to what extent jazz has strayed from the "roots" of black expression into realms with which the "folk" were unfamiliar or indifferent. Throughout the book I argue that blacks in jazz dispensed with some rich elements in African-American music—such as the rural traditions of song and dance—and that they Europeanized their music and worldviews in some pronounced ways. This may explain why jazz declined as a popular black music after 1940 and why the later jazz players formed an insular, deviant subculture cut off from the white—and black—mainstream. Here again, though, this concept needs much more research and discussion, especially since the very nature of the African-American cultural tradition (and jazz's role in it) is at issue.

The early jazz musicians' story also suggests that historians should take a fresh look at the general formation of professions and professional attitudes in America. The establishment of the traditional professions in the United States—law, medicine, and higher education—has received much recent attention from scholars, who view it as a Weberian by-product of the rationalization of industrial society. Sometime in the 1920s—and perhaps in New Orleans in the 1910s—jazz musicians came to perceive themselves as artists who possessed special skills and ways of obtaining those skills, standards that had to be upheld, and a musical style that needed to be nurtured in the marketplace and through constant professional group contact. What Louis Levy and John Paul Perhonis have called (in separate, intriguing dissertations) the growing "formalism" in jazz might be more accurately termed "professionalization."[9]

If this thesis is correct, then it would be especially interesting to explore how a group only two generations removed from slavery, often deprived of formal education, and subject to extreme racial oppression, was able to create (in a brief decade in the North) a network and a sense of purpose similar to that of the learned white professions. Was the professional paradigm part of the folk understanding of how individuals might succeed in America, and if so, was it filtered through their early identities as members of voluntary associations? It is not enough simply to marvel at their achievement nor to give the credit to the white promoters who packaged them as jazz acts: neither gets at the heart of why musicians were able to organize for the betterment of the music. After the 1930s, the fan and recording clubs, a few jazz classrooms, the union halls, and other institutions were in place or had recognized the jazz profession as worthy of support, and the musicians' professional identity was easy to preserve, but before that time it was their own cohesion that preserved and enhanced the music. Again, this phenomenon seems to bridge folk and commercial life in America in a dramatic way, or perhaps blurs the distinction we make between them, a distinction that historians of the professions in America have traditionally relied upon.

Finally, chapter 6 of this study should be considered a first step toward exploring the nature of creativity in jazz. Social and behavioral scientists, led by Howard Gardner and his colleagues at Harvard's Project Zero, have only begun to explore how creativity is stimulated in children and adults and how it is channelized and maintained. The most intriguing aspect of Gardner's work is his argument that musical creativity seems to be the product of a special set of brain functions, which is one of several essential sets of creative capacities.[10] For individual jazz musicians, we have seen, there were standard steps each took toward building a personal style, which later served as their most important professional asset. To paraphrase the statement by Wynton Marsalis with which this book began, jazz creativity seems to have been a remarkable expression of individuality in a democracy, of how a person could take a stock of techniques and create a unique, masterful style out of those elements. Viewed from Gardner's neuropsychological perspective, jazz represents an extreme fulfillment of the music "lobe's" creative potential, a musical activity radically free from any standardized expression.

Future studies ought to work toward uniting this interpretation with the sociohistorical reading of Marsalis's statement, which might argue that the United States in the 1920s—*only* there, and *only* by then—offered social realities and/or hopes that allowed for such creative musical freedom. In this book, I have argued that the converging African and European heritages, black freedom and migration, white middle-class socialization and the seeds of rebellion it nurtured, modern city life, and other factors gave individuals just enough space and time to create what had been impossible to create in a less urban, more segregated America. Perhaps only the fine-grained analysis of isolated record cuts (pioneered musicologically by Gunther Schuller, but which needs to be supplemented with the social and biographical approaches I have stressed) can show that the minds of jazz musicians actually *did* work in this important new way.

Jazz, I believe, can be integrated more fully into American

historiography. In turn, the historical study of jazz can contribute to our understanding of the relations between individuals, art, and society in the United States. With further exploration of this subject, we will know better how to interpret such statements as Max Kaminsky's, who wrote so eloquently about his colleagues and his experience in jazz in twenties Chicago: "America was still so young and new then and we all had the feeling of wanting to do something great." [11]

Notes

Introduction

1. Wynton Marsalis, untitled Regents Lecture, University of California, Berkeley, November 1987.

2. Warren I. Susman, *Culture as History* (New York: Pantheon, 1984), 105, 120–21; Nathan I. Huggins, *Harlem Renaissance* (New York: Oxford University Press, 1971), 10–11; Lewis A. Erenberg, *Steppin' Out: New York Nightlife and the Transformation of American Culture, 1890–1930* (Westport, Conn.: Greenwood Press, 1981); Elaine Tyler May, *Great Expectations: Marriage and Divorce in Post-Victorian America* (Chicago: University of Chicago Press, 1980); Kathy J. Ogren, *The Jazz Revolution: Twenties America and the Meaning of Jazz* (New York: Oxford University Press, 1989), 7. See also Lawrence W. Levine, "American Culture and the Great Depression," *Yale Review* 74 (Winter 1985), 196–223.

3. Gunther Schuller, *Early Jazz: Its Roots and Musical Development* (New York: Oxford University Press, 1968); Schuller, *The Swing Era: The Development of Jazz, 1930–1945* (New York: Oxford University Press, 1989); Olly W. Wilson, "The Significance of the Relationship between Afro-American and West African Music," *The Black Perspective in Music* 2:1 (Spring 1974), 3–22; John Storm Roberts, *Black Music of Two Worlds* (New York: Praeger, 1972); Thomas Owens, "Charlie Parker: Techniques of Improvisation" (Ph.D. diss., University of California, Los Angeles, 1974; Ann Arbor: University Microfilms International, 75-1992); Milton Lee Stewart, "Structural Development in the Jazz Improvisational Technique of Clifford Brown" (Ph.D. diss., University of Michigan, 1973; Ann Arbor: University Microfilm International, 73-24692); Scott K. DeVeaux, "Jazz in Transition: Coleman Hawkins and Howard McGhee, 1935–1945" (Ph.D. diss., University of California, Berkeley, 1985); James L. Collier, *Duke Ellington* (New York: Oxford University Press, 1987).

4. Alan P. Merriam, *The Anthropology of Music* (Evanston: North-

western University Press, 1964), esp. 243–44; Alan P. Merriam and Raymond W. Mack, "The Jazz Community," *Social Forces* 38 (March 1960), 211–22; Jeff Todd Titon, *Early Downhome Blues: A Musical and Cultural Analysis* (Urbana: University of Illinois Press, 1975); David Evans, *Big Road Blues: Tradition and Creativity in the Folk Blues* (Berkeley: University of California Press, 1982).

5. Merriam, *The Anthropology of Music;* Bruno Nettl, *Folk Music in the United States: An Introduction* (Detroit: Wayne State University Press, 1976) and *The Study of Ethnomusicology* (Urbana: University of Illinois Press, 1983). See also Marcia Herndon and Norma McLeod, *Music as Culture*, 2d ed. (Darby, Pa.: Norwood, 1982).

6. Carlo Lastrucci, "The Professional Dance Musician," *Journal of Musicology* 3 (Winter 1941), 168–72; Morroe Berger, "Jazz: Resistance to the Diffusion of a Culture Pattern," *Journal of Negro History* 32 (October 1947), 461–94; Norman M. Margolis, "A Theory on the Psychology of Jazz," *American Imago* 11 (Fall 1954), 263–91; Aaron H. Esman, "Jazz— A Study in Cultural Conflict," *American Imago* 8 (June 1951), 219–26; Howard S. Becker, *Outsiders: Studies in the Sociology of Deviance* (London: Free Press of Glencoe, 1963); Louis H. Levy, "The Formalization of New Orleans Jazz Musicians: a Case Study of Organizational Change," (Ph.D. diss., Virginia Polytechnic Institute, 1976; Ann Arbor: University Microfilms International, 1979, 76-24327); Neil Leonard, *Jazz and the White Americans: The Acceptance of a New Art Form* (Chicago: University of Chicago Press, 1962); Neil Leonard, *Jazz: Myth and Religion* (New York: Oxford University Press, 1987). See also Merriam and Mack, "The Jazz Community."

7. On drug use, see Charles Winick, "The Use of Drugs by Jazz Musicians," *Social Problems* 7:3 (Winter 1959–60), 240–53.

8. Greil Marcus, *Lipstick Traces: A Secret History of the Twentieth Century* (Cambridge: Harvard University Press, 1989); James B. Gilbert, *A Cycle of Outrage: America's Reaction to the Juvenile Delinquent in the 1950s* (New York: Oxford University Press, 1986).

9. See, for example, Charles Keil, *Urban Blues* (Chicago: University of Chicago Press, 1966); Martin T. Williams, *Jazz Masters in Transition, 1957–69* (New York: Macmillan, 1970).

10. Jack V. Buerkle and Danny Barker, *Bourbon Street Black: The New Orleans Black Jazzman* (New York: Oxford University Press, 1973); Charles Nanry and Edward Berger, *The Jazz Text* (New York: Van Nostrand Rinehart, 1979).

11. See, for example, Donald M. Marquis's discussion of the legends other musicians have woven around the early cornetist Charles "Buddy" Bolden, in *In Search of Buddy Bolden: First Man of Jazz* (Baton Rouge: Louisiana State University Press, 1978), chap. 1, and James Lincoln Collier's refutation of Louis Armstrong's alleged 4 July 1900 birthdate in *Louis Armstrong* (London: Pan, 1984), 18–21.

12. General problems associated with the use of oral histories are

discussed in Trevor Lummis, *Listening to History: The Authenticity of Oral Evidence* (London: Hutchinson Educational, 1987), and Paul Thompson, *The Voice of the Past: Oral History*, 2d ed. (New York: Oxford University Press, 1988), esp. 110–17, 137–48, and chap. 5. With regard to jazz oral histories, see Douglas Henry Daniels, "Oral History, Masks, and Protocol in the Jazz Community," *Oral History Review* 15 (Spring 1987), 146–63; Ron Welburn, "Toward Theory and Method with the Jazz Oral History Project," *Black Music Research Journal 1986*, 79–95; Burton W. Peretti, "Oral Histories of Jazz Musicians: The N.E.A. Transcripts as Texts in Context," American Historical Association meeting, 28 December 1990.

13. John Bodnar, Roger Simon, and Michael P. Weber, *Lives of Their Own: Blacks, Italians, and Poles in Pittsburgh, 1900–1960* (Urbana: University of Illinois Press, 1982).

14. Leroi Jones (Imamu Amiri Baraka), *Blues People* (New York: William Morrow, 1963); Lawrence W. Levine, *Black Culture and Black Consciousness: Afro-American Folk Thought from Slavery to Freedom* (New York: Oxford University Press, 1977), esp. 290–96; Albert Murray, *The Omni-Americans: New Perspectives on the Black Experience and American Culture* (New York: Outerbridge and Dienstfrey, 1970), esp. 54–61, and *Stomping the Blues* (New York: McGraw-Hill, 1976); Katrina Hazzard-Gordon, *Jookin': The Rise of Social Dance Formations in African-American Culture* (Philadelphia: Temple University Press, 1990); Daphne Duval Harrison, *Black Pearls: Blues Queens of the 1920s* (New Brunswick: Rutgers University Press, 1988). See also Ben Sidran, *Black Talk* (New York: Da Capo, 1973).

15. See, for example, Henry Louis Gates, Jr., *The Signifying Monkey: A Vernacular Theory of African-American Literature* (New York: Oxford University Press, 1988); Houston A. Baker, *Blues, Ideolgy, and Afro-American Literature: A Vernacular Theory* (Chicago: University of Chicago Press, 1984); Hazel V. Carby, *Reconstructing Womanhood: The Emergence of the Afro-American Woman Novelist* (New York: Oxford University Press, 1987); Sterling Stuckey, *Slave Culture: Nationalist Theory and the Foundations of Black America* (New York: Oxford University Press, 1987).

16. Quoted in Dempsey J. Travis, *An Autobiography of Black Jazz* (Chicago: Urban Research Institute, 1983), 341.

17. Frederic Jameson, "Postmodernism, or the Cultural Logic of Late Capitalism," *New Left Review* 146 (July–August 1984), 53–92.

Chapter 1: *"I Couldn't See Anything but Music"*

1. See Julio Finn, *The Bluesman: The Musical Heritage of Black Men and Women in the Americas* (London: Quartet Books, 1986), 9–37; Melville J. Herskovits, *The Myth of the Negro Past* (New York: Harper and Row, 1941), esp. chap. 7. George Eaton Simpson, *Black Religions in the New World* (New York: Columbia University Press, 1978), 12–18, discusses the especially pronounced survival of West African religion within new-world "cults."

2. See Finn, *The Bluesman*, esp. 99–150; Simpson, *Black Religions in the New World*, 217–19; Charles Joyner, *Down by the Riverside: A South Carolina Slave Community* (Urbana: University of Illinois Press, 1984), 144–50; Lynne Fauley Emery, *Black Dance: From 1619 to Today*, 2d rev. ed. (Princeton: Princeton Book Company, 1988), 154–72.

3. See Stuckey, *Slave Culture*, intro.; Levine, *Black Culture and Black Consciousness*, chap. 1; Albert J. Raboteau, *Slave Religion: The "Invisible Institution" in the Antebellum South* (New York: Oxford University Press, 1978).

4. See J. Kwabena Nketia, *The Music of Africa* (New York: Norton, 1974), esp. chaps. 2, 12, 13, and sec. 4; John Miller Chernoff, *African Rhythm and African Sensibility: Aesthetics and Social Action in African Musical Idioms* (Chicago: University of Chicago Press, 1979), esp. chap. 4; Wilson, "Significance of the Relationship between Afro-American and West African Music"; Sory Camara, *Gens de la Parole: Essai Sur la Condition et le Role des Griots dans la Société Malinké* (Paris: La Haye-Mouton, 1976), esp. chap. 7; Robert Farris Thompson, *Flash of the Spirit: African and Afro-American Art and Philosophy* (New York: Random House, 1983), chap. 3.

5. See Dena J. Epstein, *Sinful Tunes and Spirituals: Black Folk Music to the Civil War* (Urbana: University of Illinois Press, 1977), 139–58; Levine, *Black Culture and Black Consciousness*, chaps. 1, 2; Emery, *Black Dance*, 87–130; Hazzard-Gordon, *Jookin'*, chap. 1.

6. See Leon F. Litwack, *Been in the Storm So Long: The Aftermath of Slavery* (New York: Knopf, 1979), esp. 515–24; Waldo E. Martin, Jr., *The Mind of Frederick Douglass* (Chapel Hill: University of North Carolina Press, 1984), chap. 8; David W. Blight, *Frederick Douglass's Civil War: Keeping Faith in Jubilee* (Baton Rouge: Louisiana State University Press, 1989), 199–200; August Meier, *Negro Thought in America, 1880–1915* (Ann Arbor: University of Michigan Press, 1963), 4–16.

7. W. E. B. Du Bois, *The Souls of Black Folk* (1903), rpt. in *Du Bois: Selected Writings* (New York: Library of America, 1986), 365, 459.

8. Du Bois, *The Souls of Black Folk*, 430. See also Eric Foner, *Reconstruction: America's Unfinished Revolution, 1863–1877* (New York: Harper and Row, 1988); C. Vann Woodward, *The Strange Career of Jim Crow*, 3d rev. ed. (New York: Oxford University Press, 1974), chaps. 1–3. Du Bois presented a more respectful view of slave culture in *The Gift of Black Folk: The Negroes in the Making of America* (New York: AMS Press, 1924, rpt. ed. 1971), chaps. 8, 9.

9. See E. Franklin Frazier, *The Negro Family in the United States* (Chicago: University of Chicago Press, 1939), 483–84; Herbert G. Gutman, *The Black Family in Slavery and Freedom, 1750–1925* (New York: Knopf, 1977), xvii–xxiv and chaps. 9, 10.

10. Levine, *Black Culture and Black Consciousness*, 158; also 138–74. Paul Oliver, *Songsters and Saints: Vocal Traditions on Race Records* (Cambridge: Cambridge University Press, 1984), intro. and chap. 1, sketches the parallel rise of sacred and secular black traditions but offers no interpretation of their respective importance to black culture as a whole.

11. See Eileen Southern, *The Music of Black Americans* (New York: Norton, 1971), 249–51; Gilbert Chase, *America's Music: From the Pilgrims to the Present*, 3d rev. ed. (Urbana: University of Illinois Press, 1987), 213–31.

12. Tom Fletcher, *100 Years of the Negro in Show Business* (New York: Burdge, 1954), offers the fullest portrait of black minstrelsy. See also Robert Toll, *Blacking Up: The Minstrel Show in the Nineteenth Century* (New York: Oxford University Press, 1974), chap. 4; Southern, *The Music of Black Americans*, 257–77, 294–304; Oliver, *Songsters and Saints*, chap. 2.

13. See Southern, *The Music of Black Americans*, 252–54; Geneva H. Southall, *Blind Tom: The Post–Civil War Enslavement of a Black Musical Genius* (Minneapolis: Challenge Productions, 1979), and "Thomas Greene Bethune (1849–1908)," *The Black Perspective in Music* 4:2 (July 1976), 177–90.

14. Titon, *Early Downhome Blues*, chap. 1. See also Southern, *The Music of Black Americans*, chap. 11; William Barlow, *"Looking Up at Down": The Emergence of Blues Culture* (Philadelphia: Temple University Press, 1989), esp. 26–32; William Ferris Jr., *Blues from the Delta* (London: Studio Vista, 1970), esp. chap. 2.

15. Ned Cobb quoted in Theodore Rosengarten, ed., *All God's Dangers: The Life of Nate Shaw* [Cobb] (New York: Knopf, 1974), 34.

16. Hazzard-Gordon, *Jookin'*, chap. 2, esp. 79. See also Finn, *The Bluesman*, 151–230; Titon, *Early Downhome Blues*, 19–24; Barlow, *"Looking Up at Down,"* esp. 48–50.

17. I use the term "plantation" to describe these Delta communities. Although many elements of the typical slave plantation were eliminated by emancipation, the old boundaries and general social functions of many white-owned, large-scale operations persisted into the twentieth century. See Gavin Wright, *Old South, New South: Revolutions in the Southern Economy since the Civil War* (New York: Basic Books, 1986), 27–50. The most detailed examination of the persistence of slave culture among southern blacks remains Charles S. Johnson, *Shadow of the Plantation* (Chicago: University of Chicago Press, 1934), a study of Macon County, Alabama (esp. 1–46).

18. Pops Foster and Tom Stoddard, *Pops Foster: The Autobiography of a New Orleans Jazzman* (Berkeley: University of California Press, 1971), 2, 4; also 5–7.

19. Willie E. Humphrey and Willie J. Humphrey, interview digest of the Tulane Jazz Oral History Project, housed at the William Ransom Hogan Jazz Archive, Tulane University (digests or transcripts from this project cited henceforth as Tulane), 2, 6–17.

20. Edward "Kid" Ory, Tulane, 5, 14; Ernest "Punch" Miller, Tulane, 5; Milt Hinton, Smithsonian Institution Jazz Oral History Project interview transcript, housed at the Institute of Jazz Studies, Rutgers University-Newark (cited henceforth as JOHP), June 1976 3:4 (Hinton's interview is by far the longest, so I have provided month citations along with the standard volume and page numbers). See also Foster and Stoddard, *Pops*

Foster, 15. Oliver, *Songsters and Saints,* 164–68, discusses the importance of the riverside in the black Baptist traditon, and Herskovits, *Myth of the Negro Past,* 233–34, examines the African roots of the sacred role of water and rivers.

21. Ory, Tulane, 2–3, 11, 14.

22. Ory, Tulane, 2, 13, 23.

23. Herman Autrey, JOHP, 85–89.

24. Ory, Tulane, 14, 24.

25. Ory, Tulane, 14, 24–25. See also Edmond Hall, Tulane, 1. No history of American children's bands has been written, although Margaret Hindle Hazen and Robert M. Hazen, *The Music Men: An Illustrated History of Brass Bands in America, 1800–1920* (Washington, D.C.: Smithsonian Institution Press, 1987), 33–35 and passim, mentions the subject.

26. Ory, Tulane, 35.

27. For migration information, see John Chilton, *Who's Who of Jazz,* 3d ed. (New York: Da Capo, 1985); Collier, *Louis Armstrong,* 18–19.

28. JOHP: Autrey, 89; Sam Wooding, 19, 108.

Chapter 2: *"He Should Throw That Club at You"*

1. For developments in other cities, see Bengt Olsson, *Memphis Blues and Jug Bands* (London: Studio Vista, 1970); Oliver, *Songsters and Saints,* 18–20, 257–64 (on the instrumental blues in Atlanta and Dallas); Tony Russell, *Blacks, Whites, and Blues* (London: Studio Vista, 1970), 85–87 (on the swinging bands in Texas).

2. See Ronald C. Foreman, Jr., "Jazz and Race Records, 1920–32: Their Origins and Their Significance For the Record Industry and Society" (Ph.D. diss., University of Illinois, 1968), 49.

3. See Henry A. Kmen, *Music in New Orleans: The Formative Years, 1791–1841* (Baton Rouge: Louisiana State University Press, 1966); William J. Schafer, *Brass Bands and New Orleans Jazz* (Baton Rouge: Louisiana State University Press, 1977); Lawrence Gushee, "Music and Free Colored People in Post–Civil War New Orleans," Southern Historical Association meeting, November 13, 1987; Ronald L. Davis, *A History of Opera in the American West* (Englewood Cliffs, N.J.: Prentice-Hall, 1965), chap. 1.

4. John W. Blassingame, *Black New Orleans, 1860–1880* (Chicago: University of Chicago Press, 1973), 2, 63, 71.

5. Blassingame, *Black New Orleans,* 122, 124–25; U.S. Bureau of Census, *Population 1910* (Washington, D.C.: Government Printing Office, 1913), 775; Marquis, *In Search of Buddy Bolden,* 30, 78. See also Joe Gary Taylor, *Louisiana Reconstructed, 1863–1877* (Baton Rouge: Louisiana State University Press, 1974), esp. 423–27, 467–79 (Taylor notes that the city even attempted to integrate its schools during Reconstruction).

6. Blassingame, *Black New Orleans,* 2, 9, 63, 122–25, 156, 173.

7. David C. Rankin, "The Forgotten People: Free People of Color in

New Orleans, 1850–1870" (Ph.D. diss., Johns Hopkins University, 1976), chap. 5, esp. 246, 271. For the fullest examination of Creole identity, see Virginia R. Domínguez, *White by Definition: Social Classification in Rural Louisiana* (New Brunswick: Rutgers University Press, 1986). Domínguez concludes that bloodlines determined racial, class, and economic castes.

8. See Joy J. Jackson, *New Orleans in the Gilded Age: Politics and Urban Progress, 1880–1896* (Baton Rouge: Louisiana State University Press, 1969), 258–59, 318–21; William Ivy Hair, *Carnival of Fury: Robert Charles and the New Orleans Race Riot of 1900* (Baton Rouge: Louisiana State University Press, 1976), 81–89.

9. Richard Gambino, *Vendetta: The True Story of the Worst Lynching in America* (Garden City, N.Y.: Doubleday, 1977), examines the riot of 1891. See also Paul A. Giordano, "The Italians of Louisiana: Their Cultural Background and Their Many Contributions" (Ph.D. diss., Indiana University, 1978); Daniel Rosenberg, *New Orleans Dockworkers: Race, Labor, and Unionism, 1892–1923* (Albany: State University of New York Press, 1988), 36–37. Hair, *Carnival of Fury*, discusses the 1900 riot. See also Joel Williamson, *The Crucible of Race: Black-White Relations in the American South since Emancipation* (New York: Oxford University Press, 1984), 201–9.

10. See Jackson, *New Orleans in the Gilded Age*, 318; Edward F. Haas, *Political Leadership in a Southern City: New Orleans in the Progressive Era, 1896–1902* (Ruston, La.: McGinty Publications, 1988), 8.

11. Alan Lomax, *Mister Jelly Roll* (Berkeley: University of California Press, 1950), 25–26, 80–83. See also Rankin, "The Forgotten People," 285–86; and Domínguez, *White by Definition*, 195–200, 250–60.

12. See Rankin, "The Forgotten People," 285. Sister Frances J. Woods, *Marginality and Identity: A Colored Creole Family through Ten Generations* (Baton Rouge: Louisiana State University Press, 1972), shows that Creoles of color had experienced marginality since the 1700s.

13. Bureau of the Census, *Population 1910* 1:784.

14. Wright, *Old South, New South*, 60–64.

15. Ory, *Tulane*, 29–39. See also Tulane: Hall, 36; Preston Jackson, 19; Stella Oliver, 9; Gushee, "Music and Free Colored People"; Oliver, *Songsters and Saints,* 168–98; Marquis, *In Search of Buddy Bolden*, 12, 30–31. The trumpeter Bill Coleman heard similar music at Holy Rollers churches in Cincinnati; autobiography typescript, Institute of Jazz Studies, Rutgers, 3.

16. See Kmen, *Music in New Orleans: The Formative Years*, esp. chaps. 10, 12; Schafer, *Brass Bands and New Orleans Jazz*, esp. appendix 1. On Galloway, Jackson, *New Orleans in the Gilded Age*, 279, quotes Al Rose and Edmond Souchon's *New Orleans Jazz: A Family Album* (Baton Rouge: Louisiana State University Press, 1967). The evidence supporting Bolden's reputation is summarized in Marquis, *In Search of Buddy Bolden*, esp. chaps. 4, 8.

17. On police policies, see John C. Schneider, *Detroit and the Problem of Order, 1830–1880* (Lincoln: University of Nebraska Press, 1980), and Eric Monkkonen, *Police in Urban America, 1860–1920* (Cambridge:

Cambridge University Press, 1981). See also Hair, *Carnival of Fury*, 81.

18. Montudie Garland, JOHP, 81.

19. Ory, Tulane, 65; Sidney Bechet, *Treat It Gentle* (New York: Hill and Wang, 1960), 54–56; Lomax, *Mister Jelly Roll*, 57. See also Hair, *Carnival of Fury*, 178–79.

20. Ory, Tulane, 68–69.

21. Barney Bigard and Barry Martyn, *With Louis and the Duke: The Autobiography of a Jazz Clarinetist* (New York: Oxford University Press, 1986), 8. The role of ritual insult and verbal aggression in black life is explored in Levine, *Black Culture and Black Consciousness*, 344–58. The best analysis of the effects of violence on a black urban culture is in Roger Lane, *Roots of Violence in Black Philadelphia, 1860–1900* (Cambridge: Harvard University Press, 1986), chaps. 5, 6. The psychoanalytic literature on art's function as sublimation is large. See, for example, Hans W. Loewald's argument that the arts "are sublimations par excellence. . . . we seem to acknowledge and yield most readily to the magic of a great work of art." *Sublimation: Inquiries into Theoretical Psychoanalysis* (New Haven: Yale University Press, 1987), 80–81.

22. Ory, Tulane, 42–44; Ronald L. Morris, *Wait Until Dark: Jazz and the Underworld, 1880–1940* (Bowling Green, Ohio: Popular Press, 1980), 92–93.

23. Tulane: Ory, 47, 51; Willie Hightower, 2:1–2.

24. Manuel "Fess" Manetta, Tulane, 1:11, 2:8–9.

25. Blassingame, *Black New Orleans*, 228.

26. Alphonse Picou, Tulane, 4–5; Louis Armstrong, *Satchmo: My Life in New Orleans* (New York: Prentice-Hall, 1955), 37; Foster and Stoddard, *Pops Foster*, 61; Natty Dominique, Tulane, 10. On dockworkers' unions and the half-half plan (in effect from 1902 to 1908), see Rosenberg, *New Orleans Dockworkers*, 2–3, 11, 17, 32, 55; Eric Arnesen, *Waterfront Workers of New Orleans: Race, Class, and Politics, 1863–1923* (New York: Oxford University Press, 1991), esp. 95–98, 183–85. See also Blassingame, *Black New Orleans*, 234.

27. Foster and Stoddard, *Pops Foster*, 65, 69; Wingy Manone and Paul Vandervoort II, *Trumpet on the Wing* (Garden City, N.Y.: Doubleday, 1948), 148, emphasis added. See also Gushee, "Music and Free Colored People."

28. Allison Davis and John Dollard, *Children of Bondage: The Personality Development of Negro Youth in the Urban South* (Washington, D.C.: American Council on Education, 1940), esp. xvi; Charles S. Johnson, *Growing Up in the Black Belt: Negro Youth in the Rural South* (New York: American Council on Education, 1941, rpt. ed. 1967), esp. 325–27. This division of opinion is similar to the dispute between Blassingame and Rankin about racial barriers in the late 1800s. John H. Rohrer and Munro S. Edmonson, *The Eighth Generation Grows Up: Cultures and Personalities of New Orleans Negroes* (New York: Harper and Row, 1960), examined

the adult life of Davis and Dollard's subjects and concluded that "the gang, the matriarchy, and the isolated family"—not racial identification—were their primary socializers (299).

29. Jack Laine, Tulane, 8; Lomax, *Mister Jelly Roll*, quoted in Rankin, "The Forgotten People," 286.

30. Foster and Stoddard, *Pops Foster*, 63, 65. It is hard to substantiate Foster's claim that "there wasn't any Jim Crow between . . . white and colored musicians," given the incidents he himself cited. Embittered by Creole prejudices, Foster might have slighted discrimination by whites. See also Tulane: Hightower, 2; William Russell, 2:3–4.

31. Tulane: Manetta, 5, 16–17; Jackson, 20; Foster and Stoddard, *Pops Foster*, 54.

32. Georg Brunis, Tulane, 33; Foster and Stoddard, *Pops Foster*, 36; Jackson, Tulane, 22. Domínguez, *White by Definition*, 238–50, discusses racial stratification in Mardi Gras parades, and Kmen, *Music in New Orleans: The Formative Years*, 51–52, explores the early use and abuse of masks at quadroon balls. Samuel Kinser, *Carnival American Style: Mardi Gras in New Orleans and Mobile* (Chicago: University of Chicago Press, 1990), argues that "in New Orleans the defiance of the [strict race and class] taboos is acted out, not so much with the intention of making them disappear but so that they can be experienced from another, from any number of angles" (310).

33. Kinser, *Carnival American Style*, 209, 313.

34. Brunis, Tulane, 47–48. See also Henry A. Kmen, "The Music of New Orleans," in *The Past As Prelude: New Orleans 1718–1968*, ed. Hodding Carter (New Orleans: Tulane University Press, 1968), 231.

35. Russell, *Blacks, Whites, and Blues*, 102.

36. Jackson, Tulane, 19; Collier, *Louis Armstrong*, 10.

37. Bigard and Martyn, *With Louis and the Duke*, 7; Zutty Singleton, Tulane, 7. See also Kmen, *Music in New Orleans: The Formative Years*, 202–5.

38. On music in African voluntary associations see Nketia, *Music of Africa*, 42–43; Lomax, *Mister Jelly Roll*, 16. Studies that discuss voluntary association in the United States include Mary P. Ryan, *Cradle of the Middle Class: The Family in Oneida County, New York, 1790–1865* (Cambridge: Cambridge University Press, 1981); John Mack Faragher, *Women and Men on the Overland Trail* (New Haven: Yale University Press, 1979); Wilson C. McWilliams, *The Idea of Fraternity in America* (Berkeley: University of California Press, 1973).

39. Singleton, Tulane, 7; Foster and Stoddard, *Pops Foster*, 57; Ory, Tulane, 49. See also Rosenberg, *New Orleans Dockworkers*, 65; Kmen, *Music in New Orleans: The Formative Years*, 3–9, 226–27.

40. Collier, *Louis Armstrong*, 8; Lewis Porter, *Lester Young* (Boston: Twayne, 1985), 3–5. See also Chilton, *Who's Who of Jazz*, 157; Linda Dahl, *Stormy Weather: The Music and Lives of a Century of Jazzwomen* (New York: Pantheon, 1984), 20; Lee Young, JOHP, 2–3.

41. Dominique, Tulane, 8; Foster and Stoddard, *Pops Foster*, 51. See also Tulane: Laine; Dominick "Nick" LaRocca, 13.

42. Dahl, *Stormy Weather*, 15; Bechet, *Treat It Gentle*, 52; Richard B. Allen, quoted in Billie Pierce, Tulane, 2:20; Foster and Stoddard, *Pops Foster*, 32–33. New Orleans's prostitution industry is described briefly in Ruth Rosen, *The Lost Sisterhood: Prostitution in America, 1900–1918* (Baltimore: Johns Hopkins University Press, 1982), 80–81, and Buerkle and Barker, *Bourbon Street Black*, 17–20. Besides Foster, other musician-pimps included Lee Collins and Jelly Roll Morton (a rare success at the trade).

43. Foster and Stoddard, *Pops Foster*, 99; Lomax, *Mister Jelly Roll*, 21, 269–71. Susan Cavin, "Missing Women: On the Voodoo Trail to Jazz," *Journal of Jazz Studies* 3:1 (Fall 1975), 4–27, offers a sketchy analysis of voodoo's influence on jazz; more research is needed.

44. Picou, Tulane, 2:3.

45. Lomax, *Mister Jelly Roll*, 66; Garland, JOHP, 120–22.

46. Tulane: Baby Dodds, 4; Dominique, 17; Ory, 87.

47. Some writers have overstated the influence of Euro-American professionalism on jazz. For example, regarding jazz musicians' individualism, John Storm Roberts argued in 1972 that "'If the intense individuality of jazz speaking/singing/tone is not European, where does it come from?' Even he notes that "the individuality of tone of voice does stem naturally from what *is* an Africanism, the speech/song/instrument continuum" (*Black Music of Two Worlds*, 215–16).

48. Bechet, *Treat It Gentle*, 3–4.

Chapter 3: *"Therefore, I Got to Go"*

1. Vern Streckfus, Tulane, 3ff. See also Foster and Stoddard, *Pops Foster*, 113; Bechet, *Treat It Gentle*, 57–58; Warren "Baby" Dodds and Larry Gara, *The Baby Dodds Story* (Los Angeles: Contemporary Press, 1959), chap. 2.

2. Tulane: Oliver, 14; Ory, 14–16. See also Manetta, Tulane, 7.

3. The development of the river economy is discussed in Douglass C. North, *The Economic Growth of the United States, 1790–1860* (Englewood Cliffs, N.J.: Prentice-Hall, 1961), 101–21, and Susan Previant Lee and Peter Passell, *A New Economic View of American History* (New York: Norton, 1979), 71–79, 132–35.

4. Singleton, Tulane, 2. See also Jasper Taylor, Tulane, 4.

5. Hinton, JOHP, 2:24–5.

6. Tulane: Streckfus, 9; Singleton, 3.

7. On Cincinnati, see Gilbert Chase, *America's Music: From the Pilgrims to the Present*, 2d ed. (New York: McGraw-Hill, 1966), 431–33; Coleman, autobiography typescript, 2, 5–6, 12, 37; Barlow, *"Looking Up at Down,"* 276–79; John Bubbles [Sublett], JOHP, 22, 44–46.

8. See Rudi Blesh and Harriet Janis, *They All Played Ragtime*, 4th

ed. (New York: Oak Publications, 1971), 148–60; Alberta Hunter, JOHP, 6:2–3; Garland, JOHP, 23; Dominique, Tulane, 7; Lee Collins, *Oh, Didn't He Ramble: The Life Story of Lee Collins* (Urbana: University of Illinois Press, 1974), 59.

9. See Foreman, "Jazz and Race Records, 1920–32," 49; Tom Stoddard, *Jazz on the Barbary Coast* (Chigwell, U.K.: Storyville, 1982), passim; Tulane: Russell, 2:6–7; Ory, 19–20; Chilton, *Who's Who of Jazz*, 168.

10. See JOHP: Andrew Blakeney, 17–8; Garland, 45, 49; Chilton, *Who's Who of Jazz*, 53, 72; Ory, Tulane, 69–70.

11. Among the many sources on southwestern music are Ross Russell, *Jazz Style in Kansas City and the Southwest* (Berkeley: University of California Press, 1971), chap. 2; Bill C. Malone, *Country Music U.S.A.* (Austin: University of Texas Press, 1985), chaps. 1, 4; Marshall W. Stearns and Jean Stearns, *Jazz Dance: The Story of American Vernacular Dance* (New York: Macmillan, 1968), 63–91; William W. Savage, *Singing Cowboys and All That Jazz: A Short History of Popular Music in Oklahoma* (Norman: University of Oklahoma Press, 1983).

12. JOHP: Jay McShann, 6–9; Eddie Durham, 62–72; Ralph Ellison, "Living With Music," in *Shadow and Act* (New York: Random House, 1964), 187–98. See also Russell, *Jazz Style in Kansas City*, chaps. 1, 3–5.

13. Freddie Green, JOHP, 23, 67–76. See also Cootie Williams, JOHP, 20.

14. David Mannes, *Music is My Faith: An Autobiography* (New York: Norton, 1938), 212–20. See also Benny Carter, JOHP, 1:62–63; Samuel B. Charters and Leonard Kundstadt, *Jazz: A History of the New York Scene* (Garden City, N.Y.: Doubleday, 1962), chaps. 1–3; Levine, *Black Culture and Black Consciousness*, 201.

15. On unions, see Clyde E. B. Bernhardt and Sheldon Harris, *I Remember: Eighty Years of Black Entertainment, Big Bands, and the Blues* (Philadelphia: University of Pennsylvania Press, 1986), 36; Donald Spivey, *Union and the Black Musician: William Everett Samuels and Chicago Local 208* (Lanham, Md.: University Press of America, 1984), 9–11 and passim. Stanley Dance, *The World of Earl Hines* (New York: Scribner's, 1977), 9–15, and Maxine Sullivan, JOHP, 485, discuss Pittsburgh. On Ohio, see Nat Hentoff, "Jazz in the Twenties: Garvin Bushell," in *Jazz Panorama: From the Pages of the Jazz Review*, ed. Martin Williams (New York: Oxford University Press, 1964), 74–80.

16. Hunter, JOHP, 6; Bechet, *Treat it Gentle*, 116.

17. See James R. Grossman, *Land of Hope: Chicago, Black Southerners, and the Great Migration* (Chicago: University of Chicago Press, 1989), 331 n. 14; Hinton, JOHP, 11/76 2:23.

18. JOHP: Blakeney, 6; Hinton, 6/76 1:26. See also Grossman, *Land of Hope*, 14–15; Chilton, *Who's Who of Jazz*, 19.

19. See Spivey, *Union and the Black Musician*, 30–31; Bernhardt and Harris, *I Remember*, 38, 43–44.

20. Hinton, JOHP, 4/76 5:10–15, 7:23–25. On the South Side crime

organization, see Humbert S. Nelli, *The Italians in Chicago, 1880–1930: A Study in Ethnic Mobility* (New York: Oxford University Press, 1970), chap. 5, 211–22.

21. Cootie Williams, JOHP, 61. See also Chilton, *Who's Who of Jazz.*

22. Bubbles, JOHP, 11–17, 27–29.

23. Collier, *Duke Ellington,* 40; Bernhardt and Harris, *I Remember,* 63–64. See also JOHP: Bubbles, 52; Hunter, 20.

24. Collins, *Oh, Didn't He Ramble,* 43.

25. Hinton, JOHP, 4/76 3:22, 24. On the popularity of Garvey and the UNIA in Chicago, see Allan H. Spear, *Black Chicago: The Making of a Negro Ghetto, 1890–1920* (Chicago: University of Chicago Press, 1967), 193.

26. Hinton, JOHP, 4/76 3:8, 4:7, 5:16.

27. Ralph Brown, Columbia University Jazz Oral History Collection (cited henceforth as COHC), 12, 14. Many musicians fondly recalled their 1920s earning power. In JOHP, see Cootie Williams, 62, 70–71, and Lawrence Brown, 14; in Tulane, see Albert Nicholas, 3:2, Oliver, 20, and Singleton, 3; Spivey, *Union and the Black Musician,* 35; Coleman, autobiography typescript, 39.

28. Hunter, JOHP, 40; Dance, *The World of Earl Hines,* 32, 36.

29. Spivey, *Union and the Black Musician,* 38, 40; Hunter, JOHP, 59. On the importance of face-to-face contact to African-American culture, see Joyner, *Down by the Riverside,* 117–26, and James Borchert, *Alley Life in Washington: Family, Community, Religion, and Folklife in the City, 1850–1970* (Urbana: University of Illinois Press, 1980), 107–17, 220.

30. See Stearns and Stearns, *Jazz Dance,* chaps. 39–40; Hazzard-Gordon, *Jookin',* chap. 3.

31. See Fletcher, *100 Years of the Negro in Show Business,* chaps. 19, 22–23, 27–28, 31–35; Robert Kimball and William Bolcom, *Reminiscing With Sissle and Blake* (New York: Viking, 1973), esp. 84–189; Stearns and Stearns, *Jazz Dance,* chaps. 16–19.

32. Erenberg, *Steppin' Out,* 129–30.

33. Eddie Condon and Thomas Sugrue, *We Called It Music: A Generation of Jazz* (New York: H. Holt, 1947), 133. See also Leroy Ostransky, *Jazz City: The Impact of Our Cities on the Development of Jazz* (Englewood Cliffs, N.J.: Prentice-Hall, 1978), 102–7.

34. Spivey, *Union and the Black Musician,* 32; Hinton, JOHP, 4/76 8:22–25; uncatalogued (in January 1987) box of clippings and correspondence in the Balaban and Katz Theater Collection, Special Collections, Chicago Public Library. From the *Chicago Defender:* "Mayor Thompson at Savoy" (12 November 1927), 5; "Plantation Frolics at Savoy" (19 November 1927), 8; "Regal Theater Will Open" (14 January 1928), 5. See also Travis, *An Autobiography of Black Jazz,* chaps. 7, 8, 11.

35. Collins, *Oh, Didn't He Ramble,* 67–69.

36. Hunter, JOHP, 54, 2:17–18; Nicholas, Tulane, 3:2. On New Orleans's lack of floor shows, see Picou, Tulane, 2:3.

37. JOHP: Wild Bill Davison, 79–80; Mary Lou Williams, 29.

38. See Dance, *The World of Earl Hines*, 18; JOHP: Sullivan, 522; Wooding, 137–38; Ostransky, *Jazz City*, 200.

39. Dance, *The World of Earl Hines*, 25; Sissle and Blake quoted in the *Baltimore Afro-American* (23 May 1924), 4.

40. Bubbles, JOHP, 62–64. Buck and Bubbles recorded "Rhythm For Sale" twice in December 1933, but Columbia rejected both takes. Brian Rust, *Jazz Records, 1897–1942*, 4th rev. ed. (New Rochelle, N.Y.: Arlington House, 1978), 1:193. The song was copyrighted that month, #25444 in *Catalog of Copyright Entries* 12 (Washington, D.C.: Department of Commerce, 1933), 1044, but the copyright was not renewed. Sublett also described an occasion on which he and Washington forced themselves onstage after a promoter, belatedly discovering their color, forbade them from appearing. Sublett then sang "Mammy O' Mine," a nostalgic memory of the South, which "really hit the spot because I was thinking of my mother [and] . . . about the man not wanting us to be on the stage." JOHP, 126–27.

41. The major work on black inequality in the North is Olivier Zunz, *The Changing Face of Inequality: Urbanization, Industrial Development, and Immigrants in Detroit, 1880–1920* (Chicago: University of Chicago Press, 1982), in which chap. 14 discusses the deleterious job market facing black migrants in 1920. Also important are Grossman, *Land of Hope;* Spear, *Black Chicago;* Peter Gottlieb, *Making Their Own Way: Southern Blacks' Migration to Pittsburgh, 1916–1930* (Urbana: University of Illinois Press, 1987). A detailed survey on the national phenomenon is found in Florette Henri, *Black Migration: Movement North, 1900–1920* (Garden City, N.Y.: Doubleday, 1975). See also Louise Venable Kennedy, *The Negro Peasant Turns Cityward: Effects of Recent Migrations to Northern Centers* (New York: Columbia University Press, 1930, rpt. ed. 1968).

42. Huggins, *Harlem Renaissance*, 42–45, 82–83, 129–36, 188–89; David L. Lewis, *When Harlem Was in Vogue* (New York: Knopf, 1981), esp. 304–5.

43. Huggins, *Harlem Renaissance*, 10–11.

44. Chris Goddard, *Jazz away from Home* (New York: Paddington Press, 1979), 294; Carter, JOHP, 1:107.

45. Goddard, *Jazz away from Home*, 296, 302; on Ellington, see Hunter, JOHP, 3:30.

46. Goddard, *Jazz away from Home*, 284, 290; Garvin Bushell, JOHP, 75; Coleman, autobiography typescript, 73. See also JOHP: Hunter, 2:34, 3:30, Cootie Williams, 115, Carter, 1:120; Bechet, *Treat It Gentle*, 45, 127–31.

47. Dance, *The World of Earl Hines*, 150; Bushell, JOHP, 75.

Chapter 4: *"Changing, Changing"*

1. Lomax, *Mister Jelly Roll*, 108, 218; Lovie Austin, Tulane, 5. I am skeptical of Austin's statement, since Morton plainly could read and write

music in the 1920s (although no biographer has yet discussed this issue satisfactorily). Austin may have meant that Morton felt inferior to those who were *better* at reading music, but this is only speculation. In any case, Morton's isolation from darker-skinned blacks is undeniable.

2. Hinton, JOHP, 11/76 2:17–18, 24. See also Spivey, *Union and the Black Musician*, 21, 24; Drake and Cayton, *Black Metropolis*, 1:144. On clubs for light-skinned blacks in Pittsburgh, see Dance, *The World of Earl Hines*, 13.

3. Hinton, JOHP, 4/76 8:27, 9:11; 6/76 1:3.

4. Tulane: Jackson, 22, 25; Nicholas, 3:3.

5. Bernhardt and Harris, *I Remember*, 91–92. The predominant forms and themes of African-American humor are discussed in Levine, *Black Culture and Black Consciousness*, esp. 358–66.

6. Bernhardt and Harris, *I Remember*, 91–92; Cootie Williams, JOHP, 94–96.

7. Drake and Cayton, *Black Metropolis*, 1:73; Du Bois, *The Souls of Black Folk*, in *Selected Writings*, 430.

8. Dave Peyton, "The Musical Bunch," *Chicago Defender* (28 January 1928), 6, and (21 January 1928), 6; Lucien H. White, "In the Realm of Music," *New York Age* (23 July 1921), 6. See also Richard Aldrich, "Drawing a Line For Jazz," *New York Times* (10 December 1922): 8:4; Baraka, *Blues People*, esp. chap. 5; Thomas J. Hennessey's excellent examination, "The Black Chicago Establishment, 1919–1930," *Journal of Jazz Studies* 2:1 (December 1974), 15–45.

9. JOHP: Red Saunders, 5–10; Hinton, 4/76 4:13, 6:17. For a similar upbringing in Denver, see Andy Kirk and Amy Lee, *Twenty Years on Wheels* (Ann Arbor: University of Michigan Press, 1989), 11, 19, 29–30, 40–41.

10. Hinton, JOHP, 11/76 9:6–7. For a description of the South Side's numbers, or policy racket, see Drake and Cayton, *Black Metropolis*, 2:470–494. Ronald L. Morris, in *Wait Until Dark: Jazz and the Underworld*, presents a bold thesis: Gangsters across the nation were the prime benefactors of early jazz musicians, and their involvement as employers and aficionados was wholly beneficial to these players. This chapter and succeeding chapters will show why the underworld might be accorded a more ambiguous role.

11. Hinton, JOHP, 4/76 4:16. See also Quinn Wilson, JOHP, 2–4.

12. Spivey, *Union and the Black Musician*, 23, 37.

13. Dance, *The World of Earl Hines*, 10–12. On the black influx in Duquesne, see Gottlieb, *Making Their Own Way*, 70.

14. JOHP: Blakeney, 46; Lawrence Brown, 3:12; Carter, 53–54; Bubbles, 89, 186.

15. Hunter, JOHP, 24–25, 62, 2:15. See also Chris Albertson, *Bessie* (New York: Stein and Day, 1972), 136–45. Regarding the high status of butlers and chambermaids in black society, see also Kirk and Lee, *Twenty Years on Wheels*, 31.

16. Grossman, *Land of Hope*, 154, and chap. 5 in general; Coleman, autobiography typescript, 8. On masks and cross-dressing in New Orleans and Mobile during Carnival, see Kinser, *Carnival American Style*, 310.

17. Bernhardt and Harris, *I Remember*, 18, 58, 147–48. As an adult, Bernhardt met a native American in South Bend, Indiana, who "was the Indian I had seen in my dreams. . . . we became great friends" (58).

18. Mary Lou Williams, JOHP, 32–35.

19. JOHP: Juan Tizol, 4:20; Lawrence Brown, 2:19–22; Foster and Stoddard, *Pops Foster*, 145. See also Mercer Ellington and Stanley Dance, *Duke Ellington in Person: An Intimate Memoir* (Boston: Houghton-Mifflin, 1978), 153–54. Harold Courlander, *A Treasury of Afro-American Folklore* (New York: Crown, 1970), 559–64; Fanny D. Bergen ed., *Current Superstitions* (Boston: Houghton Mifflin, 1896), esp. 42–43; and Jack Solomon and Olivia Solomon, eds., *Ghosts and Goosebumps: Ghost Stories, Tall Tales, and Superstitions from Alabama* (University, Ala.: University of Alabama Press, 1981), 95–147, record beliefs regarding buttons and shoes similar to Ellington's.

20. Bernhardt and Harris, *I Remember*, 53–54. See also Kirk and Lee, *Twenty Years on Wheels*, 2–3. Levine, *Black Culture and Black Consciousness*, 262–65, discusses the importance of mobility to the first free generations of Southern blacks.

21. Bigard and Martyn, *With Louis and the Duke*, 25, 37. See also Austin, Tulane, 1; Trummy Young, JOHP, 3.

22. Hinton, JOHP, 6/76 8:25, 10:25.

23. Spivey, *Union and the Black Musician*, 35.

24. Foster and Stoddard, *Pops Foster*, 154. On rent parties see Hazzard-Gordon, *Jookin'*, 94–98.

25. Hunter, JOHP, 43, 6:5; Dahl, *Stormy Weather*, 13–15; Harrison, *Black Pearls*, chap. 7.

26. Hunter, JOHP, 6:6–7.

27. Hunter, JOHP, 6:6–7. Erenberg, *Steppin' Out*, chaps. 4, 7, cogently analyzes the use of female sexuality in New York nightclubs.

28. Hunter, JOHP, 62–64, 3:56–57.

29. Helen Humes, JOHP, 30. Daphne Duval Harrison, in *Black Pearls*, stresses that blueswomen in the North sang of migrant women's experiences in a "tough" new world of "unbridled pleasure" (63–64) as they lived in "the fast lane" of single parenthood, job-seeking, and looking for companionship in a frightening city (69). This was certainly the case, but this interpretation ignores the elegant, elite, and regal image that blueswomen (even Ma Rainey and Bessie Smith) projected onstage, which thrilled working-class audiences (while dismaying the bourgeoisie). Their popularity in part came about because they seemed to rise above their troubles. As Harrison's illustrations show, only record advertisements portrayed blueswomen as "down-home" women weighed down by cares and plain southern garb. See also Barlow, *"Looking Up at Down,"* 141–52, 157.

30. Lil Hardin Armstrong, Tulane, 2–3.

31. Hinton, JOHP, 6/76 10:12.

32. Hunter, JOHP, 35.

33. Ralph Brown, COHC, 20, 37; Spivey, *Union and the Black Musician*, 33.

34. Bigard and Martyn, *With Louis and the Duke*, 27; Scoville Browne, COHC, 7.

35. Scoville Browne, COHC, 8; Mary Lou Williams, JOHP, 11. The term "boogie-woogie" was not commonly used at the time of the situation Williams described.

36. Ory, Tulane, 85; JOHP: Hinton, 6/76 6:23; Mary Lou Williams, 11.

37. Carl Engel, "Jazz: A Musical Discussion," *Atlantic Monthly* 130 (August 1922), 186. Similar views, praising but misperceiving jazz, are expressed in Paul Whiteman and Mary Margaret McBride, *Jazz* (New York: J. H. Sears, 1926), [Sigmund Spaeth,] "When the Masters 'Jazz,'" *Literary Digest* 90 (11 August 1928), 23, and Henrietta Straus, "Marking the Miles," *The Nation* (8 March 1922), 292–94. The discourse in the twenties surrounding music and involving "Yankees," Jews and blacks is very well discussed in MacDonald S. Moore, *Yankee Blues: Musical Culture and American Identity* (Bloomington: Indiana University Press, 1985), esp. 154–57. See also Leonard, *Jazz and the White Americans*, chaps. 2, 4.

38. Tulane: Dominique, 1; Picou, 2:1.

39. Bechet, *Treat It Gentle*, 3, 142.

40. Hinton, JOHP, 6/76 3:7.

41. Edwin "Squirrel" Ashcraft, Tulane, 7; Hinton, JOHP, 6/76 8:7.

42. Browne, COHC, 7.

43. On individuality in early jazz, see Wynton Marsalis's Regents Lecture, discussed at the outset of this book, and Roberts, *Black Music on Two Worlds*, 215–16. On heroic individualism in nineteenth-century European music, see Paul Henry Lang, *Music in Western Civilization* (New York: Norton, 1941), 873–75.

44. JOHP: Garland, 19; Carter, 2:88.

45. As the ethnomusicologist Bruno Nettl has pointed out, "the difference between 'art' music and others has been a major paradigm in musicology," a distinction Nettl finds troubling. Still, I believe that it is valid to speak of Americans in the 1920s *perceiving* such a distinction very clearly, since the debate distinguishing "highbrow," "lowbrow," and "folk" had never been stronger or more influential in the nation's cultural history. Nettl, *The Study of Ethnomusicology*, 29; Lawrence W. Levine, *Highbrow/Lowbrow: The Emergence of Cultural Hierarchy in America* (Cambridge: Harvard University Press, 1988); Moore, *Yankee Blues*.

46. Hinton, JOHP, 4/76 10:13.

47. Scott E. Brown and Robert Hilbert, *James P. Johnson: A Case of Mistaken Identity* (Metuchen, N.J.: Scarecrow Press, 1986), 86–88, 218–21, 233–34; Chilton, *Who's Who of Jazz*, 275; William Grant Still, "The Men Behind American Music," *The Crisis* 51:1 (January 1944), 12–15, 29.

48. William Grant Still to Irving Schwerké, January 9, 1931, Irving

Schwerké Collection, Music Division, Library of Congress.
    49. On ghettoization on the South Side, see Spear, *Black Chicago,*
chaps. 5, 11, conclusion; Grossman, *Land of Hope,* esp. 123–28; Arnold R.
Hirsch, *Making the Second Ghetto: Race and Housing in Chicago, 1940–1960*
(Cambridge: Cambridge University Press, 1983), esp. 3–4, 15. Overviews
comparing immigrant areas and black ghettos include Thomas Lee Phil-
pott, *The Slum and the Ghetto: Neighborhood Deterioration and Middle-Class
Reform, Chicago, 1880–1930* (New York: Oxford University Press, 1978);
Sam Bass Warner Jr., *The Urban Wilderness: A History of the American City*
(New York: Harper and Row, 1972), 177–81; and Robert E. Forman, *Black
Ghettos, White Ghettos, and Slums* (Englewood Cliffs, N.J.: Prentice-Hall,
1971), esp. 26–35.
    50. JOHP: Hinton, 4/76 6:13; Carter, 1:68–69, 76–77.

Chapter 5: *"The Great Travelers"*

    1. Mezz Mezzrow and Bernard Wolfe, *Really the Blues* (New York:
Random House, 1946); Condon and Sugrue, *We Called It Music;* Hoagy
Carmichael, *The Stardust Road* (New York: Rinehart, 1946); Manone and
Vandervoort, *Trumpet on the Wing.* See also Ralph Berton, *Remembering
Bix: A Memoir of the Jazz Age* (New York: Harper and Row, 1974). With
the exception of H. O. Brunn, *The Story of the Original Dixieland Jazz Band*
(Baton Rouge: Louisiana State University Press, 1960), every jazz history
written after 1930 makes some mention of the black contribution to white
jazz. Two early white jazz musicians who discuss black leadership capably
are Bud Freeman, *You Don't Look Like a Musician!* (Detroit: Balamp, 1974)
and with Robert Wolf, *Crazeology. The Autobiography of a Chicago Jazzman*
(Urbana: University of Illinois Press, 1989), and Max Kaminsky with V. E.
Hughes, *Jazz Band: My Life in Jazz* (New York: Harper and Row, 1963).
    2. Kmen, *Music in New Orleans: The Formative Years,* esp. chap. 10;
Kmen, "Music in New Orleans," 224–30; Hazen and Hazen, *The Music
Men,* chaps. 1–3; Brunn, *The Story of the Original Dixieland Jazz Band,*
chaps. 1–2.
    3. Laine, Tulane, 3/26/57 1–6, 4/25/64 11. Laine, like Sidney Bechet
and other musicians from New Orleans, called his music ragtime, although
it bore harmonic and rhythmic features alien to the ragtime of Scott Joplin
and others.
    4. Tulane: Laine, 4/25/64 10–11; LaRocca, 1:1; Brunis, 32.
    5. Tulane: Laine, 4/25/64 3, 4/21/51 1, 7–8, 11, 1/25/59 2; Bru-
nis, 14.
    6. Tulane: Laine, 4/25/64 9; LaRocca, 13.
    7. Tulane: Brunis, 6–7, 17, 29; Laine, 5/23/60 13, 4/25/64 6; La-
Rocca, 2–3, 5–6.
    8. LaRocca, Tulane, 2, 10–11. See also Brunn, *The Story of the Original
Dixieland Jazz Band,* chaps. 1–3.
    9. Tulane: Brunis, 23; Laine, 4/21/51 6–7, 3/26/57 16, 20. Similarly

rowdy working-class picnics in Worchester, Massachusetts are discussed in Roy Rosenzwieg, *Eight Hours for What We Will: Workers and Leisure in an Industrial City, 1870–1920* (Cambridge: Cambridge University Press, 1983), 153–59.

10. Tulane: Brunis, 24–25, 29, 47–48; Laine, 3/26/57 28.

11. Tulane: Laine, 4/21/51 5, 4/25/64 11, 5/23/60 13; Streckfus, 1–2; Eddie Edwards, 30.

12. Tulane: Nicholas, 5; Laine 5/23/60 18, 1/25/59 3; Edwards, 2.

13. Tulane: Laine, 4/25/64 3, 11, 3/26/57 13; Brunis, 17–18, 36; Edwards, 27. Ray Bauduc believed that Dixieland lightly accentuated the second and fourth beats, creating the impression of two long beats; Tulane, 2.

14. Tulane: Tom Brown, 1; LaRocca, 7, 15, 21, 50; Laine, 3/26/57 29, 5/23/60 7, 4/25/64 3, 7.

15. Tulane: Laine, 3/26/57 24; LaRocca, 13; Singleton, 2. Emory S. Bogardus, *Social Distance* (Los Angeles: Antioch, 1959) is the seminal sociological work on social distance. See also Erving Goffman, *Encounters: Two Studies in the Sociology of Interaction* (Indianapolis: Bobbs-Merrill, 1961).

16. Tulane: Laine, 4/25/64 5, 5/23/60 13; Brown, 1; LaRocca, 42, 52.

17. The phenomenon of urban southern populism, cultural or political, has not been studied. The contentious historiography on rural southern populism does suggest that the agrarian political movement was accompanied by vigorous cultural expression. Richard Hofstadter, *The Age of Reform: From Bryan to FDR* (New York: Random, 1955), chaps. 2, 3; Lawrence Goodwyn, *Democratic Promise: The Populist Moment in America* (New York: Oxford University Press, 1976), esp. chap. 12; Steven Hahn, *The Roots of Southern Populism: Yeoman Farmers and the Transformation of the Georgia Upcountry, 1850–1890* (New York: Oxford University Press, 1983), chap. 2, epilogue.

18. Haas, *Political Leadership in a Southern City,* argues that "the New Orleans Democratic machine was an organization of immigrants and first-generation Americans" (72). See also Brian Gary Ettinger, "John Fitzpatrick and the Limits of Working-Class Politics in New Orleans, 1892–1896," *Louisiana History* 26 (Fall 1985), 341–65. The machine was kept out of power from 1896 to 1899 by a fragile reform coalition.

19. Laine, Tulane, 4/21/51 2, 4, 5/23/60 14.

20. LaRocca, Tulane, 46–47; Manone and Vandervoort, *Trumpet on the Wing,* 19, 30, 195. See also William Russell, Tulane, 2:3.

21. LaRocca, Tulane, 13–14. Scholarship on New Orleans ethnic and class relations includes Roger W. Shugg, *Origins of the Class Struggle in Louisiana* (Baton Rouge: Louisiana State University Press, 1939); George E. Cunningham, "Italians' Hindrance to White Solidarity in Louisiana, 1890–98," *Journal of Negro History* 50 (January 1965), 22–36; Gambino, *Vendetta;* and Hair, *Carnival of Fury.*

22. LaRocca, Tulane, 9, 10, 45–46. See also Brunn, *The Story of the Original Dixieland Jazz Band,* chaps. 3, 5, 9, 11.

23. See Eddie Sauter, JOHP, 56–58; Jack Teagarden, Tulane, 2; Kaminsky and Hughes, *Jazz Band,* 10–14.

24. Among the works that discuss the origins of white jazz in Chicago are Richard Hadlock, *Jazz Masters of the Twenties* (New York: Macmillan, 1965); John Steiner, "Chicago," in *Jazz: New Perspectives on the History of Jazz,* eds. Nat Hentoff and Albert J. McCarthy (New York: Rinehart, 1959), 137–70; Marshall W. Stearns, *The Story of Jazz* (New York: Oxford University Press, 1956), 175–78. Hugues Panassié, *Hot Jazz: The Guide to Swing Music* (New York: M. Witmark, 1936) has been superseded, but it concentrates heavily on Chicago in the 1920s (136–60). No full study of white jazz in the 1920s has ever been written.

25. Leonard, *Jazz and the White Americans,* esp. chap. 3.

26. [Chicago Plan Commission], *Forty-Four Cities in the City of Chicago* (Chicago: Chicago Plan Commission, 1942), 29–31; Melvin G. Holli and Peter d'A. Jones, *Ethnic Chicago,* 2d. ed. (Grand Rapids, Mich.: Eerdmans, 1984), 2–12 and passim; Carole Goodwin, *The Oak Park Strategy: Community Control of Racial Change* (Chicago: University of Chicago Press, 1979), chap. 2.

27. Jimmy McPartland, JOHP, 7; Nat Hentoff and Nat Shapiro eds., *Hear Me Talkin' to Ya: The Story of Jazz Told by the Men Who Made It* (New York: Holt, Rinehart, and Winston, 1955), 118–21, 124–26. For an oral history of the Rhythm Kings, see Hentoff and Shapiro eds., *Hear Me Talkin' to Ya,* 123–24.

28. McPartland, JOHP, 4, 7–11; Bud Freeman, JOHP, 1–8, and *You Don't Look Like a Musician,* 2–4.

29. For discussions of white Chicago jazz music, see Kaminsky and Hughes, *Jazz Band,* 32–33; Steiner, "Chicago," 137–70; Stearns, *The Story of Jazz,* 175–78; Hadlock, *Jazz Masters of the Twenties,* 118–19ff; Panassié, *Hot Jazz,* 139–60; and Mezzrow's fascinating appendix in *Really the Blues,* 303–15.

30. Freeman, *You Don't Look Like a Musician,* 5–6; McPartland, JOHP, 2:15.

31. Mezzrow and Wolfe, *Really the Blues,* 3, 46–7; JOHP: Davison, 2; Jimmy Maxwell, 12; and Sauter, 4–7.

32. Freeman, JOHP, 1–2; Mezzrow and Wolfe, *Really the Blues,* 1; McPartland, JOHP, 5. Condon and Sugrue, *We Called It Music,* 109 and Freeman and Wolf, *Crazeology,* 17, tell of their parents' support. See also Manone and Vandervoort, *Trumpet on the Wing,* 16; Collier, *Louis Armstrong,* 23–33, 343–44.

33. Mezzrow and Wolfe, *Really the Blues,* 88–89; McPartland quoted in George Hoefer, liner notes to *The Chicagoans,* MCA recording #1350; Freeman, JOHP, 53–54.

34. Representative sociological writings include Becker, *Outsiders,*

and Jack P. Gibbs, "Concepts of Deviant Behavior: The Old and the New," Robert A. Dentler and Kai T. Erickson, "The Function of Deviance in Groups," and Gresham M. Sykes and David Matza, "Techniques of Neutralization: A Theory of Delinquency," collected in *Deviant Behavior: A Text-Reader in the Sociology of Deviance*, ed. Delos H. Kelley, 2d ed. (New York: St. Martin's, 1984). See also Gilbert, *Cycle of Outrage*, esp. 127–30.

35. Eddie Condon, whose Irish family was fiercely populistic, might have been an exception. Condon and Sugrue, *We Called It Music*, 32–33, 128. See also Kaminsky and Hughes, *Jazz Band*, 66. On apolitical behavior among 1920s intellectuals and youth, see Caroline F. Ware, *Greenwich Village, 1920–1930: A Comment on American Civilization in the Post-War Years* (Boston: Houghton-Mifflin, 1935), chap. 8.

36. Carmichael, *The Stardust Road*, 7, 11, 26, 38.

37. Carmichael, *The Stardust Road*, 37–39.

38. Holli and Jones eds., *Ethnic Chicago*, 549–51.

39. Kaminsky and Hughes, *Jazz Band*, 31. See also Holli and Jones eds., *Ethnic Chicago* and Melvin G. Holli and Peter d'A. Jones eds., *The Ethnic Frontier: Essays in the History of Group Survival in Chicago and the Midwest* (Grand Rapids, Mich.: Eerdmans, 1977).

40. Mezzrow and Wolfe, *Really the Blues*, 3–4; McPartland, JOHP, 14.

41. Kaminsky and Hughes, *Jazz Band*, 33; Freeman and Wolf, *Crazeology*, 15. The doorman who greeted Freeman is hazily recalled in memoirs. Freeman remembered him at the Lincoln Gardens, while Dempsey Travis, among others, identified the man with the "music lessons" greeting as Bill Summers at the Sunset Café (*An Autobiography of Black Jazz*, 70). Condon and Sugrue, *We Called It Music*, 111.

42. Mezzrow and Wolfe, *Really the Blues*, 10–11, 109.

43. Freeman, *You Don't Look Like a Musician*, 7–8. Similar incidents are found in Mezzrow and Wolfe, *Really the Blues*, 104–7, and Condon and Sugrue, *We Called It Music*, 138–39.

44. Condon and Sugrue, *We Called It Music*, 107; Carmichael, *The Stardust Road*, 53, 76, 136.

45. Regarding the formation of prejudices, see Mary Ellen Goodman, *Race Awareness in Young Children*, rev. ed. (New York: Collier, 1964), 169–80; A. R. Crane, "Development of Moral Values in Children—Preadolescent Gangs," in *Studies in Adolescence*, ed. Robert E. Grinder (New York: Macmillan, 1963), 325–27; and Richard Wright, *Black Boy* (New York: Harper and Row, 1945), 30–31, 55–56. On the territoriality of urban youth, see William Foote Whyte, *Street Corner Society: The Social Structure of an Italian Slum* (Chicago: University of Chicago Press, 1943).

46. Carmichael, *The Stardust Road*, 11; Kaminsky and Hughes, *Jazz Band*, 2, 4, 14.

47. McPartland, JOHP, 16–18. Surveys of early twentieth-century race relations in Chicago include Drake and Cayton, *Black Metropolis*, 1:41–57, 73–76, and William M. Tuttle, Jr., *Race Riot: Chicago in the Red Summer of 1919* (New York: Atheneum, 1970).

48. Johnny Otis, *Listen to the Lambs* (New York: Norton, 1968), 12–13.

49. Freeman, JOHP, 14; Mezzrow and Wolfe, *Really the Blues,* 42, 271.

50. On theories of generational adaptation to American life, see Horace Kallen, *Culture and Democracy in the United States* (New York: Boni and Liveright, 1924), esp. 114–18; Margaret Mead, *And Keep Your Powder Dry: An Anthropologist Looks at America* (New York: William Morrow, 1943), chap. 3; Marcus Lee Hansen, "The Third Generation in America," *Commentary* 14 (November 1952), 492–500; Werner Sollors, *Beyond Ethnicity: Consent and Descent in American Culture* (New York: Oxford University Press, 1986), esp. chap. 7.

51. Artie Shaw, *The Trouble With Cinderella: An Outline of Identity* (New York: Farrar, Straus, and Young, 1952, rpt. ed. Da Capo, 1979), 23–26.

52. Shaw, *The Trouble With Cinderella,* 25–26, 33, 38, 53–55, 62–63.

53. On the socialization of youth, see such "Chicago school" sociologists as Louis Wirth, "Cultural Conflicts in the Immigrant Family" (M.A. thesis, University of Chicago, 1925); Wirth, *The Ghetto* (Chicago: University of Chicago Press, 1928); Frederic M. Thrasher, *The Gang: A Study of 1,313 Gangs in Chicago* (Chicago: University of Chicago Press, 1927); Harvey W. Zorbaugh, *The Gold Coast and the Slum* (Chicago: University of Chicago Press, 1929). On territoriality in Jimmy McPartland's old Chicago neighborhood in the 1960s, see Gerald D. Suttles, *The Social Order of the Slum: Ethnicity and Territory in the Inner City* (Chicago: University of Chicago Press, 1968), esp. 33.

54. The concept of prepolitical rebellion was articulated by Eric J. Hobsbawm in *Primitive Rebels,* 2d ed. (New York: Praeger, 1959) 1–6.

55. Art Hodes and Chadwick Hansen, *Selections from the Gutter: Portraits From the Jazz Record* (Berkeley: University of California Press, 1977), 18.

56. JOHP: McPartland, 7–8; Freeman, 33.

57. Kaminsky and Hughes, *Jazz Band,* 37–38; Freeman, JOHP, 33, Hodes and Hansen, *Selections from the Gutter,* 16.

58. Freeman, JOHP, 64, 87.

59. McPartland, JOHP, 51–56. See also Condon and Sugrue, *We Called it Music,* 121; Al Rose, *I Remember Jazz: Six Decades among the Great Jazzmen* (Baton Rouge: Louisiana State University Press, 1987), 79; Maxwell, JOHP, 9, 42. The relation of linguistic and musical aptitude deserves further study; see, for example, William C. Wilson, "Some Interrelationships of Verbal and Musical Listening Abilities in Elementary School Children" (Ed.D. thesis, University of California, Berkeley, 1960).

60. Condon and Sugrue, *We Called It Music,* 109; Freeman, JOHP, 44; Mezzrow and Wolfe, *Really the Blues,* 94.

61. Freeman, *You Don't Look Like a Musician,* 41; Freeman, JOHP, 53–54; Kaminsky and Hughes, *Jazz Band,* 36.

62. Freeman, JOHP, 46; Mezzrow and Wolfe, *Really the Blues,* 94.

63. Mezzrow and Wolfe, *Really the Blues,* 96; Freeman, *You Don't Look Like a Musician,* 41; Freeman, JOHP, 53, passim.

64. Kaminsky and Hughes, *Jazz Band,* 66.

65. See Helen Lefkowitz Horowitz, *Culture and the City: Cultural Philanthropy in Chicago from the 1800's to 1917* (Lexington: University Press of Kentucky, 1976); Carl S. Smith, *Chicago and the American Literary Imagination* (Chicago: University of Chicago Press, 1984), chaps. 1–3; David F. Burg, *Chicago's White City of 1893* (Lexington: University Press of Kentucky, 1976).

66. Freeman, JOHP, 2:42.

67. Frederick Lewis Allen, *Only Yesterday: An Informal History of the Twenties* (New York: Harper and Row, 1931), esp. 88–122; F. Scott Fitzgerald, "Echoes of the Jazz Age," *Scribner's* 90:5 (November 1931), 459–65.

68. Gilbert Seldes, *The Seven Lively Arts* (New York: Harper, 1924), 83–108; Sinclair Lewis, *Babbitt* (New York: Harcourt, 1922); Whiteman and McBride, *Jazz.*

69. Regarding 1920s white youth, see Paula S. Fass, *The Damned and the Beautiful: American Youth in the 1920s* (New York: Oxford University Press, 1977), esp. chaps. 6, 7. See also Paul A. Carter, *Another Part of the Twenties* (New York: Columbia University Press, 1977), esp. chaps. 1, 7; John R. McMahon, "The Jazz Path of Degradation," *The Ladies' Home Journal* 39:26 (January 1922), 26, 71; Walter Lippmann, *A Preface to Morals* (Boston: Beacon, 1929), chaps. 4, 14, 15. On how the rise in divorce in the 1920s was part of a longer demographic and attitudinal change, see May, *Great Expectations.*

70. Erenberg, *Steppin' Out,* esp. chap. 8; Ogren, *The Jazz Revolution,* chap. 5; Burton W. Peretti, "'Vulgar Sophistication': The Mingling of Rich and Poor in 1920s New York and Paris Nightlife," American Studies Association meeting, 4 November 1990. The debate over jazz and American music can be seen in Straus, "Marking the Miles," 292–94; "'Buying American' in Music," *Literary Digest* 118 (29 December 1934), 24; [Herbert F. Peyser,] "Jazz Overadvertised," *Literary Digest* 76 (15 December 192), 28–9; [David S. Smith,] "Putting Jazz in Its Place," *Literary Digest* 82 (5 July 1924), 31–32; and Engel, "Jazz: A Musical Discussion," esp. 186.

71. Condon and Sugrue, *We Called It Music,* 121–22. On the 1920s Protestant mainstream, see Carter, *Another Part of the Twenties,* chaps. 2, 3.

72. On the growth of New Orleans jazz after the exodus of the 1910s and 1920s, the best source is Jason Berry, Jonathan Foose, and Tad Jones, *Up From the Cradle of Jazz: New Orleans Music since World War Two* (Athens: University of Georgia Press, 1986), esp. chap. 1.

73. On the scholarship on adolescence in the 1920s, see Robert H. Elias, *"Entangling Alliances with None": An Essay on the Individual in the American Twenties* (New York: Norton, 1973), chaps. 1, 2; Joseph F. Kett, *Rites of Passage: Adolescence in America, 1790 to the Present* (New York: Basic Books, 1977), 197–222; Fass, *The Damned and the Beautiful,* chaps. 1, 2.

74. Carmichael, *The Stardust Road,* 7, 27; Laine, Tulane, 3/26/57 5. See also Leonard, *Jazz and the White Americans,* 52–55.

75. Ben Hecht, *A Child of the Century* (New York: Simon and Schus-

ter, 1954), 218, 221–25, 234–35, 327–44. Regarding 1920s Chicago and Hemingway's flight from it, see Kenneth S. Lynn, *Hemingway* (New York: Simon and Schuster, 1987), 130–47.

76. Malcolm Cowley, *Exile's Return: A Narrative of Ideas* (New York: Norton, 1934), 9, 25–28.

Chapter 6: *"Turn the Bitters into Sweets"*

1. On blues lyrics and their significance, see Baker, *Blues, Ideology, and Afro-American Literature,* and Paul Garon, *Blues and the Poetic Spirit* (New York: Da Capo, 1975), esp. chap. 5. A kind of guitar did originate in West Africa; Paul Oliver, *Savannah Syncopators: African Retentions in the Blues* (London: Studio Vista, 1970), 32.

2. See Joseph A. Musselman, *Music in the Cultured Generation: A Social History of Music in America, 1870–1900* (Evanston: Northwestern University Press, 1971); Levine, *Highbrow/Lowbrow,* esp. chap. 2; Burton W. Peretti, "Music, Race, and Culture in Urban America: The Creators of Jazz" (Ph.D. diss., University of California, Berkeley, 1989; Ann Arbor: University Microfilm International, 1990, 90-06472), chap. 1; Burton W. Peretti, "Democratic Leitmotivs in the American Reception of Wagner," *19th Century Music* 13:1 (Summer 1989), 28–38.

3. Marquis, *In Search of Buddy Bolden,* 112.

4. Ory, Tulane, 58–59. See also Marquis, *In Search of Buddy Bolden,* chap. 5; Hentoff and Shapiro eds., *Hear Me Talkin' to Ya,* 24–32.

5. Collier, *Louis Armstrong,* 34–40; Hall, Tulane, 15–16.

6. Jackson, Tulane, 5, 23–24.

7. Hall, Tulane, 22. Regarding written notation in the world's musical cultures, see Nettl, *The Study of Ethnomusicology,* 65.

8. Tulane: Manetta, 8; Jackson, 20; Hall, 15–16. The five black keys of the piano also make up a pentatonic scale, the foundation of most non-Western musics. Perhaps, therefore, playing only on black keys produced a sound more familiar to pianists closely tied to the blues tradition. See Max Weber, *The Rational and Social Foundations of Music,* ed. and trans. Don Martindale, Johannes Riedel, and Gertrude Neuwirth (Carbondale: Southern Illinois University Press, 1958), 13–22. My thanks to John Bracey for this observation.

9. Muggsy Spanier, Tulane, 5.

10. See Dominique, Tulane, 19–20; John Chilton, *Sidney Bechet: The Wizard of Jazz* (London: Macmillan, 1987), 38; Eddie Barefield, JOHP, 25.

11. Charles Elgar, Tulane, 1, 2, 9. The term "Dixieland" usually refers to early white New Orleans jazz only but sometimes designates all kinds of early New Orleans playing.

12. Tulane: Picou, 2:5, 3:5; Nicholas, 3; Jackson, 11. Barney Bigard's assertion that Picou could not read music is probably incorrect (*With Louis and the Duke,* 13).

13. Tom Bethell, *George Lewis: A Jazzman from New Orleans* (Berkeley: University of California Press, 1977), 26; Humphrey, Tulane, 8–9. See also Blassingame, *Black New Orleans,* 125; Chilton, *Who's Who of Jazz,* 170.

14. Lee Young, JOHP, 15. See also Porter, *Lester Young,* 5–6.

15. Garland, JOHP, 16. On Dodds and Noone, see for example Dominique, Tulane, 2:1.

16. Tulane: De De Pierce, 2:26; Dominique, n.p.

17. These effects of enhanced written literacy were similar to the epistemological effects noted in the survey by Jack Goody and Ian Watt, "The Consequences of Literacy," in *Literacy in Traditional Societies,* ed. Jack Goody (Cambridge: Cambridge University Press, 1968), 27–68. See also Jack Goody, *The Logic of Writing and the Organization of Society* (Cambridge: Cambridge University Press, 1986), esp. chap. 5.

18. Mary Lou Williams, JOHP, 4, 8.

19. Lee Young, JOHP, 14; Ralph Brown, COHC, 7. Eddie Barefield also learned off records; JOHP, 7.

20. Chilton, *Who's Who of Jazz,* 223.

21. JOHP: Carter, 8, 2:60–63; Lawrence Brown, 2:4; Bernhardt and Harris, *I Remember,* 36, 43; Durham, JOHP, 29.

22. JOHP: Hinton, 9:24–25; Bubbles, 23.

23. For examples of antijazz sentiments, see the symposium, "Where is Jazz Leading America?" *The Etude Music Magazine* 42 (August 1924), 515–31; Berger, "Jazz: Resistance to the Diffusion of a Culture Pattern," 462–71.

24. Manone and Vandervoort, *Trumpet on the Wing,* 14; Freeman, *You Don't Look Like a Musician,* 3. See also Maxwell, JOHP, 3.

25. JOHP: Gil Evans, 22–24; Davison, 2; Richard M. Sudhalter and Philip Evans, *Bix: Man and Legend* (New Rochelle, N.Y.: Arlington House, 1974), 68–72, passim, appendix 1.

26. At the age of nineteen, Freeman took lessons from Franz Schoepp, first clarinet of the Chicago Symphony (who also taught Benny Goodman); JOHP, 26.

27. Manone and Vandervoort, *Trumpet on the Wing,* 10.

28. Bechet, *Treat It Gentle,* 2–5.

29. Mezzrow and Wolfe, *Really the Blues,* 3; Hodes and Hansen, *Selections from the Gutter,* 18–19, 32; McPartland, JOHP, 18; Freeman, JOHP, 37, 84.

30. See, for example, Erich Schwandt and Andrew Lamb, "March," in *The New Grove Dictionary of Music and Musicians,* ed. Stanley Sadie (London: Macmillan, 1980), 11:650–54.

31. Kaminsky and Hughes, *Jazz Band,* 72. Roberts, *Black Music of Two Worlds,* 206–9, is the best discussion of swinging I have found. See also Schuller, *Early Jazz,* chap. 1; Alan P. Merriam, *African Music in Perspective* (New York: Garland, 1982), 76–85, chap. 19; André Hodier, *Jazz: Its Evolution and Essence,* trans. David Noakes (New York: Grove, 1956, rpt. ed. 1980), 204.

32. Kaminsky and Hughes, *Jazz Band,* 33.

33. Dance, *The World of Earl Hines*, 133. For journalistic comments on dance, see for example McMahon, "The Jazz Path of Degradation," 26, 71; "The Jazz Cannibal" [poem], *Literary Digest* 84 (10 January 1925), 37.

34. Hodes and Hansen, *Selections from the Gutter*, 18, 22.

35. Earl Hines, "Forward," Bigard and Martyn, *With Louis and the Duke*, ix; Mezzrow and Wolfe, *Really the Blues*, 89–90, 307. On timbre in African and African-American music, see Roberts, *Black Music of Two Worlds*, 213–16, and Merriam, *African Music in Perspective*, 95–96.

36. See Kaminsky and Hughes, *Jazz Band*, 16; Dance, *The World of Earl Hines*, 90.

37. Hinton, JOHP, 4/76 4:1, 6/76 1:37–40; Collier, *Louis Armstrong*, 162–63; Tulane: Dodds, 2; George Mitchell, 2. New York players, such as Bubber Miley and Jabbo Smith, used bathroom plungers for unique muting effects. On clarinets, see Nicholas, Tulane, 4; Budd Johnson, JOHP, 11; and Collier, *Duke Ellington*, 80. Barney Bigard and Albert "Happy" Caldwell (JOHP 18) continued to use Albert clarinets.

38. Lawrence Brown, JOHP, 2:18–19. Brown added, "Of course I lost that [effect] after I started playing with big bands. . . . [I] couldn't control it anymore that way."

39. Dance, *The World of Earl Hines*, 10.

40. Shaw, *The Trouble with Cinderella*, 198–99.

41. Spivey, *Union and the Black Musician*, 100; Lomax, *Mister Jelly Roll*, 39.

42. Bechet, *Treat It Gentle*, 95–96.

43. On improvisation in Western music, see H. Wiley Hitchcock, "Jazz Improvisation and the European Tradition," *Papers of the Michigan Academy of Science, Arts, and Letters* 46 (1959), 401–6, and Derek Bailey, *Musical Improvisation: Its Nature and Practice in Music* (Englewood Cliffs, N.J.: Prentice-Hall, 1980).

44. Condon and Sugrue, *We Called It Music*, 270; Hodes and Hansen, *Selections From the Gutter*, 26.

45. Condon and Sugrue, *We Called It Music*, 79. See also Schuller, *Early Jazz*, chaps. 5, 6.

46. Kaminsky and Hughes, *Jazz Band*, 112; Dance, *The World of Earl Hines*, 23.

47. Hoagy Carmichael and Stephen Longstreet, *Sometimes I Wonder: The Story of Hoagy Carmichael* (New York: Farrar, Straus, and Giroux, 1965), 21; McPartland, JOHP, 21; Manone and Vandervoort, *Trumpet on the Wing*, 46.

48. Lil Hardin Armstrong, Tulane, 2:4–5; Lee Young, JOHP, 17; Porter, *Lester Young*, 6. On cutting contests in Kansas City, see David Stowe, "Jazz in the West: Cultural Frontier and Region during the Swing Era," *Western Historical Quarterly* (1992, forthcoming), 6–9.

49. Coleman, autobiography typescript, 94–95.

50. On head arrangements, see, for example, Dance, *The World of Earl Hines*, 23; Kaminsky and Hughes, *Jazz Band*, 111.

51. Bernhardt and Harris, *I Remember*, 62, 94. Mitchell, Tulane, 4, 6;

Dance, *The World of Earl Hines*, 52. The ethnomusicologists Marcia Herndon and Norma McLeod claim that written substitutes for pedagogues, such as instruction books, have been found in a variety of world musical cultures; *Music as Culture*, 53.

52. Lil Hardin Armstrong, Tulane, 3–4. The data on the recordings are in Brian Rust, *Jazz Records, 1897–1942*, 2d ed. (London: Storyville, 1978), 1:1133.

53. Dance, *The World of Earl Hines*, 45–46.

54. Garland, JOHP, 101.

55. Cootie Williams, JOHP, 82; Dominique, Tulane, 12.

56. Cootie Williams, JOHP, 194; Ellington quoted by Phillip Elwood, "Dylan Show Sinks Like a Lolling Stone," *San Francisco Examiner* (8 September 1988), E:1.

57. Collier, *Duke Ellington*, 94–95. See also Ken Rattenbury, *Duke Ellington: Jazz Composer* (New Haven: Yale University Press, 1990), esp. chaps. 1, 2.

58. A good analysis of Ellington's style is Schuller, *Early Jazz*, chap. 7.

59. Collier, *Duke Ellington*, esp. 155–60, 182–83; Bigard and Martyn, *With Louis and the Duke*, 47. The British enthusiasm for Ellington was expressed in Constant Lambert, *Music Ho!: A Study of Music In Decline* (London: Faber and Faber, 1934), esp. 203–4, 212–15.

60. Collier, *Duke Ellington*, 22, 41–42, 158–59, 296, and passim.

61. Durham, JOHP, 22–23; Russell, *Jazz Style in Kansas City*, chaps. 5–8.

Chapter 7: *"Being Crazy Don't Make Music"*

1. See Becker, *Outsiders;* Ned Polsky, *Hustlers, Beats, and Others* (Chicago: University of Chicago Press, 1969, rpt. ed. 1985), esp. 55 (where Polsky implies that jazz musicians developed a "counter-ideology" in the 1930s); Leonard, *Jazz and the White Americans*, esp. 129–30.

2. Carmichael and Longstreet, *Sometimes I Wonder*, 46.

3. Susman, *Culture as History*, 105, 120–21.

4. Mary Lou Williams, JOHP, 31, 60; Billie Pierce, Tulane, 4; Hunter, JOHP, 6:4–5; Dahl, *Stormy Weather*, chap. 4.

5. See Dahl, *Stormy Weather*, esp. 45–47, 281–94. On Hutchinson, see Freeman and Wolf, *Crazeology*, 15.

6. Mary Lou Williams, JOHP, 48, 50.

7. Hunter, JOHP, 2:20. See also Albertson, *Bessie*, esp. 140–45; Harrison, *Black Pearls*.

8. Gender assignments for jazz instruments probably did not derive primarily from African-American ideas, as Dahl notes in her discussion (*Stormy Weather*, 35–44). For Anglo-American Victorians' gender stereotyping of musical instruments, see Russell Sanjek, *American Popular Music*

and *Its Business: The First Four Hundred Years* (New York: Oxford University Press, 1988), 2:347–48, and Arthur Loesser, *Men, Women, and Pianos: A Social History* (New York: Simon and Schuster, 1954), 267–68, 560–64.

9. Blakeney, JOHP, 42–43; Coleman, autobiography typescript, 5–7, 115.

10. See, for example, Hodes and Hansen, *Selections from the Gutter*, 19–20, and Travis, *An Autobiography of Black Jazz*, 57–58, 127.

11. Hinton, JOHP, 6/76 10:9–11.

12. Dance, *World of Earl Hines*, 42.

13. Documents regarding these groups are in Jonathan Katz ed., *Gay American History: Lesbians and Gay Men in the U.S.A.*(New York: Thomas Crowell, 1976), 39–52, 82, 530–38. See also John D'Emilio and Estelle B. Freedman, *Intimate Matters: A History of Sexuality in America* (New York: Harper and Row, 1988), 27–29, 288.

14. Berton, *Remembering Bix*, esp. 209–19 and 252; Collier, *Duke Ellington*, 199. On homosexuality among American composers, see Joan Peyser, *Bernstein: A Biography* (New York: William Morrow, 1987), 33–34, 330–31.

15. Carmichael, *The Stardust Road*, 8–10, 13–16.

16. Carmichael, *The Stardust Road*, 76–77, 91.

17. Robert S. Lynd and Helen Merrell Lynd, *Middletown: A Study in Contemporary American Culture* (New York: Harcourt Brace, 1929), 494.

18. Freeman, *You Don't Look Like a Musician*, 106; Mezzrow and Wolfe, *Really the Blues*, 104, 106.

19. Mezzrow and Wolfe, *Really the Blues*, 281–82; JOHP: Freeman, 63–64; McPartland, 2:20.

20. Victor Turner, *The Anthropology of Performance* (New York: PAJ Publications, 1986), esp. 84, 127–28, 133. Neil Leonard first applied Turner's concept of *communitas* to jazz, in *Jazz: Myth and Religion*, 66–67.

21. See, for example, Grover Sales, *Jazz: America's Classical Music* (Englewood Cliffs, N.J.: Prentice-Hall, 1984), 89–94.

22. Becker, *Outsiders*, 90 and passim.

23. On daytime jobs, see Manone and Vandervoort, *Trumpet on the Wing*, 36–43; Condon and Sugrue, *We Called It Music*, 69–76; Hodes and Hansen, *Selections from the Gutter*, 25–27. Ellington quoted in Shapiro and Hentoff eds., *Hear Me Talkin' To Ya*, 168; Dance, *The World of Earl Hines*, 32.

24. Kaminsky and Hughes, *Jazz Band*, 66, 85. Dance, *The World of Earl Hines*, 32, 36.

25. Bud Freeman and Jimmy McPartland, fascinated by black dance, were exceptions; JOHP, 19, 40–41, respectively. Sidney Bechet and Louis Armstrong were also fine dancers; see Chilton, *Sidney Bechet*, 36.

26. Ralph Brown, COHC, 5; Brunis, Tulane, 36.

27. Manone and Vandervoort, *Trumpet on the Wing*, 143 (emphasis added).

28. Mezzrow and Wolfe, *Really the Blues*, 122–23. J.L. Dillard, in

Black English: Its History and Usage in the United States (New York: Random House, 1972), 244–45, notes that *"hot*, as applied to a type of jazz, is an Africanism and . . . the same metaphor is used in French Creole."

29. Herndon and McLeod, *Music as Culture*, chap. 1, Merriam and Mack, "The Jazz Community," and Merriam, *The Anthropology of Music*, 123–44, argue that groups of musicians in cultures around the world are clannish and secretive.

30. Neil Leonard, citing Lastrucci, "The Professional Dance Musician," has especially made this argument. *Jazz and the White Americans*, 63–65.

31. Eugene D. Genovese, *Roll, Jordan, Roll: The World the Slaves Made* (New York: Random House, 1972), 434–40.

32. Mezzrow and Wolfe, *Really the Blues*, 191–93.

33. Mezzrow and Wolfe, *Really the Blues*, 187.

34. H. L. Mencken, *The American Language: Supplement Two* (New York: Knopf, 1956), 704–10.

35. Bechet, *Treat It Gentle*, 76.

36. Dan Burley, *Dan Burley's Handbook of Harlem Jive* (New York: n.p., 1944); Cab Calloway [and Ned Williams], *The New Cab Calloway's Hepster's Dictionary* (New York: Cab Calloway Inc., 1938); Manone and Vandervoort, *Trumpet on the Wing*, 143–44, 175.

37. See, for example, "Origin of the Word Jazz," *Musician* 28 (March 1923), 20; Henry O. Osgood, *So This is Jazz* (Boston: Little, Brown, 1926), chap. 2; Bushell, JOHP, 14.

38. Bechet, *Treat It Gentle*, 3; Dance, *The World of Earl Hines;* Freeman, JOHP, 36.

39. Freeman, *You Don't Look Like a Musician*, 11. On clothing and status, see Alison Lurie, *The Language of Clothes* (New York: Random House, 1981), and Richard Sennett's discussion of the "presentation of the self" since the eighteenth century, *The Fall of Public Man: On the Social Psychology of Capitalism* (New York: Knopf, 1974).

40. Bechet, *Treat It Gentle*, 93; Collins, *Oh, Didn't He Ramble*, 16; Scoville Browne, COHC, 10.

41. Benny Goodman and Irving Kolodin, *The Kingdom of Swing* (New York: Stackpole, 1939), 35, 61; James Lincoln Collier, *Benny Goodman and the Swing Era* (New York: Oxford University Press, 1989), chap. 3. For one musician's reaction to young Goodman's kneepants, see Davison, JOHP, 52.

42. Manone and Vandervoort, *Trumpet on the Wing*, 213, 98, 126. Collier, *Louis Armstrong*, 198, reproduces a still photograph from the film, showing Armstrong's leopard skin.

43. Hinton, JOHP, 4/76 5:16, 7:6; Bernhardt and Harris, *I Remember*, 63–64; Dance, *The World of Earl Hines*, 22, 32, 47, 85. Two discussions of the importance of clothes and style to urban African Americans, from very different viewpoints, are Lurie, *The Language of Clothes*, 98–100, and Alfred B. Pasteur and Ivory L. Toldson, *Roots of Soul: The Psychology of Black Expressiveness* (Garden City, N.Y.: Doubleday, 1982).

44. Condon and Sugrue, *We Called It Music*, 140, 147; Freeman, *You Don't Look Like a Musician*, 18. There were exceptions to the rule. Condon wrote that the way Bix Beiderbecke "voiced an ordinary 7th chord [on the piano] was the joy and wonder of my life. The way he dressed was my despair." *We Called It Music*, 86.

45. Thomas A. DeLong, *Pops: Paul Whiteman, King of Jazz* (Piscataway, N.J.: New Century, 1983), 82; Freeman, JOHP, 27; Condon and Sugrue, *We Called It Music*, 203, 210–12. Huggins, *Harlem Renaissance*, 88–92, gives an overview of pseudo-African costuming in Harlem nightclubs.

46. Dance, *The World of Earl Hines*, 131.

47. Condon and Sugrue, *We Called It Music*, 220, 257; Davison, JOHP, 64; Hodes and Hansen, *Selections from the Gutter*, 10, 18; Manone and Vandervoort, *Trumpet on the Wing*, 83.

48. For example, the writer John Armstrong explored the new class of restaurant waiters made wealthy by tips: "Serving the Gentry," *American Mercury* 14 (August 1928), 392–99, and "Gate-Crashers," *American Mercury* 15 (October 1928), 215–22. See also Daniel Horowitz, *The Morality of Spending: Attitudes Towards Consumer Society in America, 1875–1940* (Baltimore: Johns Hopkins University Press, 1985).

49. Mezzrow and Wolfe, *Really the Blues*, 113.

50. Hinton, JOHP, 4/76 6:19. Black Chicago's interest in gambling is related in Drake and Cayton, *Black Metropolis*, 2:470–72. See also Borchert, *Alley Life in Washington*, 187, 204; Stephen Longstreet, *Win or Lose: A Social History of Gambling in America* (Indianapolis: Bobbs-Merrill, 1977); and John M. Findlay, *People of Chance: Gambling in American Society from Jamestown to Las Vegas* (New York: Oxford University Press, 1986).

51. Scoville Browne, COHC, 12; Dance, *The World of Earl Hines*, 36; Foster and Stoddard, *Pops Foster*, 158.

52. Manone and Vandervoort, *Trumpet on the Wing*, 213; Kaminsky and Hughes, *Jazz Band*, 43; Hodes and Hansen, *Selections from the Gutter*, 13.

53. For the history of marijuana in America, see William H. McGlothlin, "Sociocultural Factors in Marihuana Use in the United States," in *Cannabis and Culture*, ed. Vera Rubin (The Hague: Mouton, 1975), 531–47; H. Wayne Morgan, *Drugs in America, 1800–1980* (Syracuse: Syracuse University Press, 1981), chaps. 2, 3; Morris, *Wait Until Dark*, chaps. 2–4.

54. Foster and Stoddard, *Pops Foster*, 162–71; Dance, *The World of Earl Hines*, 146; Collier, *Louis Armstrong*, 221–22.

55. Mezzrow and Wolfe, *Really the Blues*, 62.

56. Mezzrow and Wolfe, *Really the Blues*, 62–63; McPartland, JOHP, 44–45; Carmichael, *Stardust Road*, 53.

57. A typical and influential discussion of prewar drug use and jazz is Polsky, *Hustlers, Beats, and Others*, 168–69. Wooding, JOHP, 49. Clarence Williams quoted in Garon, *Blues and the Poetic Spirit*, 94. Mezzrow and Wolfe, *Really the Blues*, 274–78. Mezzrow's playing, with or without the aid of marijuana, has not been widely praised since the 1930s. Bud Freeman has written that "Mezz was not a talented man," and Pops Foster believed

that "he just stands up there and goes toot-toot-toot. I like him, but man he can't play no jazz." Freeman, *You Don't Look Like a Musician*, 33; Foster and Stoddard, *Pops Foster*, 167. For background on narcotics in American society at this time, see David F. Musto, *The American Disease: Origins of Narcotics Control* (New Haven: Yale University Press, 1973), esp. 200–21.

58. Leonard, *Jazz: Myth and Religion*, 71; Otis, *Listen to the Lambs*, 114; Hinton, JOHP, 6/76 10:6; Bechet, *Treat It Gentle*, 123; Evans, JOHP, 66.

59. Condon and Sugrue, *We Called It Music*, 140, 148; Hodes and Hansen, *Selections from the Gutter*, 25; Collins, *Oh, Didn't He Ramble*, 70; Manone and Vandervoort, *Trumpet on the Wing*, 90–91; Bigard and Martyn, *With Louis and the Duke*, 100–1; Bushell, JOHP, 80.

60. Freeman, *You Don't Look Like a Musician*, 19. See also Jack H. Mendelson and Nancy K. Mello, *Alcohol: Use and Abuse in America* (Boston: Little, Brown, 1985), 171–90; Freeman, JOHP, 56.

61. Davison, JOHP transcript, p. 49. After 1930, Cootie Williams avoided drinking when he played: "I found out that it makes you nervous." JOHP, 282.

62. Freeman, JOHP, 55, 2:13–15, 43–44, 59–63. On alcoholism, culture, and heredity, see Mendelson and Mello, *Alcohol*, 192–204, 231–43.

63. Sudhalter and Evans, *Bix: Man and Legend*, 329–35 and passim, is the best examination of the cornetist and drinking. Berton, *Remembering Bix*, sheds little light on Beiderbecke's alcohol problem.

64. Sudhalter and Evans, *Bix: Man and Legend*, 333–35.

65. Sudhalter and Evans, *Bix: Man and Legend*, 324–26; JOHP: Freeman, 87; Autrey, 55.

Chapter 8: *"Money-Finding Music"*

1. Hazen and Hazen, *The Music Men*, 29–40, examines the institution of the traveling band; Oliver, *Songsters and Saints*, chap. 1, discusses itinerant southern black songsters; Constance Rourke, *American Humor: A Study of the National Character* (New York: Harcourt Brace, 1931), esp. chap. 4, offers the classic analysis of itinerant entertainers in early American culture.

2. Bethell, *George Lewis*, 60.

3. Scoville Browne, COHC, 14–15.

4. Morris, *Wait Until Dark*, esp. chap. 1.

5. Edwards, Tulane, 13; Manone and Vandervoort, *Trumpet on the Wing*, 97; Dance, *The World of Earl Hines*, 167. See also Mezzrow and Wolfe, *Really the Blues*, 158.

6. Bigard and Martyn, *With Louis and the Duke*, 50. Ellington's memoirs, *Music is My Mistress* (Garden City, N.Y.: Doubleday, 1973) and Collier, *Duke Ellington*, surprisingly do not discuss underworld harassment. Joe Darensbourg and Peter Vacher, *Jazz Odyssey: The Autobiography of Joe*

Darensbourg (Baton Rouge: Louisiana State University Press, 1987), 44–45. See also Dance, *The World of Earl Hines*, 46–47, and Hodes and Hansen, *Selections from the Gutter*, 34–35.

7. Bushell, JOHP, 78a; Mezzrow and Wolfe, *Really the Blues*, 159.

8. Elgar, Tulane, 26; Collier, *Duke Ellington*, 68–69; Bigard and Martyn, *With Louis and the Duke*, 29; Hinton, JOHP, 5:24; Collier, *Louis Armstrong*, 270–73.

9. Hodes and Hansen, *Selections from the Gutter*, 27; Durham, JOHP, 59–60; Bigard and Martyn, *With Louis and the Duke*, 59; Dahl, *Stormy Weather*, 54; Dance, *The World of Earl Hines*, 67, 134.

10. Dance, *The World of Earl Hines*, 25; Hunter, JOHP, 3:9. On TOBA nicknames, see, for example, Bushell, JOHP, 52.

11. Condon and Sugrue, *We Called It Music*, 160; Bill Challis, JOHP, 56. See also Roland Gelatt, *The Fabulous Phonograph, 1877–1977* (New York: Knopf, 1977), 267.

12. Coleman, autobiography typescript, 38–39; Dance, *The World of Earl Hines*, 95; 151–53, 298; Bubbles, JOHP, 100ff. See also Ralph Brown, COHC, 32. Max Kaminsky's difficulties with promoters arose in childhood. His kid band in Boston had been forcibly taken over by Lou Lissack, an adult musician who kept all of the band's earnings. The players stripped Kaminsky of his leader's role and gave it to a more aggressive boy: "they felt Jackie would be more of a match for the Lou Lissacks of this world than I would." Kaminsky then ran home, crying. Kaminsky and Hughes, *Jazz Band*, 7–9.

13. On copyrights, see Sanjek, *American Popular Music*, 2:395; Tulane: LaRocca, 5–6, 13, 28–31, 52; Picou, 6; William J. Schafer, "Breaking into 'High Society': Musical Metamorphoses in Early Jazz," *Journal of Jazz Studies* 2:2 (June 1975), 53–60.

14. Coleman, autobiography typescript, 72; JOHP: Tizol, 4:24; Charlie Barnet, 2:12.

15. Tizol, JOHP, 41–46; Collier, *Duke Ellington*, 130, chap. 11.

16. Lomax, *Mr. Jelly Roll*, xii; Nicholas, Tulane addendum, 3:1; Schafer, "Breaking into 'High Society'"; Hunter, JOHP, 3:10–11.

17. Collier, *Duke Ellington*, 192–95; Barnet, JOHP, 2:13; Dance, *The World of Earl Hines*, 67–69, 71, 151, 298, 300. See also Travis, *An Autobiography of Black Jazz*, 45–46; Spivey, *Union and the Black Musician*, 33–34, 71, 91.

18. Freeman, JOHP, 27.

19. Gelatt, *The Fabulous Phonograph*, 15, 191–92, 210, 213–14.

20. On race records, see Foreman, "Jazz and Race Records 1920–32,"; Johnson, *Growing Up in the Black Belt*, 55.

21. Susan J. Douglas argues convincingly that to ham radio enthusiasts, "the ether was neither the rightful province of the military nor a resource a private firm could appropriate or monopolize. The ether was, instead, an exciting new frontier in which men and boys could congregate, compete, test their mettle, and be privy to a range of new information.

Social order and social control were defied." *Inventing American Broadcasting, 1899–1922* (Baltimore: Johns Hopkins University Press, 1987), 214.

22. Examples of phonograph use are noted in Ralph Brown, COHC, 7; Ashcraft, Tulane, 24; Maxwell, JOHP, 5.

23. Freeman, JOHP, 23; Carmichael, *The Stardust Road*, 104; Condon and Sugrue, *We Called It Music*, 154–55.

24. For testimony regarding record wages see JOHP: Bushell, 25, Hunter, 3:10–1, Sippie Wallace, 16, and Blakeney, 204. Barnet, JOHP, 4:4–5.

25. Davison, JOHP, 28; Oliver, *Songsters and Saints*, 9; Kid Ory's discussion of Sunset Records in Los Angeles, in Tulane, 69–70, is also revealing; Gelatt, *The Fabulous Phonograph*, 210–11, 246.

26. Dance, *The World of Earl Hines*, 134; Hinton, JOHP, 4/76 6:25. See also J. Fred MacDonald, *Don't Touch That Dial! Radio Programming in American Life, 1920–1960* (Chicago: Nelson-Hall, 1979), 2–5.

27. MacDonald, *Don't Touch That Dial!*, 2–12ff.

28. Challis, JOHP, 2:5; Gelatt, *The Fabulous Phonograph*, 218–24; Dance, *The World of Earl Hines*, 62–63.

29. Hinton, JOHP, 11/76 1:49; Bernhardt and Harris, *I Remember*, 127. See also MacDonald, *Don't Touch That Dial!*, 329–30.

30. John Gray Peatman, "Radio and Popular Music," in *Radio Research 1942–1943*, Paul Lazarsfeld and Frank Stanton eds. (New York: Harper and Row, 1944), 335–45.

31. Freeman, JOHP, 2:34; Federal Communications Commission, "Summary of Functional Broadcast Employment and Pay-roll Data," in *Financial and Employee Data Respecting the 3 Major Networks and 705 Standard Broadcast Stations, 1939* (Washington, D.C.: Government Printing Office, 1940), n.p.

32. Hinton, JOHP, 4/76 3:14. On sound in films, see Lary L. May, *Screening Out the Past: The Birth of Mass Culture and the Motion Picture Industry* (New York: Oxford University Press, 1980), 39; Frederic Thrasher, *Okay For Sound: How the Screen Found Its Voice* (New York: Duell, Sloan, and Pearce, 1946), chaps. 1–3.

33. Lawrence Brown, JOHP, 12–13.

34. Hinton, JOHP, 6/76 1:41. On theater unemployment, see Ralph Brown, COHC, 4; Robert D. Leiter, *The Musicians and Petrillo* (New York: Bookman, 1953), 60–66; George Seltzer, *Music Matters: The Performer and the American Federation of Musicians* (Metuchen, N.J.: Scarecrow Press, 1989), 23–25.

35. Leiter, *The Musicians and Petrillo*, 14. In the 1930s the AFM was able to crush the American Guild of Musical Artists, a group established to serve the needs of art musicians; Leiter, 113–15.

36. Examples of union policy are cited in Brunis, Tulane, 30, and Condon and Sugrue, *We Called It Music*, 112. See also *The Intermezzo* 5:57 (January 1928), 4 (the journal of Chicago AFM Local 10).

37. Spivey, *Union and the Jazz Musician*, 13.

38. Leiter, *The Musicians and Petrillo*, 68, 132; District Court of the United States [Chicago], Order in *Guaranty Trust Co. vs. National Theatres Corp.*(Equity No. 8412) (1928); *Intermezzo* 5:57 (January 1928), 8–9, 17.

39. Foster and Stoddard, *Pops Foster*, 144; Bigard and Martyn, *With Louis and the Duke*, 32. See also Scoville Browne, COHC, 4–5; Spivey, *Union and the Black Musician*, 59.

40. COHC: Scoville Browne, 5, 93–94; Ralph Brown, 23, 46; Saunders, JOHP, 84; Spivey, *Union and the Black Musician*, 56. See also Bernhardt and Harris, *I Remember*, 49; Darnell Howard, Tulane, 3.

41. Howard, Tulane, 1; JOHP: Saunders 93–94, Barnet 10; Scoville Browne, COHC, 3; Hodes and Hansen, *Selections from the Gutter*, 11.

42. Manone and Vandervoort, *Trumpet on the Wing*, 101; Dance, *The World of Earl Hines*, 37; JOHP: Cootie Williams, 74–75, Hinton, 6/76 2:39–42, Hodes, 32–33, Davison, 86–91.

43. Spivey, *Union and the Black Musician*, 98. On union camaraderie, see JOHP: Hinton, 7:11; Saunders, 83; Hodes and Hansen, *Selections From the Gutter*, 16; Manone and Vandervoort, *Trumpet on the Wing*, 80.

44. Leiter, *The Musicians and Petrillo*, 93.

45. Davison, JOHP, 26. On mistakes on jazz records see David Baker, "The Phonograph in Jazz History and Its Influence on the Emergent Jazz Performer," in *The Phonograph and Our Musical Life*, ed. H. Wiley Hitchcock (Brooklyn: I.S.A.M. Monographs 14, 1977), 46, and Schuller, *Early Jazz*, passim.

46. Baker, "The Phonograph in Jazz History," 45–46; Tulane: Bauduc, 1; Brunis, 40; Manetta, 6; Davison, JOHP, 29; Mezzrow and Wolfe, *Really the Blues*, 132.

47. JOHP: Challis, 22; Durham, 56, 76. See also Ashcraft, Tulane, 27–28; Sauter, JOHP, 34; Collier, *Duke Ellington*, 128.

48. JOHP: Sauter, 109; Saunders, 95.

49. Maxwell, JOHP, 2:5, 21; Shaw, *The Trouble with Cinderella*, 236.

50. Condon and Sugrue, *We Called It Music*, 145; Kaminsky and Hughes, *Jazz Band*, 11; Hodes and Hansen, *Selections from the Gutter*, 29.

51. Hodes and Hansen, *Selections from the Gutter*, 30–31.

Chapter 9: *"Wacky State of Affairs"*

1. See, for example, Gerald Abrahams, *A Hundred Years of Music*, 4th ed. (London: Duckworth, 1974), 14–15.

2. Durham, JOHP, 19; Coleman, autobiography typescript, 89.

3. Spivey, *Union and the Black Musician*, 47, 50, 53. See also Leiter, *The Musicians and Petrillo*, 63; Travis, *An Autobiography of Black Chicago*, 39.

4. Gelatt, *The Fabulous Phonograph*, 255–65.

5. See JOHP: Lawrence Brown, 3:12; Lee Young, 2:2; Blakeney, 65; Bushell, 81; Carter, 93.

6. Russell, Tulane, 9, 2:5–6; Hinton, JOHP, 4/76 8:17, 6/76 1:3. For

a fuller description of Hinton's difficulties, see Milt Hinton and David G. Berger, *Bass Line: The Stories and Photographs of Milt Hinton* (Philadelphia: Temple University Press, 1988), 53.

7. Davison, JOHP, 80.

8. Condon and Sugrue, *We Called It Music*, 165, 230, 243–45; Kaminsky and Hughes, *Jazz Band*, 67, 70. See also Davison, JOHP, 80ff; Shaw, *The Trouble with Cinderella*, 215.

9. Spivey, *Union and the Black Musician*, 46, 48. See also Mitchell, Tulane, 7; Zilner Randolph, JOHP, 88–91; WPA Writers' Program, "The Negroes of New York City—Music and Musicians" (1939), microfilm copy on deposit in the Schomburg Center For Research in Black Culture, New York Public Library, reel 3:69; Hinton, JOHP, 9:3–5.

10. Leiter, *The Musicians and Petrillo*, 106.

11. Hodes, JOHP, 21; Bernhardt and Harris, *I Remember*, 65. See also Lee Young, JOHP, 2:5–6. Neil Leonard, in *Jazz: Myth and Religion*, 102–8, argues that initiation was an integral ritual in jazz culture. It should be added that commercialism and other exigencies strongly influenced the kinds of initiation jazz musicians were expected to undergo.

12. Edwards, Tulane, 18, 31.

13. Dance, *The World of Earl Hines*, 70; Spivey, *Union and the Black Musician*, 37; Hinton, JOHP, 1:20–21; Lawrence Brown, JOHP, 3:10–11. Teagarden quoted in Condon and Sugrue, *We Called It Music*, 192.

14. Scoville Browne, COHC, 19.

15. Lawrence Brown, JOHP, 3:14; Bigard and Martyn, *With Louis and the Duke*, 52, 66; Hinton, JOHP, 6/76 3:24.

16. Hodes and Hansen, *Selections from the Gutter*, 15; Carmichael, *The Stardust Road*, 65; Manone and Vandervoort, *Trumpet on the Wing*, 55–56, 208. Georg Brunis has noted that "Wingy's a pretty shrewd boy when it comes to money. He acts illiterate, but he's pretty smart"; Tulane, 28.

17. Helen Dance's statement is in Green, JOHP, 106. Dance, *The World of Earl Hines*, 62, 88.

18. Shaw, *The Trouble with Cinderella*, 308–9. Shaw's evaluation of Americans' attitudes about industrial craftsmanship receives support in Miles Orvell's major study, *The Real Thing: Imitation and Authenticity in American Culture, 1880–1940* (Chapel Hill: University of North Carolina Press, 1989). Orvell argues that while Americans in the nineteenth century wanted manufacturers to mimic nature in making goods, after 1900 they sought items that exhibited uniquely machine-made qualities.

19. Levy, "The Formalization of New Orleans Jazz Musicians," 40–44. The idea of the mass audience as abstraction was proposed persuasively in Dwight Macdonald, "Masscult and Midcult," in *Against the American Grain* (New York: Random House, 1962), 8–10.

20. See Gelatt, *The Fabulous Phonograph*, 270–75; Leiter, *The Musicians and Petrillo*, 132; Seltzer, *Music Matters*, 39–45.

21. Collier, *Benny Goodman and the Swing Era*, chap. 12; JOHP: Quinn Wilson, 2:34–36; Carter, 86–87; Shaw, *The Trouble with Cinderella*, 341.

22. Davison, JOHP, 207; Hodes and Hansen, *Selections from the Gut-*

ter, 28–29. Bill Coleman had refused a big band job in 1929 for the same reason as Davison; autobiography typescript, 125.

23. Caldwell, JOHP, 114. See also Ashcraft, Tulane, 14; Quinn Wilson, JOHP, 39.

24. JOHP: Freeman, 35; Hinton, 6/76 2:44–45. See also Lawrence Brown, JOHP, 4:15.

25. Bigard and Martyn, *With Louis and the Duke*, 66; Shaw, *The Trouble with Cinderella*, 341–44, 347–50.

26. Mezzrow and Wolfe, *Really the Blues*, 108–9.

27. JOHP: Freeman, 2:28–29; McPartland, 64; Challis, 44–45, 47; Bernhardt and Harris, *I Remember*, 126. For a sympathetic discussion of Miller's ambitions see George T. Simon, *Glenn Miller and His Orchestra* (New York: Thomas Y. Crowell, 1974), chaps. 19, 20, esp. 216–18. Simon notes that Artie Shaw had performed Garland's original version of "In the Mood" and had met with little success (177–78).

28. Freeman, JOHP, 2:35, 40, 45–48. See also Kaminsky and Hughes, *Jazz Band*, 81; Collier, *Benny Goodman and the Swing Era*, 207–13. For negative views of Goodman, see JOHP: Evans, 83, 95, and Hodes, 47. Goodman and Kolodin, *The Kingdom of Swing*, is largely unenlightening.

29. See Collier, *Benny Goodman and the Swing Era*, chaps. 19, 22; Collier, *Duke Ellington*, 179–80; Herman, JOHP, 22; Vladimir Simosko, "Artie Shaw and His Gramercy Five," *Journal of Jazz Studies* 1:1 (December 1973), 34–56.

30. See Condon and Sugrue, *We Called It Music*, esp. 250–80; Hodes, JOHP, 37, 55–56; Kaminsky and Hughes, *Jazz Band*, 108–24; "Swing" [photo essay], *Life* 5:6 (8 August 1938), 50–60.

31. Condon and Sugrue, *We Called It Music*, 236.

32. Shaw, *The Trouble with Cinderella*, 221. See also Sauter, JOHP, 44; Condon and Sugrue, *We Called It Music*, 251.

33. Bechet, *Treat It Gentle*, 124, 165; Hodes, JOHP, 19, 47; Hodes and Hansen, *Selections from the Gutter*, 22, 29.

34. Macdonald, "Masscult and Midcult," 14, 73–74. A revealing description of the nightclub crowd may be found in Kaminsky and Hughes, *Jazz Band*, 122–23.

Chapter 10: *"The Wedding of the Races"?*

1. Woodward, *The Strange Career of Jim Crow*, 116 and passim.

2. Woodward, *The Strange Career of Jim Crow*, chap. 4; Joel Williamson, *A Rage For Order: Black/White Relations in the American South since Emancipation* (New York: Oxford University Press, 1986), chaps. 5–8.

3. JOHP: Bushell, 84–85; Hinton, 6/76 3:4, 15–16. On South Carolina laws, see Woodward, *Strange Career of Jim Crow*, 102.

4. Bernhardt and Harris, *I Remember*, 84; JOHP: Hinton, 6/76 3:5; Bushell, 90.

5. Dance, *The World of Earl Hines*, 81; Otis, *Listen to the Lambs*, 81.

6. Coleman, autobiography typescript, 56, 30.
7. Dance, *The World of Earl Hines*, 82.
8. Hinton, JOHP, 6/76 3:15–17. Compare this to Hinton's slightly different description in Hentoff and Shapiro eds., *Hear Me Talkin' To Ya*, 326–27; Bushell, JOHP, 93–94.
9. Hinton, JOHP, 6/76 3:17–19. Zilner Randolph faced a predicament similar to Payne's in Florida, when to his distress a blonde woman grabbed his hand as he was walking to the bandstand; JOHP, 2:15.
10. Tizol, JOHP, 2:11.
11. Hinton, JOHP, 6/76 3:7–8.
12. Bernhardt and Harris, *I Remember*, 107, 130. See also Evans, JOHP, 44–45 and Dance, *The World of Earl Hines*, 83.
13. The major study of this tradition is Bertram Wyatt-Brown, *Southern Honor: Ethics and Behavior in the Old South* (New York: Oxford University Press, 1982).
14. Evans, JOHP, 53.
15. Coleman, autobiography typescript, 105; Lawrence Brown, JOHP, 2:26.
16. Bernhardt and Harris, *I Remember*, 53–54; Coleman, autobiography typescript, 112.
17. JOHP: Barnet, 4:26; Tizol, 2:12; Maxwell, 31.
18. See, for example, Philpott, *The Slum and Ghetto*, esp. part 2, regarding Chicago.
19. See esp. George M. Frederickson, *The Black Image in the White Mind: the Debate on Afro-American Character and Destiny, 1817–1914* (New York: Harper and Row, 1971), chap. 9; Drake and Cayton, *Black Metropolis*, esp. vol. 1; Meyer Weinberg, *A Chance to Learn: A History of Race and Education in the United States* (Cambridge: Cambridge University Press, 1977), 69–70, 78; and Mary J. Herrick, *The Chicago Schools: A Social and Political History* (Beverly Hills: Sage, 1971), chap. 10, 305, discuss the forces behind *de facto* school segregation in Chicago. Similar forces on the West Coast are discussed in Charles Wollenberg, *All Deliberate Speed: Segregation and Exclusion in California Schools, 1855–1975* (Berkeley: University of California Press, 1976).
20. Scoville Browne, COHC, 18; Bushell, JOHP, 79–80; Garvin Bushell and Mark Tucker, *Jazz from the Beginning* (Ann Arbor: University of Michigan Press, 1988), 111–13; Dance, *The World of Earl Hines*, 74. See also Hinton, JOHP, 6/76 2:39.
21. Under union pressure Chesterfield later rescinded its decision. Maxwell, JOHP, 1:53–54, 2:19, 24, 33–34.
22. Lee Young, JOHP, 1:33–34, 2:9.
23. Coleman, autobiography typescript, 9; JOHP: Woody Herman, 48–49; Durham, 54–56.
24. Among many sources on the subject of minstrel stereotypes are Toll, *Blacking Up*, esp. chaps. 2–5; Joseph Boskin, *Sambo: The Rise and*

Demise of an American Jester (New York: Oxford University Press, 1986), esp. chaps. 4, 5; and Michael Rogin, " 'The Sword Became a Flashing Vision': D. W. Griffith's *The Birth of a Nation,*" *Representations* 9 (Winter 1985), esp. 180–84. See also the fine documentary film *Ethnic Notions,* Marlon Riggs, producer (1986).

25. Dance, *The World of Earl Hines,* 131–32, 136; Billie Holiday and William Dufty, *Lady Sings the Blues* (New York: Doubleday, 1956), 61.

26. JOHP: Lee Young, 1:33–34, 2:9; Tizol, 2:38; Hinton, 6/76 2:39. "White" bands had to look white as well; thus in the late 1930s Teddy Wilson and Lionel Hampton could not appear in films with the Benny Goodman band. Teddy Wilson, JOHP, 7.

27. Laine, Tulane, 15.

28. Rose, *I Remember Jazz,* 65; Nick LaRocca to Brian Rust, 15 and 24 November 1957, Manuscript Collection, Music Division, Library of Congress.

29. See Brunn, *The Story of the Original Dixieland Jazz Band,* 26–27; Rose, *I Remember Jazz,* 64–65.

30. Maxwell, JOHP, 2:24.

31. Whiteman and McBride, *Jazz;* Brunis, Tulane, 19, 26; Challis, JOHP, 14.

32. JOHP: Freeman, 41; Evans, 85. See also Still, "The Men Behind American Music," 12–15, 29.

33. Freeman, JOHP, 24–25, 61. Boskin, *Sambo,* 113, effectively describes how the image of the ever-happy black persisted strongly into the 1930s. On white racism in 1910s Chicago, see Philpott, *The Slum and the Ghetto,* esp. 194–211; Tuttle, *Race Riot.*

34. Ralph Brown, COHC, 33; Condon and Sugrue, *We Called It Music,* 181. Tough might have picked up this notion from the popular bandleader Ted Lewis, who did a famous rendition of "Me and My Shadow" with a black dancer behind him. Teddy Wilson, JOHP, 44.

35. Condon and Sugrue, *We Called It Music,* 130, 162; Carmichael, *The Stardust Road,* 140.

36. Hodes, JOHP, 2:22; Scoville Browne, COHC, 9; Muggsy Spanier, Tulane, 9.

37. Holiday and Dufty, *Lady Sings the Blues,* 97, 99; Hodes and Hansen, *Selections from the Gutter,* 34–36; Barnet, JOHP, 2:3, 5–6. In Los Angeles, Barnet found racial mixing in jam sessions but not in bands (43).

38. Carter, JOHP, 68; Scoville Browne, COHC, 16.

39. Hinton, JOHP, 6/76 3:25. See also Drake and Cayton, *Black Metropolis,* 180–82; Spivey, *Union and the Black Musician,* 38, 59.

40. JOHP: Bushell, 62, Barnet, 4:31, Maxwell, 31. See also John Hammond and Irving Townsend, *John Hammond on Record* (New York: Ridge Press, 1977), 136; Collier, *Duke Ellington,* 232.

41. Foster and Stoddard, *Pops Foster,* 140; Bechet, *Treat It Gentle,* 114, 168–69. The Chicago musician William Samuels agreed that when whites

tried to play jazz, "it never did sound the same [as black jazz], but they kept trying. . . . but it didn't do 'em any good." Spivey, *Union and the Black Musician*, 39.

42. Freeman, *You Don't Look Like a Musician*, 91; JOHP: Freeman, 17; McPartland, 18. A similar view is expressed in Kaminsky and Hughes, *Jazz Band*, 23–24.

43. JOHP: Bubbles, 44–46; McShann, 13–15. On "Shine" see Levine, *Black Culture and Black Consciousness*, 427–49. See also Bernhardt and Harris, *I Remember*, 54–55; JOHP: Humes, 65–66, Tizol, 10, 25.

44. This clarinetist "wouldn't leave us, saying that he got more feeling out of the music that we played, and he could really swing." Collins also knew a Japanese drummer in Chicago who passed for Chinese after the Pearl Harbor attack. Collins, *Oh, Didn't He Ramble*, 29, 81–82

45. Dance, *The World of Earl Hines*, 82; Otis, *Listen to the Lambs*, 29–30.

46. Tizol, JOHP, 2:9–10.

47. Bushell, JOHP, 89.

48. JOHP: Bushell, 89; Budd Johnson, 2:55; Kaminsky and Hughes, *Jazz Band*, 125–26.

49. W. E. B. Du Bois in *The Crisis* (April 1934), rpt. in *Selected Writings*, 1241, 783. See also Hammond and Townsend, *John Hammond on Record*, 81–85; Nancy J. Weiss, *The National Urban League, 1910–1940* (New York: Oxford University Press, 1974), 92, 174, 200–201, 232. On blacks and the New Deal, see Robert S. McElvaine, *Down & Out in the Great Depression: Letters From the Forgotten Man* (Chapel Hill: University of North Carolina Press, 1983), 28–30, 81–94.

50. See Dance, *The World of Earl Hines*, 25, 45; Foster and Stoddard, *Pops Foster*, 108; Ralph Brown, COHC, 29; JOHP: Hunter, 57; Davison, 77; etc.

51. Dance, *The World of Earl Hines*, 131.

52. Dance, *The World of Earl Hines*, 7–8.

53. Sullivan, JOHP, 506; Bernhardt and Harris, *I Remember*, 6, 20–23; JOHP: Trummy Young, 6; Hunter, 41.

54. Bechet, *Treat It Gentle*, 59.

55. Ralph Brown, COHC, 43.

56. JOHP: Challis, 51–52, Davison, 80, McPartland, 44. Among the many sources on interracial jam sessions are Foster and Stoddard, *Pops Foster*, 124; Darnell Howard, Tulane, 9; Singleton, Tulane, 4; and Mezzrow and Wolfe, *Really the Blues*, passim.

57. Carter, JOHP, 2:69; Bernhardt and Harris, *I Remember*, 47; Nicholas, Tulane, 4; Cootie Williams, JOHP, 83. On Lester Young, see Ira Gitler, *Swing to Bop: An Oral History of the Transition of Jazz in the 1940s* (New York: Oxford University Press, 1985), 34–35.

58. Bechet, *Treat It Gentle*, 164–65; McPartland, JOHP, 20; Davison, JOHP, 90–91.

59. Freeman, JOHP, 63.

60. Charles Edward Smith, "Jazz," *The Symposium* 1:4 (October 1930),

509, quoted in Polsky, *Hustlers, Beats, and Others,* 172; Maxwell, JOHP, 27–29. See also Mezzrow and Wolfe, *Really the Blues,* 3–4. Polsky notes that the phrase "white nigger" can be traced back at least to the 1850s, when Richard Francis Burton was chided by fellow British officers in India for wearing native dress.

61. Hodes, JOHP, 15–18. Leonard Feather's discussion of the 1940s, in *The Jazz Years: Earwitness to an Era* (New York: Da Capo, 1987), 81–82, 87–91, shows that Hodes and other older white musicians accused the bop movement of being antiwhite, and that these musicians struggled to gain control of *Esquire's* Jazz Poll and other publicity devices after World War Two. It is incorrect to conclude, however, that the older, antibop coterie was primarily white and racist; too many older black musicians as well disliked bop. Racial invective emanated from both camps, but the division was primarily generational.

62. Bechet, *Treat It Gentle,* 58; Cootie Williams, JOHP, 59.

63. Foster and Stoddard, *Pops Foster,* 146; Hunter, JOHP, 3:9–10. See also Lee Young, JOHP, 3:4; Hammond and Townsend, *John Hammond on Record,* 72 (WEVD's name came from the initials of Eugene V. Debs); Harrison, *Black Pearls,* 214.

64. Hunter, JOHP, 2:12. See also "William Ransom Hogan Jazz Archive" [Archive brochure] (n.d.), 6.

65. Condon and Sugrue, *We Called It Music,* 200. See also Rust, *Jazz Records, 1897–1942,* 2d ed., 45, 56, 335; Chilton, *Who's of Jazz,* 87.

66. JOHP: Freeman, 62, Herman, 19–20. See also Rust, *Jazz Records, 1897–1942,* 2d ed., 56, 335, 439–44, 541–43 (survey of Freeman's recordings); Rust, 363, 837, 1114, 1194.

67. Hammond and Townsend, *John Hammond on Record,* esp. 72–85. Hammond claims that in December 1932, the Communist party's International Labor Defense (which aided the Scottsboro defendants) asked him to organize a benefit concert at the Rockland Palace, which featured the Duke Ellington and Benny Carter orchestras as well as white performers. I could not find other evidence of this event, which might have been the first time that jazz was explicitly associated with the civil rights struggle.

68. Hammond and Townsend, *John Hammond on Record,* 70, 116.

69. Hammond and Townsend, *John Hammond on Record,* 109, 147, 175–76, 194–96, 245–69. See also Humes, JOHP, 48; Hinton, JOHP, 6/76 4:8.

70. Herman, JOHP, 23–24; Hammond and Townsend, *John Hammond on Record,* 171; Collier, *Duke Ellington,* 195–96; Dance, *The World of Earl Hines,* 154–55. See also Hodes, JOHP, 9, regarding Kapp.

71. See Collier, *Louis Armstrong,* 162; Wallace, JOHP, 23, 27; Artists' Ball advertised in *Chicago Defender* (27 February 1926), 8, described in "The Big Night" (6 March 1926), 6. Coleman, autobiography typescript, 74; Jackson, Tulane, 16; William "Count" Basie and Albert Murray, *Good Morning Blues: The Autobiography of Count Basie* (New York: Random House, 1985), 200.

72. Coleman, autobiography typescript, 21; Singleton, Tulane, 5; Freeman, JOHP, 90; Mezzrow and Wolfe, *Really the Blues*, 226–32; Rust, *Jazz Records, 1897–1942*, 2d ed., 1114.

73. Spivey, *Union and the Black Musician*, 39; Bernhardt and Harris, *I Remember*, 126; Durham, JOHP, 60–61.

74. Dance, *The World of Earl Hines*, 24, 81.

75. Holiday and Dufty, *Lady Sings the Blues*, 71–81, 82; Maxwell, JOHP, 41.

76. Mezzrow and Wolfe, *Really the Blues*, 126.

77. JOHP: McPartland, 94–95, Maxwell, 22, Freeman, 61. See also Dance, *The World of Earl Hines*, 22; Willie "The Lion" Smith and George Hoefer, *Music on My Mind: The Memoirs of an American Pianist* (New York: Doubleday, 1964), 172.

78. Shaw, *The Trouble with Cinderella*, 222–28; McPartland, JOHP, 123.

79. Hodes and Hansen, *Selections from the Gutter*, 18; Bushell, JOHP, 126–27.

80. Perhaps the closest precursor to this form of black authority over white ingenues was found in the institution of the mammy in Southern plantation mansions, discussed by Eugene D. Genovese in *Roll, Jordan, Roll*, 355–57. I am not yet prepared to accept a Freudian interpretation of this, similar to what Paul Garon argued about white blues singers: "with the black man as father = superior strength . . . the 'white bluesman' gains enormously in self-esteem, thus reaffirming his masculinity." *Blues and the Poetic Spirit*, 57.

81. Ralph Brown, COHC, 50; Foster and Stoddard, *Pops Foster*, 124; Freeman, JOHP, 59–60; Evans, JOHP, 20; Mezzrow and Wolfe, *Really the Blues*, 243. See also Spivey, *Union and the Black Musician*, 50.

82. Hinton, JOHP, 11/76 1:51, 55–58.

83. Evans, JOHP, 47; Maxwell, JOHP, 29. Some whites, such as the trumpeter Jack Purvis (who sunburned his face in an attempt to "become black") and Mezz Mezzrow, did not take racial integration as seriously. See Foster and Stoddard, *Pops Foster*, 140, and Mezzrow and Wolfe, *Really the Blues*, passim.

84. Among the jazz writers who claim that jazz advanced race relations are Panassié, *Hot Jazz*, 140, 294–95; Sidney Finkelstein, *Jazz: A People's Music* (New York: Citadel Press, 1948), 140–41; Stearns, *The Story of Jazz*, chap. 25; and Martin Williams, *The Jazz Tradition*, rev. ed. (New York: Oxford University Press, 1983), 254–56. Imamu Amiri Baraka, in *Blues People*, is the strongest dissenter from this view (see 164–65).

Epilogue

1. Carmichael and Longstreet, *Sometimes I Wonder*, 74.

2. See, for example, Hayden White, *The Content of Form: Narrative*

Discourse and Historical Representation (Baltimore: Johns Hopkins University Press, 1987); William H. McNeill, *Mythistory and Other Essays* (Chicago: University of Chicago Press, 1986), esp. chaps. 1, 2; Peter Novick, *That Noble Dream: The "Objectivity Question" and the American Historical Profession* (Cambridge: Cambridge University Press, 1988); Peretti, "Oral Histories of Jazz Musicians," esp. 14–16.

3. Rosenzweig, *Eight Hours for What We Will*; Stuart Blumin, *The Emergence of the Middle Class: Social Experience in the American City, 1760–1900* (Cambridge: Cambridge University Press, 1988); Ryan, *Cradle of the Middle Class*. On the recent impasse in community studies and quantitative methods, from a variety of perspectives, see G. R. Elton and Robert W. Fogel, *Which Road to the Past? Two Views of History* (New Haven: Yale University Press, 1983); Bryan D. Palmer, "Emperor Katz's New Clothes; or, with the Wizard of Oz," *Labour* [Canada] 13 (1984), 190–97; Eric H. Monkkonen, "The Challenge of Quantitative History," *Historical Methods* 17:3 (Summer 1984), 86–94; Kathleen Neils Conzen, "Community Studies, Urban History, and American Local History," in *The Past before Us: Historical Writing in the United States*, ed. Michael Kammen (Ithaca: Cornell University Press, 1980), 270–91; and Conzen, "Quantification and the New Urban History," *Journal of Interdisciplinary History* 13:4 (Spring 1983), 653–77.

4. Mary P. Ryan, *Women in Public: Between Banners and Ballots, 1825–1880* (Baltimore: Johns Hopkins University Press, 1990); Kinser, *Carnival American Style*; Turner, *The Anthropology of Performance*. See also Leonard, *Jazz: Myth and Religion*, chap. 5.

5. Gitler, *Swing to Bop*, 58, 61, 70, 83–84.

6. Gitler, *Swing to Bop*, 125–26; Mezzrow and Wolfe, *Really the Blues*, 281; Dominique, Tulane, 2; Collier, *Louis Armstrong*, 305.

7. Gitler, *Swing to Bop*, 58, 132.

8. Marcus, *Lipstick Traces*. Another exception to the present dearth of youth-culture studies is Gilbert, *Cycle of Outrage*.

9. The recent concentration on American professions began with Daniel H. Calhoun, *Professional Lives in America: Structure and Aspiration, 1750–1850* (Cambridge: Harvard University Press, 1965) and Burton J. Bledstein, *The Culture of Professionalism: The Middle Class and the Development of Higher Education in America* (New York: Norton, 1976). See also Gerald L. Geison, ed., *The Professions and Professional Ideology in America* (Chapel Hill: University of North Carolina Press, 1983) and Nathan O. Hatch, ed. *The Professions in American History* (Notre Dame: Notre Dame University Press, 1988). Jazz fits into the authors' concept of a profession based on education, authority, expertise, and group identity. They stress, though, that the professions arose after the Civil War out of an urge to reform the nation's ills through expertise. Jazz only partially resulted from this urge (by way of bourgeois music instructors), but this should not discourage us from considering it a profession. As Geison has argued, "there is . . . good reason to suspect that all of the existing models of professions and professionalization are inadequate to some degree." (6).

10. Howard Gardner, *Art, Mind, and Brain: A Cognitive Approach to Creativity* (New York: Basic Books, 1982), esp. chap. 13; *Frames of Mind: The Theory of Multiple Intelligence* (New York: Basic Books, 1983), chaps. 6, 14.

11. Kaminsky and Hughes, *Jazz Band*, 37–38.

Oral Histories Consulted

A. National Endowment For the Arts/Smithsonian Institution Jazz Oral History Project (JOHP). Currently owned and housed by the Institute of Jazz Studies, Rutgers University, Newark, Dan Morgenstern, director. Used with permission.

Herman Autrey
Eddie Barefield
Charlie Barnet
Andrew Blakeney
Lawrence Brown
John Bubbles (Sublett)
Garvin Bushell
Happy Caldwell
Benny Carter
Bill Challis
Wild Bill Davison
Eddie Durham
Gil Evans
Bud Freeman
Montudie Garland
Freddie Green
Horace Henderson
Woody Herman
Milt Hinton
Art Hodes

Helen Humes
Alberta Hunter
Budd Johnson
Jimmy McPartland
Jay McShann
Jimmy Maxwell
Zilner Randolph
Red Saunders
Eddie Sauter
Jabbo Smith
Maxine Sullivan
Juan Tizol
Sippie Wallace
Cootie Williams
Mary Lou Williams
Quinn Wilson
Teddy Wilson
Sam Wooding
Lee Young
Trummy Young

B. Tulane Jazz Oral History Project (Tulane). Owned in part and housed by the William Ransom Hogan Jazz Archive, Tulane University, Bruce Boyd Raeburn, curator, and also owned in part by William Russell. Used with permission.

Lil Hardin Armstrong
Edwin "Squirrel" Ashcraft
Lovie Austin
Ray Bauduc
Tom Brown
Georg Brunis
Warren "Baby" Dodds
Natty Dominique
Eddie Edwards
Charles Elgar
Edmond Hall
Willie Hightower
Darnell Howard
Willie Humphrey, Sr.
Preston Jackson
Papa Jack Laine

Dominick "Nick" LaRocca
Manuel "Fess" Manetta
Ernest "Punch" Miller
George Mitchell
Albert Nicholas
Stella Oliver
Edward "Kid" Ory
Alphonse Picou
Billie Pierce
De De Pierce
William Russell
Arthur "Zutty" Singleton
Francis "Muggsy" Spanier
Jasper Taylor
Jack Teagarden

C. Columbia Oral History Collection, Butler Library, Columbia University of the City of New York, Ronald Grele, director. Used with permission.

Ralph Brown
Scoville Browne

Index

Adolescence: 1920s white, 95, 97; and 1920s jazz revival, 174, 176; study of, 214

AFM. *See* American Federation of Musicians

African-American culture: white influence of, 14–15; oral traditions, 28; face-to-face orientation, 49–50; 1920s self-assertion, 48, 53, 54; white musicians and, 87, 89, 96–97; Ellington and, 118–19; and homosexuality, 125; and jazz culture, 130; and jazz, 214–15

African-American music: culture of, 1870–1900, 15; as extension of community, 19, 33–34, 52, 53; impact of migration to New Orleans on, 36–37

African-American musicians: combo style, 115; and alcohol, 143; and phonograph, 152; and AFM, 159; and southern roots, 182; and white jazz, 192–93; leadership in jazz, 199, 207–8

African Americans: and jazz, 2, 3, 6–8; northern communities and jazz, 7; New Orleans blacks and Creoles, 25, 27, 31, 58; and jazz profession, 215–16. *See also* Bourgeoisie, black; Northern black communities

African, West, culture, 6, 11; in the blues, 16

African, West, music, 100; characteristics, 12

Alcohol: use by musicians, 128, 139, 141–44; effects on players, 142

Alcoholism, 142–44

American Federation of Musicians (AFM): locals and segregation, 43; recording ban (1942–44), 151, 171; practices, 157–58; and jazz musicians, 158–61; Great Depression and, 165; pay scale, 165; and black employment, 201

AFM Local 10 (Chicago, white), 157–60 passim

AFM Local 208 (Chicago, black), 159, 160, 165

AFM Local 802 (New York City), 167

American Society of Composers, Authors, and Publishers (ASCAP): and music industry, 149, 150; ban on, 170

"Amos 'n' Andy," 154, 187

Apollo Theater (Harlem): seating in, 51; white musicians in, 192

Armstrong, Lil Hardin, 60, 122; in Chicago, 69; arrangements, 116

Armstrong, Louis "Satchmo," 1, 51, 52, 60, 69, 91, 108, 111, 112, 120, 127–28, 134, 137, 138, 147, 153, 183, 190; in New Orleans, 29, 33, 34; on riverboats, 39; reading Oliver's fingering, 102; timbre, 110; in cutting contest, 114; and music reading, 116; and scat singing, 127; and clothing, 135; and marijuana, 139; on Beiderbecke's alcoholism, 143;

Armstrong, Louis (*continued*)
and whites, 199, 208; and integrated recording sessions, 202; on bebop, 214
Arrangements: Dixieland, 73; Ellington's, 117–18; Mary Lou Williams's, 123; Carter's, 150
Art music. *See* European-American music
Ashcraft, Edwin "Squirrel," 72
Austin, Cora "Lovie": on Morton, 59, 231n1; Mary Lou Williams on, 122
Austin, Illinois, 82, 83, 84, 92
Austin High Gang, 82–86 passim, 91, 93, 110, 111, 138, 140
Autodidacticism: and musicians, 91–92, 107, 152
Autrey, Herman: childhood, 19; on origins of jazz, 21; on alcohol in jazz, 144

Balaban and Katz (theater chain), 51
Baltimore Afro-American, 53
Band battles: in the North, 114; integrated, 204
Baquet, Achille, 31, 81
Baquet, George: instruction by, 35
Barbarin, Paul: in Chicago, 45, 60
Barefield, Eddie: and music reading, 103
Barnet, Charlie: on Carter, 150; on record income, 153; and AFM, 160; on integration in jazz, 184, 205; in Harlem, 192
Basie, William "Count," 119, 193; and minstrel stereotype, 187; Hammond and, 203; band battle with Goodman, 204
Bauduc, Ray, 79
Beat: in Dixieland, 80; in jazz, 108–10, 193; as metaphor, 130
Bebop jazz, 4, 71, 200; rise of, 213–14
Bechet, Sidney, 45, 55, 71; in New Orleans, 31, 34, 35; on black culture, 37; and music reading, 102, 103; on music, 107–8; on innovation, 112; on jive, 132; on the word "jazz," 133; on clothing, 134; on drug and alcohol use, 141; and Great Depression, 167; on commercialism, 175–76; separatism of,

192; and integration in jazz, 198; on Condon, 199; on black jobs in New Orleans, 200–201
Becker, Howard S.: on deviance in jazz, 4, 128
Beiderbecke, Leon Bix, 83, 120, 173, 208; education, 92; musical autodidacticism, 107; rhythm of, 109; in Bloomington, 126–27; and scat singing, 127; and alcohol, 141, 142–44; emulation of his drinking, 143–44; in Harlem, 189; and clothing, 247n44
Benny Goodman Quartet: and integration in jazz, 203
Berigan, Bernard "Bunny": and alcohol, 143
Bernhardt, Clyde, 46, 65, 112, 173; in Harlem, 47–48, 167–68; on Oliver, 60; touring, 66, 183; on teachers, 106; on music reading, 115–16; on clothing, 135; on radio, 155; on racism, 179, 182; childhood and race, 198; on Mole and Lincoln, 199; in integrated band, 204–5
Bethune, Thomas Greene ("Blind Tom"), 15
Big Band Era (1935–47), 9, 171–74, 213–14
Bigard, Barney, 35, 60, 66, 70, 118; in New Orleans, 27, 33; on Morton, 112; on Ellington, 147; and royalties, 150; on AFM, 158–59; and Great Depression, 169; on touring, 172; and minstrel stereotype, 187
Billings, Josh: and clothing, 136
Biracial bands. *See* Integration in jazz
Black Swan Records, 153
Blake, Eubie, 50; on jazz, 53
Blakeney, Andrew, 63; in Chicago, 45; on women in jazz, 124
"Blind Tom." *See* Bethune, Thomas Greene
Blues, 68, 72, 110, 203; origins and definition, 16; relation to jazz, 16–17, 21; by Creath band, 41; woman singers, 122–24 passim; Brunis and Challis on, 189; Bechet on, 192; 1930s urban, 213–14
Bolden, Charles "Buddy," 20, 28, 80, 86; and creation of jazz, 26; playing

style, 101; end of career, 101
Bourgeoisie, black: in northern cities, 61–64, 118; and music, 48; and Great Migration, 197
Bradford, Perry, 153
Brass bands: in New Orleans, 26, 33–34
Braud, Wellman, 61
Briggs, Arthur, 56
Brown, Boyce, 91
Brown, Harvey, 91
Brown, Lawrence, 63, 65; on teachers, 106; style, 111; on Ellington, 150; and film music, 156; on Los Angeles, 168; on touring, 183
Brown, Ralph, 49, 69, 70; and phonograph, 105; on jive, 130; on AFM, 159; and racism, 190; on interracial theft of music, 198; on integration in jazz, 208
Brown, Tom, 77, 168; on jazz and race, 80, 81, 187–88
Browne, Scoville, 70, 72; on clothing, 134; on gambling, 138; on organized crime, 146; on AFM, 159; on New York, 168–69; on discrimination, 185; and integrated bands, 191; on white musicians, 192
Brunis, Georg, 82; on Mardi Gras, 32; in New Orleans, 32–33; childhood, 77–78; on jive, 130; on racial origins of blues, 189
Bubbles (Sublett), John, 63, 149; migration to New York, 47; in northern theaters, 53–54; on music education, 106; and minstrelsy, 193
Burnett, Chester, "Howlin' Wolf": and AFM, 160
Bushell, Garvin: in Europe, 56; and organized crime, 147; on southern dances, 178, 181; and discrimination, 185; in South, 195; on Vanderbilt, 207

California: and early jazz, 41, 82, 116; motion pictures, 156
Calloway, Cab, 169, 172, 178–82 passim; on blues, 72; and jive, 132–33
Capone, Al, 46–47, 147–48, 167, 190; and AFM Local 10, 157, 159
Capone, Ralph, 190

Carisi, Johnny: on Condon, 213
Carmichael, Hoagy, 76, 82; on rebellion, 86; in South Side, 88; and rebellion, 95–96; on World War Two, 98; on innovation, 114; on meaning of jazz, 121, 126; and marijuana, 140; on recording, 153; on Armstrong, 190; on jazz age concept, 211, 212
Carney, Harry, 89
Carpenter, Charlie, 57; on marijuana, 139; and Morris, 204
Carpenter, Elliott, 56
Carter, Benny, 63, 72–73, 189, 203; on New York, 43; on ghetto, 74; lessons, 106; and Armstrong style, 108; exploitation of, 150; on New York jazz, 171; on whites in Harlem, 191; and Trumbauer style, 199
Carter, Jack, 55–56
CBS Radio, 170, 203, 208
Celestin, Oscar "Papa," 31
Challis, Bill, 198; on Beiderbecke's alcoholism, 143; on Decca engineers, 149; on radio, 154; on recording technology, 161–62; on commercialism, 169; and Glenn Miller, 173; on blues, 189
Cheatham, Adolphus "Doc," 56
Chicago, 79, 82–94 passim, 138, 139, 198, 217; music in, 1900–1916, 41; Midway district, 41; migration to, 44, 45, 47; "valley" district, 51–52; musicians' profession in, 59–60; ethnic groups, 86–87; and the arts, 94, 98; and organized crime, 146, 147. *See also* South Side
Chicago Defender, 61
Chicagoans (1920s white jazz musicians), 8, 82–99 passim, 121, 173; style of, 115; and jazz as therapy, 127; and 1920s jazz revival, 174; racial attitudes of, 189–91; and integration, 199
Childhood of musicians: on plantations, 17–21; and race relations, 88–89, 197–98
Children's bands, 18–19, 20, 77, 78, 79, 107
Chilton, John, 43, 44, 45

Christian churches: and West African
  culture, 12; and blues, 16
Cincinnati: blacks and music in, 41, 64;
  women musicians, 124
Civil rights movement (1950s-1960s),
  204–5
Classical music. *See* European-
  American music
Cless, Rod, 83, 208
Clothing, 8; importance of in New
  York, 47–48; blueswomen's, 68;
  and jazz, 128; in American culture,
  134; and musicians, 134–37; and
  bands, 135; and racism, 181
Coleman, Bill, 64; childhood, 41; in
  Canada, 57; on suppers, 114–15;
  on jazzwomen, 124; and promoters,
  149; on royalties, 150; and poverty,
  164; on racial violence, 180; and
  segregation, 183; on integration
  and band battles, 204
Collier, James Lincoln, 3, 5, 34
Collins, Lee: in Chicago, 48; and music
  reading, 102; on clothing, 134; and
  alcohol, 141; and multiethnic band,
  194
Columbia University Oral History
  Collection, 262
Columbia Records, 116, 153, 170, 202,
  203
Combos, 115; in Big Band Era, 174–75
Commercialism, 150, 216; and jazz,
  8–9, 28, 39, 47, 145–76 passim,
  167; Ory and, 18, 19, 20; after
  1900, 145–46; and artistry, 149;
  of some musicians, 151, 162; musicians against, 162–63; Gabler and
  Paul Smith on, 175; and racism,
  185–86, 188, 190; bebop and, 213,
  214
Commodore Records, 175
Condon, Eddie, 51, 76, 83, 151, 172; in
  South Side, 88; marginalization, 96;
  on improvisation, 113; nocturnality
  of, 129; on word "jazz," 134; and
  clothing, 136; and money, 136, 137;
  on alcohol, 141; on recording, 149,
  153; and AFM, 157; against mechanization, 162–63; and Depression,
  166, 167; and 1920s jazz revival,
  174, 175; and minstrel stereotype,

  190; and integrated recording
  sessions, 202
Cook, Charles "Doc," 204
Cook, Will Marion, 55, 118
Cotton Club (Los Angeles), 165
Cotton Clubs (New York), 117–18, 172,
  185, 187
Cottrell, Louis, 37
Courtship, interracial: in jazz, 208
Cowley, Malcolm, 98
Creath, Charlie, 39, 41
Creoles of color: in New Orleans,
  24, 25; in North, 59–61; music
  education, 103; and jazz, 104–5
Crime, organized: in New Orleans, 28;
  in Chicago, 46–47, 87; and jazz,
  146–47; and AFM, 157, 158, 159;
  after Prohibition, 165
Cutting contests, 27, 114, 125

Dance: West African, 12; African-
  American, 16; in New Orleans, 34,
  77; in North, 50; musicians and,
  130, 245n25
Dance halls: in North, 50; blacks-only
  dances, 186
Darensbourg, Joe: and organized
  crime, 147
Davis, Leonard "Ham": and integrated
  recording session, 202
Davis, Peter, 33; instruction of Armstrong, 101
Davison, "Wild" Bill, 85, 198, 208;
  in Chicago, 52; autodidacticism,
  92; childhood, 107; and money,
  137; on alcohol, 142; suspended by
  AFM, 160; on recording, 161; and
  spending, 166; and Great Depression, 167; on big bands, 171; and
  Armstrong, 199
Delinquency, juvenile, 4, 84, 85, 86, 90
Delta region: and creation of jazz, 6,
  17–21
Deppe, Lois: on Hines, 109; and clothing, 136–37; on radio, 154; and
  minstrel stereotype, 186–87; childhood, 197
Deviance, 4, 5, 126; and Chicagoans,
  85–86; and jazz, 120–21, 128, 131
Disk jockeys: and jazz, 162

Dixieland, 76–82 passim; defined, 76, 79–80; as extension of white ethnic community, 77, 78, 79
Dixieland musicians: and African-American musicians, 8, 97, 187
Dixon, George, 112
Dodds, Johnny, 60, 102; and music reading, 104; and Great Depression, 166
Dodds, Warren "Baby," 60; on jazz, 37
Dominique, Anatie "Natty": and New Orleans, 30, 35; on jazz, 71; in Chicago, 41; on New Orleans playing, 37, 104, 105; on Henderson, 117; on bebop, 214
Dominguez, Paul: on Creoles, 25
Dorsey, Tommy, 171, 172, 174; on radio, 155; as leader, 173–74; and arrangements, 189
Drug use by musicians· 139–41; and jive, 132; and rebellion, 140
Drums, 92–93: in African-American culture, 12, 13; 108–9; on records, 161
Du Bois, W. E. B., 61; on African-American culture, 13, 14, 222n8; on race relations, 196
Durham, Eddie: childhood, 42; music education, 106: in Kansas City, 119; on amplified music, 162; and poverty, 164; and racism, 186; and integrated band, 205

Ear training: in Delta, 20; in New Orleans, 100, 101, 102, 104; in Kansas City, 119. *See also* Head arranging
Eckstine, Billy: on bebop, 214
Education, general: in New Orleans, 23–24; and Chicagoans, 85, 91. *See also* autodidacticism
Education, music, 103–7 passim; in New Orleans, 33, 102–4; in Southwest, 42; in New York, 43; and Chicagoans, 85; educators on jazz, 107; in Chicago, 110; and AFM, 160–61
Edwards, Eddie: childhood, 79; on organized crime, 146; on Shields, 168

Elgar, Charles, 148; New Orleans education, 103
Ellington, Edward "Duke," 71, 89, 125, 135, 161–62, 173, 174, 183, 194, 195, 202; to New York, 47; in England, 56; superstitions of, 65; achievement of, 117–19; and innovation, 117; personality, 118; on nocturnality, 129; and Greer, 141; and organized crime, 147; and royalties, 150, 151; on radio, 155, 201; and Great Depression, 165; and commercialism, 169; and racism, 182; and minstrel stereotype, 187; separatism of, 192; Hammond on, 202
Employment of musicians, 83, 155, 192; and racial factors, 185–87, 205–6. *See also* Motion picture industry; Phonograph industry; Radio industry; Promoters
Ethnicity, white, 194, 197; in New Orleans, 24, 81; in North, 89–91
Ethnomusicology: and jazz, 4
Europe, James Reese, 43, 55, 106
Europe: black musicians in, 55–57; less racism in, 56–57
European-American music: and African Americans, 15; light classics, 20, 39–40, 77; in New Orleans, 23, 37; influence on jazz, 7, 40, 43, 71–74, 100 105 passim, 119, 175; musicians' response to jazz, 56; and black bourgeoisie, 61–64; individualism in, 72–73, 112; influence on Dixieland, 78; influence on Tough, 93; improvisation in, 113; harmony, 116; and Ellington, 117, 118; reliance on social support, 164; Whiteman on jazz and, 189; definition of, 234n45
Evans, Gil, 82; autodidacticism, 107; on marijuana, 141; and racism, 183; on theft of arrangements, 189; marriage, 208; nonracial sensibility of, 209
Exploitation: of musicians by promoters, 148, 149–51

Families: African-American, 17–18, 54; and music education, 34–35

Feather, Leonard, 148; and bebop
    controversy, 200, 257n61
Fitzgerald, F. Scott: and jazz age con-
    cept, 94
Fleet, Biddy: on bebop, 213
Foresythe, Reginald, 57; and Davison,
    198
Foster, George "Pops," 35, 67; child-
    hood, 17; and New Orleans, 29,
    31, 34, 36; on Mardi Gras, 32; and
    "voodoo," 65; on gambling, 138; on
    marijuana, 139; on AFM, 158; on
    white musicians, 192, 208; in inte-
    grated combo, 201; on Mezzrow,
    247–48n57
Fox, Ed: and Hines, 148, 149, 151
France: musicians in, 55–57; expatri-
    ate writers in, 98–99
Fraternity in jazz, 9, 34, 115, 125, 169;
    women excluded from, 123–24;
    and jive, 130–31; AFM and, 160
Freeman, Lawrence "Bud": adoles-
    cence, 82–85 passim; on delin-
    quency, 85; and blacks, 88, 189;
    on race, 89; career goals, 91, 94;
    on Tough, 92, 93; and teachers,
    107; on Armstrong and Manone,
    108; on scat singing, 127; Kamin-
    sky on, 128; on the word "jazz,"
    133–34; on clothing, 134, 136; on
    musicians' status, 136; and money,
    137–38; on alcohol in jazz, 141–
    42, 143–44; on commercialism,
    151; on phonograph, 152–53; on
    radio, 155; against mechanization,
    162–63; and Great Depression,
    166; on big bands, 172; on Glenn
    Miller, 173, 189; on Tommy Dorsey,
    173; on Goodman, 174; on black
    separatism, 193; on racism, 200;
    on integrated recording sessions,
    202; on Harlem, 206; on interracial
    courtship, 208
Fuller, Walter, 146
Funeral processions (New Orleans), 32,
    79

Gabler, Milt, 174, 175
Galloway, Charlie "Sweet Lovin'," 20,
    26

Gambling, 33, 87; in New Orleans, 28;
    and musicians, 138–39
Garland, Ed "Montudie," 72; child-
    hood, 26; on training, 37; in Chi-
    cago, 41; on music reading, 104; on
    harmonies, 117
Garland, Joe, 173
Gender roles: in jazz, 8, 30, 35–36,
    67–68, 122–26; in music, 122
Gennett Records, 153, 161, 201
Ghettoization: black, 7, 214; and jazz,
    73–75
Gillespie, John "Dizzy," 214; on jazz
    historiography, 7, 8
Glaser, Joe, 138, 147, 148, 165
Goodman, Benny, 83, 171, 172, 189;
    and clothing, 134–35; as leader,
    173, 174; and Hodes, 176; and
    Hammond, 203; band battle with
    Basie, 204; and integrated band,
    205
Grear, Charles C., 66, 183; passing for
    white, 193
Great Depression (1929–40), 3, 9, 196;
    impact on jazz, 164–71
Great Migration (1915–30): and
    jazz, 7, 43–47; difficulties of, 54–
    55; interpretations of, 55. *See also*
    Migration, Black; Second Great
    Migration
Green, Freddie, 42; and Hammond,
    203
Greer, William "Sonny," 66; and alco-
    hol, 141
Grenada Cafe (Chicago), 185

Hall, Alfred "Tubby," 37
Hall, Edmond, 26; on timbre, 101; on
    music reading, 102
Hammond, John H., Jr., 148, 207; and
    Basie band, 170; and integration in
    jazz, 202–3, 204; 257n67
Hampton, Lionel: and Hammond, 203
Harlem (New York), 117, 129; migra-
    tion to, 46, 47, 48; nightlife, 53; and
    jive, 132; clothing in, 135; white
    musicians in, 189, 190, 192, 206–7.
    See also New York City
Harlem Renaissance, 2, 55, 57, 63

Harmony: West African, 12; blues, 16; in jazz, 116, 119, 193
Hawkins, Coleman, 199, 203; and Armstrong, 108; and "Body and Soul," 172; and Feather, 200
Head arranging in jazz, 8, 115, 119. *See also* Ear training
Hecht, Ben: on 1920s rebellion, 98
"Heebie Jeebies, The," 127
Henderson, Fletcher, 73, 189; arrangements, 117; and Challis, 198; Hammond on, 202–3
Herman, Woody, 174; and Ellington players, 202; and Kapp, 203
Hightower, Lottie: band, 123, 125; marriage, 125
Hightower, Willie: in New Orleans, 28, 41; marriage, 125
Hines, Earl "Fatha," 53, 63, 105, 116, 149, 199; on Chicago, 49; and swinging, 109; on timbre, 110; style of, 111; individualism of, 112; on improvisation, 113; harmonic modulations of, 117; on nocturnality, 129–30; and word "jazz," 133; on appearance, 135; on gambling, 138; and organized crime, 146–47; on promoters, 148; autonomy gained, 151; and radio, 154–55, and I oral 208, 160; and poverty, 164; on New York, 168; on commercialism, 170; on southern police, 179, 180; and discrimination, 185; childhood, 197; on integration in Pittsburgh, 205; and whites, 206
Hinton, Milt, 66, 69; childhood, 18, 62; on black labor, 46; on South Side, 48–49; on skin tone conflict, 59; on band sounds, 70; on blues, 72; on ghetto, 73, 74; college music education, 106; on Eddie South, 111; on musicians and sex, 124; and clothing, 135; on gambling, 138; on marijuana, 141; and radio, 154, 155; and union, 160; and Great Depression, 166, 167; on New York, 168; on big bands, 172; and southern dances, 178, 179, 181, 182; relations with whites, 208–9; oral

history of, 223–24n20
Hodes, Art, 83, 92, 130; in Chicago, 91; and rhythm, 108; on Manone, 109; on improvisation, 113; and money, 137; and gambling, 139; on alcohol, 141; and AFM, 159–60; on radio and recording, 163; on New York, 167; on commercialism, 168, 176; and Great Depression, 169; on big bands, 171; and racism, 190–91; on bebop controversy, 200; on Armstrong, 207
Holiday, Billie, 68; and minstrel stereotype, 187; on segregation, 191; and Hammond, 203; on Shaw, 205, 206
Homophobia in jazz, 36, 124, 125–26
Homosexuality, male: in jazz, 125–26
Hopkins, Claude, 56
"Hot" jazz (1920s), 80, 82, 83–84; described, 115; term, 245–46n28. *See also* 1920s jazz revival
Howard, Darnell, 45; and AFM, 159
Howlin' Wolf. *See* Burnett, Chester
Huggins, Nathan Irvin: on jazz, 2–3, 55
Hughes, Langston, 25, 55
Humes, Helen: and blues, 68; and Hammond, 203
Humor, African-American, 53, 60; in jazz performances, 66–67
Humphrey, James, 34, 35, 102, 104; career, 17, 18, 20
Humphrey, Willie E.: childhood, 17, 18; father's instruction, 34
Humphrey, Willie J.: music education, 103
Hunter, Alberta, 45, 47, 52, 56, 69; on Chicago, 49; on Bessie Smith, 64; northern stage persona, 67–68; self-image, 123; on promoters, 148; on royalties, 151; on race relations, 198; on radio, 201; and integrated recording session, 201

Immigrant assimilation: and white musicians, 89–90; in *The Jazz Singer*, 156
Imperial Brass Band, 35
Improvisation, jazz, 8, 16, 52, 112–13; as metaphor, 135–36, 137, 139

Initiation in jazz, 167–68, 252n11
Innovation in jazz, 18, 112, 114, 117
Instruments, musical, 84; homemade, 18, 52, 107; gender identities assigned to, 36, 124; in 1920s, 110
Integration in jazz, 9, 205, 209; and touring, 184; white and black opposition to, 191–93; whites on, 193; Hammond and, 202–4, 257n67
Intellectualism: and white musicians, 91

Jackson, Preston: on Mardi Gras, 32; in New Orleans, 32; on Chicago, 60; on music reading, 102–3
Jam sessions, 174, 175; segregation of, 191; integrated, 199–200
Jargon of musicians, 8, 130–31. *See also* Jive
Jazz: and American cultural history, 1–3, 76, 120–22, 144, 211–17; technique of musicians, 2–3, 101–19; as subculture (1940–60), 4, 5, 8, 128, 131; as subculture (1920–40), 8, 119, 128–43 passim, 144; musical culture of, 8, 100, 101–19 passim; as obsession of musicians, 19, 108–9; definition of, 21; and Great Migration, 43–44; and African-American communities, 52–54, 58–75 passim, 169, 213–14; global dissemination, 55–57, 152; white 1920s press and, 71; as African-American art music, 71–73; different black and white attitudes toward, 107; psychological benefits, 126–28. *See also* African-American music; African-American musicians; Blues; White Musicians
Jazz, historiography of, 210, 211; aficionado literature, 5; oral history, 5–6; social science scholarship, 4–5; on blacks, 235n1
"Jazz" (the word): musicians and, 71–72, 132–33; origins of, 132
Jazz age: concept of 1920s as, 94, 122, 141, 211–12
Jazz bands: and fraternalism, 35; changing composition in North, 70; rise of big bands, 115–19; and

record income, 153. *See also* Big Band Era; Combos; Jam Sessions
Jazz Oral History Project. *See* National Endowment for the Arts
Jazz Singer, The, 156
Jean Goldkette Band, 154, 198
Jenkins, Freddie: violence against, 180; and integration, 204
Jenkins Orphanage (Charleston, South Carolina), 43
Jewish Americans, 89–90
Jim Crow laws, 6, 178, 179, 193, 194, 195, 205
Jive, 128; and jazz, 130–34
Johnson, Albert "Budd": in South, 195
Johnson, Bill: in California, 41; in Chicago, 60
Johnson, Geary "Bunk": and Creoles, 31; music education, 103
Johnson, James P.: compositions, 73
Johnson, Lonnie: in Delta, 18
Jones, Jimmy: on Ellington, 117
Jones, Mildred Bryan, 62
Jook joints, 16
Jug bands, 18, 41

Kaminsky, Max, 195; on Chicago, 87, 94; childhood, 89; on Chicagoans, 91, 94, 115, 128, 217; on Tough, 93; on education, 94; on rhythm, 108; on Beiderbecke, 110; on improvisation, 113; on nocturnality, 129; on gambling, 138; against mechanization, 163; and Great Depression, 166; on Condon, 174; and promoter, 249n12
Kansas City, Missouri, 119, 123
Kapp, David, 203
Kapp, Jack: and jazz, 149
KDKA (Pittsburgh), 154
Keppard, Freddie, 60; childhood, 19; in New Orleans, 28; in Chicago, 41, 114; to California, 42; and fingering, 103
Kirk, Andy, 119; Mary Lou Williams on, 123
Krupa, Gene: and Hammond, 203; on blacks, 206

Labor, black: in South, 19; in New

Orleans, 23, 24, 25, 29; in Chicago, 45–46

Labor, white: in New Orleans, 79

Ladnier, Tommy, 20; and Great Depression, 167

Laine, Jack "Papa": on jazz and race, 31, 80, 187; and segregated bands, 31, 204; childhood, 77; and bands, 77–79, 80

Lala, Johnny, 80

Lala, Pete, 28, 40

LaRocca, Dominick "Nick," 77, 193; or jazz and race, 80, 187–88; and ethnicity, 81

Leadership in jazz, black, 76, 206–8, 258n80

Lemott, Ferdinand. *See* Morton, Jelly Roll

Leonard, Neil, 4; on jazz subculture, 83, 97, 121, 140

Levy, Louis H., 4, 170, 215

Lewis, Ted, 83, 94, 255n34

Liminality: of passing musicians, 194

Lippmann, Walter: on 1920s culture, 95

Livingston, Joseph "Fud": alcoholism, 143

Lodwig, Roy: and black musicians, 198

Lomax, Alan, 25, 31, 59, 112, 150

Los Angeles, 124, 133, 169; and jazz in 1910s, 42

Lost Generation, 8, 90 99

Lunceford, Jimmie, 135, 194

Lynd, Helen Merrell and Robert S. Lynd, 127

Macdonald, Dwight: on specialized jazz audience, 176

McKenzie-Condon Chicagoans, 115

McPartland, Dick: in Austin, 83

McPartland, Jimmy, 88, 89, 208; adolescence, 83; on delinquency, 85; and urban culture, 87; on education, 91, 92; on beat, 108, 130; on improvisation, 114; on jazz as therapy, 128; and marijuana, 140; on Glenn Miller, 173; in Harlem, 189; on integration in jazz, 193, 199, 207; on Armstrong, 199; and Tatum, 206

McShann, Jay, 119; in Oklahoma, 42; and white band member, 194

Manetta, Manuel "Fess," 105; in New Orleans, 28–29; on race relations, 31; on Morton, 102

Manley Club (Chicago), 146

Mannes, David, 43

Manone, Joseph "Wingy," 76, 130, 137, 198, 207; on New Orleans, 30; and ethnicity, 81; in Chicago, 91; and teacher, 107; on music, 107; and beat, 109; on improvisation, 114; on jive, 130–31, 133; on clothing, 135; on Chicagoans and gambling, 138; and alcohol, 141; and organized crime, 146; and AFM, 160; on commercialism, 169, 170; on Los Angeles and New York, 169

Marcus, Greil, 4, 214

Mardi Gras (New Orleans), 64, 79; race relations in, 32

Marginality, 189, 209; of Creoles, 32; of white musicians, 96

Marijuana: and jazz, 140, 141

Marriage: and musicians, 125, 208

Marsalis, Wynton: on jazz, 1, 2, 216

Maxwell, Jimmy, 82, 85; education, 92; parental instruction, 107; on radio network musicians, 162; on CBS Radio, 185, 188; and Ellington, 192; and racism, 200; and blacks, 206; nonracial sensibility of, 209

Melrose, Lester, 112; and Morton, 150–51

Memoirs of musicians, 76

Mencken, H. L., 93, 138; on jive, 132, 133

Meroff, Benny, 137, 166

Mesirow, Milton. *See* Mezzrow, Mezz

Mezzrow, Mezz, 76, 83, 200, 206, 207; rebellion of, 84–85; on Chicagoans, 85; and urban culture, 87; and blacks, 88, 89; on Tough, 93; and rhythm, 108; on timbre, 110; on scat singing, 127; on jazz as therapy, 127–28; on jive, 131, 132, 133; and money, 137–38; and drugs, 139–40; on Joe E. Brown, 146; on organized crime, 147; on bandleaders,

Mezzrow, Mezz (*continued*)
173; Bechet on, 192; proposed
integrated band, 204; interracial
marriage of, 208; on bebop, 214;
Freeman and Foster on, 247–48n57
Midway Gardens (Chicago), 204
Migration, black: 1870–90, 14; to
southern cities, 25, 36–37. *See also*
Great Migration
Mikell, Captain F. Eugene: instruction
of musicians, 106
Miller, Ernest "Punch": childhood, 18
Miller, Glenn: as leader, 173; on jazz
and race, 189
Mills, Irving: and Ellington, 148, 149,
150, 169, 204
Minstrelsy, 79, 129, 207, 210, 255n34;
black, 15, 193; after 1900, 186–87;
and jazz, 193; minstrel stereotypes
and jazz, 9, 189, 190
Mississippi River: and spread of jazz,
40–41
Mitchell, George: on music notation,
116; and WPA, 167
Mixed bands. *See* Integration in jazz
Moenkhaus, Bill: in Bloomington, 126;
on jazz age concept, 126
Morris, Ronald L.: on organized crime
and jazz, 232n10
Morris, William, Jr.: and Ellington,
203–4
Morton, Jelly Roll, 60, 66, 80, 194; on
New Orleans, 27; in New Orleans,
29, 36; childhood, 31; on jazz and
art music, 37; in Chicago, 41; and
race, 59; piano playing, 102; individualism of, 112; and music reading and notation, 116, 231–32n1;
and royalties, 150–51; and integrated recording sessions, 201
Motion picture industry, 96; and jazz,
151, 156–57; racism in, 185–86
Motion picture sound, 9, 156–57; silent
films and, 162–63
Moylen, Bennie: and Armstrong style,
108
Music Corporation of America, 158;
and jazz bands, 148, 150
Music industries, 146. *See also* Phonograph Industry, Radio Industry,
Motion Picture Industry
Music reading: in New Orleans, 41,

102–4; Dixieland players and,
78; plantation bands and, 101;
big bands and, 115–16; assump-
tions about blacks and, 185. *See also*
Notation, musical
Music teachers, 103, 105–6
Musicians: obsession with music,
107–8; and royalties, 149–50; and
AFM, 158–61; against commercialism, 162–63; as professionals,
215. *See also* African-American
musicians; White musicians
Musicians' profession, 63, 64, 193;
in New Orleans, 1870–1900, 29;
reputation of, 30; establishment of
standards, 37; and foreign travel,
57; prestige in North, 72; and
costumes, 136; and sound film,
156–57, 158; nonunion jobs and,
159–60; and professionalism in
America, 215
Musicology: and jazz, 3–4

Nanton, Joe "Tricky Sam," 118; in
South, 182, 184
Narcotics. *See* Drugs
National Association For the Advancement of Colored People (NAACP),
196; Hammond and, 202
National Endowment For the Arts/
Smithsonian Institution Jazz Oral
History Project (JOHP), 5, 261
Native Americans: influence on jazz,
42
NBC Radio, 153, 201
Nettl, Bruno, 4; on art music, 234n45
New Orleans, 17, 39–45 passim, 133,
204, 214, 215; role in creation of
jazz, 6–7, 22, 23, 24, 37–38, 41;
migration to, 1890–1917, 20–21;
musical culture of, 23, 76–82 passim, 100–105; race relations in,
23–24, 188; black neighborhoods,
1900–1920, 26; clothing in, 26,
134, 135; and departure of musicians, 40; blacks and Creoles in,
58–61; politics and ethnicity, 81;
gender roles in, 122, 123–24; and
nocturnality, 129; musicians and
jive, 130–31. *See also* Dixieland;
Migration
New Orleans Rhythm Kings, 83, 201

New Orleans University, 35, 103
New York City, 82, 109, 203; music, 1910s, 43; commercialism of, 167–69; and 1920s jazz revival, 174–75; racism in, 188. *See also* Harlem
Nicholas, Albert, 60; and music reading, 103; on Morton, 151; on Shaw, 199
Nightclubs, 50–53, 68; in New Orleans, 40; whites-only admission in, 53, 185; bargirls in, 124; and 1920s jazz revival, 174, 175, 176; integrated audiences, 196–97. *See also* specific nightclubs
1930s, culture of, 2–3
1920s, culture of, 2–3, 8; and phonograph, 152; and jazz, 94–99, 216; and radio, 249–50n21
1920s jazz revival (1938–1940s), 174–75
Nocturnality in jazz, 129–30
Noone, Jimmie, 153; migration to New Orleans, 20; in Chicago, 51, 60; and music reading, 104
Northern black communities: skin tone tensions, 58–61; class tensions, 61–64; merging of cultures in 1920s, 67–71
Notation, musical, 243–44n51; and jazz, 8; use worldwide, 102; in New Orleans, 102–4; in South Side, 106

O'Brien, Floyd: adolescence, 83; style, 111
OKeh Records, 202; 1926 Artists' Ball, 204
Old Settlers (pre–Great Migration black Chicagoans): employment, 46; on migrants, 61–62
Oliver, Joe "King," 48, 49, 51, 52, 70, 88, 111, 127, 153; migration to New Orleans, 20; migration to Chicago, 40; and race, 60; and trumpet fingering, 102; and music reading, 116; an AFM, 158; and Chicagoans, 199
Onyx Club (New York), 199; integration at, 191
Oral communication. *See* Jargon; Jive; Scat Singing
Original Dixieland Jazz Band (ODJB), 78, 79, 82, 146; recordings, 152

Ory, Edward "Kid," 70, 77, 79, 102; childhood, 18–20; and New Orleans, 25–26, 27, 31, 34, 35; migration to New Orleans, 26; and cutting contests, 27–28; on jazz, 37; on Oliver, 40; migration to California, 42; on Bolden, 101; and music reading, 101
Otis, Johnny: on race, 89, 194; on marijuana, 140–41; on southern police, 179

Page, Oran "Hot Lips": in South, 195
Panama Club (Chicago), 51, 67–68
Paradise Club (Chicago), 51
Paramount Records, 148, 153
Park Central Hotel (New York): integration at, 191
Parker, Charlie: musical innovations, 213
Passing, racial, 193–94, 209
Patriarchy: in jazz, 34–35, 123–24, 125; in Dixieland, 125
Payne, Bennie: and southern whites, 181
Perez, Manuel, 30, 60, 80, 105; instruction by, 35
Perkins, Dave, 31, 77, 101
Petit, Buddy: in New Orleans, 20, 32
Petrillo, James C., 158–60 passim, 171
Peyton, Dave, 70; on jazz, 61
Phonograph industry: and jazz, 151–53, 154, 155; and Great Depression, 165. *See also* Recording; Records
Piano and pianists, 15, 102, 241n8; in New Orleans, 29, 36; gender roles and, 124
Picou, Alphonse, 36; in New Orleans, 29; on word "jazz," 71; on music reading, 103
Pierce, De De (Joseph Lacrois): on music notation, 104
Pittsburgh, 53, 122, 136–37, 197; labor in, 46; radio in, 154
Plantation Cafe (Chicago), 49, 51, 70
Plantations, Delta, 17, 18, 19, 223n17; bands in, 17–21, 123
Police: in New Orleans, 24, 26, 27, 40; at southern dances, 179, 180–81
Pollack, Ben, 92, 134, 135, 189
Populism, southern: and Dixieland, 81, 188, 236n17

Professionalism: in United States, 215–16, 259n9
Prohibition (1920–33), 46, 68; and jazz, 147; repeal of, 165
Promoters, jazz, 147–51; and clothing, 136; and race relations, 197, 200–204
Prostitution, 33, 67, 146; in New Orleans, 27, 28, 35–36; and musicians, 29, 36, 48, 124

Race records, 152, 201
Race relations in jazz, 9, 76, 177, 198–200; in New Orleans, 30–33; Dixieland and, 80–81; and childhood of musicians, 88–89, 197–98; and jive, 133, 134; southern white ambivalence, 193–96; and greater communication, 195; in North, 196–97; private relations, 206, 207, 208–9; summary, 209–10. *See also* Integration in jazz
Race relations in United States: in New Orleans, 23–24, 27, 29, 54, 77, 78, 80–82, 188; white opposition to Great Migration, 54; black-immigrant competition, 192
Racism: and white musicians, 96; and black musicians, 125; in radio industry, 155, 185; and jazz, 177–96 passim; in 1920s, 177–78; and jazz in South, 178–82; and sexual controls on black men, 181, 182–83; in North, 184–85; in nightclub hiring, 185; in motion picture industry, 185–86
Radio industry: and jazz, 9, 151, 153–56; studio musicians, 155–56; racism in, 155, 185; and hiring of blacks, 201
Ragtime, 15–16, 42, 80–81, 82, 129
Railroads, 145, 193–94; influence on jazz, 19–20, 39, 41, 108
Randolph, Zilner: and WPA, 167
Radio Corporation of America (RCA), 170
Rappolo, Leon, 153; in New Orleans, 77
Rebellion, social, 214; and white musicians, 84–85, 97; jazz as, 121

Recording, phonograph, 141; and musicians, 152–53, 161–62; blacks and, 201–2, 203
Records, phonograph: and musicians, 9; as learning tool, 105, 152, 199
Redman, Don, 73, 189; and whites, 204
Religion: West African, and jazz, 11, 18; and African-American music, 19; and music in New Orleans, 25–26
Rent parties, 67
Rhapsody in Black and Blue, 135
Rhythm, 52; in West African music, 12; in African-American music, 15; in jazz, 108–10
Riverboats, Mississippi, 145; black bands on, 39–40, 200–201; and Dixieland, 79
Robert Charles riot (1900), 24, 27
Roberts, John Storm, 3; on art music and jazz, 228n47
Robichaux, John, 31
Royalties, music and recording, 149–50; AFM and, 158
Russell, Charles "Pee Wee," 83, 208; and painting, 93; on Beiderbecke and alcohol, 143; and Great Depression, 166

Samuels, William Everett, 51, 112; on employment, 46; on Chicago, 50; bourgeois values of, 62–63; on humor in jazz, 66–67; on jazz, 69–70; booking agency of, 151; AFM activities of, 159, 160; and Great Depression, 165; and WPA, 167; on New York, 168; on integrated bands, 204
Saunders, Theodore "Red," 62; on AFM, 159; on recordings, 162
Sauter, Eddie, 85; on recording, 162
Scat singing, 127
Schuller, Gunther, 3, 7, 216
Schwerke, Irving, 74
Scott, Cecil, 124, 150, 204
Scott, Lloyd, 204
"Second line" in New Orleans parades, 33–34

Segregation, racial, 177–79, 184, 199–200; in New Orleans, 25, 31, 32; of riverboat dances, 39; by AFM, 43, 159; on radio, 155; and jazz, 178, 183
Separatism, black: in jazz, 192–93
Sex roles. *See* Gender roles
Shaw, Artie (Arthur Arshawsky), 120; childhood, 90; on style, 111–12; on radio musicians, 162; and Great Depression, 167; on commercialism, 170; and Big Band Era, 171–74 passim; and integration, 205, 206; on Harlem, 206–7; and black culture, 207
Shields, Larry: on New York, 168
Shuffle Along, 50
Singleton, Arthur "Zutty," 41; in New Orleans, 29–30, 34; on racial origins of jazz, 80; on beat, 109–10
Slap-tonguing, 66
Slavery: impact on West African culture, 11–13
Smith, Bessie, 84; in Harlem, 64; image of, 123; and Goodman, 203
Smith, Charles Edward: on white musicians, 200
Smith, Willie: passing for white, 194
Smith, Willie "the Lion," 189; Shaw on, 206–7; on whites, 208
Snow, Valaida, 123; world travel of, 56
Social dramas, 213
Social sciences: and jazz, 4–5, 120–21; and deviance, 85–86; and adolescence, 97
Sound reproduction technology, 154, 156, 161–62. *See also* Motion Picture industry; Phonograph industry; Radio industry
South, Eddie, 62, 110–11
South Side (Chicago), 110; employment for musicians, 45; social conditions, 48; Black Belt, 51; attraction for Chicagoans and other whites, 87–88; and Great Depression, 165. *See also* Chicago
Southern Workman, The, 62
Southwest, 119; role in creation of jazz, 42
Spanier, Francis "Muggsy": on Oliver,

102; on integrated jam sessions, 191; and Feather, 200
Spending: by musicians, 137–38, 139, 166; in 1920s America, 137
Spirituals, 13, 14–15, 41
Still, William Grant, 189; on music profession, 73–74
Storyville (New Orleans), 35; policing of, 26; jazz in, 31
Streckfus, Verne, 39–40
Streckfus riverboat line, 79, 178; black bands on, 39–40, 200–201
Style, jazz, 111–12, 113–14, 216
Subcultures: in jazz, 120–22, 128–44 passim, 214–15; musical, 245–46n29
Sublett, John. *See* Bubbles, John
Suburban culture, 84, 85, 86; white musicians' rejection of, 90
Sullivan, Joe, 190; and alcohol, 141; and AFM, 157
Sullivan, Maxine: on race and childhood, 197–98
Sunset Cafe (Chicago), 51, 52, 116, 147, 185, 199; whites-only policy, 196
Supernatural: musicians' beliefs in, 65; Brunis and, 78
Suppers, instrument, 114–15
"Sweet" jazz, 94, 95, 109, 189, 201; on radio, 154
"Swing street" (52nd Street, New York), 174–75, 176; segregation on, 191
Swinging in jazz music, 109–11
Syncopation, 79–80; and West African music, 12

Tatum, Art: on radio, 155, 201; and McPartland, 206
Taverns: in New Orleans, 28. *See also* Nightclubs
Teagarden, Jack, 82; and alcohol, 141; on New York, 168
Teschemacher, Frank: adolescence, 83; style of, 111–12; Kaminsky on, 128; and gambling, 138; death, 160, 167
Theater Owners' Booking Agency (TOBA), 148

Theaters: black, 50; Broadway, 53–54, 82
Thirties. *See* 1930s
"Tiger Rag," 81, 150
Timbre: in jazz, 8, 110; in West African music, 12; of drums, 93; in New Orleans, 110
Tin Pan Alley, 94, 147–48; and royalties, 150
Tio, Lorenzo "Papa," 35, 80, 103, 104, 105
Tio, Luis, 103
Tizol, Juan, 65; and royalties, 150; on Ellington, 182; and minstrel stereotype, 187; and white listeners, 194–95
Tough, Dave, 83; early life and interests, 92–93; and alcohol, 142; against mechanization, 162–63; and minstrel stereotype, 190
Touring, band, 66, 86; in South, 9, 178–82, 183–84; effect on marriages, 125
Trumbauer, Frankie, 208; black admirers of, 199
Trumpet: fingering, 102; Armstrong et al switch to, 111; mutes, 111, 148
Tulane Jazz Oral History Project, 5, 78, 81, 114, 116, 261–62
Tuxedo Dance Hall (New Orleans), 31
Twenties. *See* 1920s

Union, musicians'. *See* American Federation of Musicians
Urban culture: white suburbanites attracted to, 86–88
Urbanization, 2; and 1920s alienation, 126–27

Vanderbilt, William K.: and Waller, 207
Vicksburg, Mississippi: music in, 18, 40–41
Victor Talking Machine Company, 79, 152, 153, 170, 202
Victorian culture, 2, 3; challenged by jazz, 8; in 1920s, 95, 96, 98
Violence: and New Orleans jazz, 26–27; organized crime and, 146–47,

158–59; by whites against black musicians, 179–80, 181
Vodery, Will, 118
Voluntary associations: in New Orleans, 34. *See also* Fraternity
Voodoo: in Haiti and Gulf, 11–12, 16; in New Orleans, 23, 36

Wages in jazz: in New Orleans, 28; in 1920s Chicago, 49, 51, 137, 158; in 1930s, 148, 164, 165, 167, 169, 186; for recording, 153; for motion pictures, 156
Waller, Thomas "Fats": in nightclub, 52; on radio, 155, 201; and Vanderbilt, 207
Warren, Earle: and race, 193–94
Washington, Ford "Buck," 47, 53, 149, 193
Wendell Phillips High School (Chicago), 59, 63
West African culture, music. *See* African, West, music
Wettling, George, 89; and painting, 93; and alcohol, 143
WEVD (New York), 154, 201
Whatley, John "Fess," 106
White, Lucien: on jazz, 61
White musicians, 3, 8, 76–100 passim; racial attitudes of, 9; migration north of, 81–82; and music education, 106–7; musical style of, 115; and jazz, 122; and alcohol, 143; and Great Depression, 166–67; and commercialism, 169–71; and racism, 192; some admired by blacks, 199; respect for blacks, 206–7. *See also* Chicagoans; Dixieland
Whiteman, Paul, 83, 94, 95; and clothing, 136; and recording, 153; and Bushell and Hines, 185; on racial origins of jazz, 189
Williams, Bernard "Cootie," 56, 60–61, 118, 201; migration to New York, 47; on Henderson, 117; on Ellington, 117; on AFM, 160; on Goodman band, 199
Williams, Clarence, 150; on drug use, 140

Williams, Mary Lou, 52, 70; and super
  natural, 65; early playing, 105; on
  Lovie Austin, 122; professional
  obstacles, 123
Williams, Ned, 132–33
Wilson, Quinn: early life, 62; on Big
  Band Era, 171
Wilson, Teddy, 191; Hammond and,
  203
Women in jazz: blues singers, 67–
  68; instrumentalists, 122–23, 125;
  integration among, 205
Wooding, Sam, 55, 56; on origins of
  jazz, 21; on drug use, 140; on radio,
  155
Works Progress Administration

(WPA): Federal Music Project, 165,
  167

Young, James "Trummy": childhood
  and race, 198
Young, Lee, 35, 104, 114; and New
  York, 168; on racism in motion
  picture industry, 187
Young, Lester, 35, 119; and music
  reading, 104, 105; and cutting
  contests, 114; and Trumbauer, 199
Young, W. H.: family instruction by,
  34–35, 104

Zulu Clubs, 32. *See also* Mardi Gras

A Note on the Author

Burton W. Peretti has taught American studies and history at the University of Kansas and the University of California at Berkeley, where he received his doctorate in history. He has published articles in *Chicago History* and *19th Century Music,* is an amateur musician, and is currently working on a book on the culture of housing discrimination in the United States.

Recent Books in the Series Music in American Life

Paul Hindemith in the United States
Luther Noss

"My Song Is My Weapon": People's Songs, American Communism, and the Politics of Culture
Robbie Lieberman

Chosen Voices: The Story of the American Cantorate
Mark Slobin

Theodore Thomas: America's Conductor and Builder of Orchestras, 1835–1905
Ezra Schabas

"The Whorehouse Bells Were Ringing" and Other Songs Cowboys Sing
Guy Logsdon

Crazeology: The Autobiography of a Chicago Jazzman
Bud Freeman, as told to Robert Wolf

Discoursing Sweet Music: Brass Bands and Community Life in Turn-of-the-Century Pennsylvania
Kenneth Kreitner

Mormonism and Music: A History
Michael Hicks

Voices of the Jazz Age: Profiles of Eight Vintage Jazzmen
Chip Deffaa

Pickin' on Peachtree: A History of Country Music in Atlanta, Georgia
Wayne W. Daniel

Bitter Music: Collected Journals, Essays, Introductions, and Librettos
Harry Partch; edited by Thomas McGeary

Ethnic Music on Records: A Discography of Ethnic Recordings Produced in the United States, 1893 to 1942
Richard K. Spottswood

Downhome Blues Lyrics: An Anthology from the Post-World War II Era
Jeff Todd Titon

Ellington: The Early Years
Mark Tucker

Chicago Soul
Robert Pruter

That Half-Barbaric Twang: The Banjo in American Popular Culture
Karen Linn

Hot Man: The Life of Art Hodes
Art Hodes and Chadwick Hansen

The Erotic Muse: American Bawdy Songs Second Edition
Ed Cray

Barrio Rhythm: Mexican American Music in Los Angeles
Steven Loza

The Creation of Jazz: Music, Race, and Culture in Urban America
Burton W. Peretti

Recent Books in the Series Blacks in the New World

My Bondage and My Freedom
Frederick Douglass, edited by William L. Andrews

Black Leaders of the Nineteenth Century
Edited by Leon Litwack and August Meier

Charles Richard Drew: The Man and the Myth
Charles E. Wynes

John Mercer Langston and the Fight for Black Freedom, 1829–65
William Cheek and Aimee Lee Cheek

The Old Village and the Great House: An Archaeological and Historical
Examination of Drax Hall Plantation, St. Ann's Bay, Jamaica
Douglas V. Armstrong

Black Property Owners in the South, 1790–1915
Loren Schweninger

The Sociogenesis of a Race Riot: Springfield, Illinois, in 1908
Roberta Senechal

Coal, Class, and Color: Blacks in Southern West Virginia, 1915–32
Joe William Trotter, Jr.

No Crooked Death: Coatesville, Pennsylvania, and the Lynching of
Zachariah Walker
Dennis B. Downey and Raymond M. Hyser

Black Towns and Profit: Promotion and Development in the
Trans-Appalachian West, 1877–1915
Kenneth Marvin Hamilton

Slaves, Peasants, and Rebels: Reconsidering Brazilian Slavery
Stuart B. Schwartz

Africa in America: Slave Acculturation and Resistance in the American
South and the British Caribbean, 1736–1831
Michael Mullin

The Creation of Jazz: Music, Race, and Culture in Urban America
Burton W. Peretti

For a complete list of books in these series, please write to: University of
Illinois Press, 54 East Gregory Drive, Champaign, IL 61820.